IMPERIAL GRUNTS

IMPERIAL GRUNTS

THE AMERICAN MILITARY ON THE GROUND

ROBERT D. KAPLAN

RANDOM HOUSE | NEW YORK

Published in the United States by Random House, an imprint of The Random House Publishing Group, a division of Random House, Inc., New York.

RANDOM HOUSE and colophon are registered trademarks of Random House, Inc.

The map on pages xiv and xv is reproduced with the permission of the National Geospatial-Intelligence Agency, United States Department of Defense. This publication has not been approved, endorsed, or otherwise authorized by the National Geospatial-Intelligence Agency, United States Department of Defense (10 U.S.C. §425).

All other maps courtesy of Maps.com: www.maps.com

LIBRARY OF CONGRESS CATALOGING-IN-PUBLICATION DATA
Kaplan, Robert D.
    Imperial grunts : the American military on the ground / Robert D. Kaplan.
        p.   cm.
    ISBN 1-4000-6132-6
    1. Soldiers—United States—History—21st century.   2. Special forces (Military science)—United States.   3. War on Terrorism, 2001–   4. United States—Military policy.
5. World politics—1995–2005.   6. Imperialism.   I. Title.
    U52.K37 2005
    973.931—dc22   2004061466

Printed in the United States of America on acid-free paper

www.atrandom.com

9 8 7 6 5 4 3 2 1

FIRST EDITION

Book design by Casey Hampton

To the memory of Marine 1st Lt. Joshua Palmer of Banning, California, born November 28, 1978, killed in action April 8, 2004

And to all the other U.S. Marines killed or wounded during the fighting in Fallujah, Iraq, in April 2004

Major Victor Joppolo, U.S.A., was a good man. . . . We have need of him. He is our future in the world. Neither the eloquence of Churchill nor the humaneness of Roosevelt, no Charter, no four freedoms or fourteen points, no dreamer's diagram so symmetrical and so faultless on paper, no plan, no hope, no treaty—none of these things can guarantee anything. Only men can guarantee, only the behavior of men under pressure, only our Joppolos.

—John Hersey, *A Bell for Adano,* 1944

Imperialism moved forward, not as a result of commercial or political pressure from London, Paris, Berlin, St. Petersburg, or even Washington, but mainly because men on the periphery, many of whom were soldiers, pressed to enlarge the boundaries of empire, often without orders, even against orders.

—Douglas Porch, professor at the Naval War College, Newport, Rhode Island, 1996

In a campaign against Indians, the front is all around, and the rear is nowhere.

—Erasmus D. Keyes, *Fifty Years' Observation of Men and Events,* 1884

CONTENTS

PACOM
THE PHILIPPINES, SUMMER 2003
WITH NOTES ON THE PHILIPPINES, 1898–1913

"Terrorists used these poor, shantyish, unpoliceable islands as hide-outs. . . . Combating Islamic terrorism here carried a secondary benefit: it positioned the U.S. for the containment of China."

CENTCOM AND SOCOM
AFGHANISTAN, AUTUMN 2003
WITH NOTES ON PAKISTAN'S NORTHWEST FRONTIER

"Because al-Qaeda was a worldwide insurgency, America had to fight a classic worldwide counterinsurgency . . . here, amid the field mice and the mud-walled flatness of the Helmand desert, there was only constant trial-and-error experimentation in light of the mission at hand."

FROM THE ARMY TO THE MARINES— FORT BRAGG AND CAMP LEJEUNE, NORTH CAROLINA
WINTER 2003–2004

"I had entered a world stripped to its bare essentials, the inhabitants of which had taken a veritable monastic vow of poverty."

CENTCOM
HORN OF AFRICA, WINTER 2004
WITH NOTES ON EAST AFRICA

" 'Who needs meetings in Washington. . . . Guys in the field will figure out what to do. I took ten guys through eastern Ethiopia. Everywhere people wanted an American presence.' A new paradigm was emerging for the military, one that borrowed more from the French and

Indian War and the Lewis and Clark expedition than from the major conflicts of the twentieth century."

"I looked around in broad daylight to see the roofscape of Al-Fallujah covered with thousands upon thousands of old mufflers and tail-pipes, guarded by U.S. Marines, standing atop the city with fixed bayonets. . . . Yet the American Empire depended upon a tissue of in-tangibles that was threatened, rather than invigorated, by the naked exercise of power."

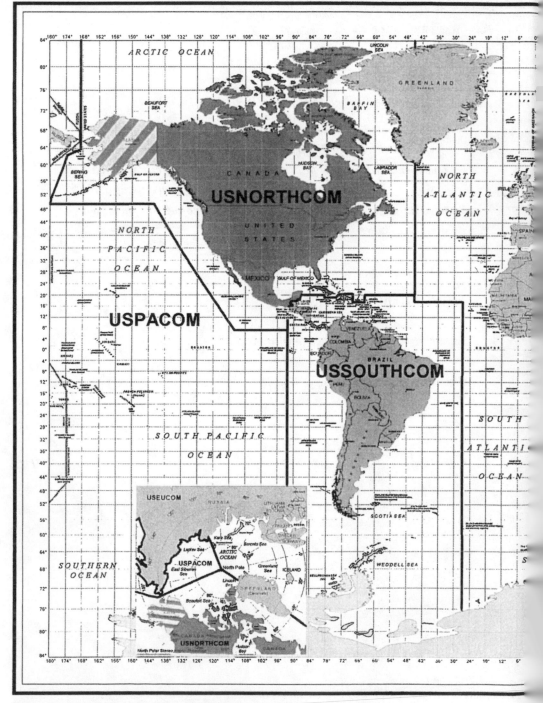

The state of Alaska is assigned to USNORTHCOM's area of responsibility.
Forces based in Alaska remain assigned to USPACOM.

AREAS OF RESPONSIBILITY

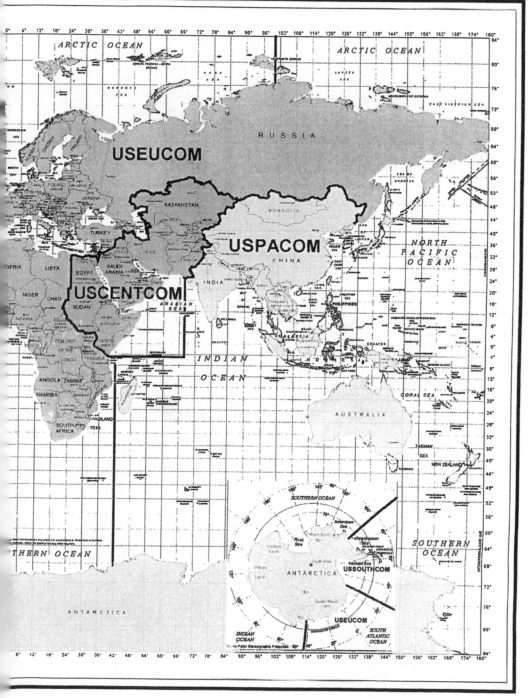

IMPERIAL GRUNTS

INJUN COUNTRY

H e was a lieutenant colonel in the First Marine Expeditionary Force (I MEF as it is written, and One MEF as it is spoken) stationed at Camp Pendleton, California. I met him before he left for the Persian Gulf in the autumn of 2002. He had just been injected with anthrax vaccine, and had been taking malaria pills for many months of his life, during missions to Africa to train local armies. He told me that in the markets of the Congo–Brazzaville condoms were used as sacks for "pencils, fruits, everything except what they're supposed to be used for"; that tribal patronage, not merit, often decided promotion in the Kenyan army; that North Korean diplomats in Africa received little financial support from their government, and in order to be self-sufficient dealt in drugs and prostitution. His skin was the color of clay under his high-and-tight crew cut, with taut cheeks and a get-it-done expression: an ancient sculpture in digital camouflage, except for the point of light in his eyes. The Romans, by their rites of purification, accepted and justified the world as it was, with all its cruelty. The Americans, heir to the Christian tradition, seek what is not yet manifest: the higher ideal. Thus, he was without cynicism. Rather, his honesty made self-delusion impossible.

"The century is only two years old," he told me, "and look at what's happened. That al-Qaeda incident on September 11 was somewhat significant. But we may have nuclear attacks and disease outbreaks that will take many more lives, and which will get us deeply involved on the ground in countries still obscure to us, the way September 11 got us involved in Afghanistan and Pakistan. It is those involvements-to-come that will shape the course of the new century."

Indeed, by the turn of the twenty-first century the United States military had already appropriated the entire earth, and was ready to flood the most obscure areas of it with troops at a moment's notice.

The Pentagon divided the planet into five area commands—similar to the way that the Indian Country of the American West had been divided in the mid-nineteenth century by the U.S. Army. Instead of the military departments of Texas, New Mexico, Utah, California, Oregon, and the West, now there was Northern Command, or NORTHCOM; Southern Command, or SOUTHCOM; European Command, or EUCOM; Central Command, or CENTCOM; and Pacific Command, or PACOM.[1]* For example, at the corner of 5 degrees latitude and 68 degrees longitude, in the middle of the Indian Ocean, CENTCOM gave way to PACOM, just as EUCOM gave way to CENTCOM at the Turkish-Iranian border.

This map bore uncanny resemblance to one drawn in 1931 for the German military by Professor Karl Haushofer, a leading father of *Geopolitik*. The United States, having vanquished Germany's budding world empire in World War II, now had operational requirements for maintaining its own.

But according to the soldiers and marines I met on the ground in the far-flung corners of the earth, the comparison with the nineteenth century was more apt. "Welcome to Injun Country" was the refrain I heard from troops from Colombia to the Philippines, including Afghanistan and Iraq. To be sure, the problem for the American military was less fundamentalism than anarchy. The War on Terrorism was really about taming the frontier. But the fascination with Indian Country was never meant as a slight against Native North Americans. Rather, the reverse. The fact that radio call signs often employed Indian names was but one indication of the troops' reverence for them.

This map left no point of the earth's surface unaccounted for. Were I standing at the North Pole, where all the lines of longitude meet, I might have had one foot in NORTHCOM and the other in PACOM; or in EUCOM if I shifted a leg. After I first saw this map in the Pentagon, I stared at it for days on and off, transfixed. How could the U.S. not constitute a global military empire? I thought.

The only way to explore such a map—to know it intimately—was on foot, or in a Humvee, with the troops themselves, for even as elites in New

* The Department of Utah included parts of present-day Colorado and Nevada; the Department of California included Arizona; Oregon included Washington and Idaho; and the West most of the central and northern Great Plains.

York and Washington debated imperialism in grand, historical terms, individual marines, soldiers, airmen, and sailors—all the cultural repositories of America's unique experience with freedom—were interpreting policy on their own, on the ground, in dozens upon dozens of countries every week, oblivious to such faraway discussions.

This was true of both officers and enlisted men, for while generals were involved at the tactical level as never before, the actions of the lowliest corporals and privates could be of great strategic impact under the spotlight of the global media.[2] It was their stories I wanted to tell: from the ground up, at the point of contact.

Truly, the increasingly decentralized nature of command—necessary in a complex world where, for instance, each region of Afghanistan required a different approach to the local militia—was giving enlisted men unprecedented decision-making powers. Such responsibility required a firm, moral belief system, of which secular patriotism could form but a part. Thus I was interested in religion, and once on base went to as many religious services as I could.

I was less concerned with war and conquest than with imperial maintenance on the ground, and seeking a rule book for its application. The project would take years. I had the earth to roam. It could not be the work of one book but of several.

Here is the first.

———

But before I recount my odyssey through the barracks and outposts of the American Empire, I must address the issue of imperialism itself, a word with which most are uncomfortable, and about which there has been much recent debate.

Imperialism is but a form of isolationism, in which the demand for absolute, undefiled security at home leads one to conquer the world, and in the process to become subject to all the world's anxieties.[3] That is why empires arise at the fringes of consciousness, half in denial. By the time an imperial reality becomes truly manifest, it is a sign that the apex of empire is at hand, with a gradual retreat more likely than fresh conquests.

It is the revealed fact of empire itself that spurs those outside it to join forces in opposition. Rome never consciously thought that it was building an empire until it already had one, and had already reached the limits of its expansion in the Near East, under Trajan in the early second century.[4] British imperialism in India reached its highest level of self-consciousness at the turn of the twentieth century, just as the British Empire was becoming impractical.[5]

Empires are works in progress, with necessity rather than glory the instigator of each outward push. The Venetian conquest of Dalmatia in 1000 began as an expedition against pirates, just as Venice's later conquest of the Morea, the Cyclades, and the Dodecanese in Greece was a defensive measure against a Turkish advance from the west. The British acquired Bermuda in 1684 to guard a stretch of the Atlantic. They took Trincomalee in Ceylon in 1795 to help guard India, and the Yemeni port of Aden in 1839 to have a coaling station for their ships en route to India through the Suez Canal.

The American Empire progressed likewise. "As both a dream and a fact the American Empire was born before the United States," writes Bernard De Voto, the lyrical historian of westward expansion.[6] Following their initial settlement, and before their incorporation as states in the Union, the western territories were nothing less than imperial possessions of Washington, D.C.

The embryonic nation that hugged the eastern seaboard of North America had found it intolerable that the guns of European powers should be at its rear: the French in the Mississippi Valley, the Spanish in the Southwest, the British in Canada and the Northwest. But it was not inevitable that the United States should have an empire in the western part of the continent. That destiny was brought by small groups of frontiersmen, separated from each other by great distances, making alliances with some Indian tribes and buying the neutrality of others. It was they who "provided just enough weight to turn and keep the balance American," writes De Voto. The result, he goes on, was an imperialist drama in "delicate equipoises, constantly oscillating."[7] He might have been describing the American military deployments of the early twenty-first century as I experienced them, for while the entire planet was a battle space for the American military, I would learn that the fewer troops that policed it the better. Small light and lethal units of soldiers and marines, skilled in guerrilla warfare and attuned to the local environment in the way of the nineteenth-century Apaches, could accomplish more than dinosauric, industrial age infantry divisions.[8]

Despite the building of the Panama Canal—one of those rare, conscious feats of empire building, accomplished by President Theodore Roosevelt—it was also not inevitable that America should have become a preeminent global power. What would the United States have become without Adolf Hitler and Hideki Tojo? It was those dictators, and the men around them, who forced the U.S. out of its self-imposed isolation in order to meet the security threat posed by Nazism and Japanese militarism. The unintended consequences of successfully meeting those challenges included the encampment of the Soviet Red Army in the heart of Europe and a civil war in China that brought a communist regime to power: new threats which led to further American imperial expansion.

Four decades later, the victory over communism, like the victories over the Nazis and Japanese, led to more unintended consequences. Breaking the will of the Soviet Union in Afghanistan in the 1980s meant the arming of radical Islamic guerrillas, who subsequently turned against the great power that had helped sustain them: the United States. Henceforth, Islamic terrorism became the sharp edge of a seeping anarchy that followed in the wake of the collapse of the Soviet empire in Eurasia, and of the decomposition of states created by European empires on other continents.

Since antiquity the collapse of empires has been a messy business, and the most benign antidote to the chaos unleashed has been the birth of new imperial domains. Consequently, the turn of the twenty-first century found the United States with bases and base rights in fifty-nine countries and overseas territories, with troops on deployments from Greenland to Nigeria, and from Norway to Singapore, all this while defense appropriations amounted to only 3.3 percent of America's gross domestic product—compared to 9.4 percent during the Vietnam War and 14.1 percent during the Korean War.[9]

Even before the terrorist attacks on the World Trade Center and the Pentagon on September 11, 2001, the U.S. Army's Special Operations Command was conducting operations in 170 countries per year, with an average of nine "quiet professionals" on each mission.* America's reach was long; its involvement in the obscurest states protean. Rather than the

---

* The term "quiet professionals" was coined by Army Special Forces commander Maj. Gen. Leroy Suddath in the 1980s.

mass conscript army of citizen soldiers that fought World War II, there was now a professional military that, true to other imperial forces throughout history, enjoyed the soldiering life for its own sake.[10]

For many of those professional troops the twenty-first century looked strikingly similar to the middle and latter half of the nineteenth, when volunteer cavalry and dragoons subdued a panoply of mobile guerrilla forces, composed of different North American Indian tribes, operating throughout the new American empire west of the Mississippi River.* Whereas the average American at the dawn of the new millennium found patriotic inspiration in the legacies of the Civil War and World War II, when the evils of slavery and fascism were confronted and vanquished, for many commissioned and noncommissioned officers the U.S. Army's defining moment was fighting the "Indians."

The legacy of the Indian wars was palpable in the numerous military bases spread across the South, the Middle West, and particularly the Great Plains: that vast desert and steppe comprising the Army's historical "heartland," punctuated by such storied outposts as Forts Hays, Kearney, Leavenworth, Riley, and Sill.[11] Leavenworth, where the Oregon and Santa Fe trails separated, was now the home of the Army's Command and General Staff College; Riley, the base of George Armstrong Custer's 7th Cavalry, now that of the 1st Infantry Division; and Sill, where Geronimo lived out the last years of his life, the headquarters of the U.S. Artillery.[12]

The range of Indian groups, numbering in the hundreds, that the cavalry and dragoons had to confront was no less varied than that of the warring ethnic and religious militias spread throughout Eurasia, Africa, and South America in the early twenty-first century. It included Pawnees in Nebraska; Arapahos in eastern Colorado; Cheyennes and Aricaras in South Dakota; Crows, Blackfeet, Flatheads, Snakes, and Cayuses in the Northwest; Utes in Colorado and Utah; Comanches, Apaches, Hopis, and Navahos in the Southwest; Shoshones and Paiutes everywhere from southern California into Oregon, Idaho, and Wyoming. The word "tribe" itself

---

* For a nostalgic firsthand account of Indian operations on the Great Plains between the Mexican and Civil wars, see Percival G. Lowe's *Five Years a Dragoon* (*'49 to '54*) (1906; reprint, Norman: University of Oklahoma Press, 1965).

was an oversimplification: the Teton Dakota, or Sioux, as they were known, who roamed from the Minnesota River to the Bighorn Mountains, were not a tribe at all but a nation composed of seven distinct groups, such as the Hunkpapas and Oglalas.

The North American Indians were a throwback to the nomadic horse peoples of the Eurasian steppe—Scythians, Turks, and Mongols—who pierced the defenses of Rome, Byzantium, and Han China.[13] Too, they invite comparison with another imperial nemesis: the nineteenth-century Pushtuns and Afridis of the Northwest Frontier of British India, who were subdivided into various *khels,* and about whom a young Winston Churchill, a subaltern and newspaper correspondent, wrote, "Tribe wars with tribe. The people of one valley fight with those of the next. To the quarrels of communities are added the combats of individuals. . . . Every man's hand is against the other, and all against the stranger."[14]

Pawnees fought Sioux and Cheyennes. Crows fought Blackfeet. Arapahos fought Shoshones and Utes. Cheyennes and Arapahos fought Comanches and Apaches. Navahos were in constant conflict with Hopis. Sioux, in their westering trek from the Great Plains to the northern Rocky Mountains, subdued a gamut of rival Indians. Yet, like the Pushtuns and Afridis, the Native Peoples of North America were also capable of uniting against the stranger. Witness the coalition of Sioux, Cheyennes, and Arapahos that defeated Custer's 7th Cavalry on June 25, 1876, at the Little Bighorn River in Montana, marring the centennial celebration of America's birth the following week.

Beyond the Mississippi and Missouri rivers, the American military found a Hobbesian world in which internecine ethnic warfare, motivated by the competition for territory and resources, was the primary fact of life. "War is the breath of their nostrils," observed Francis Parkman, the nineteenth-century historian, writing firsthand about the Sioux. "Against most of the neighboring tribes they cherish a rancorous hatred, transmitted from father to son, and inflamed by constant aggression and retaliation."[15]

Just as the stirring poetry and novels of Rudyard Kipling celebrated the work of British imperialism in subduing the Pushtuns and Afridis of India's Northwest Frontier, a Kipling contemporary, the American artist Frederic Remington, in his bronze sculptures and oil paintings, would do likewise for the conquest of the Wild West.

Remington, more than Francis Parkman, was the Kipling of early American imperialism, turning it from fact into heroic myth. Though lesser known than his British counterpart, Remington was a figure of enduring cultural importance to Army officers I met in the course of my travels. Like Kipling, Remington was to be uprooted from his time, judged relentlessly by modern standards, and found guilty of racism and jingoism.[16] And that would be something of an irony since for both men, "the white man's burden" meant only the righteous responsibility to advance the boundaries of free society and good government into zones of sheer chaos, a mission not unlike that of the post–Cold War humanitarian interventionists.*

Remington rode with the troops on scouting forays. His snapshots-in-oil idealize solitary men, the essence of hardihood and endurance, caught on the naked plain. Stern-faced cavalry officers confront Indians depicted in hot red and yellow colors, their horses in full gallop. It is a world of mixed-blood scouts clad in buckskin; of mountain men and pathfinders whose "spirit of adventure . . . is the maker of commonwealths," to quote that great Remington admirer Theodore Roosevelt.[17] In Remington's mythic universe, those early imperialists, the cavalry officers and pathfinders, appropriated the warrior ideal of their Indian enemy, which was marked by bravery and steadfastness.†

While microscopic in size, it was the fast and irregular military actions against the Indians, memorialized in bronze and oil by Remington, that shaped the nature of American nationalism.[18] America's oft-noted "optimistic ecumenicism," the basis for peace and disarmament movements, "was largely limited to the north-east of the United States," writes the British war historian Sir Michael Howard.[19] "Further west and south,"

---

* "The White Man's Burden" was a poem written by Kipling to urge the United States to intervene in the Philippines in 1899. It is essentially an idealistic poem, though it has often been quoted out of context.

† See N. Scott Momaday's terse description of the warrior ideal, in *Edward S. Curtis and the North American Indian* (New York: Simon & Schuster, 2000), p. 10. Momaday was referring not to Remington's work, but to that of the photographer Curtis. It is a small but interesting fact that members of the 101st Airborne Division, in preparation for their parachute drop on D-Day, shaved themselves in Mohawk style and applied war paint on their faces (Airborne Special Operations Museum, Fayetteville, North Carolina).

Howard goes on in a mightily perceptive passage, quite another spirit began to predominate:

> The experience of settlement, frontier defense and territorial extension was producing a war culture. . . . It assumed no progress toward a peaceful global society, but a continued struggle in which the use of violence was justified by individual conscience and brute necessity. . . . A century or so later, when global organization began to appear possible and necessary, the image that came to many American minds was not that of balancing power between states, but of protecting law and order against its disturbers . . . by a sheriff with his *posse comitatus.* If human corruption and inefficiency made this impossible, it must be provided by the efforts of a few good men following the dictates of a moral law within.[20]

A few good men: a cliché, yet a telling fact throughout the history of American expansion. As I traveled from continent to continent with the American military in the first years of the twenty-first century, my most recurring image would be one that Remington himself might have painted: singular individuals fronting dangerous and stupendous landscapes.

It is also the case that as America's pioneer spirit led it across oceans and continents, in the course of the twentieth century and into the next, American power became harder to exercise.

Despite its military might the American Empire emerged finally as more implicit than explicit, akin to Achaemenid Persia's near the close of the fifth century B.C., when the victory of a weakened Sparta over Athens in the Peloponnesian War gave Persia nominal control of the Greek archipelago in the west, even as Persia's eastern borderlands were insecure, partisan struggles ensued, and local alliances of convenience were necessary for military operations.

Indeed, America's imperium was without colonies, suited to a jet-and-information age in which mass movements of people and capital diluted the meaning of sovereignty. The Americans did not establish themselves permanently on the ground in many locations as the British had, but reliance on their military equipment and the training and maintenance that went along with it (for which the international arms bazaar was often no substitute) did help bind regimes to them in another way.* As one historian puts it, empires can be ambiguous processes rather than formal structures in which the very opposition to imperial influence constitutes proof of its existence.[21]

To be an American in the first decade of the twenty-first century was to be present at a grand and fleeting moment, a moment that even if it lasted for several more decades would constitute but a flicker among the long march of hegemons that had calmed broad swaths of the globe. The Persian empires of the Achaemenids and the Sassanids each lasted several hundred years, as did each of five conquering Chinese dynasties, to say nothing of Rome. Byzantium lasted a millennium, as did Venice. Portuguese, Habsburg, Ottoman, and British dominance must be measured in centuries, not decades. Even the Vandal empire of Genseric dominated the Western world's Mediterranean core for the better part of a hundred years while Rome was collapsing. Because it was a fomenter of dynamic change, a liberal empire like the United States was likely to create the conditions for its own demise, and thus to be particularly short lived.

Some denied the very fact of American empire, claiming a contradiction between an imperial strategy and America's democratic values. They forgot that Rome, Venice, and Britain were the most morally enlightened states of their age. Venice was defined by a separation of church and state. It had a working constitution which severely limited the authority of its doges, who were unable to act without the approval of their councilors. Its humanistic outlook made Venice the only state of Catholic Europe never to burn a heretic.[22] Liberalism at home and a pragmatic, at times ruthless policy abroad have not been uncommon in the history of some empires.

As it happened, the early twenty-first century saw the U.S. in the

---

* British historian Niall Ferguson, in a reference to the American position in the world at the dawn of the twenty-first century, puts it another way: "The technology of overseas rule may have changed—the Dreadnoughts may have given way to F-15s. But like it or not, and deny it who will, empire is as much a reality today as it was throughout the three hundred years when Britain ruled, and made, the modern world." Niall Ferguson, *Empire: The Rise and Demise of the British World Order and the Lessons for Global Power* (New York: Basic Books, 2003), p. 370.

Second Expeditionary Era regarding its global military-basing posture.[23] In the First Expeditionary Era, from the buildup to the Spanish-American War to the end of World War II, the U.S. had established bases in the Caribbean, the Pacific, and the North Atlantic, in order to expand its continental defense perimeter and protect new economic interests. The Cold War years constituted the Garrison Era, in which large, permanent frontier garrisons surrounding the Soviet Union were built in places like West Germany, Turkey, and the Korean Peninsula. The Second Expeditionary Era featured an emphasis on rapid mobility worldwide to deal with peacekeeping interventions, anti-terrorist strikes, and the containment of Iran and Iraq. The post–September 11 global footprint was to put further emphasis on mobility and the dispersion of forces, to deal with the twin threats of radical Islam and the rising power of China.

These strategies were all legacies of Rome, which was constantly requesting territory on foreign soil to build bases. Rome established hardened bases in ungovernable areas for the sake of deterrence, surveillance, and reconnaissance. Its superior road network and control of the seas enabled the rapid relocation of its forces in large concentrations at times of crisis. Rome, like Britain, followed a doctrine of "inevitable reversibility."[24] Because it knew that it could not be strong everywhere, that there would be places where it might have to withdraw ignominiously, and other places where it would not be prudent to intervene, Rome emphasized the rapid strategic reaction of its forces rather than their continual presence in too many areas.

––––––

Just as empires expand by happenstance, impelled forward by a succession of security threats, real or imagined, my journeys also followed no discernible pattern. Friendships with captains and majors helped get me to the most remote locations as much as those with colonels and generals. The American military is a worldwide fraternity. Thus people in one part of the globe led me to another part through the oddest of coincidences. A Coast Guard officer I met in Yemen would stoke my interest in Colombia. An Army officer I met in Mongolia would inform me about Bosnia. An enlisted man in the Philippines told me all about the Singaporean army. The stories themselves were evidence of a global military.

Through it all, I was not truly a war correspondent. I concentrated more on local history and scenery, because the drama of exotic new landscapes has always been central to the imperial experience. A series of books about empire—at least to some degree—had to be about travel.

The number of countries I planned to visit, while considerable, would be less important than the amount of time I spent in the barracks with the troops, and the degree to which I could be accepted by them. I wanted to see the world and their deployments from their perspective, not to judge them from mine. I wanted to devote all of my professional time to this endeavor, for half a decade at least. I wanted to cut myself off from civilians as much as possible. It was the depth and quality of an experience that I was after, particularly with the grunts.

Grunts: cannon fodder. The word best applies to Marine combat infantrymen. But in a sense even Army Special Forces sergeants belonged in the category, because of their willingness to sublimate their own identity to that of the unit. Their concern was less with their own self-preservation than with the preservation of the function they performed. If the man beside you was able to do your job, your own death would matter less. The grunts I met saw themselves as American nationalists, even if the role they performed was imperial.

The security threat that had caused the latest and, perhaps, final expansion of the American Empire was especially elusive. More so than infantry phalanxes, there were now clandestine guerrilla cells of young men and occasionally women working to wreak greater destruction than most of the armies of history ever had. Thus I began in Yemen, said at the time to have the largest al-Qaeda presence anywhere outside of the Afghanistan-Pakistan border. Yes, Yemen was relatively little known. That was the point. A world empire meant many different places.

But before I linked up with the military, I wanted to scout out America's latest version of Indian Country by myself: to view at ground level what it was, exactly, that the U.S. was up against. Yemen would constitute merely the long overture to my experience with the troops, rather than the experience itself.

Even in Yemen, though, I would meet an American officer or two:

sometimes retired, sometimes working for an international organization, who, in keeping with the implicit nature of American imperialism, like the mountain men and pathfinders of old, was clearing new trails of expansion and influence, in his own indirect and unconscious way.

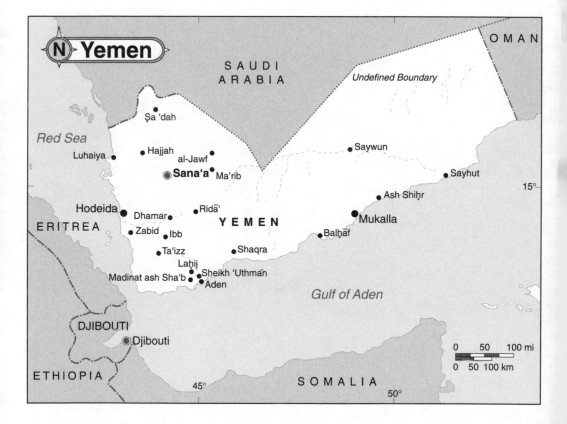

CHAPTER ONE

CENTCOM

YEMEN, WINTER 2002

WITH NOTES ON COLOMBIA

"Yemen was vast. And it was only one small country. . . . How to manage such an imperium?"

I
n November 1934, when the British traveler and Arabist Freya Stark journeyed to Yemen to explore the broad oasis of the Wadi Hadhramaut, the most helpful person she encountered was the French aesthete and business tycoon Antonin Besse, whose Aden-based trading empire stretched from Abyssinia to East Asia. Besse, dressed in a white dinner jacket with creased white shorts, served excellent wine at dinner, and was described as "a Merchant in the style of the Arabian Nights or the Renaissance."[1] In December 2002, when I went to Yemen, the most helpful person I encountered was Bob Adolph, a retired lieutenant colonel in the United States Army Special Forces, who was the United Nations security officer for Yemen.

Adolph, whose military career had taken him all over the world, had the chest of a bodybuilder and a bluff, bulldog face under wire-rim glasses and a creased ball cap. I spotted him on the other side of passport control, waiting in the dusky warehouse under fluorescent lights that functioned as the Sana'a airport.

Because of their own al-Qaeda problem, the Yemenis were suspicious of anyone with a Pakistani visa inside his passport. I was pulled over by a man smoking a cigarette and wearing a torn sweater and slippers. Adolph, seeing that I was making no progress, ambled over to him, speaking in bad but passable Arabic, gritting his teeth each time he made a point. Others were also haggling with customs and passport officers. It was a typical

.orld scene: confusion and a cacophony of negotiation in place of a standards.

After more of Adolph's pleading, I got back my passport. We headed for the parking lot. It was 2 a.m. Two beggar boys grabbed my bags and put them in the Land Cruiser. Adolph slipped them half a dollar in riyals. I was relaxed. The Arab world, while afflicted by political violence, had little or no common crime. In this sense, Islam had risen to the challenge of urbanization and modern life, and was a full-fledged success.

"This is the most democratic state in Arabia. For that reason it's the most dangerous and unstable," Adolph said, explaining that when Western-style democracy replaced absolute dictatorship in places with high unemployment rates and weak, corrupt institutions, the result was often a security vacuum that groups like al-Qaeda could take advantage of. "I've drawn up multiple evacuation plans for the U.N. staff here, updating calling-tree lists," he went on. "If the place goes down during the night, I can have all our people in Asmara the next day in time for brunch at the InterContinental there. The trick is to keep doing favors for people in the army, the police, and the tribes, and never call them in, until you need them to get your people out."

He veered to avoid another head-on. "Notice the way people drive here, you've got ten-year-olds propped up on phone books driving Granddad around town. Forget about rules and licenses. Keep all of your cash in different pockets. Despite all of the guns, ready cash always gives you more power in Yemen than a gun. Everybody in this country is a businessman, and a good one." His tone was commanding, didactic.

It was the last night of Ramadan. Though a few hours before dawn, the streets were noisy and crowded, and gaily strung with lights. Sana‘a resembled a fairy-tale vision of Arabia, with basalt and mudbrick buildings festooned with colored glass fretwork and gypsum friezes. I recalled my first visit to Yemen in 1986.

Back then, the diplomats and other area specialists had assured me that with the discovery of oil in significant amounts, the Yemeni government would soon have the financial wherewithal to extend its power into the countryside, ending the feudal chaos. The opposite had occurred. To placate the sheikhs, the government bribed them with the newfound wealth, so oil revenues strengthened the medieval periphery rather than the modernizing capital. Kidnappings of foreign tourists erupted in the mid-1990s, as the sheikhs got greedy and sought to further blackmail the government.

The government also had to compete with wealthy Wahabi extremists from Saudi Arabia and with al-Qaeda, who sometimes had more money with which to influence local Yemeni tribal leaders. With al-Qaeda targeting oil vessels off the Yemeni coast, maritime insurance rates had gone up, reducing sea traffic and consequently the amount of money from oil exports, so the regime had less money for bribes. The foreign community feared that a new wave of kidnappings might lie ahead.

For al-Qaeda, Yemen was a conveniently chaotic, culturally sympathetic country in the heart of Arabia, so much more desirable than far-afield, non-Arab Afghanistan. It might just be a matter of chipping away at the regime.

In downtown Sana'a, I noticed that people were not wearing the cheap Westernized polyesters that signify the breakdown of tribal identities under the pressure cooker of urbanization. They still wore white thobes with checkered keffiyahs or Kashmiri shawls, with the men sporting *jambiyas* (ornamental curved daggers) in the middle of their belts.

"It's tribal everything," another U.S. military source would explain to me. "The ministries are fiefdoms for the various tribes. It's a world of stovepipe bureaucracies. All the information flows to the top and none of it is shared along the way, so that only [President Ali Abdullah] Saleh knows what is going on. As for the furious demands from the Americans to fight bin Laden, we Americans are just another crazy tribe that Saleh holds close to his chest, and balances against the others. Same with al-Qaeda. Saleh has to appease and do favors for everyone to stay in power." Yeah, I thought, whichever dog is closest to biting him, he feeds.

Adolph told me that the Yemeni government controlled only about 50 percent of the country. A high-ranking Western diplomat in Yemen would hotly dispute that claim, telling me that Saleh controlled "all the main roads, oil fields, and pipelines," which, I countered, was less than 50 percent of the country. "Well," the diplomat huffed, "he controls what he needs to control." If that was the case, I thought, then why was there such a problem with al-Qaeda in Yemen at the time of my visit? The difference between Adolph and this diplomat was not in their facts, or even in their perceptions, it would turn out. Rather, like the Marine lieutenant colonel I had met briefly at Camp Pendleton, Adolph didn't know how to be subtle, or how to dissemble. He was brutally, refreshingly direct. Dealing with him saved time.

Inside the galloping Land Cruiser, Adolph knocked off the most recent security "incidents" in the country. His apartment building had been the scene of a gun battle between the son of a highly placed sheikh and government forces, with four people "KIA" (killed in action). Several more had been killed during a firefight between the al-Haima and Bani Mattar tribes outside Sana'a. Two bombs had exploded near the homes of government officials in the capital. In nearby Ma'rib there had been an attempt to assassinate the regional governor, Abdullah Ali al-Nassi, when tribesmen blocked the road and opened fire on his vehicle. The reasons for all this violence remained murky. As for al-Jawf and other areas on the Saudi frontier, there had been so many bombings and gun battles that Adolph hadn't bothered to investigate or keep count. All this was a prelude to the assassination of a leading Yemeni politician and the murder of three American missionaries.

Adolph, trained as a hostage negotiator by Great Britain's New Scotland Yard, told me what to do in case I was kidnapped: "Don't protest. Be submissive. Show them pictures of your family to establish a relationship. After the first few hours, ask to see the sheikh. If they take you to meet him, it's all right. It's an authorized kidnapping, for the sake of convincing the authorities to give the tribe a new road or water well. They'll tell you the negotiations should be completed in a few days; figure two months. Foreigners have been known to gain weight in the course of being held hostage in Yemen. Each family in the village will host you for a while, to divide the cost of your food. But if they don't take you to see the sheikh the first day, start to worry. Then it may be an unauthorized kidnapping, and it's okay to think of ways to escape."

He slowed the vehicle as we got closer to his apartment in a wealthy area of Sana'a where many expatriates lived. High walls, armed guards, and concertina wire were everywhere: the paraphernalia of paranoia.

I was headed for Injun Country, Adolph told me. He meant the desert wastes of northern Yemen abutting the Saudi border, a border that the Yemeni government was attempting to demarcate, even as local tribesmen were blowing up the new border markers. The next day I had an appointment with a sheikh who could provide me with guards and a guide, a sheikh for whom Adolph had done favors.

Sheikh Abdulkarim bin ali Murshed, forty, looked older than he was: something not uncommon in a country where extreme poverty and a high birthrate literally sped up time. Well over half of the people in Yemen hadn't been born when I had first visited sixteen years before. From his father, Sheikh Murshed had inherited control of one hundred thousand Khawlan tribesmen who lived east of Sana'a. They were part of the Bakil tribal confederation, the largest in Yemen. The Bakils were less powerful than President Ali Abdullah Saleh's more cohesive Hashid confederation, which resided along the northern spine of the mountains of the High Yemen. President Saleh's political rival, Abdullah al-Ahmer, leader of the Islamic Islah (Congregation for Reform) party, was a fellow Hashid, of the al-Ahmer branch. Consequently, the president needed allies from the Bakils to counter some of his own Hashid tribesmen, and Sheikh Murshed was both willing and ambitious for power.

With the blessing of both Saleh and some *khawajahs* (wealthy white foreigners), including the Americans, Sheikh Murshed had established a nongovernmental organization (NGO) called Human Solidarity. He had business cards and a half-empty office where nothing seemed to be going on. Like the political party system in Yemen, the office was mainly a Westernized facade, behind which lay a vibrant traditional means of power: the tribe.

Adolph introduced me to Sheikh Murshed less than twenty-four hours after I had arrived in Yemen. This was at the start of the three-day Feast of Eid al-Fitr which concluded Ramadan, a time when such a meeting should have been impossible to arrange. But Adolph had a holiday gift for the sheikh: "an American *jambiya*," as he put it with a wide, overbearing smile, as he towered over the sheikh. It was an authentic, foot-long Texas bowie knife in a handsome red case.

Adolph showed me a stack of such bowie knives inside red cases that he had bought for $80 apiece. "I should be able to deduct these on my taxes as a legitimate business expense," he told me, "but of course I can't. I've given one to the chief of police, and have another for the president's half brother. In male-dominated tribal societies like Yemen, manliness goes a long way. It's how you get people to do things for you." Adolph's apartment was filled with knives and swords—from West Africa, the Horn, and Yemen.

Sheikh Murshed told me that as a friend of Adolph's, I would be his guest in the tribal areas. Thus it would cost me nothing for the vehicle, the bodyguards, and the guides I would be lent for my journey. If I wanted to show my appreciation, however, through a donation to his NGO, that was up to me. In other words, the negotiation had begun. The first group of guards with whom he put me in contact wanted $350 a day. I ended up paying $100 a day, plus a donation to the sheikh's NGO.

Soon after our first meeting, the sheikh invited me to chew ghat at his medieval tower house, perched on a hilltop on the outskirts of Sana'a. The sheikh's *mafraj,* upper-story room, was filled with about twenty tribesmen reclining on pillows on the floor. Late-afternoon sunlight fell through the stucco friezes and colored glass windows. The sheikh sat with his Makarov pistol, Kalashnikov assault rifle, and notebook, using a spittoon to rid his mouth of excess ghat leaves and mucus as he listened to supplications. The ghat was stuffed in plastic supermarket bags beside the pile of assault rifles on the machine-made carpets. An antique telephone sat on a chipped wooden stand. It never rang, but the sheikh talked incessantly on his new cell phone. Mounted on the wall beside faded family photographs was a television turned to Al-Jazeera, the all-news Arabic-language station out of Qatar that the Yemenis thought of as provocatively Westernized, even as Americans saw it as hostile to the West.

Arguments raged into the evening over the best way to improve security and living conditions in the troubled desert regions of al-Jawf and Ma'rib. The sheikh listened, not interrupting, but he always had the final word. He heard numerous supplications, including a request to help a man whose brother had been arrested for allegedly stealing funds from the central bank. The idea that a good lawyer and an independent judge would provide justice was not especially considered; only the sheikh, it seemed, could guarantee a fair resolution of the matter. "In Yemen, the *kabili* [tribal] system is stronger than the government, stronger than Islam even," one of the supplicants told me. This was the essence of underdevelopment, a situation in which the government bureaucracy works on the basis of family ties and who-you-know, rather than on impersonal laws and principles.

The ghat spurred conversation. If it is chewed properly—the soft stems and leaves bunched into a rear corner of the mouth, resting on the lower teeth until a greenish mucus forms—the plant has an exquisitely subtle effect at once energizing and relaxing, like having five cups of espresso without feeling overwound. Ghat's effect was creeping. It incited you sexually. It was common for men after the afternoon chew to take a siesta with their wives. A water-intensive crop, ghat was a principal reason for the desertification of the country. Groundwater supplies in Yemen were expected to last no more than a generation or two, while Yemen's population growth rate of 2.8 percent was among the highest in the Middle

East.* Ghat, which had no export potential, was increasingly being grown at the expense of cash crops like coffee, further exposing the local economy to catastrophe as underground oil reserves diminished.

The next person I saw as soon as I arrived in Yemen, again courtesy of Adolph, was Brig. Gen. Ali Muhsen Saleh al-Ahmer. Gen. Ali Muhsen, half brother to President Saleh (they shared the same mother), was said to be the second most powerful man in Yemen after Saleh himself. Ali Muhsen controlled an armored division that protected the capital. He had the reputation of being a buttoned-down, capable organizer, close to the fundamentalist Islah movement, as well as to gun-running sheikhs and perhaps to some in al-Qaeda, too. It was Ali Muhsen who helped Saleh get support from the radical "Afghan-Arabs" (Yemeni veterans of the Afghan war against the Soviets) when his regime was threatened by civil war in the mid-1990s. But American pressure following September 11, 2001, had been so severe that both Ali Muhsen and Saleh felt they had no choice but to accommodate President George W. Bush. The Americans made a deal with this former "bad guy": giving Ali Muhsen's regiment a chunk of the American military aid package was the only way that Washington could do business in Yemen.

Ali Muhsen reminded me of a tribal leader that a young Winston Churchill describes in his first book, *The Story of the Malakand Field Force:* "He was a great man, which on the frontier means that he was a great murderer. . . . A strong man who has felt the grip" of an imperial power "is the best tool to work with."[2] It was Ali Muhsen's ties to the radicals that gave his half brother, the president, the political protection he needed to move closer to the Americans—temporarily, that is. And also to distance himself from the Americans swiftly and credibly if that, too, became necessary.

Late at night during Eid al-Fitr Ali Muhsen received Adolph and me in his heavily fortified compound in Sana'a. The flamboyant *jambiya* that Ali Muhsen wore over his tribal dress testified to the value of its lineage; it had likely been passed down for generations. Syrupy tea, nuts, and raisins were served. Adolph presented Ali Muhsen with a bowie knife, "a gift from one soldier to another." Ali Muhsen smiled as he put his hand gratefully on Adolph's. For Adolph in this situation, being a former U.S. Army officer

* World Bank estimates.

was more important than being a U.N. security officer. But the two functions were really inseparable. For sensitive security details like Yemen,
where expatriates were truly at risk, it was not unusual for the U.N. to have
Americans, or at least other Anglos, in positions of authority. While the
United States and the United Nations often seemed at odds on the world
stage, on the ground in Yemen the distance between them seemed less
consequential.

"I'm ready to roast your communications minister alive," Adolph complained. "I need to set up a radio call network for my staff in case of emergency and he won't see me." Ali Muhsen suggested he would settle
Adolph's problem. Adolph didn't believe him, and went on complaining
for a while. Ali Muhsen appeared to respect him for that.

Adolph introduced me in flattering terms and I made small talk with
the general. To ask a direct question—or to consider this an interview—
would have been an abuse of hospitality. In a place like Yemen the truth
emerges by accident, when talking of other matters. The fact that the general had received me would serve as the best form of protection were I un-
lucky enough to be kidnapped. The excess of nervous-looking armed
guards in the sitting room and nearby courtyard testified both to Ali Muhsen's real authority and to the anarchy swirling around it.

Less than seventy-two hours after I had arrived in Yemen, during the most
important holiday of the Muslim year, when government offices were
closed, Adolph, with his passable Arabic, had arranged a trip for me
through an area where westerners had been denied the right to travel, and
had gotten me a brief audience with the country's most shadowy figure.
Adolph impressed me as neat, orderly, a bit anal-retentive even, as well as
unpretentious.

Robert B. Adolph Jr. was born in 1952 in Chelsea, Massachusetts, one
of nine children in a poor Catholic family. He started working when he
was eleven. He was thrown out of high school five times, finishing 313 in
a class of 330. He joined the U.S. Army after high school and was sent to
Germany, becoming a staff sergeant, and later a member of Army Special
Forces. "In the military, for the first time in my life, people told me that I
wasn't stupid." Encouraged, Adolph, by way of a mail-order correspon-
dence course, got a college degree, something he was still intensely proud
of. Later, he would earn a master's degree in international relations from
American University in Washington, D.C. His military education in the

course of becoming a Special Forces officer included Belgian commando school, Russian language school, a combat swimmer's course offered by the Danish army, and Ranger and parachute jump master schools. In Germany he commanded two military intelligence companies. Serving in Egypt he learned to be wary of most scholarly books about the Arab world. "The books I read never mentioned that to improve a society you have to give the money to women, never to men. In the City of the Dead in Cairo," he went on, "I adopted a poor family: Dad wanted a TV set, Mom wanted a sewing machine to start a little business."

In 1992 he was sent to Cambodia as an American military observer to the U.N. peacekeeping mission. "It was the first time that I was in a place with no government. The Khmer Rouge were doing a bargain-basement business with the Thai army in gems and logging. I learned that if someone puts an AK-47 in your face, you move back slowly, bend at the waist in a supplicating manner, with your palms together as though you are about to pray. They usually put their guns down when you do that. Being in Cambodia for six months was like being raped. Nothing I had been given to read in the course of my education prepared me for what I encountered.

"It didn't make me cynical. It just helped me get things done on the ground." He set up an anti-malarial program in northern Cambodia, getting a French crew to bring in mosquito nets on C-130s (Adolph's French, I learned, was like his Arabic) and a Canadian trucking company to distribute them. "The hardest thing, though, was to convince rural Cambodians that malaria was from mosquitoes, not from bad spirits."

Upon retirement from the U.S. Army in 1997, Adolph became an advisor under contract with the State Department to the Bosnian Ministry of Defense. The next year he became the chief security officer for the U.N. peacekeeping mission in Sierra Leone, where he had to evacuate several hundred civilian staff under threat from the sadists of the Revolutionary United Front (RUF). "Whether it's the RUF, al-Qaeda, or Serbian Chetniks, one unifying factor is that none of these people know how to have a normal relationship with a woman, and that lies at the root of their cruelty," he told me, sucking on beer suds one night in his apartment. "RUF commanders would force boy soldiers to rape old women in their own village at gunpoint, so that the boys could never go home again. It is the kind of discipline unsocialized teenagers understand."

Sierra Leone had been a frustrating assignment for Adolph. In Special

Forces he had learned that "the mission was everything"; in the U.N. he had to work in an environment where, as I knew from my own reporting, the mission was secondary to diplomatic necessity.

For example, Nigerian peacekeepers were not in Sierra Leone to keep the peace, but in some cases to steal alluvial diamonds. The RUF controlled the diamond fields. The Nigerians made deals with the RUF. They used their own peacekeepers as mules to get the diamonds back to Lagos. The Nigerian government was getting money from the international community for each peacekeeper it dispatched to Sierra Leone, but the Nigerian soldiers themselves were not always paid by their own government. Guinean and Zambian peacekeepers were also not paid, though their governments were getting money from the U.N. for every soldier dispatched to Sierra Leone. The result was that they surrendered without a fight to hunter-warrior guilds dressed in wigs and shower caps.[3]* If the U.S. was going to subcontract out its imperial burden to the U.N., the U.N. would have to be able to fight on the ground as well as it talked before the television cameras.

Two weeks after he left Sierra Leone, the U.N. sent Adolph to Yemen. Here the mission was everything, to judge by the blunt way he had spoken to Gen. Ali Muhsen about the communications minister.

⸻

"Family, Village, Tribe, Guns—*Tinker, Tailor, Soldier, Spy.* That's Yemen," began the U.S. Army colonel dispatched to Sana'a from CENTCOM in Tampa, Florida. Terrorism is an entrepreneurial activity dominated by enterprising self-starters. And as the colonel explained to me as we lined up for food in Adolph's apartment, "In Yemen you've got nearly twenty million aggressive, commercial-minded, and well-armed people, all extremely hard-working compared to the Saudis next door. It's the future. And it terrifies the hell out of the government in Riyadh."

The buffet dinner included a dozen men. Aside from me, a U.N. official, the French defense attaché, and two diplomats from the American Embassy, the rest were American military officers running one program or another in Yemen: Yemeni commando training, de-mining, and so on. They were a bunch of working-class guys. There was much talk about "how dumb" they all were, especially from the U.S. defense attaché, Army

* For a blow-by-blow account of United Nations military incompetence in Sierra Leone see Damien Lewis's *Operation Certain Death* (London: Century, 2004).

Col. Gralyn Harris, a former wrestler at the University of Connecticut who happened to speak fluent Arabic. I had also gone there, I told him. I said that he was the first fellow graduate I had met in more than two decades as a foreign correspondent. "What shit is that?" he laughed.

The conversation drifted to jobs after retirement from the service that paid as much as $70,000 per year. There was a lot of clear, ungrammatical, mincing-no-words comparisons of one country and culture with another, observations that were relevant even as they might be difficult to print. This was a world where people were judged less by their ideas than by the practical implementation of them; here virtue was in the results. If there was such a thing as an American Empire, it was here at this party.

Bob Innes, tall, red-haired, and extremely personable, was a fireman's kid, born in 1950, who had grown up in an Irish-Italian neighborhood on Brooklyn's Flatbush Avenue, near Ebbets Field. "I never got over the Dodgers deserting Brooklyn for Los Angeles," he told me. "The three greatest villains of the twentieth century were Hitler, Stalin, and Walter O'Malley," the Dodgers' owner. Innes was now building from scratch a Yemeni coast guard.

"I was the product of a mixed marriage," he began in homey deadpan. "My mother was from Brooklyn, my father from the Bronx. In the late 1950s my father retired to fireman's heaven, Arizona: the real mythic west of the Apaches, that's before it became suburban and upscale," he sneered. On the streets of Phoenix, Innes learned Spanish from his Mexican friends. With good grades he got accepted to Stanford, which his parents couldn't afford. With no scholarship from Stanford, he went to the U.S. Coast Guard Academy in New London, Connecticut.

Though we live in the jet age, 70 percent of all intercontinental cargo travels by sea, making the seas more strategic than ever. Most countries that claim to have navies really have coast guards. Though the U.S. Coast Guard consists of only thirty-eight thousand seamen and five thousand civilians, it is the largest coast guard in the world, as well as the world's seventh largest navy. At first Innes served off the coasts of Greenland, Canada, Wake Island, and South Vietnam. "I saw the last U.S. aircraft leave Tan Son Nhut, where it was decided which dependents got on and which didn't.

"What did I learn from the experience in Vietnam?" he asked himself out loud, letting the silence formulate his next statement. "I learned that honor and integrity are personal qualities, not institutional ones, not ones we should expect the state to always have. If you don't like the policy, tough. Bad things happen in this world. You do the best you can in your job, and let the crybabies write the books."

In the 1980s, Innes administered Coast Guard training programs in West Africa and every place in Latin America except for Bolivia and Paraguay, which don't have seacoasts. His Spanish had become fluent. He was reading Cervantes in the early-seventeenth-century original text. He arrived in Monrovia, Liberia, in April 1980 just as Master Sgt. Samuel K. Doe staged a coup against President William Tolbert, and body parts were being paraded in the streets. "West Africa was Haiti on a pan-continental scale. The problems in South America weren't even close. The high culture that in South America is a thing of beauty no longer exists in West Africa. But then there was Colombia. . . ."

Innes was in Colombia from 1987 to 1990 as the U.S. Coast Guard, police, and naval attaché. He also worked for the Drug Enforcement Administration. "Yemen can be hell in a handbasket, but it's paradise compared to the Colombia of that era."

Manuel Noriega held the reins of power in Panama, providing a haven for insurgents and narco-traffickers along the Panamanian-Colombian border. The Iran-Contra scandal raged still, which hindered Washington from providing the Colombian military the support it needed to battle the guerrillas and drug lords. The period also saw a closing act of the deadly drama between cocaine kingpin Pablo Escobar and the Colombian government.

Innes told me of an incident in the Amazon region of southeastern Colombia in the late 1980s. In one village, he and the Colombian troops accompanying him found all of the adults crying because their children had been kidnapped. Unlike previous kidnappings, no one had demanded a ransom. He and a force of local soldiers took a boat upriver. In a clearing they discovered a dozen bodies of children with various body organs removed in a not so delicate fashion. The local police chief and others believed the carnage was committed by smugglers and dealers in the lucrative underground trade in body organs for transplant. A wealthy and unknowing foreigner from another continent—Innes never found out who—had a child who desperately needed a liver transplant. Such a foreigner would be willing to pay anything to find a liver that matched for his child, and he wouldn't necessarily ask about how it was done.

"In Colombia," Innes continued, "there was no distinction between military conquest, enslaving Indians, kidnapping, narco-trafficking, or a black market for body organs, so long as it turned a profit. Drugs are the lure that promises to break the cycle of poverty. By local standards the cartels were not inhuman. For many, drugs represented a means of escaping abject poverty."

Narco-trafficking was, among other things, an economic weapon of the rising middle and upper-middle classes against the government, the traditional families, and the oligarchs who controlled the coca, the sweet coal, and the emeralds—the real wealth of the country.

"Violent, untimely death," he went on, "was normal for young men in many parts of Colombia. It's an intimate fact of their lives, it's what most of them expected. Because they know they are going to die young and in pain, they want to do right by their families, breaking the cycle of poverty. Narco-traffickers knew this. In Colombia, minors would never be tried and sentenced as an adult regardless of the crime, so criminal organizations sent children to commit horrible acts on their behalf. The narco-traffickers kept their promises to these kids, financially rewarding their families if they were killed or caught. There is a big show of moving the kids' parents into new little homes, and of sending the siblings off to private schools. That is more than the state could ever do for them. In Colombia, every pubescent teenager could be your assassin. In Yemen, crime operates within limits. Islamic law provides a vigorous moral compass."

I should go to Colombia, I thought.

Innes retired from the Coast Guard in the late 1990s and was recalled to active duty after September 11, 2001.

"I was mowing my lawn in Louisiana when the twin towers were hit. Now I've got forty guys under me, only forty, but they're a beginning. These guys," he told me, getting intense, "were kicked out of the other Yemeni armed services, because they were smart, they spoke English, they asked too many questions and so nobody here trusted them. They were demoralized. 'No,' I tell them. 'Don't you all understand! Before [Robert] Clive consolidated India for the British in the eighteenth century, Yemen, right through the Middle Ages, was the haunt of those like Sindbad the Sailor. Aden was among the largest ports in the world for a thousand years. The coast here constitutes an incredible strategic geography. When you look at the expanding desert, the maritime environment is the only non-bleak future this country has.'

"After the [French tanker] *Limburg* was hit by al-Qaeda," Innes went on, "insurance premiums for ships entering Yemeni waters went up 254 percent for a while. Yemen needs a twenty-first-century coast guard, like Jordan and the UAE [United Arab Emirates]. And these people are willing to learn; they're not like others in the region who just want to hire mercenaries."

Innes had $8 million of the $22 million in military aid that the U.S. had awarded Yemen after President Saleh and his half brother signed on to the War on Terrorism. Innes's ambition for the Yemeni coast guard was infectious. He told me how in "five to seven years," his 40 guys would increase to 2,500. They would patrol the coast from Saudi Arabia to Oman, from the Red Sea through the Bab el Mandeb Strait to the Gulf of Aden. "Their mere existence will drive down maritime insurance rates. I have forty-four-foot motor lifeboats for them, a real heroic, forgiving boat. The French boats from Djibouti are crap."

Two weeks later I happened to be in Aden, visiting the Prince of Wales Pier, a somber, gray, churchlike edifice that the British had built in 1919, at the start of their last phase of High Empire. Here, in the heart of "Steamer Point," from where British rule over Aden and its hinterlands had emanated, was an off-limits construction site, the spot that Bob Innes had chosen for the headquarters of his new Yemeni coast guard.

The month before I had come to Yemen, on November 3, 2002, a missile fired from an unmanned CIA Predator aircraft had incinerated a vehicle in which a suspected al-Qaeda leader, Abu Ali al-Harithi, was traveling along with five others in the Ma'rib region east of Sana'a. Since then, foreigners—Americans especially—had been denied permission by their embassies to enter the area, for their own safety. My plan was to pass through the northern, al-Qaeda–strewn badlands of al-Jawf and Ma'rib en route to the Wadi Hadhramaut, four hundred miles to the east, and then head south to the Arabian Sea where al-Qaeda was also active. I wanted a visual sense of the socioeconomic stew in which al-Qaeda flourished.

Leaving Sana'a, I and Abdullah, the driver whom Sheikh Murshed had found for me, entered a horrid maze of sandstone and black lava escarpments, buttes, and mesas that formed steep, wind-chiseled canyons. The canyons quickly emptied into an ashen wasteland speckled with ruins identified with the biblical kingdom of Sheba. An hour after leaving Sana'a, we pulled over by a roadside market to buy ghat for the afternoon chew.

Immediately I was amid filthy cinder-block storefronts, crowded like an inner city with young men in dirty white thobes, old keffiyahs and blazers, and armed with *jambiyas,* bandoleers, and Kalashnikov assault rifles.

It was like a John Wayne western, except that the men were wearing skirts. A young boy pulled out his *jambiya* and pointed it at my face, laughing manically as he did so. Blunt and difficult to remove from their sheaths, *jambiyas* are rather impractical as a ready weapon, and more often than not represent the stabilizing influence of tribal custom: the Yemeni social glue that kept down the rate of random crime. The AK-47s were another matter. "Once you have a gun, why bother to learn to read and write," the Yemeni soldier whom Abdullah had picked up interjected, after I had asked a particularly hostile knot of young men if they attended school. They didn't.

Estimates for the number of firearms in Yemen went as high as eighty million, four for every Yemeni. The U.S. intelligence community speculated at the time that Yemenis had more assault rifles and grenades per capita than any other nation in the world. The small arms threatened to raise Yemen's age-old tradition of quaint tribal wars to a debilitating level of anarchy.

Between Sanà'a and Ma'rib, a distance of 125 miles, I counted eleven military checkpoints signaled by oil drums filled with sand and cement. The government presence in this desert was greater than ever before, and that was no small achievement. The soldiers at these checkpoints were neither drunk nor vicious like the kind I had experienced in Sierra Leone, or like the lizard-eyed mafiosi I had seen in former Soviet Georgia. Yemen was not a failed state. It was just a somewhat weak one, like so many others around the world. That's what made the canvas which continued to unroll before my eyes so daunting.

The Global War on Terrorism—or GWOT, as the U.S. military called it—represented merely the current phase of American imperialism. But terrorism was both a cause and a symptom of the political weakness of states like Yemen. So, in a sense, the U.S. was fighting the unwieldy process of modernization itself.

The military checkpoints were freelance enterprises, where underpaid soldiers charged a few thousand riyals ($20) to jump in the car with a foreigner and protect him until the next checkpoint or two. Officially, the main road between Sana'a and Ma'rib was in government hands. But between one checkpoint and the next—indeed, two hundred yards away from any of the checkpoints—anything could happen. Mudbrick battlements visible from the road hid the encampments of rebellious tribal sheikhs, some with their own artillery pieces. The crowded markets selling

guns and ghat multiplied as we skirted the region of al-Jawf ("The Depression"), an especially lawless region plagued by a continuum of mysterious
bombings and tribal firefights.

We pulled into a roadside café—a few broken tables and chairs set on
a corroded wooden pallet. Two Toyota pickup trucks stormed in, filled
with rowdy young men in their early teens, most with bad teeth, pockmarked complexions, and broken fingernails. Every one of them had an
AK-47, often with the safety latch off. Older men, also armed, were the
drivers. The lone soldier accompanying us sat morosely sipping his tea, as
though trying to hide. The fact that Yemen had among the lowest per
capita income and highest population growth rate in the world was for me
no longer a statistical abstraction.[4]

The sheikhs who controlled these young men were often wealthy: from
highway robbery, the sale of guns and other cross-border contraband, and
bribes offered by both the Yemeni government and Saudi Wahabis. With
the money the sheikhs bought sheep and camels, and more guns and ammunition; they didn't build schools and women's health clinics. It was a
conscious choice, not a matter of poverty. I thought of warriors straight out
of the *Iliad,* armed with cell phones and other information-age paraphernalia.

To counter this trend, the U.S. Embassy in Sana'a was overseeing a foreign aid program in the Ma'rib region that included the building of schools
and a hospital. But the general instability this close to the capital, plus the
heightened tension following the CIA's Predator attack, made it a difficult
choice whether or not to expose civilian aid workers to kidnapping and
worse. (To wit, the U.S. Embassy was a sealed-off fortress, with multiple
gates, two-way mirrors, and iron teeth coming out of the ground to block
vehicles. Most of the diplomatic staff were males without dependents.)

Given these facts, it was left to the military assistance team from
CENTCOM to provide the liberal humanist alternative. The money for
military assistance that wasn't going to Bob Innes's coast guard, or to
bribe Ali Muhsen into supporting his half brother's new alliance with the
Americans, was being spent on the training of Yemeni elite units. Nobody
expected President Saleh to take control of these desert tracks east and
north of the capital. However, the U.S. did hope that better-trained Yemeni
commandos would eventually be able to project power at will, facilitating
the introduction of civilian aid workers.

It was a Hobbesian state of affairs. Thomas Hobbes, the English philosopher, was by seventeenth-century standards a modernizer, because he believed that the breakdown of the medieval order, through the establishment of a central governing authority, was necessary for liberal progress. In Yemen the soldier took precedence over the aid worker because it was only the soldier who could provide the elemental security, without which there could be no central authority in the first place.

Leaving al-Jawf for Ma'rib, we now had two armed guards riding with us, along with an escort of soldiers in a separate truck that we had picked up at the latest roadblock.

Ma'rib, described by the Elder Pliny in his *Natural History* as a town six miles in circumference, had been the capital of biblical Sheba. It was now a gridwork of dusty streets littered with wrapping paper and discarded bottles. The ratty storefronts rested on high cinderblocks, smelling of oil and petrol combined with choking gray dust. Except for a flock of women clad from head to toe in black, the whole place had the atmosphere of a male dormitory. Given the recent Predator attack, I was told to tell people that "I was Australian."

Who here was al-Qaeda? I asked myself, licking my fingers after devouring a greasy chicken in a sidewalk restaurant filled with armed youngsters. Perhaps nobody. It didn't matter. The point was that these foul, densely populated encampments in Yemen's northern desert, adjoining the most unstable parts of Saudi Arabia, constituted a fertile petri dish within which radical groups such as al-Qaeda and its offspring could breed. Here was the demographic and cultural battlefield that the U.S. security establishment would have to penetrate. Similar battlefields lay all over the world.

———

The fact that Ma'rib was an oasis became noticeable only when I looked down on it from afar: from a sun-baked archaeological mound coated in moondust holding the crumbled debris of antiquity, with nineteenth-century mudbrick towers tilting crazily in each direction. The tourist stand had long collapsed. A few soldiers followed on foot close behind me. From the top of the mound I saw a thin band of drab vegetation.

For a thousand years, from the eighth century B.C., the great dam of Ma'rib, whose massive, honeycombed walls were still visible, joined with an elaborate system of terrace irrigation to make much of this desert truly green. Biblical Sheba (the Sabaean kingdom) had been part of an antique cluster of civilization every bit as fabulous as the Nile Valley in Egypt and the environs of Carthage in Tunisia. The pharaonic Egyptians called this corner of Arabia the Land of Punt; to the Hebrews it was Ophir. As I shall explain, Yemen's internal disarray was a natural by-product of this history, which in turn was a result of geography.

Yemen, or *Yaman,* is a word of ancient connotation. In Arabic it literally means "right hand," the part of Arabia south of the Gulf of Aqaba that, from the standpoint of Greco-Egyptian geographers like Ptolemy, lay to the "right" of Alexandria. Yemen, with a quarter of Saudi Arabia's land area, yet with a population almost as large as Saudi Arabia's, has since the classical age been the demographic core of the Arabian Peninsula. Here in the peninsula's southwest corner sweeping basalt plateaus rear up into volcanic plugs and sandcastle formations, framing a network of oases that since antiquity has sustained large urban populations.

Separated from one another by mountain fastnesses, and rich from the production of funerary spices on the cliff sides, from 800 B.C. to A.D. 500 half a dozen tribal kingdoms in this part of Arabia (Sabaean, Hadhramauti, Himyarite) fought internecine wars, even as their merchants cultivated contacts with Africa and southern Asia. From India came diamonds and sapphires, lapis lazuli, and pepper; from Africa, ivory and ostrich feathers. Sabaean merchants and their rivals exported frankincense and myrrh at a time when such spices sweetened every funeral altar in the known world. Yemeni kingdoms grew rich on their individual strips of the great incense highway. Freya Stark writes that "they became imperial and aristocratic, builders of tall cities; they colonized Somaliland and Ethiopia."[5] Yet, because each was checked by the other, in spite of their imperial demeanor, none of them developed into an empire that was able to rule the whole of present-day Yemen.

These ancient kingdoms were followed by an equally bewildering assemblage of medieval Arab dynasties—Ziyadids, Zaydis, Rasulids, and so forth—both Shiite and Sunni, as each valley and oasis remained a sovereignty unto itself. Indeed, the Rasulid period from 1229 to 1454 stands out as the only example of effective government over most of Yemen through modern times.[6]

The Ottoman Turks officially conquered Yemen in 1517. But their four-hundred-year hold over the interior was nothing but a series of bloody failures, with the Shiite Zaydis withdrawing into their mountain hideouts of northern Yemen following each victory. To the south, the British officers who manned the Aden Protectorate were kept busy maintaining short-lived truces among the Qu'aiti, Kathiri, and other tribes in the Hadhramaut and adjoining wadis. The historian Jan Morris mentions that "the last true expression of High Empire" for the British was the system of tenuous treaties among the Hadhramauti chieftains negotiated by Harold Ingrams of the Colonial Office and his adventurous wife, Doreen, which came to be known as the *Sulh Ingrams* (Ingram's Peace).[7]

But internecine violence never truly ceased. A civil war from 1962 to 1968 in northern Yemen, between the forces of a conservative imam and revolutionary officers supported by Gamal Abdel Nasser's Egypt—a war which gradually disintegrated into the usual tribal feuding—claimed two hundred thousand lives before a military-run republic emerged. Meanwhile, in southern Yemen, Britain's Aden Protectorate gave way to a Marxist state, where, in 1986, Moscow's attempt to change the leadership of the Yemeni Communist party led to a month-long intertribal war in which ten thousand people were killed. As in Afghanistan, the Soviets found that Yemeni governments were easy to change but that once installed they were undermined by clan divides.

North and South Yemen officially united in 1990, as the South Yemeni state collapsed in the course of the worldwide dissolution of the Soviet empire. But unlike in Eastern Europe, the experiment with democracy failed here. Indeed, it led to another civil war in 1994, this time along north-south lines, in which the north emerged victorious; seven thousand people died in the fighting.

Ali Abdullah Saleh, a former army lieutenant colonel, took power in North Yemen in 1978. Though he couldn't control all of this Afghanistan-like country, he was still doing better than the Turks or the British before him.

The anachronistic trinity of family, village, and tribe that has divided Yemen since antiquity had one positive element, though: it prevented the kind of stultifying, overly centralized tyranny existent in places like Iraq and Syria. And with no danger of Saleh becoming such a tyrant, the CENTCOM concept of training Yemeni elite units to project power in the cindery badlands held out the only hope of liberalization, through the extension of central authority. But to succeed, the three-thousand-year legacy of separate Yemeni kingdoms would have to be overcome.

We continued east, passing through the edge of the Empty Quarter, the utter desert that, while associated with Saudi Arabia, crept over into

Yemen. It was late when we entered the Wadi Hadhramaut and stopped for *salta,* a spicy stew filled with beans and lentils. Reclining on a rush mat in the gaslit darkness, I noticed that the bread I had been served was similar to Indian *nan,* and that the men had darker, more oriental features than in Sana'a and Ma'rib. Instead of thobes they were wearing plaid loincloths, like men I had seen in India, Burma, and Indonesia. It was testimony to the copious family and trading links with South and Southeast Asia that Hadhramauti merchants had maintained for centuries; the Nizam of Hyderabad, in south-central India, recruited his bodyguards exclusively from Hadhramauti tribesmen.[8]

Despite a history of insular tribal feuds, this hundred-mile-long oasis, inhabited since 1000 B.C., was part of a rich cosmopolitan world obscure to the West. The rise of radical Islam in Indonesia in our own time has its roots in Islamic learning centers established in the early eighteenth century by Hadhramauti traders, whose twenty-first-century business networks derive from those begun by the Sabaean and Himyaritic spice merchants of antiquity.[9] Such networks offered convenient pathways for a group like al-Qaeda to conduct its financial operations, particularly as Osama bin Laden's family came from the nearby Wadi Do'an. Caravan trails, revived by bin Laden's organization, provided the Hadhramaut with direct links to Mecca and other places in Saudi Arabia.

I awoke the next morning to a racket of birds amid pink oleanders, highlighting fields of alfalfa and date palms at the bottom of soaring, crumbly canyons. In towns dubbed "mini-Manhattans," because of the six- and seven-story mudbrick buildings stacked one against the other, hordes of young boys filled the narrow alleys. The jewelry stores had been boarded up and replaced by hardware and motorbike shops after the collapse of the nascent tourist boomlet of the early 1990s. This was when kidnappings increased and the Hadhramaut became known as an al-Qaeda hideout. In the shell of a dilapidated hotel, once owned by a Hadhramauti trading family from Singapore, I had a Pepsi with a devout young man who told me that "people here have different opinions about Osama than you do in America, so I think it is better that we do not discuss it."

From the Wadi Hadhramaut it took five hours to reach Mukalla on the Arabian Sea, where the French oil tanker *Limburg* had been bombed by al-Qaeda in 2002. Mukalla teemed with Somali refugees, Ethiopian street urchins, and Islamicized Yemenis recently returned from Saudi Arabia.

The Wahabi attempt to radicalize Yemenis was having more success in the formerly Marxist south, where fundamentalism was the natural reaction to communism and its assault on religion.

At sunset I took a walk on Mukalla's beachfront. Red volcanic rocks pressed against steamy seawater with scabby white buildings in the background. The beachfront was divided into two parts: one for men and teenage boys; another for women and their young children. The women were veiled and most of the men had beards. Garbage was everywhere. Yet it was a peaceful communal space, with throngs of the proletarian faithful enjoying the first evening breezes. Mukalla offered the urban fundamentalist counterpart to the wild tribalism of the northern desert and the exotic cultural stew of the Wadi Hadhramaut. To judge by the recent firefights, Mukalla's al-Qaeda cells had eluded capture by Yemeni commandos. Here was yet another battlefield that awaited successful penetration by U.S. intelligence agencies.

Yemen was vast. And it was only one small country. I looked at the teeming working-class crowd all around me, so pure and devout, each young woman with several children. To judge by the threadbare Western polyesters of the men, the folkways of the tribe were slipping away faster in Mukalla than in Sana'a, making religion here less traditional and inevitably more austere and political.

How was America to cope with this crowd and so many more like it, from Morocco to Indonesia? "Rome is no longer confined to Rome: henceforth she must identify herself with half the globe, or must perish," writes the French novelist and historian Marguerite Yourcenar, assuming the voice of the Emperor Hadrian.[10]

How to manage such an imperium? It was time to find out.

CHAPTER TWO

SOUTHCOM

COLOMBIA, WINTER 2003

WITH NOTES ON EL SALVADOR

"The future of military conflict was better gauged in Colombia than in Iraq. . . . In Colombia I was introduced to the tactics that the U.S. would employ to manage an unruly world."

H ow do you infiltrate and police the world, if such a thing were even possible?" I asked.

"You produce a product and let him loose," retired U.S. Army Maj. Gen. Sidney Shachnow told me.

Back from Yemen, I had arrived at a horse farm in Southern Pines, North Carolina, a manicured landscape of calm hills, shaved lawns, freshly painted white picket fences, and carefully tended private roads less than an hour from the ratty sprawlsville that dominated Fort Bragg, home of U.S. Army Special Operations Command. Gen. Shachnow owned horses. Yet, with his spartan tastes and rugged, growly voice—his accent a blend of darkest Eastern Europe and working-class Boston—he didn't seem to fit with this fantasy landscape. Gen. Shachnow had spent his life fitting into places he shouldn't have. Sid Shachnow, a Jewish Holocaust survivor, was a veteran of two combat tours in Vietnam. With forty years of active military service, he was one of the deans of the Army Special Forces' old boys network.

Born in 1933 in Lithuania, Shachnow spent three years of his boyhood in a Nazi concentration camp, and then supported his family in Allied-occupied Germany by selling contraband on the black market. He had watched his mother being raped by a drunken Lithuanian partisan—a fact that slipped out during one of our conversations, when he also told me about his attempt to get his family's property back in Lithuania.[1] "The number of Jews in Vietnam and in the world of Special Forces where I spent my life, well, you could fit them in a small car," he said, shrugging.

We talked no more of it. Being Jewish was nothing he wore on his sleeve. He had married a Catholic girl and his Jewish family had virtually disowned him; the marriage, still strong, was at the half-century point. Besides, the world of liberal Jews was not one with which he could always be comfortable. "The shots of the last helicopters leaving Vietnam still nauseate me," he said. "I remember getting Broadway tickets while on leave from the service, with a note written on them saying, 'Don't wear your uniform to the theater.' "

The layers of Shachnow's personality were like armored breastplates. Every aspect of his lined face and short, wiry body seemed hard and chiseled. Awards, citations, and decorations lined the walls of his home and the guest quarters. I imagined Ligustinus, the Roman centurion who had served in Spain, Macedonia, and Greece. Ligustinus had spent nearly half his life in the army and was rewarded for bravery thirty-four times.[2]

Shachnow had enlisted in the Army out of high school, and rose to sergeant first class before attending Officer Candidate School at Fort Benning, Georgia. He had survived concentration camp guards, got married with no money to a girl of another faith, raised a family of four daughters, gone from private to two-star general, and lived in a magnificent home, all because of decisions he had made on instinct and impulse. He implied that if the U.S. was going to monitor and regulate the world with a minimal number of troops and without large-scale wars, then it would require the ability to replicate soldier personalities like himself.

"An SF [Special Forces] guy has to be a lethal killer one moment and a humanitarian the next. He has to know how to get strangers who speak another language to do things for him. He has to go from knowing enough Russian to knowing enough Georgian and Arabic in a few weeks, depending upon the deployment. We need people who are cultural quick studies."

Shachnow was not talking about area expertise; that took too many years to develop and, in any case, was not always practical for Special Operations Forces (SOF), a bureaucratic category which included Army Special Forces (the so-called Green Berets), Rangers, and psy-ops (psychological operations); Navy Special Boat Units and SEALs (Sea, Air, and Land commando teams); Air Force para-rescue units, and so forth. Special Operations Forces did not have the luxury of knowing in which part of the world they would have to intervene. Rather, Shachnow was talking about a knack, about a way of dealing with people, about implanting charisma almost. The right men would find things out and act on the information they gathered, simply by knowing how to behave in a given situation.*

"The Special Forces who dropped in to help [the warlord Abdul Rashid] Dostum, the guys who grew beards, got on horses, and dressed up like Afghans, were not ordered to do so by Gen. Tommy Franks. It was a decision they made in the field.

"That's why I joined SF," Shachnow continued. "In Vietnam, when I commanded my own infantry battalion, there was someone to pitch my tent, blow up my air bag, make me coffee, and drive my jeep. If you're the ego-trip sort of guy you like that. In SF you pitch your own tent and blow up your own air bag. I joined Special Forces because it forced me to think; it kept me from getting bored."

Shachnow introduced me to the world of Army Special Forces, where I would start my odyssey with the American military. Later I would move on to other branches of the armed services, in no particular order, often shuttling back and forth. Comparison is the heart of all serious scholarship, and thus my keenest perceptions about SF would come only after many trips with non-SF units.

U.S. Army Special Forces traced their origins to the World War II–era Office of Strategic Services (OSS), specifically the Jedburgh teams who were dropped behind enemy lines in Nazi-occupied France, and Detachment 101, which operated in Burma.[3] Jedburgh is an area of Scotland where local Scots had conducted guerrilla war against British invaders in the twelfth century. The Jedburgh concept meant placing small teams in hostile terrain, to train and organize much larger groups of guerrillas in unconventional warfare so that the teams became force multipliers.[4]

The OSS, disbanded after World War II, gave birth to the Central Intelligence Agency (CIA) in 1947 and to the 10th Special Forces Group in 1952, based at Fort Bragg, which had responsibility for operating behind enemy lines in Europe in the event of war with the Warsaw Pact nations. President John F. Kennedy, whose respect for unconventional warfare dated to his experiences as a PT boat commander in the Pacific in World War II, expanded the role of Army Special Forces, particularly in Southeast Asia, and awarded them an official headgear, the green beret.[5] But the

* Women did not serve in the Special Operations community.

term "Green Berets" is rarely used by Special Forces troops themselves. They prefer simply "SF."

SF's real signature was not sartorial but organizational: its emphasis on twelve-man teams.

In places like Yemen, the right men, men like Shachnow, had the best chance of finding the right hinge—the fragile axis upon which political developments in a given country can turn. The Spartans turned the tide of battle in Sicily by dispatching only a small mission, headed by Gylippus. His arrival in 414 B.C. kept Sparta's allies, the Syracusans, from surrendering to the Athenians. It broke the Athenian land blockade of Syracuse, rallied other Sicilian city-states behind Syracuse, and was crucial to the defeat of the Athenian fleet the following year.

The notion that vast historical forces could be tipped by the right individuals exerting pressure in the right spot has always offered an attractive antidote to fatalism. As such, it was reprised by President Kennedy, who, in the second decade of the Cold War, believed that relatively small-scale unconventional, covert operations could be an alternative to massive nuclear retaliation. Kennedy also believed that the nature of war itself was changing. As he told the 1962 graduating class of West Point: "This is another type of war, new in its intensity, ancient in its origin—war by guerrillas, subversives, insurgents, assassins, war by ambush instead of by [conventional] combat. . . . It requires . . . a whole new kind of strategy, a wholly different kind of force, and therefore a new and wholly different kind of military training."[6]

Kennedy could have been describing the world of the early twenty-first century. Though his vision of unconventional war was to bear mixed results in Vietnam, his larger analysis would prove clairvoyant.*

——————

Special Forces was particularly active in Colombia, the country that Coast Guard Capt. Bob Innes in Yemen had described to me in grisly detail. Thus Colombia was where I wanted to go. It was the third biggest recipient of U.S. foreign aid after Israel and Egypt. American interests there were hard to overestimate.

* See Richard H. Shultz Jr.'s *The Secret War Against Hanoi: The Untold Story of Spies, Saboteurs, and Covert Warriors in North Vietnam* (New York: HarperCollins, 1999) (footnote 6) for a lucid analysis of the problems of unconventional war in Vietnam, and of Kennedy's attraction to it.

Colombia is the third most populous country in Latin America after Brazil and Mexico, and half as close to the United States as Europe. It has vast untapped oil reserves; America was already getting more oil from this region of South America than from the Arab world. Colombian narco-terrorists had forged strategic links with radical Islamists: proof that while the frontier of Indian Country used to begin eight miles west of Fort Leavenworth—where the Santa Fe and Oregon trails separated—it now circumscribed the earth, and was not confined to the Middle East.

While the world's last totalitarian, Cold War regimes in Iraq and North Korea were grabbing headlines that winter, the future of military conflict was better gauged in Colombia, which represented a severer form of social breakdown than Yemen or almost anyplace else in the Middle East. The effort in Iraq, with its large-scale mobilization of troops and immense concentration of risk, could not be indicative of how the U.S. would act in the future. It was in Colombia where I was introduced to the tactics that the U.S. would employ to manage an unruly world.

Colombian guerrilla groups had forsaken controlling twentieth-century ideologies in favor of decentralized baronies and franchises, built on terrorism, narco-trafficking, kidnapping, counterfeiting, and extortion of oil pipeline revenues from local governments. With hundreds of millions of dollars annually from cocaine-related profits, and with documented links to the Irish Republican Army and the Basque separatists—who advised them on kidnapping and car bomb tactics—the Colombian guerrillas were an exotic variant of al-Qaeda, in the sense that they had no stake in any legitimate world order.

While Yemen boasted the largest per capita number of small arms in the world, Colombia led the world in kidnapping: three thousand in 2002 alone. Colombia produced 80 percent of the world's cocaine. More so than Yemen, Colombia was less a country than a series of fortified city-states, perched eight thousand feet up in the Andean Cordilleras, surrounded by ungovernable, fast-buck tropical lowlands. In those sweaty forest tracts, loyalty to the elected government in Bogotá was, as one Army officer at Fort Bragg told me, "about twentieth on the inhabitants' list of priorities."

Even as U.S. leaders denied that America had imperial intentions, Colombia—so remote from public consciousness, and yet the recipient of so much American aid—illustrated the imperial reality of America's global situation. In Colombia, cocaine armies had constituted an intractable insurgency long before al-Qaeda did. To better understand the so-called War on Terrorism, it was worth beginning with the so-called War on Drugs.

—

Thus, I flew to Miami, the headquarters of U.S. Southern Command.

SOUTHCOM traced its origins to 1903, when the first U.S. Marines arrived in Panama to protect a railroad connecting the Atlantic and Pacific oceans. It had responsibility for Central and South America, and the Caribbean.* Only in 1997 did SOUTHCOM move its headquarters from the outskirts of Panama City to Miami. The many decades in Panama, the large number of Latinos in the U.S. military, and the fact that so many non-Latino troops in SOUTHCOM spoke Spanish made it the most insular, old-fashioned, and colonial of all the area commands.

The flags flying at the Miami headquarters called to mind the Spanish-American War of 1898 and lesser, constabulary escapades south of the border. The ethnic Cubans, Puerto Ricans, Dominicans, and Mexicans in SOUTHCOM's ranks were the American equivalent of the field-savvy Hindustani- and Pushto-speaking Anglo-Indians who had served Britain's Indian army so well. Officers and enlisted men spent entire careers in SOUTHCOM, to a degree uncommon in other theaters, moving from El Salvador to Honduras, then to Panama, to Peru, Ecuador, Colombia, and so on: "the *cucaracha* circuit," as it was affectionately known. The battalion coins for the Army's 7th Special Forces Group, the group assigned to Latin America, were engraved in Spanish rather than in English: "Fuerzas Especiales" rather than "Special Forces." Seventh Group was the only SF group that approximated the standards of the original 10th Group in terms of linguistic and area expertise.[7]

SOUTHCOM's identity was further defined by a feeling of inferiority. With Europe the principal Cold War battleground, and Asia the secondary front because of the threat posed by "Red" China and North Korea, the American military in Latin America had for decades been given short shrift, even as it had a vast area to defend. The answer to this predicament was aggressive intelligence operations and Special Forces' training of local armies, combined with coercive diplomacy.

The results were not always pretty: witness the murder of thousands of

* Mexico is covered by Northern Command.

innocent civilians in the aftermath of the 1973 coup against Salvador Allende in Chile. Yet for a relatively small investment in money and manpower, the U.S. neutralized an aggressive Soviet and Cuban campaign at its back door, helping to pave the way for the democratic transitions and market liberalizations of the 1980s and 1990s. In 1967 in Bolivia, Special Forces helped hunt down and kill the hemispheric agitator Ernesto "Che" Guevara.* In the 1980s in El Salvador, 55 Special Forces trainers accomplished arguably more than 550,000 troops in Vietnam: teaching the Salvadoran military to slow down a communist insurgency, even as it transformed itself from a 12,000-man, ill-disciplined constabulary force to a more professional 60,000-man army.† El Salvador showed that you didn't need many people to fight these small wars, but the ones you deployed should be the best.[8]

"Economy of Force" was what Maj. Gen. Geoffrey C. Lambert at Fort Bragg and SOUTHCOM hands in Miami called the strategy of the Cold War decades—their way of talking about the right hinge. Actually, Economy of Force was a strategy practiced by all the great empires of antiquity, which had prevailing but not unlimited amounts of military power, so that necessity required them to be both light and lethal, leading to a reliance on mobile strike forces and client states, which was particularly the case with Rome.[9]

In Latin America, an Economy of Force strategy had produced friendly regimes that in almost every case were better than what the Cubans and Russians had in mind. Even in Chile, despite the human rights iniquities of

---

* SOUTHCOM provided a fifteen-man Special Forces Mobile Training Team to train a Bolivian Ranger battalion, which killed Guevara. Guevara had hoped that the U.S. would respond with a massive gringo intervention; in fact, Washington's response was measured. Guevara's company made the additional mistake of trying to recruit native Bolivian Indians whose Quechua and Aymara languages they didn't speak. See John D. Waghelstein, "Ruminations of a Pachyderm or What I Learned in the Counter-insurgency Business," *Small Wars and Insurgencies* (London: Cass, Winter 1994), p. 362.

† The Special Forces operation in El Salvador was certainly not a complete success, nor were many aspects of the Vietnam War a failure. Moreover, the congressionally imposed limit of 55 SF trainers at any one time—a reflection of the Vietnam syndrome—was not always adhered to; in fact, the real number on the ground was often higher. Still, it was an exceedingly small number. The U.S. approach to El Salvador showed that as much help as the U.S. gives a besieged ally in a small war, ultimately, military and humanitarian assistance must operate under a reasonably strict ceiling, so that the war remains the ally's to win or lose.

dictator Augusto Pinochet following Allende's overthrow, the military regime there subsequently lowered infant mortality from 79 to 11 per 1,000 births, and reduced the poverty rate from 30 percent of the population to 11 percent.[10] Such melding of the political reality south of the border did not run the risk of quagmires, for throughout the Cold War there were relatively few official Americans on the ground in any one Latin American country.

SOUTHCOM's Economy of Force concept now offered a beautiful logic for the seemingly intractable world of the turn of the twenty-first century, in which everyone (humanitarian interventionists included) admitted that nation-building, whether it was in Bosnia, Afghanistan, Iraq, or Colombia, was fraught with danger, difficulty, uncertainty, and great expense.

Don't try to fix the whole society. Rather, identify a few key pivotal elements in it, and try to fix them. For example, because a national army is essentially unreformable without wholesale social and cultural change, work to improve only its elite units, using men from America's own military elite as trainers. That had been the motor for change in El Salvador, where political violence per month was reduced from 610 murders in 1980 to 23 in 1987.[11] It was the strategy in Colombia, too.

The exterior of the American Embassy in Bogotá, Colombia, was a replica of the one I had seen in Sana'a, Yemen. Both were "Inman buildings," a reference to Adm. Bobby Ray Inman, who in 1985 chaired an advisory panel that set tougher security standards for U.S. embassies. There were the fleet of armored cars whose drivers always altered their routes, the bomb-blast walls, the hundred-foot setbacks, sliding electronic gates, and active vehicle restraints (AVRs), also known as Delta barriers, that popped up from below the ground.

The Bogotá embassy compound was a world of acronyms, a particular feature of America's entire national security community at the dawn of the twenty-first century. Acronyms formed the private language that only the initiated understood, like the Latin and Greek once spoken by the upper echelons of the British Empire. Inside the embassy was the NAS (narcotics affairs section), which ran the CD (counter-drug) program. Adjacent to the main building, in a one-level prefabricated unit, made of two sheets of aluminum separated by foam, was the TOC, or tactical operations center, for the 3rd Battalion of the 7th Special Forces Group. The TOC was also known as the FOB, the forward operating base for the 3rd Battalion.*

The 3rd Battalion, like all Special Forces battalions, was divided into three companies that were in turn divided into six twelve-man detachments, many of which were strewn across Colombia. The FOB was manned by one of these detachments, ODA-773: Operational Detachment Alpha-773. The Alpha signified that this was a front-line SF team, even if it currently functioned in a support role.

In a corner office of the FOB sat the 3rd Battalion's commander, Lt. Col. Kevin A. "Duke" Christie, the effective leader of all Green Berets in Colombia. Like Coast Guard Capt. Innes in Yemen, he was a New York City fireman's kid, though from Queens rather than Brooklyn. Duke Christie had joined Army ROTC at Florida State University. The first time he was shot at was by urban guerrillas in Lima, Peru, in the 1980s. He served afterwards in Bosnia and Pakistan, trained paratroopers in Kenya, spoke French and German, and was forgetting his Russian, even as his Spanish was coming along. Gangly and muscular, with sharp features and short, corn-colored hair combed upward in 1950s style, Duke Christie was one of those personable guys you could begin your first conversation with in mid-sentence, though when I first met him at SOUTHCOM headquarters in Miami he had been somewhat subdued. One of the best officers in his command, Capt. Adam Kocheran, a West Point graduate about to enter medical school, with a pregnant wife, had just been killed by a claymore mine in a training exercise in Puerto Rico.

The battle update brief for Friday, February 7, 2003, prepared for Duke by his staff, began at 8 a.m. at the FOB in Bogotá. Around a three-sided arrangement of Formica tables with fans whirring sat Maj. Albert Quiros, Capts. Bill Pittman and Luciano Gonzales, Chief Warrant Officer III Pat Gleason, and other officers. All were in BDUs (battle dress utilities, green camouflage uniforms for U.S. troops in the tropics, tan for those in the desert Middle East). The first subject was a "Nairobi scenario," a reference to the 1998 al-Qaeda bombing of the American embassies in Nairobi, Kenya, and Dar es Salaam, Tanzania.

---

* For diplomatic reasons, it was politically unacceptable for SOUTHCOM to have a forward operating base inside Colombia. Thus, it was technically a battalion headquarters and not an FOB, though that's what everyone called it.

"The threat level at the embassy from narco-terrorists has increased significantly," noted Maj. Quiros dourly. "Where?" Duke asked. "At this embassy, and at your hotel," Maj. Quiros replied, looking at me in a manner both genial and threatening. A diagram of the embassy grounds was taped on a stretched camouflage poncho that served as a wall partition. Maj. Quiros outlined which officers would control what "fields of fire" in case the embassy was attacked, who would keep the "comms" (communications) going, and who would stay behind here in the "cheesebox" to blow up the safe boxes that held stacks of classified documents.

The brief continued. A congressional delegation would be arriving. Along with the congressmen and their staffers, it would include a few Marine escorts, meaning that some U.S. troops would have to be moved out of Colombia temporarily to preserve the "force cap." The force cap was a congressionally mandated limit on the number of uniformed U.S. troops that could be in-country at any one time to prevent mission creep. In El Salvador, with a population of five million in the 1980s, it had been fifty-five Special Forces trainers. In Colombia, whose population approached forty million, it was four hundred troops, including roughly seventy Special Forces trainers. The force caps were arbitrary, based more on political trade-offs in Washington than on any substantive analysis of what was required to get the job done. They simply reflected the fear of another Vietnam, even though the difference between having a few hundred elite troops in a country and hundreds of thousands of draftees was vast. Nevertheless, in an imperfect world, force caps were the ultimate guarantors of an Economy of Force strategy.

There was a discussion about the ammunition problem. Imperialism was less about conquest than about the training of local armies. Reliance on American techniques and weapons systems, and the relationships established between American officers and their third world protégés, helped give the U.S. the access it needed around the globe. And when Army Special Forces agreed to train a third world army, it also supplied the ammunition and equipment used in the training.

Arranging transport for the "palletized ammo" from Fort Bragg on C-130s and C-27s was turning out to be a chore. (The military shipped everything in aluminum pallets.) "It's a bleak world out there as far as available aircraft are concerned," reported Chief Warrant Officer Gleason in a flat Nebraskan accent.

Pat Gleason, like many noncommissioned sergeants and warrant officers I would meet in the course of my travels, was quietly amazing. From his laptop he ran the equivalent of a small travel agency and moving company, shuttling troops and equipment between the eastern United States, Puerto Rico, and Colombia. His Green Beret specialty was HALO (high altitude, low opening). He could jump out of a plane at night at 25,000 feet, opening the parachute at 3,500 feet. He spoke fluent Spanish and had served all over the Americas. With only one year at Campbell University in Buies Creek, North Carolina, he had a knowledge of South America (of the mores of the Chilean military, of political attitudes in rural Bolivia, and so on) that was nevertheless encyclopedic. Duke called him the team's "collective, historical memory."

There was, too, the issue of the new communications gear. Signals Capt. Bill Pittman, a West Point graduate from Georgia, said it was time "to raise the bullshit flag" about the plan to replace the old PSE-5 Delta "commo" system with a flyweight triband multi-channel package that bundled voice, data, secret, and nonsecret communications. The former system required a network of cumbersome outdoor antennae. The latter ran everything from secure telephones to unclassified PowerPoint briefings off a single eight-foot satellite dish. But it was complicated to operate and repair. Pittman worried that the operator-trainers wouldn't stay long enough in Bogotá to transfer their knowledge, and the new system would end up as a broken toy that everyone stared at and didn't know how to use properly.

All in all, it was a typical morning brief, thousands of which were held by the American military around the world every day.

I had dinner with Capt. Pittman the following night in Bogotá's glitzy Zona Rosa district, a few blocks from my hotel. It was a night I won't forget. Admiring the clean streets, bicycle paths, and sidewalk ramps for the handicapped from the restaurant window, and refreshing my palate with sorbet between courses, I might have been in any upscale American suburb. Compared to Caracas, Venezuela, where I had been some years before, Bogotá was low-key and dressed-down. The wealthy lived in apartments rather than in villas. It all seemed so thoroughly American. Then I saw that Pittman was distracted.

"What was that?" he said to the waiter, noticing the window shake. The waiter shrugged, unknowing.

We returned to our conversation. Pittman mentioned that Colombia was a bit reminiscent of the Pacific theater in World War II: jungly, disease-ridden, and chillingly violent in its hinterlands, and yet somewhat relegated by American policymakers because of larger events elsewhere. I told him that Bogotá reminded me of Santa Monica and Tel Aviv. Five minutes after Pittman had noticed the window shake his cell phone rang. It was the FOB informing him that five minutes before a big car bomb had exploded a few blocks from our restaurant and my hotel.

The concussion blast inside the exclusive El Nogal club, a haven for the Bogotá elite—accomplished with 440 pounds of fertilizer-based explosive—killed 32 people and wounded 260. Locals compared it to the 1995 Oklahoma City blast. It was the work of the Fuerzas Armadas Revolucionarias de Colombia, or FARC. Americans were not among the casualties, but the car bomb and a smaller blast the next day occurred near the American Embassy and hotels frequented by Americans.

The FARC's origins dated to the communist agitation of the 1920s in rural Colombia, which came in the wake of the Russian Revolution, though in Colombia there had always been more banditry than Marxist philosophy, so that the fall of the Berlin Wall had little effect here. Indeed, it was difficult to know what the war was about anymore.

Lured by billions in annual cocaine-related profits, these leftist guerrillas, as well as rightist paramilitaries formed by local landowners in response to guerrilla outrages, drifted easily from a unifying ideology to localized anarchy, in which franchises arose built on murder and extortion. By the 1990s, Colombia's homicide rates had tripled from already high levels, making Colombia more dangerous than even Brazil, Mexico, Nicaragua, and Panama.[12] The tradition of an amoral paganistic Christianity, combined with the struggle over drug revenues, fed the sickening violence. Colombia demonstrated that the most basic human right is not freedom of speech but personal security.[13]

The FARC, with its seventeen thousand or so fighters, no longer represented the shaggy-haired university idealists of the Cold War era, but a criminal army built on the forced recruitment of teenage boys and girls, in which desertion led to the slaughter of one's family. FARC leader Mañuel Marulanda, perhaps the world's oldest living guerrilla, might still have harbored ideals. But with an income variously estimated at $500 million annually in protection money from the cocaine business, the FARC was Karl Marx at the top and Adam Smith all the way down the command chain.

To wit, the FARC frequently set up roadblocks that would last for days, checking the names of drivers and passengers against a computer database to see if their bank accounts made them worthy of kidnapping. In Colombia, ideology was dead, as were historical grievances. Ethnic conflict had never been an issue. It was all about money.

_____

Because Colombian society was sick, so was its military. While U.S. Army Special Forces couldn't reform the whole Colombian army, it could improve some of the host country's elite units, which could then project power into the FARC-controlled badlands. The training of foreign armies provided the Green Berets' basic function.* And they didn't just train the commandos from foreign armies; they trained the trainers themselves— the foreign lieutenants and sergeants who, in turn, would pass on Special Forces techniques to their own subordinates.

To see the training up close, I had to travel about the country to various bases. Thus, Lt. Col. Duke Christie and I left Bogotá one afternoon in an armored pickup truck. Duke carried his M-4 assault rifle and 9mm Beretta pistol. The precautions seemed absurd. The journey from Bogotá southwest to Tolemaida took only two hours over a well-traveled route that was generally safe from roadblocks and kidnappings (few other routes in the country could claim that distinction). It was partly a "force protection" issue. For a journalist to be kidnapped or harmed in another way while under the protection of the Special Forces would have been a public embarrassment. But as I would increasingly discover in the course of my travels, force protection was a debilitating obsession with the U.S. military.

Bogotá, at 8,560 feet, is one of the coolest spots in Colombia. Yet it wasn't long before our car was careening down a choppy sea of ragged, bluish green slopes, smothered in vines and strewn with cedars, tamarinds, and bananas, with evergreens gradually giving way to palms and bougainvillea. The bosky realm was suggestive of the coastal forests of Portugal, another climatic fault zone, except that this landscape was wilder and more chaotic. After the refreshing clarity of the higher altitudes, the air now had the somber closeness of a fish tank.

As it got dark, we turned into Colombia's National Training Center at Tolemaida. For the Colombian military, Tolemaida combined the func-

---

* Douglas Porch, professor of strategy at the Naval War College, in his 1996 introduction to Col. C. E. Callwell's *Small Wars: Their Principles and Practice* (1896; reprint, Lincoln: University of Nebraska Press), notes that a key feature of imperialism is the use of host country or "client" armies in place of one's own.

tions of Fort Bragg, with its Army Special Forces; Fort Rucker, Alabama, with its aviation units; and Fort Benning, Georgia, with its Officer Candidate School, noncommissioned officer school, mechanized infantry school, and school for Army Rangers (which in Colombia were called Lanceros). Decades of democracy notwithstanding, the military was still the most respected institution in Colombia, more so than the Catholic Church, according to polls. Tolemaida was a manifestation of that fact. The level of maintenance was high: trimmed lawns, whitewashed sidewalks, speed bumps, nice supermarkets, and playgrounds for the children of Colombian military families.

Just as the Indian and Pakistani armies copied the dress and mannerisms of the British, Colombian army uniforms were modeled after American ones, with Colombia's special forces wearing the same green berets and red flashes as U.S. elite units. The lone, original sartorial touch was the black kerchiefs that Colombian soldiers wore around their necks in South American cowboy style.

The assault rifles—the workhorse of late-twentieth-century armies— were also different. Rather than the American M-16 or its variations (such as Duke Christie's M-4), the Colombians packed Israeli-manufactured Galils. The Galil was modeled after the Soviet Kalashnikov, yet it was compatible with the American 5.56mm bullet, instead of the Russian 7.62mm. The Israelis had developed the Galil in order to benefit from the Soviet rifle's firing dependability and convenient folding-stock design, while still relying on American ammunition.

After driving at high speed for another quarter hour through the sprawling Tolemaida base, we pulled up at an isolated barracks, the temporary home of ODA-781, a U.S. Army Special Forces A-team.

Opening the steel door of the air-conditioned armored pickup, I gasped from the humid, knee-buckling heat of Colombia's equatorial lowlands. Capt. Chris Murray, ODA-781's commander, was there to greet us. Capt. Murray had a velvety voice and smile that mothers everywhere fall in love with, even as his uniform hid a muscle mass straight out of a bodybuilding magazine. Chris Murray, thirty-five, was an African-American who had joined the Army after graduating from high school in Rockaway Beach, a working-class area of Queens, where I, too, had grown up. Murray was a commissioned officer thanks to attending Officer Candidate School at Fort Benning.

Murray led me inside to my quarters, a corner bunk at the end of a long, corrugated iron shed where the heat was relieved here and there by loud whining fans. Duke smiled, as happy as I would ever see him. "The barracks," he exclaimed, "the last remaining thoroughly unrepentant masculine environment in the Western world!"

Militaries are the ultimate reflections of national cultural achievement, or the lack thereof. Here was America's brawn, organizational know-how, and technological advancement, condensed as though in a museum case on foreign soil. Atop bunks and storage bins, on long foldout tables, and on metal shelves under fluorescent lights, I saw piles of black boots, Listerine, shaving cream, and pictures of loved ones alongside ammunition cases, bandoleers, speed loaders for jamming ammo, and magazines for 9mm and 5.56mm bullets. There were boxing gloves, a trapeze-like arrangement of mosquito nets, torches, briefing books, and laptops. CDs and floppy disks lay alongside blasting caps, communications gear, night vision goggles, signal flares, chem-bio masks, M-3 medical kits, flak vests, machetes, M-203 grenade launchers, 60mm and 80mm mortars, and bipods for heavy guns. There were two black suitcases, each containing a water purification system. There were all sorts of web gear, MREs (meals ready to eat), and Peltors (earphones that filtered out gun sounds but not voices on the firing range).

There were stacks of Beretta pistols, first used by the Army during the invasion of Grenada in 1983, when the Beretta replaced the Colt .45, which had been in service since Gen. John "Black Jack" Pershing's 1916 expedition into Mexico against Pancho Villa. The Beretta uses a smaller bullet than the Colt, but it has less recoil, carries more rounds, and as a last-ditch weapon is easier to handle. There were also the new modular integrated communications helmets, snugger fitting and lighter than the previous models, yet with a tighter Kevlar weave that provided better protection against bullets. Most importantly, there were the squad automatic weapons, which for Army Special Forces were M-249 "Minimis" from the Belgian design, and M-4s with collapsible stocks and shorter barrels for urban combat.

What made the M-4 an improvement over other assault rifles was its modular rail system, on which one could add several accessories—grenade launcher, shotgun barrel, optical site, and carrying handle—making for a truly custom-designed weapon. Unlike the rest of the Army, Special Forces abjured uniformity. Everybody's rifle and web gear were slightly different. You packed what worked for you in the field, not what the regulations demanded. A few years back, someone had noticed that the Israelis manufactured a nifty collapsible litter for bearing the wounded. Special Forces officers started ordering them over the Internet; nobody waited for the Army to go through the procurement process. The litters were now known simply as "Israelis."

Hanging from the ceiling in the middle of the barracks, between the two long lines of bunks, was a large American flag. Salsa music blasted from speakers as everyone peeled off their uniforms and headed for the showers. I realized I would be the only one without at least one tattoo on my body.

The members of this A-team hailed from Georgia, South Carolina, Arizona, New Jersey, the Dominican Republic, and Puerto Rico, with several from Ohio. All spoke Spanish. Sgt. First Class Ivan Castro, putting on a pair of shorts, gave me his life story without prompting. "Yeah, my family is from Puerto Rico. I was born in Hoboken, New Jersey, St. Mary's Hospital. My wife is a speech pathologist. When I go back to Puerto Rico to visit my relatives I like it for a day or so, then I hate it. I can't wait to leave. All the dirt and crime," he said, looking down in a self-reflective way at his tattoos.

Sgt. Castro was a "bravo," that is, a weapons specialist. A-teams were usually commanded by a captain, with the rest of the detachment all noncommissioned officers, either sergeants or chief warrant officers, each with an occupational specialty. "Charlie" meant the engineer, "delta" the medic, "echo" the communications expert, and "foxtrot" the intelligence officer. Between the commanding captain and the noncoms was an "18 Zulu," the operations or team sergeant, who held the rank of master sergeant. He was the heart and soul of the detachment.

Capt. Murray's 18 Zulu was Master Sgt. Mike Fields of Akron, Ohio. Fields, a stocky guy of average height, with close-cropped red hair verging early on gray, was terse and self-contained. He seemed hard to get to know, and he was. As soon as everyone had showered and changed, he conducted a briefing about "deconflicting the range issue." He ran through a detailed accounting of eighteen thousand rounds of ammo in addition to blasting caps. Then he outlined the problem: the team needed three rifle ranges for the next day's training of Colombian troops, but only one range was available, so he had decided that communications training, which didn't require a range, would be held alongside rifle training. "That way," Fields said, "we don't have people wasting time, loitering." Capt. Murray smiled throughout. The fact that his team sergeant seemed to be the real leader of this A-team was an obvious truth that Murray was not only comfortable with but proud of.

Murray, the ambitious working-class African-American from Queens, was an officer, an aristocrat of sorts, who handled the bilateral relations with his Colombian counterparts at the Tolemaida base. Each member of ODA-781 trained the Colombians on his own occupational specialty: weapons, intelligence, demolition, and so forth. They all reported to Fields. It was in Colombia where I began to see that the genius of the American military was less technological than social, a reflection of American society whose telling feature was the relative absence of class envy. Chris Murray hadn't been completely satisfied as a noncommissioned officer, so he went to Officer Candidate School. Mike Fields, on the other hand, seemed born to his job as a noncom. As I evaluated more A-teams in Colombia, I continually saw master sergeants with affection for their captains, and captains who positively idolized their team sergeants. American democracy spawned rich and poor, but the basis for its revolutionary dynamism was the *great middle.* The American military was the clearest example of that. As I would see in my travels, few militaries in history had produced such impressive middle ranks.

Rather than dine on MREs in the barracks, a bunch of us piled into Capt. Murray's armored car and drove out of the base into the nearby town of Tolemaida. On a ratty sidewalk stall I had one of the best steaks in my life. Salsa music blasted a few feet from us. Here was a simulacrum of pleasure after a twelve-hour training day. Under a scrap iron shed lit by fluorescent lights, in sour heat and humidity, sweating Colombian girls, their shoulders and bellies exposed, squeezed between the tables and chairs serving us the steaks and fries. Disco lights jumped inside a nearby dance hall. A motorcycle roared by with a family of four on it. A little girl with braids played with a doll a few feet from me, separated by a locked iron grille at the bottom of a flight of stairs.

"Let's go," said Lt. Col. Christie quietly. "It's GBNT [Green Beret nap time]." It was only 9 p.m. when we settled the bill; I was the only one who had ordered a beer. Back at the barracks, it being "Mefloquine Monday," everyone took their weekly malaria pill before going to sleep.

The day began at 5:45 a.m. with a five-mile run followed by weight lifting. By 9 a.m. the heat and humidity were unbearable. Duke and I spent much of the day on a series of firing ranges—shadeless except for a few thorn and cashew trees—with Master Sgt. Mike Fields and Sgt. Ivan Castro, each of whom had a detachment of Colombian soldiers to work with.

The Colombian anti-guerrilla commandos under training were hardened volunteers; it would have been a waste of time and resources for Green Berets to train draftees. These Colombians were short, extremely muscular, very dark complexioned, and flat featured. Some were black. They bore the blood of slaves and indigenous Indians, unlike the tall and light-skinned inhabitants of Bogotá's fashionable Zona Rosa. Colombia's wealthy could buy their way out of the military, and in any case did not consider the military a path of social advancement. America's all-volunteer military appeared more typical of the society it was supposed to defend, though it really wasn't. Discount the exceptions. In fact, SOUTHCOM had few Jews, and the only soldiers from the Northeast were working-class African-Americans, ethnic Puerto Ricans, and Dominicans.*

Despite the heat Sgts. Fields and Castro were in full kit, loaded down with weapons, magazines, flares, Chemlites, map cases, and other survival items, as though out on a mission. They looked movie-quality impressive, and that was the point. Because the military at ground level is a world of practice and technique, not of theory, the techniques of the trainers would be accepted only if the trainers themselves looked, acted, and performed the part perfectly.

Carving up the bull's-eye from 100 meters away with an M-4 to prove the benefits of adjusting (zeroing) one's scope, or repeatedly changing magazines in under three seconds, might seem like showing off. But if you couldn't prove your expertise with an assault rifle, no one would trust your advice about weaponry. The world of the military is not like the world of social science, in which one can be an academic superstar without having a day's experience inside the crucible of government, with its humbling crises. In the high testosterone world of the military, teaching demands proof on a daily basis that you are the best. Adolescent it may be, but at least it is honest.

Ivan Castro was a former drill instructor, and it showed. He paced back

* According to *The Economist,* "The harder-jawed a region, the likelier it is to put its young into the army. The generally Republican, pro-gun south contributes a lot more soldiers than the Democratic north-east, both in absolute numbers and percentages of the regional population. A Texan is eight times more likely to be in uniform than a New Yorker." Mar. 22, 2003, p. 28.

and forth in full kit in the pulverizing sun, towering above his Colombian protégés, who were kneeling beside hills made by leaf-cutter ants. Castro's subject was how to sit in a "360-degree cigar formation" while on reconnaissance, in order to rest in the field without being surprised by the enemy. "How do you sit and rest on recon?" he asked didactically in choppy Puerto Rican Spanish. "You take your hats off to listen. You don't talk to the guy next to you. If you talk to anyone, it is to God. You lean against your pack, but you don't nap. Each of you has a field of fire that together covers 360. Practice your SOPs [standard operating procedures], especially your hand signals. And remember SLLS [Smell. Look. Listen. Silence]."

Throughout the long hot afternoon and into the evening, he would teach them the Australian technique of peeling back in retreat, without allowing for a gap in fire, after making contact with the enemy. It was harder than it looked: to keep the fire up, then to keep the fire up even in the dark, then in the dark in a tangled thicket, then in the dark in a tangled thicket with smoke bombs exploding all around you. *You see them. They see you. You kill them. You peel back.* Because the real event would elicit such fear and confusion, your only hope was grueling repetition, so that it became instinct. Castro worked twelve hours in the heat that day, speaking in a steady, nurturing tone, working individually with each soldier until the unit performed the drill perfectly.

"All I can give is 110 percent; nothing in life is better than what I've been doing today," Castro shouted at me, his hearing impaired by earplugs. Soldiers talked in clichés. It is the emotion and look in their faces—sweaty and gummed with dust—that matters more than the words. After all, a cliché is something that only the elite recognizes as such.

Laughing now, Castro gave me another acronym: "*P*roper *P*lanning, Good *R*econ, *C*ontrol, *S*ecurity, *C*ommon *S*ense—PUERTO RICANS SUCK COCK."

I spent another part of the day with the team sergeant, Mike Fields. Besides being ODA-781's effective managing director, he taught several classes. In the morning he ran a tape drill in Spanish for an AMOUT (advanced military operation in urban terrain). Since the firing range lacked buildings to practice on, Fields used tape on the ground to simulate the various structures that the Colombian anti-guerrilla team would infiltrate. He went over basics that drew on the U.S. Army's *Ranger Handbook*: isolating a building and covering all of its sides before entering; entering the building from the highest point; securing one building before moving on to the next; shining a flashlight in the enemy's face to momentarily shock him and make him easier to kill.[14]

I learned that a really good sniper will take his bullets from the same box, since gunpowder grain is not always measured out evenly; that the green-tipped 5.56mm bullet that the Americans used in Somalia and Afghanistan, while it pierced Kevlar, caused less damage inside the body, so it took two or three shots to "take a bad guy down."

Fields was full of compacted technical knowledge. He never wasted a word or body movement, and he had even nerves. The year before he had been thrown from a helicopter and bounced off a third-story building. He broke a pelvic bone, was laid up for forty-five days, then spent ninety days on crutches. He looked bored when I asked him about it, but perked up when I asked him to explain how he had machine-tooled an M-16 scope onto a Galil. Fields's schedule was so jam-packed that the only time I could get him alone to talk was to meet him for breakfast the next day at 6 a.m. at the Colombian army canteen.

When we met for breakfast Fields seemed nervous talking to me. He said that he had his name mentioned in a newsmagazine once, and while nice words were written about him, it was something he didn't especially appreciate. He seemed utterly without ego, channeling all his psychic energy into the technical task at hand. One shouldn't expect soldiers to be interesting, I thought. War is work, and like all work it is for the literal minded. Fields was the opposite of the foreign correspondents who love to tell bar stories. His stories were probably much better, but he was bored by them. The only thing that interested him was the next task.

Fields also spoke in clichés that he didn't recognize as such. Like many in this A-team, he was in his mid-thirties, married, his family back at Fort Bragg. He had attended junior college in Texas, then spent a year at Akron University in his hometown before quitting. "School wasn't for me. I needed direction. I joined the Army." The next sixteen years he spent in Sinai, South Korea, and then Honduras, Guatemala, "El Sal," and other places on the *cucaracha* circuit.

"A twelve-hour day is, I guess, a short one," he said flatly. "I'm away from my family six months a year. I have responsibility for all the enlisted men. I write the ratings for each guy except the chief warrant officer and the captain. I write the training schedules, control the budget. I make sure we have trucks, logistics, ranges. I answer for everything that does and does not happen. But my primary job is training COLAR [the Colombian army]. Ultimately, nothing else matters except getting a few of their special units to the point where they are capable of taking out the FARC leadership. I'm a trainer."

"How good is the Colombian army?" I asked.

He looked at me hard, then down at his eggs and plantains. The Colombian army was the only Latin military that had fought beside the U.S. in the Korean War, and Fields and his team deeply respected that. "But their noncommissioned officer class is weak," he said. "Their corporals and sergeants don't take the initiative when their officers are around." Colombian society had a rigid social hierarchy and that hurt the army. Without strong noncoms, it was hard to have well-functioning small units. And without that, it was hard to hunt down narco-terrorists.

I left Fields as he jumped into a discussion about stringing a wire for a Barker-Williams antenna. It was part of the process of relocating the commo gear. I'll explain:

——

The evening before, following the long day on the firing range with Fields and Castro, the team had learned that it suddenly had to move barracks immediately: all of the equipment, everything. And they had to move into a few "crackerboxes" which offered a lot less room than the old barracks. It was no way to treat the Americans. A Colombian colonel whose unit was not being trained by ODA-781 had made the decision.

Morale could not have been good at that moment. Yet nobody complained; nor was there the slightest display of annoyance, as everyone returned from the range and methodically began the moving process. Unloading communications gear from a truck, someone said he hoped that the World Trade Center wouldn't be replaced by "some weepy memorial. Build something bigger even, taller; that's what America's all about." By midnight the bathrooms had been cleaned, the weapons, the office equipment, and other things all unpacked in their new places, and the fans installed to cut some of the equatorial heat.

All of these guys, most of whom had kids and were of the same caliber as Mike Fields, brought home no more than $4,000 a month after taxes. Unlike in civilian life, salaries were determined completely by rank, so everyone knew what everyone else was making and it was not impolite to ask. It was not rare for noncommissioned officers to be on food stamps.* If a member of ODA-781 was killed in combat or in a training accident, his family received $200,000 in servicemen's group life insurance. That was all. "Governed by necessity, the best-disciplined army is so good that it requires neither rewards nor punishments," writes Israeli military historian Martin van Creveld, paraphrasing ancient Chinese philosophy. The best-disciplined army behaves "as if it were a single personality."[15] That was ODA-781 all right. In a few hours they all would get up to run five miles, after which Fields would meet me for breakfast.

Espinal, half an hour by car away from Tolemaida, is a gridwork of corrugated iron huts and modular living units resembling shipping containers. It is the home of the Carabineros, the police units of Colombia's Defense Ministry, and of their counter-narcotics jungle fighters, known as *junglas*. In many developing countries the police have a full-fledged war-fighting capability. It sounds sinister, conjuring up the very image of a South American police state. But there were times in the 1990s when Colombia's police enjoyed a more liberal reputation than its civilian government, tainted as it was by drug-financed campaign contributions.

In any case, chameleon-type units that merged army and police functions were the wave of the future in a world of unconventional, low-intensity conflict. The *junglas*—the police equivalent of the Lanceros—were particularly well regarded. They had better noncommissioned officers than Colombia's army, and were able to do certain types of assaults better than the army could, such as rappelling from helicopters. Officially, the *junglas* were merely a counter-drug force. But because the U.S. was now fighting terrorism with drug war money, it had become the job of another Special Forces A-team, ODA-784, to train the *junglas*.

ODA-784 was commanded by Capt. Jim O'Brien of Portland, Maine. Jim O'Brien, a West Point graduate in his late twenties, was broad-chested with a shock of red hair and a big eager smile. He positively oozed enthusiasm. He looked like the all-American kid on a milk carton. "I've been waiting to command an SF team since I was eight," he told me. "This was

* A. J. Simons, *The Company They Keep: Life Inside the U.S. Army Special Forces* (New York: Free Press, 1997), pp. 189–90. The author writes that some noncom families live in trailers and turn on the heat only at night in the winter. "Others heated with wood they chopped themselves."

all I ever wanted to do. Though, I have to admit, I thought that I had reached the height of my ambition when I became the scout leader of a recon platoon in Germany."

O'Brien's formative experience had been in the former Yugoslavia. By his mid-twenties, he was the veritable mayor of a small Kosovo town, settling disputes over land and other matters. Yugoslavia prepared O'Brien well for Colombia. Both were places where politics and criminality were inextricable, where ideological goals provided a mask for murder and racketeering, where one or two men could strike fear into a whole town, and where the landscapes were heart-wrenchingly beautiful.

Capt. O'Brien showed me ODA-784's hootch. Here was another salsafied 7th Group A-team, with Latin music blasting out of speakers amid guns, laptops, communications gear, and topographical maps. There were also the tattoos: of Chinese dragons, wives' names, barbed-wire patterns. In Lima, Peru, the whole team had bonded by getting tattoos from the same parlor. The team sergeant, Timothy Norris of Longview, Texas, who had been with George Bush the Elder on the latter's seventy-fifth birthday parachute jump, told me the first thing that A-team medics do upon arrival at a new deployment is to inspect the tattoo parlors, to make sure the equipment is sterilized.

ODA-784 trained the *junglas* at a nearby *finca* (plantation). It was an immense amphitheater of rolling fields sectioned by copses, with a glorious monotony of sawtooth mountain peaks and sandpaper hills in the foreground. You might have been in Greece or Turkey. But amid the poignant weather-stained walls of an abandoned church were African bees, boa constrictors, and caimans. I saw a group of about a hundred *junglas* sitting in a field taking notes, getting a human rights lecture from one of their officers. Members of O'Brien's A-team looked on. They had trained this particular officer on the subject.

In the Special Forces community, human rights was considered an aspect of psy-ops. In the 1980s in El Salvador, Col. J. S. Roach, a member of the U.S. Army's operational planning team, had pounded home the point that violating human rights never makes sense from a "pragmatic perspective," because it causes you to lose civilian support, without which you cannot root out insurgents. "Human rights wasn't a separate one hour block at the beginning of the day. You had to couch it in the training so that it wasn't just a moralistic approach."[16] Human rights abuses didn't come to an end in El Salvador. Still, third world military men were more likely to listen to American officers who briefed them about human rights as a tool of counterinsurgency than to civilians who talked abstractly about universal principles of justice.

"This whole scene may look inspiring to you, but don't be fooled," one Green Beret told me. "These soldiers know that the FARC and other groups will rape their sisters, torture their fathers, and the international community will do nothing. They see how people are kidnapped daily and held in awful conditions for years. But if any of these guys now taking notes were to accidentally shoot a guerrilla, without first trying to apprehend him peaceably, by Colombian law he would be liable for prosecution."

Colombia was Latin America's oldest democracy, even as its government could not protect its citizens from armed insurgents. The Colombian parliament treated the struggle against the FARC, the leftist ELN (Ejército de Liberación National), and the rightist paramilitaries not as a war but as a police action, meaning that every death had to be investigated by the civilian authorities, even if it occurred in the midst of a battle or commando raid.

Lt. Col. Duke Christie and Capt. Jim O'Brien were neither lawyers nor professors; they were Special Forces trainers. They knew what kind of motivation worked to get young men to risk their lives, and what kind didn't. And in Colombia, human rights was a theory drawn up by a fair-skinned elite in Bogotá who had been influenced, in turn, by their cosmopolitan friends in Western capitals, with the contradictions paid for in blood by the darker-skinned, broad-faced Indian castes sitting beside me, taking notes in the hot sun. Laws in Colombia were often not a sign of the country's democratic vibrancy, but of its impotence: of the need of Bogotá's elite to cover its backside with legalities.

In the barracks of both American and Colombian soldiers, a book was passed around, in Spanish and in English translation: *In Hell* by "Johnnie." There was no publisher's identification. It was the anonymous memoir of a FARC assassin who had escaped the organization. The author describes the forced recruitment of teenage boys and girls into guerrilla ranks, and their executions after they tried to desert and were caught. There is an account of a young girl defecating and menstruating while crying for her mother as a noose is tied around her neck. The executions are carried out by other young recruits, who, under the watchful eyes of older commanders, are made to cut off the limbs of the dead bodies and drink the blood.

Another story, not in the book, but very similar to those in it, I heard from an official American briefer: about a policemen who fought to the last against the FARC as they assaulted a village near Espinal. The FARC tore up this man's testicles with fishing wire, then cut off his head and played soccer with it. Afterwards they went to the man's home, shot his children, gang-raped his wife, and tied her in a sheet that they set afire with gasoline. "Given what will happen to these policemen if they fight as we teach them to, yet still end up being caught, it's tough lecturing them about how they should respect human rights," said one Green Beret.

Green Berets in Colombia believed that promoting human rights meant one thing: loosening their own ROEs (rules of engagement). Current ROEs state that Special Forces teams can only train and advise Colombian troops, but cannot join them on the battlefield. Yet Green Berets talked frequently about "going beyond the base perimeters and advising from forward positions." Some suggested that they provide cover fire from the air for Colombian ground troops, as well as fight alongside the men they trained. The roots of such bravado were several:

- The professional ambition of Green Berets was to give battle, not merely to train others to do so. If their attitude was less aggressive than it was, they would not have volunteered for their jobs in the first place.
- They were selfless, a trait associated with a narrow field of vision. Like Master Sgt. Mike Fields, they lived for the particular technical task at hand, and were willing to die, provided there would be someone behind them to pick up the task where they had left off. Their favorite reading material was the *Ranger Handbook*.
- They hated routine. In Bosnia, the general staff was so timid of casualties that troops "couldn't even take a crap at night inside the base perimeter without putting on full armor." But as Duke explained, "If you're never off duty, you're never on duty," because even heightened alert, as in Bosnia, gets dull. New and loosened ROEs for Colombia would break the routine.
- They were too young to have an active memory of Vietnam, so they were unburdened by it. They quietly disparaged older generals who were hesitant about loosening the ROEs, for fear of getting too deeply involved in a distant war. They knew that loosening the ROEs

for Colombia, or adding a few more Green Berets, did not constitute sending half a million regular soldiers into harm's way, as in Vietnam.

- Because their only experience with power had been with the American version of it in the last days of the Cold War, and in the post–Cold War and post–September 11 eras, they saw American power as incorruptible. They could not understand why American power was not applied more often and more vigorously. The motto of Special Forces was "De Oppresso Liber," To Liberate the Oppressed.
- As captains, chief warrant officers, and sergeants, they thought tactically, not strategically. Tactically, it made sense to loosen the ROEs. Strategically, it might have caused political and legal problems with the host country, overshadowing the tactical benefits.

The best example of how military tactical thinking in Colombia differed from diplomatic and legal thinking had to do with the murderous right-wing paramilitaries. The paramilitaries were narco-terrorists, the same as the leftist FARC and ELN. Numbering some ten thousand, they controlled 40 percent of the coca-growing regions and killed people with electric saws at roadblocks. But tactically speaking, it made sense for the Colombian government to align itself with the right against the left; then, after the left had been defeated, or forced to negotiate, to roll the paramilitaries into the regular army, where they could be professionalized. The strategy had worked to a degree in El Salvador. "The paramilitaries are bad guys, but they're *good* bad guys," one Green Beret explained. "That's why Espinal is safe. It's why you can go to the restaurants and stay at a local hotel rather than be restricted to the base: because the town is run by the AUC [Autodefensas Unidas de Colombia]," the paramilitaries.

The war against the guerrillas was in its thirty-eighth year. Colombia's agony went on and on. If aligning with one group of thugs to defeat another group of thugs would end the bloodshed and kidnappings sooner, how was that not virtuous? Diplomats and generals thought too often in abstractions; noncoms and middle-ranking officers saw truths on the ground.

Back in Bogotá, I learned that a single-prop Cessna 208 Caravan with four American contractors and one Colombian aboard had developed engine trouble over southern Colombia. It had been forced to crash-land in a

FARC area, where at least two of the five passengers had been shot dead. The plane was on a surveillance mission for the State Department's counter-drug program, mapping out coca fields for future spraying and eradication. It was equipped with sensitive electronic equipment. A Special Forces A-team stationed at Larandia, a Colombian army base fifteen minutes by helicopter from the crash site, had been put on alert; so had another A-team in the vicinity which specialized in search-and-rescue operations. The American major who commanded the two detachments in southern Colombia—and who, by coincidence, happened to be in Bogotá for the day—agreed to take me down there with him the next morning, February 14.

At a secluded section of the airport in Bogotá, I met quite a rogues' gallery. There would be eight of us on the ninety-minute flight south to Larandia: FBI; ATF (Alcohol, Tobacco, and Firearms), a private defense contractor, a fellow from the intelligence community, a Special Forces medic, and my new traveling companion, Special Forces Maj. John Paul "J. P." Roberts. All except for the medic were in civilian clothes; everyone except me and the contractor was packing either an M-4 or a 9mm pistol. The medic brought along extra body bags. The ATF guy, a long-haired Navy veteran who had fought in Desert Storm and had a Beretta strapped under his shoulder, told me that it would be his job to inspect the downed plane: to assess whether the crew had been able to destroy the equipment with thermite grenades before they were captured and killed.

As we waited to board, there was much anger regarding the FARC and the feeble policy against it. "They're a bunch of sadistic, crazed, chickenshit motherfuckers," one of my fellow passengers told me. "It's what you get when you marry Colombian energy and ambition to ideology and coke profits." "You can't give in; the only sane policy is to kill these guys," said another.

"That fucker Pastrana!" yet another exclaimed, referring to former Colombian president Andres Pastrana, who had compromised with the FARC and ELN, giving them safe havens that they had used to build criminal mini-states, from where they conquered more territory. For example, there was the "Ho Chi Minh Trail," a two-lane highway laid by the FARC under the cover of a jungle canopy in the coca-growing breadbasket of Putumayo near Ecuador, lined with military bases, discos, schools, playgrounds, hospitals, and so forth for the guerrilla troops and their families.

The propellers of our CASA 212, owned by Evergreen Corporation, another U.S. government contractor, whirred up and we all inserted earplugs. I eyed the small oxygen tank next to me. We'd be flying close to sixteen thousand feet and the cabin was unpressurized. We bumped upward through gnarled and heavily bearded peaks the shimmering, spellbinding green of moss and emeralds. As we edged south, the chaos of hillsides became so unreal in their greenery that I thought of the serrated backsides of iguanas. Colombia was like the earth on the third day of Creation, primitive and untamed, bubbling and spewing smoke, with dense forests and jungle quiltworks. The bird and insect life was the most prodigious in the hemisphere, save for Brazil.

Colombia is the size of the entire southeastern quadrant of the U.S. God could not have designed a better landscape for anarchy and guerrilla outlaws, or a more malignant one for strong, central government: a "Paradise of snakes," as Joseph Conrad puts it.[17] Whereas Mexico and Chile had been mastered by central valleys surrounding their capitals, and whereas the capital cities of Venezuela, Uruguay, and Argentina had become commanding nodes of economic power in their respective countries, Colombia, since pre-Columbian times, "has had no naturally centralizing topographic feature."[18] The capital, Bogotá, was never able to dominate such cities as Medellín, Cali, and Cartagena, separated from each other by wilderness badlands and towering cordilleras, as the Andes split apart at their northern extremity.

From its inception, Colombia was always too big and too small. The Spanish conquest reified topographical divisions, with different groups of conquistadors coming north from Peru and south from Panama, and establishing themselves on different sides of the cordilleras. The urban concentrations in the cool and easily defended highlands had little need of each other; nor did the inhabitants of these cities in the mountains have the possibility or incentive to develop the seemingly impenetrable jungle lowlands split by the tributaries of the Amazon and Orinoco. As late as 1911, the *Encyclopaedia Britannica* could still write, "The larger part of this territory is unexplored, except along the principal rivers, and is inhabited by scattered tribes of Indians." At the turn of the twentieth century, Bogotá was harder to reach than just about any other capital city in the world.

In fact, Colombia was little more than a network of city-states, despite the creation by Gen. Simon Bolívar in the early nineteenth century of Gran

Colombia, designed to include Colombia, Venezuela, Ecuador, and later Panama. Bolívar's vast commonwealth was simply ungovernable, and decades were lost in a grand guignol of revolts straight out of Conrad's novel *Nostromo* (which, by the way, deals with an imaginary republic, Costaguana, located somewhere near the joint of Central and South America). Colombia was a world of slaves and Indians exploited by Spanish colonizers, whose priests were as fanatical and bloodthirsty as modern-day Iranian ayatollahs. Church-state conflicts were the cause of eight civil wars, not to mention smaller rebellions.

But Colombia was also the most self-sufficient country in the hemisphere, with storied quantities of coffee, cattle, gold, emeralds, and oil. Gold and coffee created obscene concentrations of wealth, as later would drugs. The early-twentieth-century "Republic of Coffee," as Colombia was then known, would mutate into a veritable late-twentieth-century Republic of Cocaine.

Eventually, the lowland forests were cleared and precious wood plundered, as well as rubber in the Amazon basin after the spread of automobiles had created a demand.[19] The upshot was the rise of a violent frontier society that, through crime and migration, threatened the urban civilization in the highlands. Two hundred thousand people died between 1945 and 1964 in a nationwide bloodletting among peasants, set against each other by liberal and conservative hierarchs.[20] The nightmarish spectacle was "so empty of meaning" that it was called simply *La Violencia*.[21]

Coast Guard Capt. Bob Innes in Yemen had not been exaggerating when he told me that this part of Latin America was more dangerous than the Middle East. Even after the gruesome murder of journalist Daniel Pearl by al-Qaeda, you had to wonder if it might be worse, given the record of amputations and other tortures here, to be captured by the FARC. In Yemen you could travel in anarchic areas under tribal escort; in Colombia there was often no safety except in full kit, inside a Humvee with a mounted machine gun. Because Colombian guerrillas stole uniforms of government soldiers and police, it was not always clear who was manning the roadblocks. A larger percentage of Colombia than Yemen was considered by the American military to be Injun Country.

The task that the U.S. appeared to have in both Yemen and Colombia was similar. And it was similarly impossible: to make countries out of places that were never meant to be countries.

Yet the U.S. could not, at this moment in history, fail to rise to the challenge that Colombia presented. Not only was Colombia so much closer to the U.S. than the Middle East, but cocaine and other illegal drugs even in the post–September 11 era arguably constituted a greater risk to American society than Islamic extremism, barring a truly catastrophic terrorist attack. Moreover, a newly elected Colombian president was offering the U.S. a tantalizing window of opportunity for progress against the insurgents. Alvaro Uribe appeared willing to prosecute a full-scale war, and deploy large numbers of specialized police units in the most violent towns of Colombia. He was a dynamic workaholic who had filled his cabinet with people like himself. He was physically as well as politically brave, visiting remote regions of the country in spite of death threats. Uribe's ascension, combined with the real danger of an alliance between Colombian and Middle Eastern terrorists, meant that the U.S. had to go all the way here.

Plan Colombia signified the ultimate U.S. interagency strategy for healing a troubled foreign country: hundreds of millions of American taxpayers' dollars annually for a gamut of programs, from Special Forces to Counter Drugs, Judicial Training, Human Rights Monitoring, Child Soldier Rehabilitation, Maritime Enforcement, Alternative Crop Development, Environmental Support, and so on. The armed passengers beside me aboard the CASA 212 were evidence of the sharp, rough-and-tumble edge of several Washington bureaucracies.

The U.S. goal was not to completely pacify Colombia. That would have been too ambitious. The goal was to break up the leadership networks of the guerrilla groups through assassination and other means, thereby reducing them to an even lower level of banditry. "We aim to balkanize them and kill their centers of gravity," one American military official said. That was the way that the Khmer Rouge had ultimately been dealt with, though here the model wasn't Cambodia in the 1990s, but El Salvador in the 1980s.

El Salvador was the inverse of Vietnam, where, instead of applying Economy of Force through the exclusive use of Special Operations teams, President Lyndon Johnson had dispatched more than half a million troops. "El Salvador" was, too, a code phrase within Army Special Operations Command for the kind of qualified success possible in the messy world of nation-fixing—a success so slim it barely went noticed, or could be labeled as such. Richard W. Stewart, the historian for the Special Ops community, writes thus about the role of Special Forces in El Salvador from 1980 to 1992, during the country's civil war:

> How successful was the Special Forces and U.S. advisory effort in El Salvador? . . . Despite military setbacks and the increase of international support to the enemy (including weapons from Nicaragua and Cuba, and diplomatic recognition from France and Mexico), the El Salvadoran military fought back and beat the guerrillas to a standstill. When the "final" offensive of the FMLN [Farabundo Martí Liberación Nacional front] was launched in 1989, the El Salvadoran military faced a few minor defeats, but rallied and decimated the rebels. The FMLN was forced to seek victory with a political solution; a military victory was no longer an option for them. Special Forces had helped make that . . . possible.[22]

The 1991 report submitted by the General Accounting Office to Senator Edward Kennedy did not differ substantially from that assessment. It said there had been "a significant decrease in political violence against civilians during the past 10 years. . . . U.S. military trainers . . . have exposed the Salvadoran military personnel to internationally recognized human rights standards and democratic principles."[23]

Despite detailed media coverage of specific human rights atrocities, the basic trend in human rights over the course of the decade was positive, especially when one considers the small number of Special Forces trainers deployed in the field.*

Nobody kidded himself that Colombia would be another El Salvador, where the fall of the Berlin Wall helped reduce support for a strongly ideological guerrilla movement. Moreover, the U.S. military had been in El Salvador for more than a decade, long enough to develop a learning curve.

---

* Though dated by events, an incisive analysis on what succeeded in El Salvador and what didn't was prepared by four Army lieutenant colonels, A. J. Bacevich, James D. Hallums, Richard H. White, and Thomas F. Young: *American Military Policy in Small Wars: The Case of El Salvador* (Washington: Pergamon-Brassey's, 1988). See p. 25 concerning the reduction in political murders. The media and the State Department, in the minds of many Special Forces operators I interviewed, evince a zero-defect view on human rights violations, so one incident can delegitimize an entire multi-year effort. According to Special Forces, this is an unreasonably high standard that runs counter to the gradualist approach adopted by the media and State Department on the implementation of democracy and free markets.

Perhaps, I thought, as I adjusted my oxygen mask in the plane, the crash of the day before would constitute a spike in the learning curve in Colombia, for it highlighted all the contradictions of America's involvement here.

"If Washington decides to pull out of Colombia just because a bunch of us get killed, then we shouldn't be here in the first place," Duke Christie had told me. One of the rationalizations for the strict rules of engagement was that everyone up the command chain in the Pentagon wasn't sure he could justify American deaths in Colombia. The politicians and higher-ups thought that this demonstrated their deep concern for American soldiers' lives; the Green Berets thought it demonstrated political cowardice.

Meanwhile, every day American pilots crisscrossed Colombian guerrilla country in flimsy planes, conducting spraying and surveillance operations, and ferrying American troops from base to base. The inevitable had finally happened. Yet from the way people talked—and the concerns Duke and his fellow officers had about being pulled out of Colombia altogether—the policy suddenly seemed up for grabs.

The hatch door opened as we gave up altitude, revealing stagnant curvilinear rivers, oily green fields, and broadleaf foliage, with parasitic orchids in the mango canopy. As the CASA 212 set down near wire-mesh, sand-filled barriers (HESCO baskets), the sound of jungle parrots began the moment the propellers went silent. It was early morning and depressingly hot, hotter than Tolemaida and Espinal. We were 2 degrees latitude north of the equator. A UH-60 "Lima" model Black Hawk and two UH-1N Hueys hovered by us. The Hueys, the besieged nature of the base, and the landscape itself recalled the Vietnam of a third of a century earlier. I noticed that the airfield was covered in pierced steel plank, collapsible metal sheets for laying instant runway on loose tropical soil; the plank seal indicated that it had been manufactured in 1967, and had been used for the first time in Vietnam.

"Yeah, every Tuesday this base is about to be overrun," someone half joked. Maj. J. P. Roberts barked about getting "the host nation's commo freeks [frequencies]," and the need "to unfuck the time line" of yesterday's crash, the capture of the crew, the recon follow-ups, and so on. Maj. Roberts was short, clean-cut, compact, and poker-faced. He seemed to have a somewhat cold and surly nature. In his late thirties from western Pennsylvania, he had a twin brother who was also an Army Special Forces major. As a major, his B-team at Larandia commanded several A-teams here.

There is a term in the U.S. military, "iron majors," though it might really apply to all middle-level officers, from noncommissioned master sergeants and chief warrant officers to lieutenant colonels. In a sense, majors ran the military, regardless of who the chairman of the Joint Chiefs of Staff happened to be. Up through the rank of captain, an officer still hasn't closed the door on other career options, but becoming a major means you've "bought into the corporation," Maj. Roger D. Carstens had explained to me back at Fort Bragg. "We're the ones who are up at 4 a.m. answering the general's e-mails, making sure all the systems are go."

But it was only when you got outside the United States that you realized the power and responsibility wielded by not only majors, but captains and master sergeants, too, to say nothing of a lieutenant colonel like Duke Christie. While policy specialists argued general principles like nation-building in Washington and New York seminars, these young middle-level officers were the true agents of the imperium.

A plane had gone down, at least one American body needed to be recovered, and several Americans on official government business were missing inside a hornet's nest of narco-terrorists. SOUTHCOM commander Army Gen. James T. Hill was flying in from Miami; SOUTHCOM's Special Operations commander, Army Brig. Gen. Remo Butler, was flying in from Puerto Rico; Ambassador to Colombia Anne Patterson likely rated the incident her top priority; and yet Maj. Roberts would be shaping decisions on the ground. He had slept only two hours the night before and would be making judgment calls during the course of the day that would effect his entire career. More so than civilian life, the military was about being your best under the worst of circumstances.

The barracks for ODB-780, where Maj. Roberts had his office, featured the usual clutter of drying towels and mosquito nets among piles of mortar base plates, mounted guns, bore sights, aiming sticks, and multiband inter-team radios. Fans whined, creating pockets of relative comfort. I laid down my pack and filled my canteen with purified water. A young, enthusiastic noncom launched into an explanation about the heat ribbing on the M-60mm dropfire mortar beside me.

Maj. Roberts emerged only to disappear into a classified briefing with ODA-785 and -776: the two A-teams that, along with the FBI, ATF, a search-and-rescue unit of DynCorp (another private defense contractor), and shadowy civilian others, would be headed in two helicopters to the site of the crash and the place where the bodies had been found.

Compared to these civilians, the Green Berets looked positively innocent; the civilians were grizzled old Special Forces veterans of Vietnam, now working for private contractors and government agencies at the rough edge of the counter-drug program. Some had long hair and looked like country music stars. Another had a shaved head. Each had his weapon of choice: a Beretta, an Austrian-manufactured Glock pistol, an M-4 rifle. This was the world of the contractors.

The Pentagon, the State Department, the CIA, and others had learned that there were many intelligence-related details more efficiently handled by private firms, which did not incur quite the degree of oversight by the media and Congress. The Americans aboard the plane that had gone down were technically civilians doing contract work for the U.S. government. But their work was classified, and in a slightly earlier era their jobs might well have been handled directly by the CIA. The men were examples of the privatization of war and clandestine operations.

Maj. Roberts, in the midst of a crisis, had no time for me. I wasn't supposed to be here. The next day, a *Washington Post* reporter would be turned away at the entrance to the base. Information that would be public knowledge in weeks, or days even, was still classified. I noticed a television turned to CNN in the corner of the barracks. There was an "orange" terror alert. President Bush had given a pep talk to sailors embarking for the Persian Gulf, Liberian rebels were closing in on the capital of Monrovia, rebels in the Ivory Coast were threatening to take the capital of Abidjan, twenty-nine people had died in political riots in Bolivia, and the government of Austria was blocking the transit of American troops from Germany to Italy, en route to Kuwait and Iraq. At the mention of the last news item, a noncom came over and cursed the screen, the media, and Hollywood.

Outside in the glaring sun two other noncoms were sitting with their feet propped up on ammunition cases. One had served previously in the 5th Special Forces Group, with responsibility for the Middle East.

"How was 5 Group?" I asked.

"It sucked."

"Why?"

"Because it sucked. It just did. The Paks, the Kuwaitis, the Gypos [Egyptians] are all equally worthless. Not up to COLAR standards, Muslim armies have even worse noncoms and middle management than South American armies."

The other noncom, Mike Davila, an 18 Delta medic, was a Mexican-American from near Brownsville, Texas. His voice was as soft and friendly as his body was huge. Chewing on a piece of shelf-stabilized bread from an MRE, he told me that the year before he had been on a small Special Forces mission in eastern Peru, near the Brazilian border. He had seen riots where people had burned down a college. It was at a time when the world media was reporting that democracy and stability had returned to Peru. "I've noticed that poor people naturally follow the ones with an education, and that the ones with an education are often corrupt," Davila said. "You can't always equate education with good character."

Hungry myself—I still hadn't eaten breakfast—I wandered across a dirt field to a canteen-restaurant, where under a scrap metal shed a waitress in a tank top and tight jeans brought me coffee and eggs with hot pepper sauce. There was another restaurant on the base, by a lake filled with piranha. It, too, featured waitresses who dressed and flirted almost like strippers and had the saddest stories of guerrilla atrocities to tell. I would hear one grizzled civilian contractor remark, "If my daughter ever dressed like that, I'd string her up."

The helicopters filled with the two A-teams departed for the crash site as news arrived that a bomb had gone off in the town of Neiva, ninety miles to the north, with eighteen dead and thirty-seven wounded on the day before President Uribe was supposed to visit. It had been meant for him and was detonated by mistake.

I got a lift to the airfield. In the hangar an American flag had been hung in preparation for the arrival of the bodies. Amid the jigs and jack stands, I waited, along with a medic and some of the contractors, for the helicopters to return. The conversation drifted. I learned that the way you get a cow to jump out of a plane was simply to prod it, while a donkey required a halter; cows and donkeys had been regularly dumped out of planes to provide food for pro-American insurgents throughout the Cold War.

After an hour the helicopter that had gone to retrieve the bodies finally landed. The medic and one of the contractors pulled on purple gloves and went out to help the DynCorp rescue team load the two body bags onto

"Israelis" and carry them, ducking under the rotors and out of the man-made wind into the hangar. Only one of the dead was American; the other was the lone Colombian crew member.

The medic broke open the first body bag. A 7.62mm AK-47 assault rifle bullet shot at the skull from such close range causes a hydrostatic explosive effect, which made the victim momentarily difficult for even a friend to identify. It was an execution. The dead contractor, Thomas Janis, fifty-six, of Montgomery, Alabama, had been the recipient of a Bronze Star for valor in Vietnam. He had a son and a step-grandson in Kuwait, both waiting to be deployed to Iraq. It emerged later that rather than run into the trees for cover, as he had instructed the others, he stayed behind to destroy the sensitive equipment on board; that's where the FARC found him. Talk about making sacrifices for your country!

The other body was that of Luis Alcides Cruz, a noncommissioned Colombian intelligence officer based here in Caquetá Province. His body did not look as bad as Janis's, though he might have suffered more. His neck was dislocated and a rifle bullet had gone through his back.

The previous morning, the Cessna, in the midst of mapping coca fields for eradication, had developed catastrophic engine trouble. The pilot, Thomas Janis, brilliantly glided the plane down to a belly flop at the edge of a ridge. Though only a few minutes' flying time from Larandia, the small mapping team was in the midst of FARC territory. Janis and Cruz, to judge by the medic's examination, had not been injured in the crash. There might have been a shoot-out with guerrillas, who saw the plane come down and rushed to the scene. The two men had been murdered and their bodies dumped in the first wooded area north of the crash site. The bullet in the back indicated that Cruz may have been trying to run away. The other three, all Americans, were taken hostage.

When news of the crash reached Bogotá, Lt. Col. Christie immediately mobilized the two ODAs in southern Colombia and ordered them to heli-copter fields. But the rules of engagement did not permit A-teams to go on such a mission in enemy territory. Duke knew this. Yet, as he later told me, "Since we had an SF capability so close by, I wanted to give my superiors the option of changing the ROEs for this extraordinary circumstance." Indeed, one of the teams, ODA-776, had been specifically trained for this type of search-and-rescue mission.

But twenty-four hours would go by before the two ODAs would get permission from the higher-ups to board the helicopters. In a hostage situation, akin to a kidnapping, the first twenty-four hours are crucial, particularly the first night following the abduction. It may be the only time when a rescue squad can effectively keep the perpetrators from moving their prey out of the vicinity. All the satellite and other high-tech surveillance that the Americans would subsequently bring to bear on the crisis would never make up for that original twenty-four-hour delay. The middle-level officers had been ready to move, but then "Washington" took over.

When I returned to ODB-780's barracks that evening, thirty-six hours had gone by since the three had been taken hostage. Maj. Roberts observed reflectively, "By now you've got dehydration, heat exhaustion setting in, bug bites, it gets harder and harder for them. All the FARC needs is one terrain feature between it and its pursuers, and they're safe in this environment."

Roberts had just finished a huddle with his chief warrant officer, Terry Baltimore, a smooth and charismatic ball of fire who gave the demoralized B-team a pep talk.

"I know," Baltimore began, "we were all packed, organized, up all night, and ready to assist the A-team secure the crash site. But the decision to disengage us, to keep us out of the op, and have the A-team wait until today to enter the field was taken above our pay level. I'm sulking with the best of them. But now we have to help the host nation plan to capture as many FARC as possible, so that we can interrogate them and find out where the three AMCITS [American citizens] are.

"COLAR is running the show," he went on, "but it has done no force-to-force ratio analysis. The host nation had the initiative last night, but lost it and we did not go in until today. The host nation needs us to come up with options, to help them map out where the roadblocks should be, so that we can establish traffic patterns that can, in turn, help us determine where the FARC is concentrating its troops, and where the AMCITS might be. If we don't start templating, we'll miss the whole fucking puzzle."

It was getting late and I needed a place to sleep. I was about to see if a bed was available in the B-team barracks when a big, friendly Green Beret came over and asked if I wanted to stay over in his hootch. "It's more comfortable than here, if the air-conditioning works." He was Capt. Mike "Mick" Braun of Wolcott, Connecticut. He had served in Bosnia and now led ODA-785, one of the A-teams that after a twenty-four-hour delay had finally got to the crash site. ODA-785's specialty was combat diving, not out of place here; southern Colombia had more navigable river mileage than usable roads. Capt. Braun's hootch had twelve guys packed on bunks in a small room, filled with drying towels and a jumble of charging computers and intra-squad radios. But the air-conditioning worked, and after opening my sleeping bag, I quickly fell unconscious.

Morning brought acquaintance with Capt. Braun's two sidekicks, both sergeants first class: Juan Perez, a tall, mustachioed Cuban-American from Los Angeles who had a cigar in his mouth before his first cup of coffee; and Bo Wynn, an avid deer hunter originally from Tampa, Florida, who had tattoos of boats and barbed wire on his chest and gladly explained to me the workings of a Remington 7.62mm M-24 sniper rifle.

"We lost the initiative after we were made to stand down the first night," a frustrated Sgt. Perez told me as I opened my eyes from a night's sleep and grabbed my notebook. "We're so afraid of getting our guys killed that we let 'em get captured."

They told me the whole sad story of the previous two days. At 9:10 a.m. on February 13, soon after the Cessna Caravan had gone down, they got their "get ready" orders from Duke Christie's forward operating base in Bogotá. They called their team in from training and quickly packed their webs, to be reinventoried at the B-team barracks: canteens, rehydration packets, bandages, compasses, flares, Chemlites, maps, intra-squad radios, GPS (Global Positioning System) units, 9mm and 5.56mm magazines, knives, Berettas, M-4s with grenade launchers, and 40mm grenades. Sgt. Bo Wynn would also carry a quickie saw for breaking down doors. At 10:10 a.m. they were at the airfield. They waited four hours in the hot sun for the execute order to board the helicopters. It never came. Then they were told to "stand down."

Sgts. Perez and Wynn called it demoralizing and humiliating to be prevented from entering a combat zone in front of the very Colombian battalions they had been training.

At 7 p.m. that night the bureaucratic process restarted, with a "warning order" for the next day, followed by a "plan" at 9 p.m., a "written order" at 12:30 a.m. February 14, an "op order" at 5 a.m., and an "up-top intel update" at 6:10. This was all before Maj. Roberts's classified brief that morning which I had been barred from attending. Finally, at 10:45 a.m. they were boarding the helicopter to go to the crash site, where they established a 360-degree security perimeter while the ATF team inspected the equipment on board the Cessna, which, it turned out, had been sufficiently destroyed by the crew members before their capture. Photos of the "crime scene" also had to be taken for use by the FBI and Colombian prosecutor's office. Everyone thought that the designation of a war zone as a civilian "crime scene" was quixotic. For years such legal fictions had tied the Colombian government in knots in its war against narco-terrorists.

"What was the terrain like?" I asked.

"Pothole heaven," Sgt. Perez said. "You move only in a zigzag, sixty-degree inclines all over, no shade. Great guerrilla country. But here is what the higher-ups miss, for the same reason it's great anti-guerrilla country. A half dozen SF guys, fluent in Spanish, traveling load-lite, living off the land, with good comms and helicopter locations for infil and exfil, and we'd find out a lot more in a few days than a whole battalion clunking around."

Braun, Perez, and Wynn were three well-spoken men with tattoos, guns, and serious reading material all over their hootch: Braun had been dipping into the complete works of James Fenimore Cooper. Wynn, though frustrated by the timid military-diplomatic policy of the previous days, nevertheless told me that "everyone has his place and I accept mine. I'm just happy being a sergeant. What do I know?" His tone was truly humble.

I was beginning to love these guys. They had amassed so much technical knowledge about so many things at such a young age. They could perform minor surgery on the spot. Yet each had such a reduced sense of self compared to everyone I knew in the media and public policy worlds. In the barracks, egotism was expressed purely in terms of team pride.* Here hierarchy and authority were looked upon as supreme virtues, giving each officer and noncom a role and a function in a noble cause. Everybody had read Stephen Ambrose's *Band of Brothers,* and related more to the World War II paratroopers in the story than to their contemporaries in civilian life.[24]

By mid-morning, the mood at the base had subtly shifted from an emergency to a long-haul operation. I hitched a ride back to Bogotá with Brig. Gen. Remo Butler on the Casa 212. Brig. Gen. Butler, an African-

* See David Brooks's insightful commentary about the reduced sense of self in the part of America that voted for George Bush in the 2000 election: "One Nation, Slightly Divisible," *The Atlantic Monthly,* December 2001, p. 63.

American, was a huge, gregarious, delightfully profane man. "I helped ap-
prove your trip down here," he told me, "but I had no idea who you were!"
Thank God for the majors on his staff, I thought.

I had an embarrassing moment on the flight back. In Larandia, before
taking off, I had drunk a lot of water because of the heat, and suddenly at
fourteen thousand feet with my body fast cooling I desperately needed to
urinate. There were no facilities.

I spoke to the pilot. He said, "No problem, I'll open the hatch, piss out
the back."

"Are you kidding? I'll get sucked out."

"You've been watching too many movies, *man*. This plane isn't pres-
surized; you won't get sucked out. I'll open the hatch."

I wasn't brave enough. I took a discarded mineral water container and
used that, capped it, and flung it out. The pilot counted a few seconds and
said, "It must be frozen by now at this altitude." A projectile of frozen piss
falling over FARC country. Gen. Butler laughed.

A few days later I was back at fifteen thousand feet in the unpressurized
Casa. Duke and I were headed northeast to Arauca Province, on Colombia's border with Venezuela. Arauca, the size of New Hampshire, was
the most violent region of Colombia, the heart of Injun Country. America's imperial destiny was to grapple with countries that weren't really
countries. No place in Colombia, and few places in the world, illustrated
that as much as Arauca, where the Green Berets had several teams deployed.

In Arauca Province three generations of people had grown up loyal to
the insurgents. Kidnappings and car bombings occurred on a daily basis.
There were twelve thousand hectares of coca fields set to be targeted
by the counter-drug program. Big oil was here: Occidental Petroleum
had a pipeline from Arauca northwest to the Caribbean, which was frequently attacked by terrorists. Arauca boasted a strategic location abutting
Venezuela, where the radical-populist (yet democratically elected) president, the ex–Army general Hugo Chavez, was providing Colombian guerrillas with rear bases. Control of Arauca gave the Colombian guerrillas a
corridor for exporting narcotics to Venezuela, in exchange for weapons
and munitions that, in turn, were smuggled into the region by Arab gangs
based in the Venezuelan port of Maracaibo.[25] There were credible reports
that Hamas and Hezbollah had established havens on the Venezuelan

island of Margarita near Caracas.[26] Venezuelan authorities were providing thousands of local identity cards to Syrians, Egyptians, and Pakistanis.[27]

A supporter of Fidel Castro in Cuba and Saddam Hussein in Iraq, Venezuelan president Chavez had fingerprints all over the narco-terrorist operation in South America. U.S. intelligence found that the small GPS systems carried by FARC gunrunners constantly indicated positions inside Venezuela. With help from Venezuela, the ELN narco-terrorists had learned how to sabotage the oil pipeline with satchel bombs.

The stakes for the U.S. were high. It was getting 34 percent of its oil imports from Venezuela, more than from the entire Middle East. The economic threat posed by Chavez was, to a degree, more important and more insidious than that posed by radical regimes in the Arab world. Chavez had an interest in FARC and ELN attacks on Colombian oil installations, since it made the U.S. even more dependent on Venezuelan oil.

In late 2002 the Bush administration had dispatched several Special Forces A-teams to the border towns of Arauca and Saravena, where President Uribe was building new police stations to be patrolled by forty-six-man units, also trained by American Special Forces. Uribe had targeted the whole province as a "rehabilitation" zone, to be pacified and governed directly from Bogotá. Arauca symbolized how the counter-drug war had, following September 11, been transformed into a regional war for governance. And it wasn't just the Venezuelan border area that required help; the FARC was also importing arms and precursor chemicals, and exporting drugs, over the Brazilian and Peruvian borders.

———

Descending through the clouds I saw a pool-table-flat lesion of broadleaf thickets, scrap iron settlements, and gravy-brown rivers. There was something frightening and uncharted about Arauca. As a young traveler in the 1970s in Cairo, I had met an American couple my own age who had recently arrived in the Middle East by cargo ship from South America. They had hitchhiked and taken buses all the way down through Central America into Colombia, and then continued by road into Ecuador, Peru, Bolivia, and Argentina, before boarding a ship in Buenos Aires. It had been grueling and adventurous, but not suicidal, as such a trip would be today along significant parts of the same route. I myself had just been in Yemen, which was far more dangerous to travel through now than it was when I first visited there in the mid-1980s. For those who rarely ventured beyond the

cocoon of the post-industrial Western democracies, the world was liberal-
izing and becoming more convenient. But many parts of the planet had become more dangerous and out of reach.

Just over the treetops now, shacks and sagging clotheslines gave way to
rutted roads in dry, reddish savanna. Maj. William "Bill" White, commander of five Special Forces detachments in the towns of Arauca and Saravena, met us at plane-side flanked by Green Berets in Kevlar and full kit,
inside a Humvee that was fitted with a mounted MK-19 40mm grenade
launcher.*

As I stepped off the tarmac, two Colombian soldiers, badly wounded in
a car bomb detonated the hour before in nearby Arauquita, in which the
explosive device was coated with human feces to cause further infection,
were being carried off a Russian-made Mi-17 helicopter on stretchers.
They were taken to an infirmary where one of Maj. White's Special Forces
medics was waiting to treat them. Half of their bodies were caked with
blood. The day before in Arauca, White informed me, the Colombian police had managed to deactivate two other bombs. The day before that there
had been an assassination attempt on a local politician. The day before that
an electricity tower was bombed, knocking out power in the region. Going
back more days in Arauca Province there had been the usual drumroll of
roadside kidnappings, street-corner bicycle bombs, grenade strikes on police stations, and mortar attacks against Colombian soldiers with propane
cylinders packed with nails, broken glass, and feces. White had prepared
a list of violent incidents over the past thirty days in the province. It was
single-spaced and ran more than two pages.

Maj. Bill White, thirty-seven, was an Army brat who had grown up in
Fayetteville, North Carolina, next to Fort Bragg. His sense of humor was
as dry and pale as his complexion. "I don't look a day over forty," he
quipped.

The journey from the airstrip to the army base was only a few hundred
yards along a public road. So were the Kevlar, Humvee, and mounted gun
really necessary? I asked. "Yes," White said, staring intently at the road.
The tension here was noticeably higher than at Larandia.

Near the Green Beret compound we passed two young men being led
away in handcuffs. They were the ELN operatives accused of setting off
the car bomb in Arauquita by remote control with a cell phone. They

---

* "Humvee" is, in fact, another acronym: high mobility multi-wheeled vehicle.

smirked like real punks. Next in my line of sight came the Colombian army barracks, with its concrete trench used for washing clothes and mess kits, and for pissing and shitting. A medic described the Colombian troops inside as "nice little soldiers full of parasites, fungus, and jock itch."

The Green Beret compound was hidden behind three layers of black sandbag walls and concertina wire. An entire shipping container was used to store ammo. Special Forces was ready for a siege. Maj. White brought me to a baking-hot corner of the barracks where he had a laptop and blank wall arranged for a PowerPoint briefing. "I keep it real hot in here," he joked; "that way you'll ask fewer questions and we'll get through this thing faster." I thanked him for his consideration. I had seen the same PowerPoint briefing about Arauca twice already, at Fort Bragg and at SOUTHCOM in Miami.

Still, he had some new information for me. The day before in Arauca forty people had been killed in action during a shoot-out between left- and right-wing paramilitaries. The FARC was moving back and forth across the border with help from the Venezuelan national guard. The oil spills from ELN satchel bombs had caused an ecological disaster, an issue that might have been better publicized in the U.S., because, as one Green Beret deadpanned, "You can bet that people back home will get more upset about despoiling the environment than about Colombians being shot and tortured."

Disgust about Colombian democracy and human rights laws, which made it particularly hard to prosecute car bombers and other narco-terrorists, was greater here than at the other Green Beret compounds. "The FARC has an intelligence operation one block from the police station in Arauca town," Maj. White explained, "but the intelligence gathered by the police against the FARC is still insufficient for a court-ordered phone tap. Meanwhile, the mayor's been killed, the airfield's been bombed, and the governor's personal assistant has been assassinated. My Colombian counterpart whose troops we're training," White continued, "doesn't want to know more than two hours in advance about our plans for visiting the airfield or the town, since he doesn't trust his own staff not to leak it to the FARC. Come on, let's go see the town."

"Yeah," I responded. All the briefings in the world were not as revealing as the indefinable essences gleaned from visual contact.

Under vast skies and pummeling mid-afternoon heat, the armored car and Humvee equipped with a mounted gun rolled through the town of

Arauca, a desultory, low-level gridwork of scrap iron and red-tiled roofs, blotched walls, cafés with molded plastic chairs, and awnings made of the same plastic material used for garbage bags. The few decent-looking dwellings had iron grates over the doors and windows. Weeds, garbage, and rusted shacks mixed with flowers, agaves, and sagging banana leaves. Sidewalks disappeared into scraggly bush. I saw half-naked people with unreadable expressions wearing thongs and baseball caps.

Every parked car and bicycle looked deadly. The steel armored doors, Kevlar, and weaponry offered some protection. But they were also a pretense. The enemy was invisible and could incinerate us at any moment. The only defense in this terrorist environment was offense, which the restrictive rules of engagement forbade. After a truck had unexpectedly pulled out into the street, slowing our convoy, causing us to scan the rooftops and parked vehicles, and causing me to sweat more than usual in the fetid climate, Duke Christie remarked, "If five firemen get killed fighting a fire, what do you do? Let the building burn? I wish people in Washington would totally get Vietnam out of their system." Translation: he and his men were willing to take quite a few casualties in Colombia to defeat the narco-terrorists; it was the politicians who were afraid of casualties, not the American military.

Lifting his eyes on this ratty hellhole of a town, Maj. White asked rhetorically, "Where has all the oil money gone? Tell me. You see any signs of development here?"

Occidental Petroleum received 8 percent of the annual oil profits from the Arauca region, leaving 92 percent in Colombian hands. That 92 percent, assuming honest administration, should have been $30 million annually. Even in 2001, when the pipeline was shut down for two hundred days because of sabotage, there still should have been enough millions in profits "to build a brand-new town," White calculated in his dry and laconic way.

For generations, the wealthy urban sophisticates in the highlands had barely been aware of this malarial outback. "If you lived here, you'd be ELN or FARC, too," another Special Forces officer remarked. "That is, if they didn't rape, murder, and extort money from you, and from the local authorities. The truth," he went on, "is that everyone here is just scared. Everyone thinks the government will eventually give up and leave the area back in the hands of the rebels."

Our convoy reached the Arauca River at the edge of town, one of those unhappy, bile-colored, sluggish rivers so common in the third world. The collapsed mud banks were partially supported by sandbags. Venezuela lay on the other side a hundred feet away, where there were more weeds, clotheslines, and scrap iron hutments. Officially there was a border here; in fact, there was none. The narco-terrorists crossed easily, back and forth, getting help from Chavez.

Later I spoke with an American intelligence officer in the area. He worried that "the Colombian military was following America's Vietnam strategy: building up troop levels while avoiding risk. The Colombian army, police, air force all think Black Hawk helicopters are the answer to everything," he went on; "that's the way we used to think. They're not sufficiently improving their noncommissioned officer class, while their generals are content to play it safe. Thus, little happens. In Peru, [Alberto] Fujimori told his generals that they couldn't retire until the war with the Shining Path [terrorists] was won. Here Uribe talks tough, but you don't see the follow-through in the field with aggressive, small unit tactics like you did in Peru."

I concluded that the deployment of Special Forces to train host country troops in Arauca was more of a political statement by the Bush administration in support of President Uribe than it was a substantive attempt to break the back of decades of guerrilla control in this scraggly back-of-beyond.

I found a bunk beside two Army civil affairs specialists who were here to jump-start various education and health programs: Maj. Mike Oliver of Derby, Connecticut, and Capt. Carl Brosky of Plant City, Florida. Brosky had served in Bosnia and Rwanda. He had dark hair and a permanent introspective manner. He told me about families digging up the graves of loved ones in Bosnia following the Dayton Peace Accords and moving them to places where they wouldn't be mutilated by people from a hostile ethnic group returning to the area. In Rwanda he had been in charge of water purification for a refugee encampment. He spoke softly about how he had watched a family of five come to the yard outside his office to die, because they knew that a truck would properly transport their bodies to a gravesite. They were on the verge of death by starvation, he said, and "they knew—just knew—they were all going to die. When the town was covered by mud from a volcano it was the best thing that ever happened to it." Like other soldiers I had met who spoke the truth, he did not mean it cynically. He just didn't know how to dissemble for the sake of making a proper impression on a stranger. His blunt honesty left him with stores of idealism for the work he was doing.

He and Maj. Oliver had books strewn all over their bunks. They said that civil affairs in the U.S. military really had its origins during the Mexican War with Gen. Winfield Scott. I started reading a book they gave me on the subject, but was so tired I fell asleep on the pages.

After years of drifting through lonely hotel rooms, I found barracks life a pleasure. You could leave your valuables about and not worry about locking your room, since everything was safe with these guys. They were not rambunctious young recruits. They were married, had families, and some of their wild years were behind them: you had to have served in the regular Army before you could even apply for Special Operations. Camaraderie was a constant. Like a family, someone was always willing to help you or lend you what you needed. If you wanted company, there was always somebody to talk to. If you were bored, there was always a DVD to watch on one of the laptops. If you wanted to be left alone to read or write, people always gave you your space.

The town of Saravena was even more violent than Arauca; thus the most violent in the country. The very extremity of the situation granted further insights into what the Green Berets could and could not accomplish.

It lies only seventy miles to the west, along the border. But as this was Injun Country, we flew. A half hour later I was on the tarmac in Saravena, greeted by Capt. Gil Ferguson of Jackson, Mississippi. The first thing he did was point out to me the remains of the terminal building blown up by guerrillas the previous summer with four cylinder bombs. A 40-pound empty propane gas cylinder, he explained, would be slipped inside a 120-pound one to serve as the mortar launcher. The 40-pound cylinder would then be stuffed with standard explosives—in addition to bits of nails, screws, scrap metal, broken glass, and human feces—and fired out of the 120-pound cylinder with a gunpowder charge. The *rampa,* as Colombians called it, could hit a target three thousand meters away. The broken glass was forbidden by the Geneva Convention.

Saravena was so violent that the Green Berets never left the base here. "I've been here for months and I have never seen the town of Saravena," Capt. Ferguson said. The sandbags at the compound were piled higher than at Arauca; the strands of concertina wire were laid thicker. It was dustier and hotter here, too. Amplifying the claustrophobic atmosphere, the three dozen Green Berets and support staff were not even permitted under the rules of engagement to patrol the area beyond the base, known to be friendly to the insurgents and within the range of the *rampas*—for which the compound's corrugated roof provided little protection.

"The ELN and the FARC are too smart to fight us," Master Sgt. Jose Cabrera told me, shaking his head. "If they want to kill us, they'll just use cylinder bombs."

"It's like Iwo Jima," Duke Christie observed, "no place to hide," referring to the February 1945 battle on a bare volcanic island in the western Pacific where U.S. Marines were rained upon by Japanese shells.

Following the destruction of the Marine barracks in 1983 in Beirut, and of military apartments at Khobar Towers in Saudi Arabia in 1996, U.S. generals and civilian politicians needed a saying, I thought: *Thou Shalt Not Be Sitting Ducks*. American troops, particularly elite units, should never be concentrated in any place where they could not patrol the immediate environs aggressively. Yet that was the situation here. The current rules of engagement which limited the Green Berets to training details only might have placated the U.S. Congress and made for smooth bilateral relations with Colombia, but they were dumb tactics. And they were morally wrong, since they denied the troops the means of self-defense.

The first night here Duke spent several hours listening to complaints about the restricted rules. He allowed everybody to talk, letting himself get beaten up. Morale at Saravena was genuinely bad. The boredom was reflected in the long evening hours spent weight lifting; everybody joked that it was like prison. Saravena was the classic case of a deployment for the sake of political symbolism, in which the military logic had not been properly thought through.

"If they would just loosen the ROEs, give us the assets and some helicopter platforms, this whole guerrilla siege of Arauca Province would be over in six months," Capt. Ferguson said. He wanted to do what he had been trained to do: fight, go into battle with the Colombian forces he was training. A graduate of the Air Force Academy, Gil Ferguson had switched over to the Army the moment he learned that he couldn't be a fighter pilot. Once in the Army he gravitated to Special Forces. From Mississippi, he adored the New York City lingo of television's *Law & Order*. His crony was his team sergeant, Master Sgt. Cabrera, a native of the Dominican Republic via New York City.

Jose Cabrera, forty-two, in the Army for twenty-two years, was the ultimate sergeant: the nucleus of the United States military and why it was so good. Cabrera had a refrigerator-thick build. He was street-smart, ambitious, intellectually curious, and proactive to the extent that he had practically developed his own little native intelligence service for Saravena run from inside the barracks. Trained as a combat diver, he was a veteran of America's war against the Cali drug cartel, and also of Just Cause, the 1989 invasion of Panama to oust dictator Mañuel Noriega. Based in Cali in the 1980s, he worked in photographic intelligence. In Just Cause, his job was to interrogate pro-Noriega lawyers and policemen. He had also served in Ecuador, Peru, Bolivia, and Paraguay. Because of Sgt. Cabrera and others like him, SOUTHCOM was a model of the kind of linguistic and area expertise that all the area commands required in an age of imperial responsibilities.

Over a dinner of ham, fried rice, and Gatorade at the Colombian officers' club, Cabrera summed up the local situation: "murder, extortion, blowing up power lines, and yet there is no opposition, no sign of a communal spirit. People struggle only to survive or to reach the next rung, where they can skim too. There are better places to grow coca," he went on; "the ELN is here in such numbers only because of the oil." Oil had not brought development but terrorism.

Cabrera brought me daily casualty reports from the internecine guerrilla fighting between the FARC and ELN, which in his mind was good news: let the narco-terrorists kill each other. He told me about a new class of improvised claymores: glass and nails stuck in melted tar; barbed wire wrapped around dynamite; bolts and nails sunk in fertilizer inside a milk can. Then he told me about how the ELN had hired a top lawyer to get their Venezuelan explosives expert released early from prison.

One day Cabrera introduced me to four members of a Colombian army motorcycle platoon that investigated car and bicycle bombs. They were solid little men in their early twenties. Their faces were the hue of the soil, with the broad features and impassive expressions of indigenous Indians. Sitting on camp chairs amid the sandbagged walls of the Special Forces compound, they explained that they were volunteers from Bogotá and Tolima, because nobody local could do their job without endangering their families. The week before there had been five of them. Now one was dead. They had arrived at the scene of a car bomb. After they moved the crowd away and cordoned off the area, a second bomb had gone off, sending one of them ten meters in the air. He lost his torso and died on the spot.

While these four soldiers were risking their lives daily, other Colombian soldiers were secretly helping the terrorists. I learned of an incident a few days earlier. A Colombian army unit was notified that it would be dispatched to arrest several guerrilla leaders at a meeting in Saravena. Some of the Colombian privates then made calls from their cell phones. When the unit arrived at the site, the tables and chairs for the meeting were set up but no one was there. Having presumably got word of the raid, the guerrillas had fled.

"We've told the Colombians," Ferguson said, clearly exasperated, "that we're not going to get anywhere in this war, despite the training we're giving their counter-guerrilla battalions, if they can't even confiscate cell phones from their privates. But they haven't done it."

I thought of what the intelligence operative had told me in Arauca: Uribe's tough anti-guerrilla rhetoric had little follow-through in the field.

The following day I observed training. The purpose was to stage an ambush. But before that could be done, a security perimeter and rally point near the ambush site had to be established.

Sgt. Dave Ogle of Spokane, Washington, was standing knee-deep in bramble so thickly matted and dense that visibility was only a few feet. Members of the Colombian army's 30th Counter-Guerrilla Battalion were walking single file ahead of him. Setting up a 360-degree security perimeter is easy in an open field, but it took skill in this endless thicket. Having gotten his Colombian troops in a massive circle, each soldier lying on the ground, facing out from the center, covering twenty degrees or so with his rifle, unable to see each other yet aware where all the others were, Ogle next had them practice finding an objective rally point, a place which was "out of sight, sound, and small arms range of the objective area."[28]

The plan was to ambush a pickup truck on a nearby dirt road. The day before, the Colombian army had accomplished the task smoothly. This time Ogle and the other sergeants added a surprise: a Green Beret was hidden under an old blanket in the back of the pickup. As soon as the Colombians jumped out of the bush to surround the pickup, the Green Beret shot the squad leader, who dropped his M-60 machine gun. But none of the other Colombians assumed command; nor did any of them think to retrieve the M-60 from the dead man.

"Both the assumption of command and the gun died along with the commander," Sgt. Ogle remonstrated afterwards in Spanish. He ended in an upbeat manner, though, with the necessary clichés: "Do your best. Do what's right. Do what you're supposed to do."

He and the other sergeants stayed out with the trainees through the worst of the muggy midday heat. At dusk we plodded back to the barracks, where under the fluorescent lights, Sgt. First Class Javier Martinez of Oxnard, California, who had wanted to join the Army since he was six, mentioned that the hardest field maneuver to teach the Colombians was charging directly into an ambush. "Directly assaulting an ambush line is counterintuitive," he explained. "It demands a lot of self-confidence in your team and in your commanding officer. But the technique was used successfully in Vietnam. You can find it in the *Ranger Handbook*."[29]

"Yeah," someone responded. "But how do we get these guys to believe us, if we're not allowed to go out on patrol with them against the FARC and ELN? Every time they go out on an op without us, we lose face." Only if they were attacked could the Green Berets violate the rules of engagement.

Suddenly we heard gunfire. I turned my head. Capt. Ferguson frowned and said, "It's just night practice at the range. We should be so lucky."

––––

Policing the world meant producing a product and letting it loose, Maj. Gen. Sid Shachnow had told me back in North Carolina. That product had been produced all right, but it hadn't been let loose in Colombia. The American contractors taken hostage from that downed plane in southern Colombia were still being held captive two years later—a situation that might have been avoided had the two A-teams gotten permission to deploy to the crash site twenty-four hours earlier. As in Vietnam in the early 1960s, the effect of Special Operations Forces was blunted by the unwillingness of policymakers to utilize them more effectively as a policy instrument.* It was partly because of such timidity that the Johnson administration had been left with no other options than to escalate the war in Vietnam with conventional troops, or get out completely.

In Colombia, though, as the months rolled on, some forward steps were made. President Uribe reclaimed rebel areas, thanks to the training provided by Green Berets. The level of violence dropped somewhat, and Uribe, who had lost none of his political courage, went on to become the most popular leader in modern Colombian history. Imperial progress was

* This is one of the themes in Shultz's *The Secret War Against Hanoi.*

slow and imperceptible. It could not be measured in news cycles, and was always subject to reversal.

The problem for the U.S. military, even at the tactical level of infantry, was that its capabilities were simply too potent for the restrained diplomacy born of an age of media intrusion. Thus the challenge was to go unnoticed. The next place I went, I saw what one man could do when given absolute freedom, and when nobody was looking.

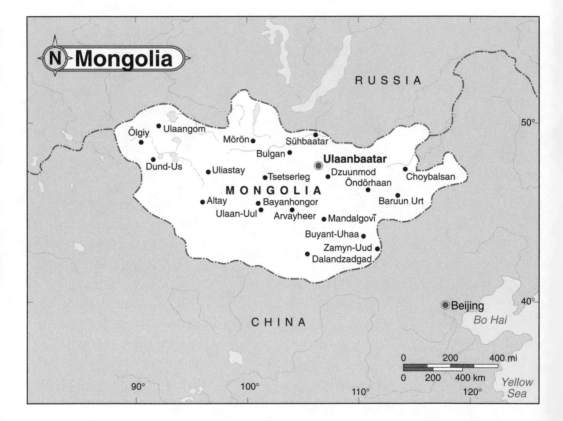

N Mongolia

RUSSIA

50°

Ölgiy   Ulaangom
        Mörön   Sühbaatar
              Bulgan   Ulaanbaatar
Dund-Us
        Uliastay   Dzuunmod   Choybalsan
              Tsetserleg   Öndörhaan
        MONGOLIA
                        Baruun Urt
        Altay   Bayanhongor
Ulaan-Uul   Arvayheer   Mandalgovĭ
                  Buyant-Uhaa
              Zamyn-Uud
              Dalandzadgad

Beijing   40°
                Bo Hai

CHINA

0   200   400 mi
0   200   400 km

Yellow
Sea

90°   100°   110°   120°

CHAPTER THREE

PACOM

MONGOLIA, SPRING 2003

WITH NOTES ON MACEDONIA, BOSNIA, AND
TAJIKISTAN

*"Mongolia was a trip wire for judging future Chinese intentions. . . . Col.
Wilhelm was determined to make the descendants of Genghis Khan the
'peacekeeping Gurkhas' of the American Empire."*

I n the early spring of 2003 an American-led host, spearheaded by the
First Marine Expeditionary Force (I MEF) and the Army's 3rd Infantry and 101st Airborne divisions, captured Baghdad, racing from
Kuwait across 350 miles of hostile Mesopotamian desert to the Iraqi capital, seizing it and other cities along the way, and doing so with greater
speed and efficacy than German Panzer divisions moving across Russia in
1941 and the Israeli Defense Forces moving across Sinai in 1967. Because
conventional war played to the strengths of the Pentagon brass, they out-
did the military achievements of Xenophon at Cunaxa in 401 B.C. and of
Alexander the Great at Gaugamela in 331 B.C., both of which lay along the
invasion paths. The three-and-a-half-week campaign would be compre-
hensively documented by hundreds of journalists who were implanted
with the Marine and Army divisions.*

But while the public at the time identified America's imperium with an
expeditionary force of several hundred thousand troops in Iraq, more often
than not this empire was being created and maintained elsewhere by just a
few individuals here and there. Mongolia, whose obscurity did not render
it unimportant, was the best example of that.

---

* This included my colleague at *The Atlantic Monthly*, Michael Kelly, who gave his life for
the enterprise. Embedded with the 3rd Infantry, he was killed April 3, 2003, on the outskirts of Baghdad.

As I MEF and the 3rd Infantry, assisted by Special Operations Forces, tried to consolidate their hold over Iraq following the collapse of Saddam Hussein's despotic regime, a small event went unnoticed. A contingent of 175 Mongolian soldiers made plans to deploy to Iraq, to assist American troops in policing that conquered country. It constituted the first entry of Mongol troops into Mesopotamia since 1258, when Hulagu Khan, a grandson of Genghis Khan, exterminated most of the population of Baghdad, the capital of the Abbasid caliphate.

Hulagu also destroyed the irrigation system, reducing Mesopotamia to a malarial swamp from which it never quite recovered. Tamerlane, another Turkic-Mongol, reconquered it in 1400. Mesopotamia next became a battleground for Sunni Turks and Shiite Persians, with the Turks eventually consolidating it as a backwater of the Ottoman Empire. The collapse of the Ottoman sultanate at the end of World War I led to a British-created state that threw Kurds together with Sunni and Shiite Arabs. Following the British departure, one Iraqi ruler violently toppled another. Only the most ruthless of dictators could contain Iraq's sectarian passions, hence Saddam.

The arrival in Mesopotamia of America's liberal world empire was an attempt to reverse that doleful historical pattern. The fact that America did, in fact, constitute a world empire was best demonstrated by distant Mongolia's inclusion in it. "Mongolia is a vast country completely surrounded by two anti-American empires, Russia and China," S. Galsanjamts, a member of Mongolia's National Security Council, told me. "It is therefore a symbol of the kind of independence America wants to encourage in the world."

Before seeing how one good man encouraged that independence, it is necessary to set the stage with some history.

For nearly a millennium, from before the collapse of Rome to the dawn of the Renaissance, Inner Asia—Mongolia in particular—was the source of much of the destruction and epochal change wrought upon Europe and the Middle East. Pouring out of a desolate steppe prone to extreme temperatures and hemmed in by the Altai, Pamir, and other mountain ranges, Turko-Mongol nomads recurrently descended upon sedentary peoples lying to the south and west. Between the fourth and twelfth centuries, Huns, Avars, and Magyars, as well as Khazar, Petcheneg, and Cuman Turks, all beat similar paths out of North-Central Asia into southern Russia, the Great Hungarian Plain, and the Balkans.[1] China, too, which lies to the southeast of Mongolia, suffered the whirlwind onslaughts. The Great Wall was less a defense against men than against their horses, without which the nomads were powerless.[2]

But the barbarians of Asia's interior tableland were shrewd, making a pact with one Chinese faction against the other, or siding with an exiled pretender. In his definitive tome, *The Empire of the Steppes: A History of Central Asia,* the French scholar René Grousset writes that the "periodic descents by the hordes of the steppe . . . became one of the geographic laws of history."[3]

There was an opposing law, too, which brought about the "slow absorption of the nomad invaders by ancient civilized lands."[4] To wit, the Moghul Empire in northern India, with its sensuous fusion of Persian-Turkic architecture, was the by-product of stationary anthills of civilization being invigorated, rather than ravished, by steppeland nomads, founded as the Moghul Empire was by Muhammad Babur, an early-sixteenth-century Mongol king and descendant of Tamerlane. History in Eurasia had always been determined by large-scale migrations. And that was something the United States had to keep in mind, given that as the earth's largest landmass Eurasia was still the heart of geopolitics.

Of all the Turkic and proto-Turkic multitudes that washed out of the high plateau of North-Central Asia, the most notable came from just north of the Gobi Desert: the thirteenth-century Mongols led by Genghis Khan who, as Grousset writes, "integrated the steppe . . . and became the steppe incarnate, from Peking to Kiev."[5] It was Genghis—the "Great Khan" and "Lord of the Earth"—who replaced clan-based battle units with mixed squads of ten, which allowed for a monolithic cavalry that crossed tribal lines and represented all the peoples of Central Asia.[6]

Following his imperial election in 1206, Genghis (a Persianized spelling, actually; he is called "Chingis" by Mongols) required only twenty years to unify the steppe and begin his conquest of sedentary China and Iran. By the middle of the thirteenth century, the conquering squadrons of his descendants would cover 90 degrees of longitude across the swath of Asia, a quarter of the earth's circumference.[7]

The descriptions of the thirteenth-century Mongols by the Chinese annalists and the medieval French traveler William of Rubruquis are, in fact, strikingly similar to those of the fourth-century Huns written by the Roman historian Ammianus Marcellinus: they were short and stocky, with broad faces, leathery skins, straight black hair, flat noses, and eyes like thin crevices. History may record nothing so terrifying as the sight of a Mongol cavalry, in all its stench and ugliness, girdling the horizon, and advancing "at a jog trot in an awe-inspiring silence," before charging with "diabolical shrieks and yells."[8] Tuluy Khan, the most brutal of Genghis's sons, in 1221 killed several times more people in Merv, in Turkestan, with swords and axes than the 225,000 killed in Hiroshima and Nagasaki.[9] Up to 30 percent of the population of Central Asia and adjacent areas was decimated by this Mongol war machine.

Still, the great civilizations of northern India would never have come into being without these Turko-Mongol incursions. It was the Mongols who unified Cathay and Mangi, respectively the northern and southern empires of China. Kublai Khan, another of Genghis's grandsons, established China's Yuan dynasty, with Beijing as its capital. In 1267 he began to construct a new complex of palaces to the northeast of Beijing, known as the "City of the Khan," Khanbaligh, the Cambuluc of Western travelers to Kublai's court, whose luxury was celebrated by Marco Polo.

The late-eighteenth-century English historian Edward Gibbon, who considered these Central Asian hordes the "remote authors of the fall of the Roman empire," writes thus in defense of the Mongols:

> The Catholic inquisitors of Europe, who defended nonsense by cruelty,
> might have been confounded by the example of a barbarian, who antici-
> pated the lessons of philosophy, and established by his laws a system
> of pure theism and perfect toleration.[10]

Under Kublai Khan's reign in China, Gibbon continues, "letters and commerce, peace and justice, were restored," and "the great canal of five hundred miles was opened."[11] Kublai's Chinese khanate lasted no more than a century, though, as the Mongols lost their old nomadic hardiness and slipped into the decadence of sedentary life. They were subsequently toppled by their Chinese subjects, even as China's civilization had been revitalized by the steppeland occupiers. "Conquering a country while mounted is easy," Genghis had said, anticipating the problem with China, "dismounting and building a nation is difficult."[12] It was something the U.S. would learn in Iraq eight hundred years later.

Following Genghis's conquests, the process of dismounting and nation-building was truly begun by Ogodai Khan, the most intelligent of Genghis's offspring. Ogodai, who completed the Mongol conquest of northern China, Iran, and southern Russia, settled in the city of Karakorum in the center of present-day Mongolia (the region where the Hsiung-nu, or Huns of antiquity, had their capital), and in 1235 surrounded it with a defensive wall.[13] Gibbon observes that a "change of manners is implied in the removal . . . from a tent to a house."[14] In Karakorum, the sterile immensity of the plateau and forest was tempered by painting, sculpture, silverware, and the mosques and Nestorian churches of foreign traders.

Karakorum was visited by the Franciscan William of Rubruquis, who set out from Constantinople in May 1253 on a mission from Louis IX of France (Saint Louis) to Mongka Khan, yet another of Genghis's grandsons, who had taken up the Nestorian faith and turned his grandfather's empire into a functioning bureaucratic state. By mid-summer, Rubruquis had traveled east from the Black Sea and Crimea, penetrating the heart of the Mongol imperial domain at its western edge in present-day Kazakhstan. In late autumn, he had rounded Lake Balkhash, and crossed into northwestern China and then Mongolia proper. Having arrived at the *ordu* (tented palace) of Mongka Khan, Rubruquis was granted an audience with the sovereign on January 4, 1254. In his account, he writes:

> when the felt before the doorway was raised we entered, chanting. . . . This place was all hung with cloth of gold. In the middle stood a brazier in which burned a fire of thorns, wormwood roots, and cattle dung. The grand khan was seated on a little bed, dressed in a rich furred robe which glistened like the skin of a seal. He was a man of middle height, aged about forty-five, with a somewhat flattened nose. The khan ordered us to be served with *cerasine,* made of rice, as clear and sweet as white wine. He then sent for many kinds of birds of prey, which he set upon his fist and viewed attentively for some time. After that he ordered us to speak. He had a Nestorian as his interpreter.[15]

Karakorum, which Rubruquis would reach the following April, and where he would meet a Parisian goldsmith, represented, along with Kublai Khan's Cambuluc, the high-water mark of medieval Mongol civilization, when the empire founded by Genghis stretched from Hungary to Korea, and as far south as the Persian Gulf and Vietnam: the largest land empire in history.

Later the Mongol Empire unraveled to the point where the Mongolian heartland itself became disunited by tribalism. By the end of the seventeenth century it was incorporated into Manchu China. There Mongolia languished until the seismic political shocks of the early twentieth century: the crumbling of the Manchus' Qing dynasty in 1911 and the Bolshevik Revolution in 1917 that tore imperial Russia apart.

The weakening of central authority in both Beijing and St. Petersburg led to Outer Mongolia declaring its independence, even as Inner Mongolia to the south remained a part of China. It would be in Inner Mongolia in the following decade where the celebrated American explorer and China scholar Owen Lattimore, in the words of his son, David, experienced "a kind of epiphany."[16] Seeing a camel caravan alongside a railway track, Lattimore wrote:

> There lay the loads, between the lines of camels and the lines of railway wagons: a distance of two paces, perhaps four paces, bridging a gap of two thousand years, between the age when caravans had padded back and forth into the obscure distances dividing the Han Empire from the Roman Empire, and the age of steam, destroying the past and opening the future.[17]

In Outer Mongolia, that steam-driven future had already led to a political maelstrom. First the Chinese tried to reclaim it. Then in 1921 came the "Mad Baron," Roman Nicolaus Fyodorovich von Ungern-Sternberg, a thirty-four-year-old Baltic soldier-baron, Buddhist convert, and paranoid alcoholic. Ungern-Sternberg, who with his disheveled blond hair and exhausted expression resembled a figure in a Byzantine icon, believed himself the reincarnation of Genghis Khan brought back to earth in order to re-create Greater Mongolia.

The Mad Baron's ragged army of Cossacks, czarist White Guards, Austro-Hungarian prisoners of war, and other war-criminal types pillaged Urga, the Outer Mongolian capital, after having driven out the Chinese. He and his troops gang-raped women to death, baked people alive in ovens and in the boilers of locomotives, fed ethnic Chinese to wolves, and stripped Jews naked in the bitter cold and mutilated their children, among other well-documented atrocities.[18]

Yet, by ousting the Chinese from Outer Mongolia, the Mad Baron unwittingly opened the door to Lenin's Red Army. Though he vowed to erect an "avenue of gallows" from Urga to Moscow, from which would "swing Bolshevik and Jew alike," the Bolsheviks captured and executed him later in 1921 in the course of establishing the Mongolian People's Republic.[19] Urga thus became known as Ulan Bator, "Red Hero," more recently spelled as Ulaanbaatar. For seven decades thereafter, Mongolia languished in the limbo of a Soviet satellite, the second country in the world after Russia itself to become communist.

It was in the turbulent period of 1922–30, a time when the Soviets were still establishing themselves in Mongolia—when the Gobi was still accessible to Americans—that Roy Chapman Andrews of the Museum of Natural History in New York conducted several expeditions there, scouring the desert for dinosaur fossils. Chapman Andrews was a charismatic, larger-than-life big-game hunter and scholar-adventurer who uncovered the first skeleton of *Velociraptor,* the star dinosaur in Steven Spielberg's movie *Jurassic Park.* Chapman Andrews would later become the prototype for the fictional archaeologist-explorer Indiana Jones in the movies of George Lucas.[20]

Three quarters of a century later, after central authority had once again dissolved in Russia upon the dissolution of the Soviet Union, even as China was continuing to reemerge as a great power, an American Army officer in the style of Roy Chapman Andrews was dispatched to Mongolia to make it a military ally of the United States. The deployment of this particular American officer occurred against the following backdrop.

Mongolia, with one of the world's lowest population densities, was being threatened by the latest of Eurasia's great historical migrations— that of an urban Chinese civilization determined to move north. The Chinese coveted the oil, coal, uranium, and empty grasslands of their former Manchu possession. Given that a resurgent China had already absorbed Tibet, Macau, and Hong Kong on the mainland, Mongolia, which on the map looked like a big piece of territory that had been bitten away from China, was fast becoming a trip wire for judging future Chinese intentions.

Cognizant of Mongolia's geographic encirclement by Russia to its north and by China to its south, west, and east, the American secretary of state James Baker III had pointedly told Mongolians during a visit in July 1991 to consider the U.S. "your third neighbor." But that bold vision languished for a decade, until the arrival of regular Army Lt. Col. Thomas Parker Wilhelm.

Lt. Col. Wilhelm was determined to make the descendants of Genghis Khan the "peacekeeping Gurkhas" of the American Empire. It was an apt metaphor. The Gurkhas, the fighting tribes of Nepal which had won the respect of the British on account of their toughness and adaptability, were originally of Mongolian origin.[21]

Of average height with a sturdy, fireplug build, Tom Wilhelm was a perpetually exploding canister of energy. His forceful manner and animated voice communicated *ready, aim, fire* in each sentence. He walked fast and his train of thought was faster still. Either way, I found it hard keeping up with him. Everything about him was a series of exclamation points. His eyes under his dark, short, slightly receding hair literally drank up the Gobi landscape. He could quote from memory Robert Service's poetry of adventure and wanderlust. In e-mails to me before I came out to Mongolia, he went on about Central Asian history and the medieval traveler William of Rubruquis, before ending his missives with "GO ARMY, BEAT NAVY! CHEERS FROM THE STEPPE, TOM."

Wilhelm had a maniacal laugh. In his office at the American Embassy in Ulaanbaatar he kept two saddles and a tent. He hunted. He fished. He owned a World War II–vintage motorcycle with a sidecar. He traveled with a jar of McIlhenny's Tabasco Brand Pepper Sauce that he used liberally. I remember him popping hot green peppers into his mouth at a Mongolian border post while talking up the benefits of Harris Falcon-II Series tactical hand-held radios to a Mongolian colonel. "They're the best radios in the world, they'll last forever, you'll love them," he said. "Tom Wilhelm," a friend of his in Washington had warned me, "is what happened when Huck Finn grew up."

As with other American officers and noncoms I had met, for Tom Wilhelm the mission was everything. Not to take bureaucratic risks—or to shade the truth for the sake of a diplomatic or career advantage—was in his eyes unmanly, the worst of offenses. "I'm the guy who gutted the DOD's [Department of Defense's] environmental program for Mongolia, because it was unimplementable, and I didn't see what we were getting out of it," he told me as soon as we had met in Ulaanbaatar, just after he had been promoted to a full bird colonel. "Gutting the environmental program was the first policy step towards getting Mongolian peacekeepers on the yellow brick road to Baghdad."

When Wilhelm had arrived in Mongolia in 2001, there was no focus to defense relations, only a hodgepodge of unrelated aid and training programs that had not been staffed out in detail in either Washington or Ulaanbaatar. Nor did Mongolia's post-communist military have a realistic vision of its own future. It wanted a modern air force, but it was unclear just what such an air force would do, even as there was no expertise to maintain and sustain transport planes or fighter jets.

Wilhelm, with the active support of Ambassador John Dinger (like Colombia, this was another example of interagency cooperation), implemented a "three pillars" strategy for Mongolia, to which he convinced the Mongolian military to sign on.

- Secure Mongolia's borders not against a conventional military threat from China, which was impossible to do, but against illegal border incursions including Chinese migration and transnational terrorism— for example, the Turkic Uighurs of western China. Aided by the Chechen mafia and al-Qaeda, the oppressed Muslim Uighurs conceivably represented the future of terrorism in Central Asia.
- Prepare the Mongolian military to play an active role in international peacekeeping, in order to raise its profile in global forums and thus provide it diplomatic protection from its large, rapacious neighbors. The planned dispatch of Mongolian troops to post-Saddam Iraq elicited shrill cries of annoyance from Russia and China, which had opposed the U.S. invasion. But it was the first building block of this pillar.
- Improve Mongolia's own capacity to respond to internal disasters.

To achieve these goals, Wilhelm scrapped existing aid programs and added new ones that would support the three pillars, such as a humanitarian dental project in a key Mongolian-Chinese border area. Even as a lieutenant colonel, Tom Wilhelm was a policymaker by another name.

But there was another reason that I traveled to Mongolia to meet Wilhelm. Tom Wilhelm—known as "Mean Mr. Tom" to warlords in Bosnia, and "Aga Tom" to aficionados of the civil war in Tajikistan—had witnessed the messy collapse of communism in Eurasia on the ground in several theaters, where his very presence indicated the consequent rise of American power. Fluent in Russian, he was the ultimate area expert for the former Soviet empire and its shadow zones, from Yugoslavia to Mongolia.

Ulaanbaatar, where Wilhelm and I met, was a composite of any number of ex-communist capitals that I had seen in the Balkans, the Caucasus, and Central Asia, with an added touch of bone-chilling Anatolian-like bleakness. Dominated by gray cement and brown dirt, it had barely a tree in sight. The apartment blocks resembled penitentiaries. The stench of lignite lasted deep into spring. Yaks fed on weeds in garbage-strewn lots on the city's outskirts, where people inhabited traditional *gers* (circular felt tents). Underground utility pipes housed the homeless and shipping containers functioned as kiosks. Because of the SARS epidemic, people went about with white masks over their mouths and noses, adding a strange, futuristic element to the cityscape.*

Ulaanbaatar was a far cry from the town founded in the mid-seventeenth century as a trading post at the junction of several caravan routes, known as Urga. Roy Chapman Andrews, observing Mongol horsemen mingling with camel drivers from Turkestan in Urga's dusty streets, compared it to "an American frontier outpost of the Indian fighting days."[22]

The American Indian analogy went far in Mongolia, for the Plains Indians were descendants of the very peoples who had migrated from this part of North-Central Asia across the Bering Strait and down into North America. Gen. Joseph Stilwell, the American commander in China during World War II, remarked that the "sturdy, dirty, hard-bitten" Mongols all had "faces like Sitting Bull."[23] The Mongolian long-song took you back to the chants of the Sioux and Apaches. Helping matters were the cowboy hats that Mongolians wore along with their traditional robes. As Wilhelm never stopped saying, "Mongolia is real Injun Country."

———

There was other romance, too. Ulaanbaatar was once the Sacred City of the Living Buddha. The Buddhist lamaseries of Gandantegchinlen Khiid and Daschoilon Khiid, revived since the fall of communism, were cavernous, dusky red and leafy gold worlds of chanting, saffron-robed monks and hammered brass prayer wheels. Sculptures of frightening servant deities sat in dilapidated wooden cases sanctified by dust, reminiscent of faded black-and-white photos in an antiquarian's library. The seventy-five-foot-tall gilded gold statue of Buddha at Gandantegchinlen Khiid, built to replace the one destroyed by the communists, was a loud, happy spirit of beauty and wonderment. It was a welcome contrast to the bone gray

---

* SARS, severe acute respiratory syndrome, caused panic in Asia in the spring of 2003. The Centers for Disease Control and Prevention in Atlanta said that the masks were of only minimal help, yet the Mongolian authorities insisted that everyone wear them.

steppe, apartment blocks, and statues of local communist bosses that had curiously not been torn down, and which people passed by in silence.

The American Embassy in Ulaanbaatar was different from the American embassies in Sana'a and Bogotá. It was a small building, with less imposing security, befitting the threat assessment. Mongolia had been under the Soviet jackboot for seventy years, a generation longer than the satellite states of Eastern Europe, so public opinion was particularly pro-American. There were no anti-war demonstrations at the time of the invasion of Iraq. On the walls of the embassy's corridors were splendid old photographs of Chapman Andrews's expeditions in the Gobi in the 1920s, with the Stars and Stripes snapping in the breeze above Fulton trucks.

Newly promoted Col. Tom Wilhelm greeted me in a gray suit, white shirt, tie, and suspenders. His jobs included defense attaché, Office of Defense Cooperation chief, and liaison for Pacific Command. Actually, he was an Army FAO (foreign area officer), part of a cadre of U.S. military experts in local cultures that blended the role of soldier and diplomat.

The morning I arrived, Col. Wilhelm was busy with a number of tasks. He had to personally thank the parents of a Mongolian-born U.S. Marine fighting in Basra, Iraq, and plan for the visit of the chief of the Mongolian military, Maj. Gen. Tsevegsuran Togoo, to Washington, and the visit of fourteen American brigadier generals to Mongolia. Also due to arrive here was the Third Marine Expeditionary Force commander, Lt. Gen. Wallace Gregson. That last visit was the most important. If there were ever a land invasion of Asia, in the Korean Peninsula for example, III MEF would play a role just as prominent as I MEF had played in Iraq.

The majority of Mongolia's foreign military training and assistance came from the U.S., and Wilhelm was only one of three full-time defense attachés here. The other two were Russian and Chinese, and they rarely left the capital. Americans were uncomfortable with the idea of empire, even as the responsibility was thrust upon them in places like this.

————

"I chose to come here, and not to work on the JSTAFF [joint staff] at the Pentagon, because in Mongolia I knew that I could make a difference," Wilhelm told me as we packed for a nine-day trip along the Mongolian-Chinese border. "Mongolians are the only optimistic people in post-Soviet Central Asia," he went on. "In the *Stans* they're all cynical."

The *Stans*—Turkmenistan, Uzbekistan, and so forth—were an assemblage of dysfunctional one-man dictatorships, in which Brezhnevian-era central committeemen were behaving like medieval khans, searching for a glorious past that eluded them because of artificial borders drawn by Stalin, which had resulted in ethnically divided populations. In Mongolia, by contrast, a place with few ethnic tensions, the greatest of the true khans, Genghis, had been reborn as a unifying national hero following the Soviet collapse. Genghis, unlike Hitler or Stalin, was not burdened by any racist or utopian ideology. He was simply a conqueror, albeit among history's bloodiest, so given enough centuries he could metamorphose into a useful and benign symbol.

The Soviets detested the legacy of Genghis Khan's thirteenth-century Mongols. It was their destructive onslaughts that had orientalized Russia, denying Russia the experience of the European Enlightenment. Because the Communists had banned all public displays of veneration for Genghis, after the Soviet Union's collapse he became a luminary instantly. His visage now appeared on carpets, altars, the currency, and beer and vodka bottles. Because his presence overshadowed that of every politician in this fledgling democracy, it discouraged any of them from trying to become big shots, or dictators; thus was democracy strengthened here.

For that and other odd reasons, Mongolia seemed full of promise. So was our mood as Wilhelm donned his baseball cap, suspenders, and cargo pants in the style of an Austrian mountaineer, and slipped oriental prayer beads into one of his pockets for good luck. Next he stuffed his BDU (battle dress utility) into his Army kit bag, in order to wear it at upcoming meetings with Mongolian officers at the Chinese border.

Like any good policymaker—for that was what, in essence, he was—Wilhelm relied on a vivid ground-level sensibility regarding the country in question. Such ground-level sensibility was not a matter of squeezing a large number of meetings into a day or two of travel outside the capital. The keenest insights could never be had by efficient management of time. You refined your instincts about places like Mongolia—or Colombia or Yemen, for that matter—by, in effect, wasting a lot of time. You needed to be able to forget about the capital and slip into the bizarre and tedious inefficiencies of the countryside, with its monotonous travel and meetings that often didn't go anywhere, in order to have a better understanding of what you were dealing with. That is what Wilhelm meant to do on this trip, though he never put it that way.

Ulaanbaatar's train station was a poured-concrete neoclassical pile that for a third world train station was surprisingly quiet and well organized. Our Russian-built train reeked of lignite as a shapely female conductor, wearing a white mask against SARS, had the stove already going for tea. Joining us in the compartment was Maj. Dabarch Altankhuu (Golden Sun), our translator. Mongolians, like American Indians, had naturalistic names. Maj. Altankhuu, dressed in jeans and a work shirt, was a young, stocky, and clean-cut officer who had learned English at the Defense Language Institute in San Antonio, Texas.

As the train slipped out of Ulaanbaatar, Wilhelm, wearing a little boy's smile, declared: "I just love train travel." Being dinnertime, he whipped out from his rucksack a bottle of red wine, black Russian caviar, soft-boiled eggs, cheese, and pickles, and we had ourselves a feast. Then he proceeded to pump Maj. Altankhuu for information on the up-and-comers in the Mongolian military. I looked out the window at bark-brown and tungsten-hued ridges streaked with snow beyond the last of Ulaanbaatar's scrap metal junkyards.

Mongolia constituted a vast spectacular emptiness: Mars except with oxygen to breathe. Only 2.5 million people lived in this country two and a quarter times the size of Texas, and close to a million of them were in Ulaanbaatar. For Peter Fleming, that most intrepid of early-twentieth-century British travelers, Mongolia was a barren tableland of "little horses and great frosts."[24] Here geology mattered more than civilization. Unfolding like a streamer before my eyes was a steppe of gaunt and grumbling hills. Not a tree or piece of scrub was in sight, not even a *ger.* One of the pretty conductors brought tea.

Deep inside East-Central Asia, Mongolia is dominated by a "basin-like plateau," much of which lies from three thousand to five thousand feet above sea level.[25] Looming to the north are the Khangai and Altai ranges, rising to fourteen thousand feet. The climate is among the world's most extreme, with temperatures in Ulaanbaatar varying from 100 degrees in summer to −43 degrees in winter. "It was a desolate country," writes Roy Chapman Andrews, "for every wave in this vast land-sea was cut and slashed by the knives of wind and frost and rain, and lay in a chaotic mass of gaping wounds—canyons, ravines, and gullies, painted in rainbow colors, crossing and cutting one another at fantastic angles as far as the eye could see."[26]

Today's Mongolia, the former Outer Mongolia, has the elongated shape of a sheepskin. We were headed southeast—and downhill—from Ulaanbaatar, into the warmer lowlands of the Gobi Desert, as far as

Zamyn-Uud on the Chinese border. This was close to where Marco Polo had passed en route to China in the thirteenth century.

For much of history, the overwhelming majority of Mongolia's inhabitants were nomadic herdsmen. The Khalka tribe formed the majority in an ethnic mosaic that included Kazakhs, Uzbeks, Buriats, and Torgots. The Chinese began settling here in the early eighteenth century by order of the Manchu emperors. The current hostility between the Mongolians and the Chinese dates from this time. While the Mongolian was at home on the back of his pony, the Chinese infiltrated through agriculture. As Chapman Andrews writes,

> The Great Wall was built to keep the Mongols out, and by the same token it should have kept the Chinese in. But the rolling, grassy sea of the vast plateau was too strong a temptation for the Chinese farmer. Encouraged by his own government, which knows the value of just such peaceful penetration, he pushes forward the line of cultivation a dozen miles or so every year.[27]

At sunset we saw a signature image of Mongolia's nomadic spirit: galloping across the hard, baked steppe and keeping up with the train was a lone horseman, standing upright in his unpadded wooden saddle, wearing a pointed fur cap. "It's like the Great Plains 150 years ago," Wilhelm exclaimed. After two years here his enthusiasm hadn't abated. When darkness reduced the world to the rumbling sound of the train, he began to tell me his life story.

———

Tom Wilhelm was born in 1959 in Evansville, Indiana. His father worked for Martin Marietta, a defense contractor. His job brought him to Orlando, Florida, soon after Tom's birth. "I grew up in Orlando, B. M.—Before the Mouse," he said, referring to Disney World. "It was a quiet little town back then, with a lot of veterans always talking about World War II. The military was an important part of our lives. I was a nationally ranked backstroker and class president with good grades. You know," he continued, sounding embarrassed, "the typical high achiever, and got into West Point. When I got there I found out I was Joe Average.

"West Point's official motto is 'Duty, Honor, Country,' but the everyday mantra is 'You Must!' Electives at other colleges are required subjects here. You take a full load of engineering, math, science, history, psychology, philosophy, foreign languages, and other hard courses besides the military training that continues through the summer. For me that included airborne training and jungle warfare school in Panama. If you flunk just one class, you get a bus ticket home the same day. You don't even get to spend the night in your dorm room. It was certainly an experience, but it was only a moment. As soon as you're commissioned you're just another second lieutenant in the U.S. Army. The only information that appears on your uniform is your last name, WILHELM. You never mention that you went to West Point. The Army hates elitists."

After West Point came something harder still: Ranger school at Fort Benning, Georgia. The Army Rangers hark back to Rogers's Rangers, organized in 1756 by the New Hampshire native Maj. Robert Rogers, who recruited nine companies of American colonists to fight for the British during the French and Indian War. Rogers was the first to incorporate the guerrilla fighting methods of the frontier into an organized military doctrine, the nucleus of today's *Ranger Handbook.*

"At Ranger school you learn what you're capable of," Wilhelm continued. "It's where you meet yourself, stripped of illusions. When we'd run up a hill in full kit a school bus would follow beside us, to pick up stragglers, who got shipped out immediately—without even a chance to wash off the sweat and dust. You swam rushing rivers in winter with a full pack, boots, and rifle. The *Ranger Handbook* has been my bible ever since. In the Army infantry, without that Ranger patch on your BDU, you're suspect."

Having become an Army Ranger, Wilhelm was appointed a platoon leader of an air assault infantry unit of the 101st Airborne Division, stationed in Fort Campbell, Kentucky. It was the early 1980s, the last years, it would turn out, of the old Vietnam War Army. Robbery and drugs were still rife in the barracks. Disciplining soldiers was a big part of his job. "That was all gonna change. I'll get to that later." In 1983 he was sent to helicopter flight school at Fort Rucker, Alabama, and afterwards assigned to the 172nd Infantry Brigade, based in Fairbanks, Alaska.

After a tour as an Army bush pilot, Wilhelm commanded an arctic infantry company, patrolling the Aleutian Islands with Eskimo scouts, occasionally spotting signs of SPETSNAZ (Soviet special forces) units which operated in remote parts of Alaska, a little-known aspect of the Cold War. Fighting in the Arctic demanded a unique set of infantry skills. "When the temperature is forty below," Wilhelm explained, "you can't afford to break a sweat, because once you stop sweating you'll turn into a Popsicle.

You've got to stay dry, even when you're pulling a sled loaded down with gear. Therefore, everything has to be planned and carried out far more methodically than in temperate climates. It was the best job of my life." But that's what he said about all the jobs he had in the Army.

In 1985 he was sent to the Canadian Land Forces Command and Staff College at Kingston, Ontario, a bastion of British colonial tradition where you wore a tie after six and were given your own napkin ring at mess. "There was a lot of esprit. Everything was deliberate, meticulous, with a fierce sense of a warrior ethic, despite the lack of opportunities Canada had to prove it. I never worked harder writing op orders. The Canadians didn't blink; they just kept demanding more detail. I get angry whenever someone belittles the Canadian military."

About this time Wilhelm decided to become a foreign area officer (FAO) for the Soviet Union and its environs. Henceforth he would be a soldier-diplomat, a risky career choice given that the regular Army's main mission was fighting wars, not diplomacy. Total immersion in Russian at the Defense Language Institute in Monterey, California, and graduate school in Russian and Eastern European studies at the University of Kansas followed in quick succession. Then, on his own initiative, and with his own money—with a wink and a nod from the U.S. Army—Wilhelm applied and got accepted to Leningrad State University. "I've built my career in the gray areas," he explained.

He slept in the dorms with Soviet students and queued at neighborhood buffets for sticky rice, black bread, and sour milk. "But the ice cream made it worth it. Russian vanilla ice cream is the best vanilla ice cream in the world!" he exclaimed. Like everyone else in Leningrad, he learned to chase down rumors about consignments of fresh fruit. Waiting in line once in a rainstorm for bananas, he saw the heavyset woman in front of him turn completely naked as the cheap cotton slip she was wearing stuck to her body and became transparent. She laughed along with everyone around her.

It was a life spent learning specific skills—the Russian language, arctic survival, helicopter piloting—rather than theoretical constructs. And there was no letup. At the Russian Institute in Garmisch-Partenkirchen, Germany, Wilhelm studied Soviet mapmaking and Soviet arms control mathematics, which he soon learned had nothing to do with mathematics.

"The Cold War was a sequence of tactical responses," he explained. "Each side developed a new weapons system to negate the other side's.

The Soviets had reduced the whole process to various math equations. Then I learned about 'Coefficient K,' which stipulated that the Politburo always had the power to revise all the other math." For example, toward the end of the Cold War the Soviets came out with the T-80 tank, which they touted as superior to its American counterparts. In that case, responded the Americans, the Soviets would have to reduce their forces in Europe to compensate for the imbalance created by the new tank. The Politburo then revised the math data and indicated that maybe the T-80 wasn't such a breakthrough after all. "This was my first hard lesson in the politization of warfighting," he said.

Wilhelm was thirty years old and an Army captain when the Berlin Wall fell, an event that would change his life. At first he was made a leader of an on-site inspection team for policing arms control agreements between the U.S. and the Soviet Union that had been accelerated by the wall's collapse. The following decade would take him all over the former East Bloc, and to war-torn Tajikistan, Macedonia, Bosnia, and back to Tajikistan. His knowledge of Russian and other Slavic languages would get him repeatedly into war zones, something the Cold War likely never would have.

—

I went to sleep in the dark and rattling train compartment amidst smells of cheese, lignite, and dirty socks, remembering the China scholar Owen Lattimore's phrase about the melancholy of travel: "a winelike melancholy, tenuous but soft, like the delicate, plangent, muted syllables of Verlaine, fortuitously remembered in a Mongolian sunset."[28] I awoke to a full moon at dawn, with snow like powdered sugar glinting on the wrinkled face of the desert. We were now in the real Gobi (Mongolian for "gravel-covered plain"). A Bactrian camel, hairy from the long winter, stood silhouetted at a lonely station platform. Wilhelm, playing with his orange prayer beads and adjusting his ball cap after a few hours of sleep, said, "Now where would you rather be: here, or stuck in traffic, staring at the car ahead of you on I-395 going to work at the Pentagon?"

The train pulled into Zamyn-Uud. Scanning the compartment one last time, Wilhelm, quoting the next-to-last page of the *Ranger Handbook* with Maj. Rogers's own standing orders, declared, "Don't forget nothing."

The new station building sat like a stage prop against the gravel steppe. Waiting for us at the foot of the platform in the freezing April cold were three Mongolian officers wearing dress greens, leather coats down to their ankles, and ridiculously large service caps in standard Soviet style, dubbed "satellite dishes." They shunted us into a Russian-made jeep called a UAZ, short for the Uralski Aftomobilni Zavod (Ural Automobile Factory). Noting that it was a large-sized and late-model UAZ, Wilhelm declared, "Looks like we'll be living in tall cotton." The UAZ was about as big as a small SUV, but without the amenities and with none of the comfort.

Our hotel was two hundred yards farther along the railroad tracks, a poured concrete blockhouse with hard beds, hideous furniture, and cracked windows. Wilhelm quickly changed into his BDU with its Ranger and paratrooper insignias, and black beret with the U.S. Army flash, along with an eagle, the insignia of his colonel rank.* We all gathered in Wilhelm's room. Col. D. Battsengel, the leader of the Mongolian delegation, ordered breakfast brought up: *buuz,* or mutton ball dumplings in goulash, fatty cold cuts, and salty camel's milk tea. We cleaned the plates.

"The American military will eat anything, anywhere, anytime," Wilhelm pronounced to our hosts. Maj. Altankhuu translated. (Though Wilhelm's Russian was fluent, his Mongolian was basic.) They all laughed. Asking the name of a Mongolian officer a second time, Wilhelm apologized, "I always ask for a name twice. When I remembered a woman's name the first time, I knew she would be my wife." Laughter again. Wilhelm's friendly banter and broad smile never let up.

After small talk about wrestling and martial arts, Col. Battsengel told us he was from northeastern Mongolia, where Genghis Khan was born and was likely buried. Col. Battsengel told us he was opposed to the current search for Genghis's remains by archaeologists, saying it was bad luck. I noticed the endless knot of eternity, a Mongolian shamanistic symbol, on his dress greens. Wilhelm, pointing to another shamanistic symbol on Battsengel's uniform, mentioned that it appeared on a cloth given him by an old man who had traveled to the U.S. Embassy from an outlying village. The symbol, according to the old man, would force "your Iraqi enemies to bow down to you in supplication."†

Formally welcoming us to East Gobi Province, Col. Battsengel said that the tempo of development was about to pick up dramatically with the establishment of an economic free zone, manufacturing plants, and a casino

---

* The black berets were introduced by the then–Army Chief of Staff, Eric Shinseki.
† As it happened, that prediction proved correct for Operation Iraqi Freedom, but not for the insurgency that followed.

on the border that would increase the population of Zamyn-Uud from ten thousand to thirty thousand. The Chinese were pushing hard for a casino gambling industry in Mongolia, which favored their business acumen and organizational skills. The Chinese had other plans, too.

The Chinese wanted to start large-scale animal husbandry operations in southern and eastern Mongolia, which would ruin the earth's last uninhabited steppe. They had their eyes on the Gobi's mineral deposits. They wanted to build a modern road network into Mongolia's Gobi Desert from Inner Mongolia, and they were underbidding everyone else for construction projects. Meanwhile, northern Mongolia was being deforested; every other freight train we saw was filled with logs headed for China.

Despite seven decades of virtual Soviet occupation, Mongolians were less afraid of the Russians than of the Chinese. This was less because of the long Manchu occupation in the eighteenth and nineteenth centuries than because of the threat China now represented. Russia's was the disintegrating empire, China's the rising one, with the Chinese migrating in large numbers into adjacent Russian Siberia.* Having once conquered Mongolia by moving the line of cultivation northward, China was poised to conquer Mongolia through globalization. The Chinese border post was in eyesight of our hotel: a brightly lit, well-engineered arc, signifying the post-industrial monolith encroaching on Zamyn-Uud's sprawl of felt tents and scrap iron huts.

The Chinese had flooded Inner Mongolia with Han Chinese immigrants, just as they had flooded Tibet and the Turkic Uighur areas of western China's Sinkiang Province. The Mongolians worried that they would be next. Uppermost in their minds was the fate of the Tibetans, co-religionists with whom they shared the same form of Buddhism. Mongolia's national security doctrine had a phrase about "ethnic purity," reflecting its fear of Manchu-like penetration.

The paranoia in Mongolia about SARS, a disease which seemed to come from China, was telling. In Mongolian minds, it might take only one epidemic to wipe out a substantial part of this sparsely populated country, easing the path for another Chinese demographic conquest. The Mongolians had been particularly grateful for American diplomatic support in encouraging the Dalai Lama's visit to Ulaanbaatar the previous November, a

---

* The Siberian city of Chita, northeast of Mongolia, was reportedly 40 percent ethnic Chinese by 2003.

visit the Chinese tried to block by temporarily cutting rail and air links to Mongolia.

"In my blood I don't like the Chinese," declared a high-ranking Mongolian official in an interview I had conducted in Ulaanbaatar. "The Russians dominated our politics for seven decades but did not incorporate us into the Soviet Union. The Chinese have the possibility to absorb us utterly." I recalled Gen. Stilwell's comment in 1923 about the Mongols' determination never again to be incorporated into China.[29]

But greater than the fear of a strong China among Mongolians was the fear of an internally weak China, or a breakup of China even.

To wit, to Mongolia's southwest lay China's Sinkiang Province, populated heavily by Muslim Uighur Turks, who harbored a Balkan-like hatred of their Han Chinese overlords. Throughout history, China's control of this desert region bordering Pakistan, Afghanistan, and the ex-Soviet *Stans* ebbed and flowed. In the minds of Muslim Uighurs, western China was really "East Turkestan." In the early twentieth century the Uighurs had even set up an Independent Muslim Republic of East Turkestan headquartered in Kashgar, in western China, with hazy Pan-Islamic ideals.[30] A weakened China, along with continued instability in the former Soviet *Stans* and the North Caucasus, spelled trouble for Mongolia, we were told. It conjured up the prospect of Central Asian terrorism and drug trafficking spearheaded by Uighurs and Chechen criminals.

Col. Battsengel drove us beyond the last border checkpoint. Here in no-man's-land there was only a plinth marking the frontier. A Chinese officer a few feet away on the other side of the plinth watched silently as Col. Wilhelm in his BDU and black beret went right up to it, careful not to step beyond for fear of provoking a diplomatic incident. Cameras clicked away at us from a window on the Chinese side.

This was a border that mattered. It would matter more as China loomed over the horizon—beyond the present conflagrations in the Middle East—as the greatest conventional challenge to American power. Yet America's response was often subtle, as I would see.

————

We returned to Zamyn-Uud, where, in a nondescript house amid a sprawl of *gers* and huts, we found a long line of Mongolians waiting in a hallway in traditional *dels,* or robes. Many were children accompanied by their parents. In an adjacent room, U.S. Air Force Tech. Sgt. Dan Elliot of Huntington Beach, California, greeted us. He was the chief of a four-person dental mission dispatched to this side of the Mongolian-Chinese border by Pacific Command. The mission fell within the humanitarian component of Col. Wilhelm's three pillars strategy. By treating an average of a hundred patients daily in this and nearby border towns, Mongolians saw the benefits of American self-interest.

Sgt. Elliot briefed Col. Wilhelm. First he introduced the other members of the team, who nodded as they were busy with patients: Dr. Mark Uyehara, an Air Force lieutenant colonel from Honolulu; Dr. Charles F. Craft, a captain in the U.S. Public Health Service from Lincoln, Nebraska; and Air Force Tech. Sgt. Lorrin Savage from Newport News, Virginia.

"The goal here, sir," Sgt. Elliot told Col. Wilhelm, "is load-light, low-tech, small footprint." He meant that here in the Gobi more good could be done by traveling with minimal equipment, using the most basic technology least compromised by power outages, and keeping the mission as unobtrusive as possible. *Slip in, slip out, take five minutes to set up and pack up, spend the rest of your time and energy with your patients.* "We stay low-key and crank out patients, sir."

Sgt. Elliot pointed out the cheap hardware store lamps for illuminating patients' mouths and the locally purchased gas burners for hot water sterilization. The dental chairs came from nearby shops and offices. The team had advertised its mission to the community through the local radio station. All the equipment fit into six small trunks, including presents for the kids treated along the way. It was like battlefield surgery. The American military was most impressive when it knew how to be low-tech, the same way as guerrilla fighters.

In Colombia, high-tech items were less significant than training on basic tactics like peel-back retreats and direct charges into ambushes with old-fashioned grenades and assault rifles. Each war, each training mission, brought with it new lessons that had little to do with technology. Because America, under all its post–Cold War presidents, was active militarily overseas, its armed services were improving tactically by leaps and bounds.

Wilhelm complimented Sgt. Elliot and the rest of the team on the good work. As we were leaving, Elliot said, "Drink some of that camel's milk, sir. It's what keeps people's teeth here so healthy." With his fair face, unblinking eyes, and organizational skills, Sgt. Elliot was another example of America's superb cadre of noncommissioned officers.

Later, at Col. Battsengel's office, we were plied with camel's milk, greasy mutton, and horse meat for lunch. There was a portrait of Genghis Khan, but none of *our beloved leader,* as in all the other Central Asian countries I had visited that venerate the current dictator. Mongolia, miraculously, still comprised a traditional culture that remained undiluted and uncompromised by communism or globalization. The diet, even at the upper levels of the military, was still a purely nomadic one: meat and milk products with no fruits or vegetables, for nomads lived off their animals and did not stay long enough in any place to cultivate the land. The only foreign cultural import was vodka.

After lunch we piled into the UAZ and headed southwest along the border from Zamyn-Uud. This part of the Gobi, inside no-man's-land, was flat, featureless, and gravel strewn, utterly disorientating. No matter what direction I fixed my eyes, it all looked the same. Here I got my first intimation of how the Gobi abounded with wildlife, more so than anyplace I had seen in sub-Saharan Africa. There were swarms of finches, ruddy drakes, and black-tailed gazelles (Asiatic antelopes), the last of which we used the UAZ to chase down, barely catching them at forty-five miles per hour, exactly as Roy Chapman Andrews had described doing in his book *Across Mongolian Plains.* The horizons were so far you intuited the curvature of the earth. On a one-foot rise, the only landscape feature in this flat emptiness, stood a golden eagle about two feet tall. Next we came upon herds of goats, horses, and Bactrian camels guarded by a few border police. The goats, enclosed in a corral of sheep dung, were a source of food; the horses and camels were used for patrolling.

The Bactrian camels, with their cartoon-like faces and thick winter coats that they shed in blanket-like masses, appeared almost prehistoric. They were far more imposing than the single-humped, smooth-skinned dromedaries of the North African and Middle Eastern deserts. These homely queens of the desert, with heads like floor mops, got their name from the ancient kingdom of Bactria, between the Oxus and the Hindu Kush, that was easily subdued by Alexander the Great. Mongolia and the Gobi in particular contained most of the world's surviving Bactrians.

Near the corral was a *ger* inhabited by a family of nomads. They invited us inside for camel's milk and homemade vodka. The *ger,* ubiquitous throughout Mongolia, is a large, round felt tent. Everywhere else in Central Asia it is known by its Turkic equivalent, *yurt.* We were careful not to step on the door board as we entered; that brings bad luck and was a crime punishable by death in Genghis's time. Continuing with the prescribed etiquette, we walked to the left, or clockwise, around the side of the tent to the back, the place for honored guests. This made sense as the kitchen—a few pots on a stove fueled by dried dung—lay off to the right of the door. The center of the sloping roof was open to the sky. From there hung the ceremonial blue scarf, or *khatag,* which blessed the *ger.* The spokes of the roof frame, or *toono,* represented the wheel of life. The altar behind us, fragrant with juniper incense, included a small carpet with a portrait of Genghis. There was a clean pagan simplicity to it all.

"I'm culturally at home," Wilhelm announced to the gathering, as he sprinkled vodka in the air three times in Mongolian fashion before swallowing a small glassful. "I'm in the Gobi, among Mongolians, and among soldiers." The statement, like so many others he made, endeared him to the locals. It demonstrated, too, how imperialism can entail the aesthetic appropriation of a foreign landscape. The tradition of British literary travel writing would have been impossible without the British Empire. Tom Wilhelm was a man of empire here in Mongolia. He was a more grounded, less mystical version of Francis Younghusband, the early-twentieth-century British army officer and Central Asian explorer who had led a military expedition to Tibet as a preventative to Russian infiltration there.

Heading back to Zamyn-Uud for the night, Wilhelm continued telling me about his life.

His arms inspection team had worked out of a "cheesebox" on Rhein-Main air base in Germany, on call for surprise inspections in recently liberated East Bloc countries. Then in the summer of 1992 came Provide Hope, a humanitarian program for giving away excess military supplies (pallets of winter clothes, blankets, tea, etc.) to the victims of the civil war in Tajikistan, a war which would result in more casualties proportionate to the population than any other civil war in the second half of the twentieth century.[31] Wilhelm, as a Russian foreign area officer, was dispatched immediately to Dushanbe, the Tajik capital in the midst of a descent into anarchy, where he would link up with CARE International.[32]

Now a captain, the only order he got from his superiors was "Don't get yourself killed." The rest he had to figure out on his own.

Capt. Wilhelm now found himself the leader of a different sort of team, one of young and inexperienced civilian relief workers pining for discipline and organization. "I had to figure out who needed to be bribed in order to get our relief supplies out of the railway station in Dushanbe and into secure warehouses." Without a functioning government, and with thousands of ethnic Russians fleeing the country, the railway station was a place of chaos. "Over tea and vodka with the stationmaster, I realized that my team had something he could use. The SeaLand containers holding the humanitarian supplies were exactly what the Russians needed to get their possessions out. Because I controlled the market on storage, we struck a deal."

Wilhelm next had to get the stuff into the countryside. "I got no intel out of the capital. The only useful intel came from the Russian troops nearest to the latest shoot-out." He found himself writing battle doctrine for humanitarian convoys that needed to be escorted by Russian Hind helicopter gunships through terrain so rugged distances were more vertical than horizontal: from canyon floors to high mountain passes. (The last helicopter Wilhelm would pilot in his career was a Russian Mi-8 in Tajikistan, in order to survey the autonomous region of Gorno-Badakhshan.) "If your relief convoy is escorted by local militia and someone attempts to rob one of your trucks, do you ask the militiamen to shoot? At what point does a threat to a humanitarian convoy necessitate losing lives in a firefight?" he asked himself.

This was a question for which the *Ranger Handbook* provided no guidance. The *Ranger Handbook* is about combat: how to kill and avoid being killed. "Nobody much spoke about ROEs until the humanitarian and peacekeeping operations of the 1990s," Wilhelm explained, "since during the Cold War we were either in an armed conflict or we weren't. Now we needed subtle rules for subtle situations."

That summer of 1992 saw fighting in Yugoslavia spread from Croatia to Bosnia, while the Caucasus, Moldova, Transdniestria, and Tajikistan all erupted in civil wars and rebellions. For untold millions across the southern swath of a former communist imperium, it was among the bloodiest and saddest times in history, even as many Americans turned away from the world in semi-isolationist ignorance.

Yet a pivotal drama had begun to unfold for both the Russian and American militaries. The collapse of the Soviet Union was causing civil conflict on the communist empire's periphery. Throughout its history, the Soviet army had been a top-down institution in the most extreme sense. Because of the totalitarian nature of Soviet society, the lower ranks did little more than follow orders. That tendency was reinforced by the terms of the bipolar nuclear standoff, which necessitated that all key decisions be made at the highest levels in Moscow. But what had begun in Afghanistan now spread to the Caucasus and Tajikistan, places where the Soviet military found itself in the midst of dirty little wars. Consequently, in Wilhelm's words, "The generals in Moscow had to rely on their twenty-six-year-olds in the field to figure out what to do."

Figuring out what to do meant that these young Russian officers and noncoms had to overcome an iron law of Russian bureaucracy, *initsiyativa vsegda nakazevema* (initiative is always punished).

Wilhelm bonded with these young Russians, because he was in a similar position himself, writing a new rule book for what a Cold War American military, with its fixation on Armageddon in Germany's Fulda Gap, had not prepared him for. It would be in the Balkans where that learning process would continue for him, and for the American military.

Following several months in Tajikistan, Wilhelm, now a major, was suddenly pulled back to Rhein-Main to lead more weapons inspections in the former East Bloc. Flying on a C-130 transport from one country to another, he watched the noses of MiG fighter jets cut off and steel wrecking balls destroy tanks. But his career was in danger. He had had too much education and not enough infantry experience. He became a "major non-select for the CGSC," meaning he was not among the majority of middle-ranking officers selected to study at the Command and General Staff College at Fort Leavenworth, Kansas, which automatically put him in the bottom 20 percent of all majors slated for future promotion. The U.S. Army, still in its Cold War mode, was not impressed by his hybrid soldier-diplomatic-academic–relief worker career pattern.

To balance out his résumé, Wilhelm was assigned to the 3rd Battalion of the 12th Infantry Division, stationed in Baumholder, Germany. As the executive assistant to the commander, he worked long hours, seven days a week. "Like Ranger school, it was another meet-yourself experience. I loved it." He kept the job for three years, during which time he continued to develop doctrine, based on his experience in Tajikistan, for MOOTWA—military operations other than war.

Then, in 1995, his unit was assigned to the United Nations peacekeeping force in Macedonia.

The next morning in Zamyn-Uud we woke to rain and freezing weather. The day before we had driven on well-worn desert tracks made by other

UAZs. Now we headed out on a longer excursion southwest along the border and left the dirt tracks entirely. Here the Gobi only appeared flat; the vast ocean of stubble fields was so bumpy my head was constantly banging against the roof. After an hour we came to a *zastaf* (border fort), a few single-story barracks with distempered white walls and leaden green roofs. Before alighting, we drove on a little further to pay homage at an *ovoo,* a shamanistic cairn for making offerings to the gods.

Wilhelm, I, Maj. Altankhuu, and the other Mongolian soldiers with us walked around the *ovoo* three times, clockwise, throwing stones at it, in the traditional manner. Then we sprinkled camel's milk on it—a truly sacred gift—and placed the juniper incense, tea bricks, candies, and small vodka bottles that we had brought into the *ovoo*'s crevices, just as other worshippers were doing. Finally, we lined up in single file to tie *khatags* (ceremonial scarves) around the uppermost stones. "It's a pretty good *ovoo,*" Wilhelm said, nodding like a connoisseur.

A fat Mongol woman in a black *del* and orange sash was on her hands and knees in supplication. This *ovoo* had been a stop on the Silk Road long before the Mongolian-Chinese border existed. Destroyed by the communists, it had been rebuilt in 1990. *Ovoo*s were pre-Buddhist. They represented the purest and ultimate form of worship, signifying less superstition than a stark and simple submission to larger forces. Now that we had paid it the proper respect, we would be welcomed at the *zastaf.*

A young soldier wearing a fur hat and greatcoat, with frostbite on his cheeks, saluted smartly as we entered. Then came the dress parade, with a dozen or so troops, a few officers and their wives and children, and the post dog all standing at attention for review. It was like a frontier fort of the Old West. This was not merely a military base but a small community in the wilderness, something that Wilhelm truly admired. Protecting a remote border was seen in Mongolia as a vocation, a way of life. Such an outpost would not be considered complete without at least some women and children.

In a bare and freezing room, the officers' wives served us tea mixed with salt, mutton fat, and camel's milk. The women were thin, wore tight blouses, and were quite attractive. While we shivered inside our heavy jackets, they looked comfortable in shirtsleeves. Wilhelm took notes as the *zastaf* officers complained about how the cold weather shortened battery life for their Kenwood walkie-talkies, about the shortages of spare parts and diesel fuel, and how their solar panels didn't work in bad weather. Wilhelm said he would try to get them new FM radios. In place of solar panels, he suggested wind generators.

The neat and frigid barracks were lined with maps and shamanistic designs. The border guards used old-model Kalashnikovs, with wooden stocks rather than collapsible metal ones. Outside, several dozen horses stood stoically in a freezing drizzle; the afternoon desert sky looked as dark and dreary as coal. A network of concrete trenches and pillboxes indicated the closeness of the Chinese border. Gen. Purev Dash, the deputy commander of the border patrol service, whom I had met in Ulaanbaatar, told me that his men used camels and horses for patrols "not because we are poor and primitive, but because such animals offered the surest means to scout the desert." Wilhelm's plan was for a mobile patrol force mixing fast ponies and Bactrian camels with light, high-tech communication gear.

"You arrived with the rain, that is a blessing," Lt. B. Altanzul (Golden Flame), a lively and inquisitive fellow, told us after several vodka toasts. We were tired and a bit drunk, so we just let the conversation flow. Owen Lattimore writes that "nothing shuts off the speech of simple men like the suspicion that they are being pumped for information; while if they get over the feeling of strangeness they will yarn as they do among themselves," revealing "the rich rough ore of what they themselves accept as the truth about their lives and beliefs."[33] Lt. Altanzul was not a simple man, yet after we sat and got a little drunk with him, without directly asking him a political question, he began to talk about the U.S. and Iraq, the issue of the moment.

"I saw the demonstrations against the war on television," he remarked suddenly, "yet America acted anyway. As a military man, that impressed me." When another officer asked us if the U.S. would defend Mongolia, as it had Kuwait in 1991, Wilhelm replied bluntly, "Probably not. The U.S. can only help Mongolia defend itself. That's the reality." Wilhelm loved Mongolia, but his primary concern was U.S. interests, and he was honest about that.

Driving back to Zamyn-Uud, Wilhelm talked about northeastern Macedonia, where U.S. and combined-Nordic battalions were patrolling the border with Serbia in the early 1990s.

"I was a major; my bosses called me an 'iron major,' no damn joke, the deputy commanding officer on the ground. 'This is great,' we all told ourselves, 'we're in a war zone,' what all soldiers live for. There were American generals saying the Balkans were a waste of time, that we should have been doing Bradley fighting vehicle exercises in Germany instead. What a bunch of crap! Finally, we're actually using our training, and these Cold War dinosaur generals want us to train for a war that would never happen. I'll bet you the reenlistment rate for the soldiers who served in the Balkans was greater than that of those who stayed in Germany. The Balkan deployments were the best thing for the morale of U.S. soldiers at the time. They paved the way for how we fight now."

Wilhelm's men monitored the smuggling of fuel across the unmarked Serbian-Macedonian border. They tracked Serb patrols. They learned to integrate themselves with the Finns, who were part of the Nordic battalion but not part of NATO. They patrolled in full kit several times a day. "The Scandinavians started patrolling without weapons because the atmosphere seemed peaceful. Not us. Our sergeants, who didn't have poli-sci degrees, were smart enough to insist that we lock-and-load all the time. We were defining real peacekeeping, which is like war-making, since you monopolize the use of force in a given area.

"Macedonia," he went on, "was the dictionary definition of exotic: dark-eyed women, little teahouses, intoxicating music, and no laws or rules. It was paradise after Germany. Somalia was over. Bosnia for us hadn't started yet. Macedonia was the only game in town. Majors and master sergeants were defining national policy at the fingertip level. It was really in the post–Cold War years that you started hearing the term 'iron major.' "

The full flowering of the middle ranks had its roots in the social transformation of the American military which, according to Wilhelm, happened a decade earlier, when the rise of Christian evangelicalism helped stop the indiscipline of the Vietnam-era Army. "This zeal reformed behavior, empowered junior leaders, and demanded better recruits," he said. "For one thing, drinking stopped, and that killed off the officers' clubs, which, in turn, broke down barriers between officers and noncommissioned officers and changed the recipe for junior leader development. Our noncoms gained the confidence to do the jobs that those of higher rank and experience had previously done. Our majors do the job of colonels in other armies; our sergeants perform like captains. The moral fundamentalism," continued Wilhelm, a liberal who voted for Al Gore in 2000, "was the hidden hand that changed the military for the better. But you try to get someone to admit it! We never could have pulled off Macedonia or Bosnia with the old Vietnam Army. It lacked the discipline and talent to abide by the restrictive ROEs and complex political-military battlefield.

"In Macedonia," Wilhelm said, "I brought the broom back to the Wizard of Oz. The Army demanded I get experience as a field grade officer. Well, I did."

On December 14, 1995, Wilhelm, who hadn't seen his family for the better part of a year, was on leave in Peoria, Illinois. He had just finished cutting down a Christmas tree with his father-in-law when he saw on television that the Dayton Peace Accords had been signed. He was summoned the next day to the Balkans by Maj. Gen. William Nash, who was about to assume command of Task Force Eagle, with responsibility for the northeast sector of Bosnia.

In Macedonia, Wilhelm had learned the evolving, unwritten doctrine of insertion of forces in a zone of separation. In Bosnia he built on that. He established joint military commands in these zones between the Serbs and the Bosnian Muslims.

Establishing a joint military command, Wilhelm explained, meant "finding the top thug in each village and his counterpart on the other side of the ethnic divide, then finding a secure, neutral place for them to meet, and putting in place the force protection so that each of these local warlords could get to the meeting without being assassinated. The real purpose of the first meeting," he went on, "was not to talk, but to show the thugs who was the boss—and it was us, not them. It was to teach them that unless something was facilitated by us, it wasn't going to get done.

" 'We're the foremen,' I'd say to each local warlord, 'and you're the workers. Without all of our hands on the wheelbarrow, it ain't going to move.' Once they realized the fighting was over, they began making demands on us for water and electricity, which was exactly what we wanted.

"We're still in 1995 now," he continued. "Bosnia was a cold, muddy place, and the people were cold and muddy, too. There wasn't much brotherly love. They had just shot the shit out of each other and were living in the rubble they made for themselves. They seemed tired, though. Their morale was low. That was all good news. Those were things we could exploit."

Wilhelm got wind that the diplomats had worked out a deal for the Russians to join the peacekeeping force. The Russians would be subordinate to Maj. Gen. Nash, who assigned Wilhelm the role of integrating them with the other NATO peacekeepers. "The reason you're here, corporal," Gen. Nash told then-Maj. Wilhelm, "is to keep the Russians out of trouble." Nash had meant the word "corporal" as a generic term for lower- and middle-ranking officers. "Nash had given me a one-sentence mission, which implied that he trusted me to figure the rest out. He knew that I knew that the Russians were professional and well disciplined, and would work well within the brigade. My job was to incorporate them into this complex, fast-moving machine of ours, and to protect them from our own media that was constantly looking for mistakes."

Wilhelm broke off talking as the UAZ pulled into Zamyn-Uud. It was dark and we had another meal of meat and camel's milk and vodka toasting to endure. Peter Fleming had been continuously hungry during his trip across China to India in 1935. That seemed easier to endure than being force-fed meat and alcohol all the time.

The next morning Wilhelm and I went for a walk. Zamyn-Uud's clapboard houses, with their uneven sidings and dumb ornamentation fronting the dust-blown desert, reminded us of the bad construction that each of us had seen throughout the ex–Soviet Union and its former communist satellites. "It's like everything in sight was put together by a high school shop class," Wilhelm remarked. But then his zest returned, as he fingered his prayer beads.

"The values the Mongols have are those of our pioneer forebears 150 years ago, when they settled the frontier. They were full of optimism and busy with chores, emptying the wash pail, getting the fire started in the morning. What a tough life it was—freezing in a wagon train threatened by Indians. Yet few regretted it. Anything could happen and it was all good—that was the central tenet of the pioneer spirit." Wilhelm's parting gift to Col. Battsengel was a lavish coffee table volume of Frederic Remington's paintings of the nineteenth-century American West.

Battsengel introduced us to Col. Kh. Ranjinnyam, a bearish, scruffy, and friendly-looking man who would be our guide on a northeasterly journey along the Chinese border, into an area where Mongolia sticks out into Manchuria. Col. Ranjinnyam's UAZ followed ours until we had driven a few miles beyond Zamyn-Uud. Then we got out and, in the midst of the desert, toasted farewell to Col. Battsengel with a few glasses of Absolut, the only high-quality vodka we had on the journey.

Following final farewells, we transferred to Col. Ranjinnyam's UAZ and set out over a tableland of sagebrush and tumbleweed, stopping after twenty miles at a *zastaf*. I was freezing despite my long underwear. The outhouse was an eighth of a mile away in the ceaseless wind. This *zastaf* had the same spartan minimalism as the one we had seen the day before, with the floors painted a lovely autumnal yellow, and the smell of fresh bread and drying jerky on the roof, a bit of which a petite girl in a blue smock put in our soup along with horse meat. Horse meat, I had decided, tasted as good as beef.

Another twenty miles brought us to another border post and another line of soldiers in fur hats and greatcoats holding ancient AK-47s and standing at attention alongside women and children in the bleating wind on a knife-carved steppe. Here Wilhelm gave yet another short speech of thanks, on behalf of the people of the United States of America.

It turned out that the meal at the previous *zastaf* was only a pre-lunch snack. Here we were brought veritable masses of food. Eyeing the beds beside the eating table, Col. Ranjinnyam announced that it was time for a nap. Within a moment he was snoring loudly. Wilhelm, Maj. Altankhuu, and I followed suit. When I awoke Col. Ranjinnyam was already sitting up in bed, his hair and uniform in disarray and pouring himself another glass of vodka, like a character out of a Russian short story. "It's time to go," he announced.

More *zastafs* and lonely soldiers looking like throwbacks to the czarist army. The landscape of the Gobi kept shifting: small glaciers and glinting streams that wove through gravel fields beside volcanic slag heaps, followed by horizonless uplands of igneous rock engulfed in late-afternoon shadow. Then came vast dirt expanses that gradually shed their stubble, so that by dusk there was nothing in sight but empty sand, with the desert unfurling like a long, haunting echo, a warbling note held at the back of the throat until eternity. I thought of the sound of a *morin khuur,* the traditional Mongolian fiddle capable of the most astonishing sounds with only two horsehairs.

We stopped for the night at Ulaan-Uul (Red Rock), a regiment-sized encampment for the border force. Wilhelm and I shared a small icy room where he continued his reminiscences of Bosnia. I didn't ask questions. I just let him talk. Homer must have been a middle-ranking officer like Wilhelm, I thought, a great oral historian.

"The Russians were in Uglevik, Republike Srpske, to patrol a sector in the U.S.-led area of operations," Wilhelm said. "They had American brigades on either side of them. They had their own JMCs [joint military commands] to set up. Again, there was no doctrine for this. Daily patrols were the guts of the Dayton agreement, and I went on many patrols with the Russians, enduring their combat rations of tinned fish and buckwheat. Their BTR-8os [Bronetransporter, the Russian armored personnel carrier] dispelled the myth of cramped and clunky Red Army fighting vehicles. They were quite comfortable and user-friendly, with plenty of room for a squad in full kit to prep equipment and swap positions.

"We went to one village where the church had been destroyed," Wilhelm went on, "and the Serbs had their headquarters on the wrong side of the street. They had had twenty days to move it to the right side of the street, as stipulated by Dayton, and they hadn't. I took out the copy of Dayton that I carried around with me and read it out loud. The Russian lieutenant with me repeated it to the Serbs. I told the Serbs we would bomb their headquarters with an Apache if they didn't move it. I called in an Apache to do a flyover. The Serbs were in disbelief that they couldn't drive a wedge between us and the Russians. 'Let's go now,' my Russian companion told me. 'Let's give them their own space to absorb the bad news.' An American would have stayed and drunk tea with the Serbs. But the Russians live more in an ambiguous world of negotiations without rules, especially because of their experience with civil wars in the Caucasus and Central Asia. They have a better sense of these things.

"My Russian lieutenant and I seized weapons that were hidden in haystacks," Wilhelm continued. "We destroyed anti-aircraft guns mounted on trucks. We called in Apache missions. That's when I started to be called 'Mean Mr. Tom,' because I kept threatening both the Muslims and Serbs with Apaches if they didn't abide by Dayton by disarming and dismantling their checkpoints.

"I've logged more hours in a Russian ACV [armored combat vehicle] than in an American one over my lifetime," Wilhelm said. "I was taken in and accepted by a brotherhood that had seen exceptional combat in Chechnya and Afghanistan, and listened to them bitch about lousy chains of command and problems in Russia. Many national armies in Europe wouldn't fight when push comes to shove. I've seen them corrupted by too much U.N. work and not enough real combat. But hell, the Russians would fight! Nothing about the American military in Bosnia impressed the Russians so much as our own sergeants whipping out GPS devices, which the Russians didn't have, and calling in Apache strikes. Through us, the Russians learned the real power of technology, not the false power of it."

The real power of technology, Wilhelm went on, is that it provides an objectivity even an enemy trusts. It has a calming effect. Because of the GPS devices, there were no arguments about whether this or that outpost was on the wrong side of the cease-fire line. "The false power of technology," Wilhelm believed, was exemplified by the nuclear chains of command, which were elaborate theoretical constructs never meant for actual use. "The Cold War wrought a whole bureaucratic culture that had no battlefield reality. The Cold War armies were not great armies because all the decisions were made by generals and politicians. In great armies the job of generals is to back up their sergeants. That's just my opinion, but I know I'm right."

That was the other thing about American sergeants whipping out GPS devices in Bosnia which had impressed the Russians. Even if they had GPS equipment, in the Russian military calling in an air strike would be a decision only a colonel would make. Yet the Russians, in Wilhelm's opinion, had middle-level officers almost as good as those in the U.S. military, the result of combat experience in complex environments like Transdniestria, Ossetia, Abkhazia, and Tajikistan, not to mention Chechnya and Afghanistan. And because their empire was collapsing, the Russian military found itself frequently in combat situations that, in turn, were encouraging reform at the lower and middle levels. "I would have followed Col. [Alexander] Lentsov into combat anywhere," said Wilhelm, referring to his Russian commander in Bosnia. "On a tactical level, we have more in common with the Russians than with many of our allies."

But while the lower levels of the Russian military, according to Wilhelm, were dealing with the reality of contemporary conflict, the general staff in Moscow remained locked in a Cold War mindset. In fact, it was becoming even more conservative because of the bitterness over an American-dominated unipolar world. It saw missions like Iraq not as potential learning experiences, but as deployments to be opposed simply because the Americans were leading them.

In the spring of 1996, Wilhelm left Bosnia. By the fall he was back in Tajikistan.

The next day we entered a landscape of rolling hills speckled with scree and yellow stubble grass. Between the blackest shadows, grazing in an ethereal light, was a herd of bighorn argali, or Marco Polo sheep—the "supreme trophy of a sportsman's life," according to Roy Chapman Andrews, because even in the 1920s they were so rare.[34] A hunting license in Mongolia for one of them now cost $20,000. They were as large as horses almost. Wilhelm was ecstatic: "All we need now is to see a snow leopard." We followed them in the UAZ to the edge of a range of clay hills, where below us the great Mongolian plain fell away as if into the sky. Wilhelm gave me his Russian-made monocular to get a closer look. It was like peering back in time, as if seeing the light of a distant star. Marco Polo had seen these sheep in his travels through the Gobi. He described their horns as a "good six palms in length."[35] They were now practically extinct, and would certainly be so if this desert were exploited for its oil and coal. A little while later we saw a *khulan,* a wild ass with large, funny ears that was also extremely rare.

That day Wilhelm and I had to endure large meals at six *zastafs,* with vodka toasts at every one. This was in addition to drinking the blood of a black-tailed gazelle that Col. Ranjinnyam had shot with his Makarov pistol from the UAZ. Having swallowed a glass of blood and eaten the animal's testicles and eyeballs, Wilhelm told me, "Like I said, this is better than rush-hour traffic on I-395 en route to the Pentagon." He never tired, never stopped laughing and slapping the Mongolian officers on the back. Maj. Altankhuu confided to me, "Col. Wilhelm is a great man. He makes us like America so much."

According to Mongolian lore, the three manly sports are horse racing, archery, and wrestling.[36] At the turn of the twenty-first century, racing gazelles with a UAZ and target shooting with Makarovs and AK-47s had become variations of horse racing and archery; thankfully, I had no wrestling to endure. But we stopped for a marksmanship contest at a spot in the desert where we all got ticks, so we didn't reach the next border regiment until 11:30 p.m. As I threw my pack on the bed, in the adjacent dining room I heard Wilhelm let out yet another maniacal laugh. Walking over I saw a large roasted pig, head and eyes and all, placed on the table, and Col. Ranjinnyam imploring us to eat. "The liver of the gazelle I shot will be served to you at breakfast," he said, apologizing.

"You have to understand," Wilhelm told me, "that in this culture food is a gift. And they are showing respect for us and for America by shower-ing us with gifts."

Thus, we ate, again.

The next morning, while eating the gazelle liver, Wilhelm talked about his second posting to Tajikistan. It began in October 1996 when he became America's first defense attaché to the newly independent post-Soviet re-public, whose four-year-old civil war had finally begun to wind down. The ethnic Pushtun Taliban had just captured the capital of Kabul in neighbor-ing Afghanistan. Central Asian leaders, not to mention Russia and the Shiite clerisy of Iran, were fearful that the Taliban, aided by Pakistan and Saudi Arabia, would try to spread its ideology of Sunni fundamentalism throughout the region. Thus, they demanded an end to the Tajik civil war because it was getting in the way of containing the new Taliban regime: Tajikistan was now needed as a rear base to help the ethnic Tajik guerrilla leader Ahmad Shah Massoud recapture Afghanistan. The fact that the civil war in Tajikistan had descended into localized warlordism gave the vari-ous faction leaders, who were fast losing control, a further incentive to stop the fighting.

But the Tajik capital of Dushanbe still constituted one of the lower cir-cles of hell when Wilhelm arrived back there. Much of his time was spent keeping up with the activities of a colorful cast of warlords: Rakhmon "Hitler" Sanginov, Jagga "the Sweeper" Mirzoyiev, Makhmud "the Black Robin Hood" Khudoberdiev, Abdumalik "the Shark" Abdullojonov, Khur-shed "Tyson" Abdushukurov, and Yakub Solimov, who played the theme song from *The Godfather* whenever he received guests at his home.

The Tajik economy consisted of a cotton monoculture, one aluminum smelting plant, and heroin, which all of these men fought over. "In Tajik-istan," Wilhelm said, "I learned that warlords are not the products of great, scheming political minds. Our intellectuals have described them as far more complicated than they really are. They are just simple opportunists, who aren't distracted by larger thoughts about national security or any-thing else." For example, Makhmud Khudoberdiev, a captain in the Soviet army in Afghanistan in the 1980s, happened to have the keys to the armory in Kurgan-Tyube in southern Khatlon Province. "The fact that he had the keys to the armory made him a warlord. He got three tanks running; that's all it took to make him famous."

Wilhelm attended the "final" fall of the town of Tursunzade near the border with Uzbekistan three times, once lying in a ditch in a vicious fire-fight. "On the firing range, bullets make one kind of sound; when they're coming at you they make another." Wilhelm's wife, Cheri, and their two young children, Parker and Daley Alice, had come with him to Tajikistan. "I had been separated from them for so long because of the deployment in Bosnia and other assignments. We were all finally together in a war zone. There was no electricity, no heating; it was so cold we all slept together in the same bed to keep warm. The tap water was the color of Coca-Cola. We shared a toilet with our armed guards. I went boar hunting occasionally. It was the greatest time of our lives."

As the war ended and the infamous Sodirov brothers—Rizvon and Bahrom—were cut out of the peace deal, they began taking Western hostages. The Wilhelms were evacuated two times. During one of the evacuations, Wilhelm was sent to Tampa, Florida, the headquarters of Central Command, which was soon to incorporate the former Soviet Central Asian republics into its domain. Wilhelm was summoned to meet the CENTCOM commander in chief, Marine Gen. Anthony Zinni.*

"I found Zinni in the weight room, pumping iron," Wilhelm related. "A typical Marine general, I thought. He had only one question for me, the big one. Given that I was a force protection risk—after all, my family and I had to be evacuated—what was I doing in Tajikistan in the first place that made me so necessary there? I told him that I was the only guy that he had on the ground in a country with a civil war and next to a country where the Taliban were fighting a collection of warlords called the Northern Alliance. Fine, he told me. Go back to Tajikistan then. That's a good general: If he gets the right answer to the right question he's finished with you. He trusts you to figure out the rest."

Wilhelm returned with his family to Tajikistan one last time, until a contract was put out on his life, forcing them to leave for good. He had been promoted to lieutenant colonel. He then found out that he had been short-listed for a battalion command, placing him in the top 10 percent of his peer group. He never got that battalion command. But the fact that he had risen from the bottom 20 percent—unselected for the Command and General Staff College at Fort Leavenworth—to the top 10 percent through such an unconventional career path constituted proof of how the Big Army had changed since the fall of the Berlin Wall.

* When Zinni's term ended, he was succeeded by Army Gen. Tommy Franks.

"I'll never be a general, so this is the only band I'll ever have," Wilhelm remarked, as the small border force band banged out a variation of a Red Army tune from the 1940s. The detritus of a dead empire was apparent in other ways, too, at this regimental outpost. Near the parade ground was a row of rusted and wheelless armored personnel carriers from the days when the Soviets had used Mongolia as a buffer against China, in the wake of the Sino-Soviet split. Out here there was no way to crush these vehicles, break them down, or recycle them in any way. They were literally ruins of a gone age.

After reviewing the band, we packed our gear into the UAZ and continued our journey northeast along the Chinese border. The plan today was to stop at a few *ovoo*s en route to Shiliin Bogd Uul, an extinct volcano considered by the Mongolians to be holy. "What's the point of all this, militarily speaking?" I half complained to Wilhelm.

"None," he replied, smiling. "Col. Ranjinnyam and the others want us to climb the holy volcano. It's real important to them, so we have to do it. These are the kinds of things the Chinese and Russian defense attachés would never do with the Mongolians. That's why they trust us. Yesterday was a Roy Chapman Andrews day; today will be a Bruce Chatwin or Peter Fleming day." Yesterday, he meant, was given over to Boys' Own activities of hunting gazelles and target shooting. Today we would savor the aesthetics of landscape and culture.*

We stopped to inspect a pair of shattered Turkic statues, standing like mysterious totems in the midst of the desert. They may have been built by the Hsiung-nu (Huns) and dated apparently to the early centuries of the Common Era. No one seemed to know. The guidebooks contradicted each other. We also came upon a statue of Toroi-Bandi, a local bandit who had harassed the Manchu Chinese. Symbolically, the statue faces the Chinese border. It had been turned into a holy site next to an *ovoo*, to which we gave offerings.

We then passed a region of giant crescent-shaped sand dunes rising over a felty marshland. The Gobi was the most varied desert I had ever seen. It had everything: dunes and marshes; hard dirt steppes and gravel plains;

---

* But it must be said that Fleming was no slouch at hunting. Much of what he ate in his journey across China he had shot himself. He would die tragically in a hunting accident in Scotland at the age of sixty-four.

pure sandy desert and slag heaps; clay hills, mountains, and glacial slopes. In the late afternoon we arrived at the sacred volcano of Shiliin Bogd.

The gaunt, hump-shaped rock that we ascended granted a view to the south and east of a shimmering desert, knobbed with the ranks of many dead volcanoes and scarred with moraine ice, as if the moon were coated in sawdust with the black rims of its craters sticking through. This was the western edge of Manchuria, the point where the last vestige of the Western classical world—with its Hun, Turkic, and Mongolian hordes that had ravaged Rome and its shadowlands—gave way to Sinic civilization. "It is a paradise for wolves," Col. Ranjinnyam said.

We circled the *ovoo* at the summit three times, then prepared a barbecue with the ducks that Col. Ranjinnyam had shot earlier in the day, and which Wilhelm had dressed. In a toast to Wilhelm, Col. Ranjinnyam said that he respected the American and Russian armies above all others "because they suffered and won World War II. I want soldiers like Genghis," he went on, "but, of course, without the cruelty of those days."

At the end of the meal we passed around hot rocks from the barbecue to juggle in our hands, a local tradition that Mongolians claim is good for the upper-body joints. Then we took the shoulder blade of a sheep and punched a hole in it, so that no one could cast a spell on us. Wilhelm enthusiastically explained all these traditions to me. "I love my job," he repeated.

———

Completing our visit to the border regiments, Col. Ranjinnyam accompanied us in his UAZ for the long drive to the town of Choir, located in central Mongolia, southeast of Ulaanbaatar. Outside Choir was a deserted Soviet air base that Wilhelm wanted to inspect, with an eye toward its future use by the United States.

The two-mile-long runway needed only modest repairs and could handle any kind of fixed-wing aircraft in the U.S. arsenal. Beside it was a long line of hardened aircraft shelters, reinforced-concrete bunkers in the shape of semi-pyramids to protect fighter jets from aerial bombardment. A gigantic sign proclaimed "Praise to the Communist Party Central Committee." The Choir base had been built in the 1970s, a consequence of the Sino-Soviet split a few years earlier. It constituted a forward front for the U.S.S.R. in a possible conflict with China.

Why in the world would the U.S. ever need a base in Mongolia? one might ask. In the 1990s, Wilhelm had thought the same thing in regard to

Tajikistan. Then came September 11, 2001, and back-of-beyond Tajikistan, with its southern border facing Taliban-controlled Afghanistan, suddenly became a possible staging area for U.S.-led coalition operations.
"That's when I learned never to say 'never,' " Wilhelm said. With Mongolia's eastern border only five hundred miles away from North Korea across
Manchuria, in an unpredictable, fast-changing strategic environment an air
base here could be an asset.

There was no thought of making Choir an American base, the way it
once had been a Soviet one. Rather, for a relatively small amount of money
the runway and a building or two might be repaired and kept up, so that
American planes and Air Force personnel could use them at any time.
Given the political instability throughout Central Asia, the Pentagon was
intrigued by a Eurasian "footprint" strategy in which the U.S. would have
basing options everywhere, without having a significant troop and hardware presence anywhere.

Choir itself was nothing but a series of skull-like concrete tenements
surrounded by steppe. A building complex that had once housed 1,850 Soviet military families, including a theater and shops, had been stripped of
all its windows and heating pipes. "It used to be so lively," said Maj. Altankhuu, "it was the place where all Mongols wanted to go in the evening."

Overlooking a field of broken glass, where the last tenement block met
the flat and empty Gobi, was a concrete statue of a generic Soviet commis-
sar strutting forward in the sneering, aggressive style of Lenin. The statue
of Father Soviet had begun to flake and crumble, though, on account of its
gargantuan size, it might be here forever: the ultimate Ozymandias, with
only a few yaks and stray dogs to admire it.

The statue brought to mind not just brutality and domination, but also
cheapness. "Another thing constructed by a high school shop class," Wilhelm observed, laughing.

"We should be careful of our own ambitions," I said. "We don't want to
end up like the Soviets."

"There is nothing we need to build here," he answered, "except relationships."

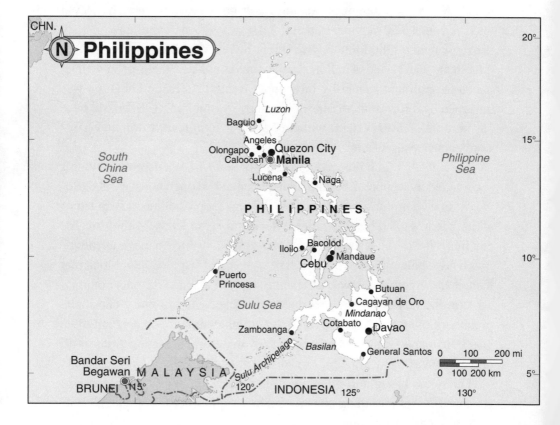

CHAPTER FOUR

PACOM

THE PHILIPPINES, SUMMER 2003

WITH NOTES ON THE PHILIPPINES, 1898–1913

"Terrorists used these poor, shantyish, unpoliceable islands as hideouts. . . . Combating Islamic terrorism here carried a secondary benefit: it positioned the U.S. for the containment of China."

ew vistas are as laden with fateful patriotic memory as the one seen from the grounds of Camp H. M. Smith outside Honolulu, Hawaii, home of U.S. Pacific Command (PACOM).* From the cluster of yellow World War II buildings that served as PACOM headquarters until 2004, when a new building opened on the site, I saw in one sweep the whole tragic landscape of December 7, 1941.

From left to right I gazed down upon Hickam Field; Pearl Harbor, with the U.S.S. *Arizona* Memorial off Ford Island—a mass grave for 1,177 sailors and marines; the shadowy lava peaks of the Waianae Range, behind which Japanese bombers hid in the moments prior to their assault; Wheeler Air Force Base; and Schofield Barracks, the forward post of the 25th Infantry Division, memorialized by James Jones in *From Here to Eternity.*

The Hawaiian island of Oahu, like the Deep South and the Great Plains, screamed *military.* Uniformed Americans were ever-present, so different from the Northeast where I lived. There, with the exception of Fort Drum in northern New York State, home of the Army's 10th Mountain

---

* Marine Maj. Gen. Holland McTyeire ("Howling Mad") Smith is the father of amphibious training of the U.S. armed forces. Before the outbreak of World War II, the Alabama-born general foresaw the need for U.S. soldiers and marines to land on enemy beaches in the face of hostile fire. See Robert Sherrod's *Tarawa: The Story of a Battle* (New York: Duell, Sloan and Pearce, 1944), pp. 133–34.

Division, the major bases had been closed and scaled back decades before. It was one of the lesser noted causes of the Northeast's anti-militarism, in comparison to the rest of the country.*

I had stopped at PACOM for briefings en route to the Philippines. While in Mongolia, I received a message from Maj. Gen. Geoff Lambert at Fort Bragg, asking if I wanted to be embedded with Army Special Forces in the Philippine islands of Mindanao and Luzon. It was an easy call. While the media was focused on Afghanistan and Iraq, the southern Philippines had quietly become a laboratory for drying up an Islamic insurgency, as well as for small-scale nation-building.

As the majestic view from its headquarters indicated, PACOM enjoyed all the grandeur that poor little SOUTHCOM lacked. PACOM had its roots in America's old Pacific Army, which existed from the 1899–1902 Philippine War to World War II. The Pacific Army had arisen from the ashes of the Indian fighting force of frontier days. It was as close to a British colonial institution as the U.S. had ever produced. Its snappy uniforms were made by Chinese tailors, and were worn by men who talked of jungle marches, of the treacherous Moros of Mindanao and the Sulu Islands, and of the headhunters of Luzon. America's Pacific soldiers of the early twentieth century belonged "to the Bamboo or Carabao or Pineapple armies" of the Philippines and Hawaii. They had their own marching songs like "The Monkeys Have No Tails in Zamboanga." Their officers played polo with the local Pacific island elites, while the lower ranks kept exotic village maidens as mistresses. When their ships docked in Honolulu the troops were serenaded by regimental bands and decked with flower leis.[1]

The character and ambience of this colonial-style army was brutally captured for posterity in Jones's *From Here to Eternity*, a saga of thirty-year lifers rather than of citizen soldiers, for whom the military is simply "The Profession." Robert E. Lee Prewitt, Jones's main protagonist, is inspired to join the Army out of Harlan County, Kentucky, not because of the stories he heard from older men about World War I, but because of the ones they

---

* The Northeast certainly has military facilities—the Hanscom Air Force Base in Portsmouth, New Hampshire; the Soldier Systems Center in Natick, Massachusetts; the U.S. Military Academy at West Point, New York; the Naval War College in Newport, Rhode Island; and so on. Nevertheless, no military facility in the Northeast serves as the home of thousands of uniformed troops and their families, and none has generated a retirement community of former military men and women, as bases in the heartland and in the South have.

told him about fighting the "Goddam" Muslim Moros in the Philippine insurrection.[2]

The surviving remnants of that world were visible in the open-porched quadrangles at Schofield Barracks and the line of wood-framed, hip-roofed houses at nearby Fort Shafter, with their mint green facades and screened porches, encased in a graceful clutter of flowering trees and venerable palms. Through the early twenty-first century, Army general officers. assigned to PACOM in Oahu were still living in these elegant termite-infested structures, listed on the National Historic Register.

America's Pacific troops still accounted for the bulk of its overseas soldiery, just as they had a hundred years before. Whereas SOUTHCOM had a paltry 1,271 dedicated troops, CENTCOM 22,046, EUCOM 112,000, and NORTHCOM 133,407, PACOM had a whopping 280,840 troops in addition to 75 warships, 35 submarines, and 1,679 combat aircraft.[3] CENTCOM fought wars in Iraq and Afghanistan with troops borrowed from PACOM.

History and current reality accounted for the extreme imbalance among the area commands.* The Pacific, specifically the Philippines, had been the setting of America's first great overseas war. The Pacific theater had been one of the two great components of World War II. Afterwards, the only large-scale and sustained conflicts in which Americans fought and died were in the Pacific—Korea and Vietnam. The very size of the Pacific Ocean meant PACOM bore responsibility for 51 percent of the earth's surface. India, the two Koreas, China, and the numerous archipelagoes of the South Seas, including Indonesia—the most populous Muslim nation—also meant that PACOM's area included 60 percent of the world's people. And these were mainly highly educated, high-technology populations with expanding militaries, difficult relations with each other, and increasing dependence on imported oil.

Moreover, America did a third of its trade with the Far East. The Strait of Malacca between the Malay Peninsula and the Indonesian island of Sumatra was the busiest waterway in the world. There were nuclear stand-offs on the Korean Peninsula and the Indian subcontinent. Islamic funda-

---

* Defense Secretary Donald Rumsfeld considered this imbalance irrelevant, arguing that troops everywhere belonged to him and the President, to be moved around as they saw fit. But outside Washington, the proprietary attitude with which the various area commands referred to their troops was striking. Also, Rumsfeld's argument presupposed a powerful defense secretary as well as a president focused constantly on military matters. As the 1990s showed, a less forceful defense secretary coupled with a distracted president allowed some area commanders to become barons in their own theaters.

mentalism infected the bigger archipelagoes, while some of the smaller ones were failed states like the Solomon Islands. Looming over all of this was the rising power of China. The Pacific theater could make a grand strategist's head spin.

The briefings at PACOM packed the following theme, even if the briefers themselves did not fully spell it out. Forget central governments and national sovereignty. The Philippines, Malaysia, and Indonesia constituted one vast, interconnected archipelago, whose innumerable remote islands made it a crossroads for international terrorism. Terrorists used these poor, shantyish, unpoliceable islands as hideouts for training and rest and rehabilitation. Combating Islamic terrorism in this region carried a secondary benefit for the United States: it positioned the U.S. for the future containment of nearby China.

Keep in mind that this was largely the Army's perspective, and that of the Special Forces in particular. PACOM had other realities and points of view. The overriding fact of the Pacific theater was oceanic distance, which led to a reliance on the Navy and Air Force. Following the destruction of the Japanese navy and merchant fleet in World War II, critical SLOCS (sea lines of communication) had to be maintained for U.S. commerce and potential military operations against the Soviet Union. Though the Soviet threat became irrelevant, the sea lane threat from China continued to grow.

Thus, except for the Korean theater, the Army had always been the minor element in PACOM. The PACOM commander was traditionally a Navy admiral. The head of SOCPAC (Special Operations Command, Pacific), with operational control for Army Special Forces in the theater, was often an Air Force brigadier general. The Navy and Air Force thought more abstractly than the Army. They put more emphasis on fleet diplomacy in the Taiwan area and in the containment of North Korea than in unconventional wars in the Philippines and in collapsed states like East Timor. Indeed, because North Korea was still a major threat, PACOM remained somewhat in a Cold War mode of nuclear Armageddon.* Finally, there was the pall of the Vietnam experience, which made PACOM particularly averse to land adventures in Asia. As one Army officer complained in mid-2003: "CENTCOM lives and breathes the unconven-

---

* Though the Korean Peninsula was technically under its own separate command from PACOM, it was the centerpiece of any regional strategy.

tional post–Cold War world. So does EUCOM, with its peacekeeping and humanitarian rescue operations in the Balkans, Africa, and the *Stans;* while the biggest deal in SOUTHCOM is Special Forces in Colombia. But PACOM is twenty years behind the times, afraid of messy little wars and of a transparent humanitarian affairs role for SF. As for North Korea, it's liable to melt down in the most unconventional of ways."

September 11 eased PACOM out of its Cold War–era torpor. When President George W. Bush and his advisors scanned the world for places to get down and dirty with Islamic terrorism, the stark fact of the Philippines, a pathetically corrupt and heavily populated archipelago ridden with Islamic insurgents, became impossible to ignore. And that was a job for Special Operations Command.

In historical terms America had come full circle. It was in the Philippines where America's epic experience in the Pacific had begun in earnest the century before, when President William McKinley dispatched a naval expedition to Manila Bay from Honolulu. The victory over Muslim insurgents in the Philippines at the start of the twentieth century—a corollary to the Spanish-American War of 1898—constituted the second milestone in the imperial progress of the United States, following the consolidation of the American West.

Throughout the nineteenth century, side by side with westward expansion, the United States Navy and Marines had been establishing, to quote Abraham Lincoln's secretary of state, William Henry Seward, an "empire of the seas."[4] Built on trade and influence much more than on outright occupation, America's mercantile, seaborne empire bore a certain resemblance to that of Venice. Driving it was the same pioneer optimism and bravado that had been expanding the borders of white settlement into the south and west of the continent, encouraged further by the economic dynamism that ensued from the industrial North's victory in the Civil War.

U.S. sailors and marines staged repeated landings in Argentina, Peru, Nicaragua, Uruguay, Mexico, Chile, and Panama (then part of Colombia). The aggressive incursions in Latin America, designed to prop up and topple governments, and to protect American diplomats and the trading interests of an expanding nation, were replicated in the Caribbean, and also in the Pacific.

In 1887 the U.S. Navy gained exclusive access to Pearl Harbor, following the economic integration of Hawaii with post–Civil War America. The

Navy also raided China, and great and small islands from Sumatra to the Marquesas. The United States opened Japan to American trade, purchased Alaska, charted and claimed the Midway Island group. And after a drawn-out series of sea engagements and negotiations, it acquired an island in the Samoas.[5]

America's entry into the Philippines began at dawn May 1, 1898, when Commodore George Dewey's nine ships, having passed Corregidor Island off the Bataan Peninsula under cover of darkness, entered Manila Bay and destroyed a slightly larger Spanish flotilla. Like so many signal episodes in history, Dewey's victory was both the culmination of vast political and economic forces and an accident of circumstance that might easily have not occurred, for it was not instigated by events in the Pacific at all, but by those in the Caribbean, where Spain's repression of Cuba led President McKinley—urged on by expansionists including Assistant Secretary of the Navy Theodore Roosevelt—to declare war on the Spanish empire.

The invasion of the Philippines marked the first time that the U.S. had deliberately set out to conquer a large piece of territory overseas in order to occupy it. That would not happen again until the invasion of Iraq more than a century later. Though it began with Commodore Dewey's glorious overture, the first major conflict for the United States outside its continental limits descended within a few months into a military night-mare, as well as a domestic trauma of a kind not to be seen again until Vietnam.[6] The mistakes that the U.S. made in the Philippines, the varied experiences that the U.S. military had there, and the plethora of tactical lessons that American troops learned in the course of years of jungle war-fare offered a far richer repository of information in terms of the war, peacekeeping, and nation-building challenges of the turn of the twenty-first century than the experiences of World Wars I and II combined. And had the U.S. military paid more attention to its successes and failures in the Philippines—what worked and what didn't—it would have dealt with Vietnam better than it did.

The Philippine War was a gory, real-world experience writ large: the kind that both the American media and public, both then and now, could not and cannot bear. As a result, the military's overall performance in the Philippines gained an undeservedly bad reputation. The instances of bru-tality committed by American troops, partly a response to the brutality of the Filipino insurgents, allowed a somewhat naive and muckraking press in the U.S. to smear the entire campaign. Thus, the painful military lessons gained in the Philippines were either ignored or forgotten by the same Army that would have to fight later in Vietnam, writes Brian McAllister Linn in *The U.S. Army and Counterinsurgency in the Philippine War, 1899–1902*.[7] Nevertheless, the larger truth, in the words of Max Boot, in *The Savage Wars of Peace,* is that U.S. actions in the Philippines constituted "one of the most successful counter-insurgencies waged by a Western army in modern times."[8]

―――

Following Dewey's successful entry into Manila Bay, the American military assisted Filipino insurgents in their takeover of the Spanish-run archipelago. But just as they would in Iraq and elsewhere, the Americans wrongly assumed that because local elements welcomed the ouster of a despotic regime, they would automatically remain friendly once the regime was toppled. Freedom was "understood in differing ways," explains the Filipino historian Samuel K. Tan. The United States "pursued the quest of empire in the name of freedom to civilize the world," while for Filipinos freedom had little to do with elected government and everything to do with a "mystical relationship between the people and the natural environment."[9]

After the Spanish were defeated, tensions mounted between the new Philippine government headed by a young ethnic Tagalog, Emilio Aguinaldo, and the American liberators, even as Aguinaldo was losing control over his own faction-ridden armed forces. By February 1899, Philippine anarchy and misplaced American idealism ignited into a full-scale war between American troops and a host of indigenous guerrilla armies.

The collapse of central authority led to the complete regionalization of the conflict, with various guerrilla leaders transforming themselves into local warlords.[10] The American strategy was to pacify each region and turn it over to a civilian commission for reconstruction, to be headed by an Ohio judge, William Howard Taft, recently appointed by President McKinley. But it was this very civilizing strategy of the American occupiers that accounted for much of the war's brutality, for it was a direct threat to the warlords' authority over their own populations.

The American expeditionary force would peak at 69,000 Army, Navy, and Marines, commanded by Army Gen. Arthur MacArthur, a Congressional Medal of Honor winner from the Civil War. Most of Gen. MacArthur's officers and troops were volunteers from states west of the Mississippi River, whose predominant military experience, if they had any, had been fighting the Indians. Of the thirty American generals in the Philippines, twenty-six had been in the Indian wars.

As with the Indian wars, in which tactics were somewhat different for each tribe, the American forces in the Philippines, scattered among four hundred isolated garrisons on different islands, fought many separate conflicts. Middle-level American officers in the Philippines at the end of the nineteenth century, lacking radios and helicopters, often had no possibility of following instructions from general headquarters. Thus, they became policymakers in their own patch of jungle, acquiring area expertise, and developing their own counterinsurgency campaigns specifically suited to the political, military, and cultural situation in each micro-region. They improvised by trial and error. By reporting their successes and failures to their superiors, they influenced policies up the command chain.

It became a war of company commanders impatient with paperwork and routine. William H. Taft told Secretary of War Elihu Root that "the pacification of the Islands seems to depend largely on the character of the military officer in charge of the particular district."[11]

That was the military the way it was supposed to be, with generals backing up decisions of subordinates who were closer to the action. Tom Wilhelm had told me much the same thing.

For example, in the extreme north of Luzon, Lt. Col. Robert L. Howze, a Texan who had won the Medal of Honor in the Indian wars, set up a school system and a local government, making the transition from a combat commander to a provincial governor.[12] Yet it was Lt. Col. Howze's very success, along with the paucity of troops at his disposal—there were only five companies confined to a few towns—that led the guerrillas to cut telegraph lines, attack convoys, and threaten civilians who cooperated with the Americans. Howze's response was decisive. He organized aggressive patrols that ravaged the whole region, killing and surrounding the guerrillas, allowing them to die of hunger and disease, even as he offered amnesty to the simple villagers who had been coerced into helping the *insurrectos.*

In one instance, Howze told his commanders: "warn [civic officials] that the feeding, sheltering and harboring of the *Insurrecto* element must at once cease, or the vicinity will be laid to waste, even to the extent of destroying their crops."[13] Howze created a local intelligence service like the native scout units being set up by the British in India, even as he established village governing councils, which were the first rudimentary step toward self-rule.

The native intelligence services that the Americans established were "hard to beat," in the words of Brig. Gen. Frederick Funston.[14] A Kansas native with trekking experience in the Dakota badlands, Gen. Funston, the commander of a district in another part of Luzon, set up his own spy service, which he rewarded with large payments. When some of his spies were kidnapped, he would kidnap the family of a prominent guerrilla. He even organized a native strike force that he personally led into battle. "By conciliating powerful ethnic and social groups, using native auxiliaries, and conducting military operations which struck at the guerrillas but left the populace relatively untouched, he was able to destroy opposition in slightly more than a year," Linn writes.[15]

While in some parts of the archipelago the U.S. military was able to exploit ethnic divisions, in other parts it was foolish to try. In some parts a purely military strategy was called for; in others a civil affairs and humanitarian component was an absolute necessity. There was one constant, though: both military victory and social reform were possible only when, as Linn observes, "the Army could separate the guerrillas from civilians," thus preventing the guerrillas from obstructing civic organizations.[16] It was this overriding truth that would form the basis for the Army Special Forces plan to undermine international terrorism in the Philippines a century later.

On July 4, 1902, when President Theodore Roosevelt proclaimed the Philippine War over, 4,234 American soldiers had been killed in the conflict and 2,818 wounded.[17] Overall, 200,000 people died, mainly Filipino civilians.[18] Fighting in the Muslim south would go on for years. One could well argue that it was all unnecessary in the first place, a political blunder of the highest magnitude by the McKinley administration, in which America's idealism and naïveté led it on a path of destruction and brutality. But the strictly military part of the equation looked different. As Max Boot writes:

> the success of the U.S. counterinsurgency effort was due not to committing atrocities—24,000 soldiers [in the field] could hardly hope to terrorize 7 million people into submission—but to paying attention to the rudiments of counterinsurgency strategy. In Vietnam . . . the army squandered its resources on fruitless search-and-destroy missions. In the Philippines, by contrast, it concentrated on cutting off the guerrillas from civilian assistance by garrisoning the countryside. While the men grumbled about the monotony of life in the *boondocks* (an Ameri-

canization of the Tagalog *bundok,* meaning "mountain"), their very isolation forced them to become well acquainted with their area and the people who lived there.[19]

The military victory, however messy and brutal, was followed by decades of American rule that the journalist and historian Stanley Karnow calls "a model of enlightenment" compared to European colonialism.[20] Samuel Tan, the Filipino historian who is critical of American policy in other respects, concurs, describing American rule as the historical engine that brought modernity to the Filipino masses.[21]

The Americans forbade themselves to buy large tracts of land. They avoided schemes like opium monopolies. They redistributed land to peasants from wealthy church estates, and built roads, railways, ports, dams, and irrigation facilities. American expenditures on health and education led to a doubling of the Filipino population between 1900 and 1920, and a rise in literacy from 20 to 50 percent within a generation.[22]

The Philippines, in turn, affected the destiny of twentieth-century America to a degree that few faraway countries have. Taft's leadership of the Philippine Commission propelled him to the presidency of the United States. Capt. John "Black Jack" Pershing, who would head the expedition against Pancho Villa in Mexico and command American forces in World War I, was promoted to brigadier general over nine hundred other officers after his stellar performance in leading troops against Islamic insurgents in the southern Philippines. Douglas MacArthur, son of Gen. Arthur MacArthur, came to the Philippines to command an American brigade and returned for a second tour of duty as the indigenous government's military advisor. One of Douglas MacArthur's aides in Manila was a middle-aged major, Dwight D. Eisenhower, who honed his analytical skills for World War II by attempting to organize a Philippine national army. The Japanese victory over Gen. Douglas MacArthur's forces on the Philippines, MacArthur's last stand on Corregidor Island in Manila Bay before retreating to Australia, the subsequent Japanese atrocities committed against both American and Filipino prisoners of war during the Death March on the nearby Bataan Peninsula, and MacArthur's triumphal return to the Philippines in the battle of Leyte Gulf, all became part of the Homeric legend of World War II that bound Americans to their military, and gave the American and Filipino peoples a common bond.

Indeed, anyone who doubts that America is, or was, an imperial power should come to the Philippines, where the white baronial U.S. Embassy fronting Manila Bay occupies the most beautiful downtown real estate in the same way that British and French embassies do in their former colonies; where the Americans have their own hill station for cool weather retreats, like British hill stations in India; where leading local military officers, businessmen, and politicians are graduates of West Point just like the leading personages of former British colonies have been graduates of Sandhurst; and where the country's romantic hero is not a Filipino but the protean figure of Douglas MacArthur, who, in the Filipino mind, rescued the country from the butchery of the Japanese occupiers.

Yet there is a deeper, less appealing truth about American colonialism in the Philippines: As far as the life of the average Filipino has been concerned, it may not have made much of a difference at all. Throughout the twentieth century, the Philippines remained among the most dysfunctional, intractable, and poverty-stricken societies in Asia, with African-like slums and Latin American–style fatalism and class divides. The journalist James Fallows bluntly observes that a damaged culture, not Ferdinand Marcos's dictatorial rule from the mid-1960s through the mid-1980s, was the root cause of the country's problems.[23] In the early twenty-first century, almost two decades after Marcos had been overthrown, Philippine democracy had become so corrupt and inefficient that Filipinos complained constantly that "at least under Marcos you knew who to bribe."

Karnow notes that Filipinos were easily co-opted by the Spaniards and later by the Americans because they had little sense of their own identity— something that is in stark contrast to the Vietnamese and Indonesians, who could gaze at stone temples that symbolized an indigenous historic grandeur. The only real history the Philippines had was a colonial one.[24]

Before the Portuguese explorer Ferdinand Magellan fell upon the archipelago in 1521, flying the flag of Spain, the Philippines (named for the Spanish king Philip II) had merely been a jumble of Malay tribes, eight different languages, and seventy Tagalog-related dialects spread over 7,107 islands, without a central governing authority. Spain more or less invented the Philippines, providing it with a lingua franca and a common religion, Roman Catholicism, practiced by all save for the Muslim minority in the south. By giving land grants to Spanish settlers, which were passed on to rich mestizo families, Spain also created an oligarchy that has ruled the country ever since, whether it was under American auspices, dictatorial fiat, or democratic constitutionalism. Indeed, the closer one looked at how the Philippines actually functioned, and the closer one got to the Muslim areas in the south, the less important the advent of democracy in the mid-1980s seemed.

———

I arrived in the Philippine capital of Manila late at night, and left at noon the following day to link up with American forces at Zamboanga in southwestern Mindanao, the same Zamboanga that American soldiers had sung a song about a hundred years earlier.

It has been said that with its strip malls and faux-classical architecture reminiscent of Washington, D.C., no place—not even the cities of India with their Victorian Gothic buildings—is stamped with a colonial legacy to the degree of Manila. I had a few hours to walk around. Outside the Spanish walls of old Manila, I found teeming poverty, white pristine mansions, and fast-buck Americanization that bore eerie resemblance to cities in northern Mexico. It was a testament to just how much America had imposed itself on this capital, almost seven thousand miles across the ocean from San Francisco and Los Angeles.*

Manila is vast and sterile, despite its location on a magnificent historic bay, with yawning, ruler-straight boulevards lined by faded and sharp-angled concrete towers, reflecting the alienating modernism of the 1970s. The spaces between the skyscrapers are filled by squalid hutments plastered with ratty and rusting signage. The beggars wear flip-flops and oversized ball caps. The Philippine capital conjures up the tackiness and vegetal gaudiness of Mexico and Central America grafted onto the demographic immensity of Asia.

Flying south to Mindanao, I stared through the plane window at a dazzling emerald squiggle work of islands and bays defaced by a torn mosaic of human habitation. The Philippines comprises 84.5 million people, about 40 percent of whom are under fifteen years old, with Muslims growing disproportionately to the rest of the population. There is a look to poverty from the air. Rather than the finely wrought, computer chip complexity of post-industrial Western cities, third world cities and towns seen from ten thousand feet up appear more like a ragged psoriasis. Dennis Downey, a Green Beret lieutenant colonel, would later tell me: "Below Luzon it's the *Odyssey*. In the eyes of people from Manila the area to the

———

* It was also testament to the fact that under Spanish rule, administration of the Philippines was often subcontracted out to Mexicans.

south is ungovernable, uneducated, and unchristian, with small islands changing hands daily."

Approaching Zamboanga, a break in the dense, ashen cloud cover of a monsoon rain revealed a shattered coast barely rising above the turquoise mirror of the Sulu Sea. Then came a glassy trapezoidal tilework of rice fields and seaweed farms, the mossy felt of well-jungled, broccoli-colored hillsides, and a seemingly unending concentration of sloping corrugated iron roofs painted in various loud colors. Unlike Colombia's tropical badlands, the Zamboanga peninsula of Mindanao was thick with humanity.

While Manila was heavily marked by Spanish and American colonial influence, that was not the case with Mindanao and the Sulu Islands. The dozen or so Muslim sultanates that had dotted the southern Philippines were never completely subjugated by the Spanish. It took the Americans until 1913 to quell large Muslim uprisings, even as smaller ones never ceased. The problem that the U.S. had with Islamic terrorists in the Philippines and elsewhere in the early years of the twenty-first century was simply the most recent chapter of a very old story. The first so-called *clash of civilizations* between America and the Muslim world occurred here in the southern Philippines at the beginning of the twentieth century.

Islam, which had spread across the world from the Middle East, implanted itself in Malaya and the Indonesian islands of Java and Sumatra in the thirteenth century, with Muslim missionaries arriving in the southern Philippines from Borneo in the fifteenth century. When the Spanish arrived a hundred years later, they grouped the various tribes and ethnicities practicing Islam under the appellation "Moro," or Moor, for with the reconquest of Muslim Spain a recent memory, the Spaniards looked down upon these southern Filipino Muslims and beheld their historic enemy. The word "Moro" remained a pejorative until the mid-twentieth century, when Moro nationalists transformed it into a symbol of collective identity.[25]

Although a distinct Islamic ethnicity had arisen as a reaction to the Christianizing influence of Spanish rule, Islamization was undergirded by deep cultural ties among southern Philippine Muslims that surmounted barriers of dialect and jungle terrain.[26] Islamization was further reinforced in the early twentieth century by the Americans, who, as part of an attempt to modernize the Philippines, refused to recognize traditional sultans. The undermining of the local headmen—by erasing differences between the various Moro communities—unwittingly united the Muslim Moros as never before. From 1902 to 1913, America's attempt to impose democracy here led to a more militant Islam.

Because of their fierce adherence to Islam coupled with their exotic dress, blood feuds, and love of hand-to-hand combat, the Moros became a truly romantic opponent in the eyes of America's Pacific soldiery. The Moros were America's own colonial equivalent to the fierce and individualistic Pushtuns whom the British fought on the Northwest Frontier of India.[27] The Moros had suicidal warriors called *amoks* and religious fanatics called *juramentados*. The Americans developed the .45-caliber pistol (the Colt .45) in 1911 because the .38-caliber pistol, it was said, "would not take a Moro down." Moros attacked at night from the high ground so they seemed invincible. They were emboldened by hallucinogens and amulets that they believed offered special powers.

The Moros' last stand against the Americans took place in 1913 on the island of Jolo in the Sulu chain; it was not unlike that of the Indians at Wounded Knee in South Dakota twenty-three years earlier. Women and children deserted their villages to join the menfolk in battle. Capt. John Pershing conducted a series of troop withdrawals and negotiations to isolate the noncombatants, even as he planned for a decisive assault that would lead to the Moros' defeat.[28]

Yet the Moro spirit of rebellion against the Christians in Manila never died, even after elected Filipino politicians replaced American imperial overlords. Following World War II and Philippine independence in 1946, young Moros went to study in the Middle East, particularly at the al-Azhar University in Cairo. They returned home to become religious teachers, often in slum communities, channeling their economic and theological grievances into a political cause.[29] The Muslim separatist movement got a further boost with President Marcos's declaration of martial law in 1972. Between 1972 and 1977, Muslim insurgents fought the Philippine military to a stalemate. The fall of Marcos ultimately led to an autonomous region ruled by the Moro Islamic Liberation Front.

In 1991, Moros who had fought in the Afghan jihad against the Soviet Union founded a more radical Islamic group in the southern Philippines called Abu Sayyaf, or Bearer of the Sword. Thus did the Philippines emerge as a central spoke of international terrorism, with terrorists moving in small boats across a broad area from Indonesia and the Malaysian state of Sabah on Borneo, north through the Sulu Islands to Mindanao.[30] Many, if not most, of the major al-Qaeda attacks on the West were planned here in Southeast Asia.[31]

It was in Afghanistan that Abu Sayyaf's founders, Abdurajak Janjalani and Abdul Murad, befriended Mohammed Jamal Khalifa—Osama bin Laden's brother-in-law—and Ramzi Yousef, the organizer of the first World Trade Center bombing in 1993. In 1995 in Manila, Abdul Murad and Ramzi Yousef planned an attack on Pope John Paul II during the pontiff's upcoming visit to the Philippines. As they were mixing explosive chemicals for the operation in their Manila apartment, a fire erupted that led to Murad's capture. The Philippine security services "tortured the dog meat out of him," an American military source told me. "But it wasn't until they threatened to turn him over to the Israeli Mossad that he cracked."

Murad gave Philippine investigators the password to his computer that was recovered from the burned-out apartment. On the hard disk they found the details of several terrorist plots, including one to use eleven jetliners to crash into CIA headquarters and other prominent buildings in Washington and New York. Ramzi Yousef was eventually captured in Pakistan. Both he and Murad were later extradited to the U.S. and sentenced in district court in Manhattan to 240 years in prison.

Meanwhile, back in the southern Philippines, the al-Qaeda–aligned Abu Sayyaf had launched a campaign of ritualistic beheadings, kidnapping, and rape against Filipinos and foreigners. Its victims would include two American Christian missionaries from Kansas, Martin and Gracia Burnham. Martin Burnham was killed and Gracia Burnham freed during an American-assisted Philippine rescue operation in 2002. Abu Sayyaf was given safe havens and camp facilities by the Moro Islamic Liberation Front. It got money and trainers from al-Qaeda and Jemaah Islamiyah, a transnational terrorist group that operated throughout Thailand, Malaysia, Indonesia, and the Philippines. Jemaah Islamiyah would be linked to the nightclub bombing in 2002 in Bali that killed more than two hundred people.

Besides Abu Sayyaf and Jemaah Islamiyah, the southern and central Philippines were also plagued by guerrilla outfits like the communist New People's Army and the Misuari breakaway faction of the Moro National Liberation Front. In truth, like Yemen and Colombia, the Philippines was a country that was not really a country, with the central government unable to project its power in part because of a difficult geography. Moreover, in the 1990s the decay of security structures that came with the advent of democracy, both in Indonesia and the Philippines, provided an opening for international terrorism.

———

The inability of a democratic Philippine government to govern large areas of its own territory—with al-Qaeda-related terrorism the result—became a principal concern of the United States in the wake of September 11, 2001. The response was Operation Enduring Freedom, which, while predominantly focused on removing the Taliban regime in Afghanistan, also had a Philippine component.

Enduring Freedom in Afghanistan combined conventional military elements with Special Operations Forces and a militarized CIA. But the effort in the Philippines was almost exclusively a Special Operations affair. It was run by Special Operations Command, Pacific, a division of PACOM in Honolulu, which brought in assets such as the Marines and Army Special Forces from Okinawa, Japan, and Fort Lewis, Washington; Navy SEALs and Special Boat Units from Guam; and Air Force Special Operations units and regular Army helicopter crews from South Korea.

The Americans referred to the arrival of these combined assets as "Joint Task Force 510." The democratically elected Philippine government had a different name for it: Exercise Balikatan (Shoulder to Shoulder), to give its public and local media the impression that it was all part of a normal joint maneuver. That was true to an extent: As in Colombia, the Special Forces operation was exclusively "by," "through," and "with" the host nation. That gave the operation political legitimacy among Filipinos. But it also imposed severe limitations on the Americans, which would result in international terrorists remaining at large.

The base of operations was Zamboanga, the center of the Spanish colonial administration in Mindanao, and of the American effort against the Moros a century earlier. September 11 had brought American troops south of the main island of Luzon, and into the Muslim south of the Philippines, for the first time since World War II.

Enduring Freedom—Philippines began in earnest in January 2002. The "force cap" negotiated by the American and Philippine governments limited the number of uniformed American personnel to six hundred (compared to four hundred in Colombia). The focus would be on expelling the Abu Sayyaf guerrillas from Basilan, the large and strategic island to the south of Zamboanga. It would be accomplished less by military actions than by an unusual kind of humanitarian assistance program. By the time

I arrived in July 2003, the operation had been successfully completed, with a number of Abu Sayyaf leaders killed and the group scattered to smaller islands, reducing Abu Sayyaf to the banditry from which it had first emerged. Yet the joint task force was still in place in Zamboanga when I got there, and various Special Forces A-teams were still training Philippine units nearby and in Luzon to the north.

I came to the Philippines to tell the story of what had taken place on Basilan, and to observe what was still going on.

I was met at the airport in Zamboanga by two U.S. soldiers in full kit and body armor, inside a van with darkened windows. They took me to Camp Navarro, a Philippine military base that was the headquarters of the American Joint Special Operations Task Force that had officially replaced the larger Joint Task Force 510, following the successful ejection of Abu Sayyaf from Basilan. The Americans treated all of Zamboanga outside of Camp Navarro as hostile, hence the guns and flak jackets. A large Muslim population coupled with an incompetent government police force of "Barney Fifes" made Zamboanga a perfect venue for the kind of terror attacks on American soldiers that would generate headlines around the world for a day or two. The local Chinese business community, the city's only real middle class, had its own private security force.

From inside the van I found Zamboanga (Malay for "land of flowers") a generic third world city: ratty, smoky with pollution, and jammed with trishaws, jeepneys, and mopeds. Roads were completely flooded from the monsoon rains; bright flowers sprouted like weeds. People were texting on cell phones while dodging water buffaloes in the streets. Vast, seemingly impenetrable mazes of wooden shacks led incongruously to a shopping mall similar to that in a middle-sized American town. With more than six hundred thousand inhabitants, Zamboanga was a somewhat less overwhelming version of many cities in India that I had seen, with the following distinctive features that I would get to know better:

- Much of the city was a warren of slums resting on stilts in the water, connected by narrow channels plied by wooden *bancas,* boats with bamboo outrigging. Out in the Basilan Strait sat houseboats inhabited by Samas, the Bedouin of the Sulu Sea and Moro Gulf. These fishermen moved back and forth between the southern Philippines and the Indonesian and Malaysian coasts of Borneo. They provided a convenient means for slipping terrorists in and out of the three countries.

- Zamboanga is located astride the fault line between Christianity and Islam. From inside the fungal black walls of Fort Pilar here, the Roman Catholic Spaniards had, for hundreds of years, governed the Muslims of Mindanao and the Sulu Islands. Three thousand Moros had stormed Fort Pilar in 1720. The Americans occupied it in 1898. It was taken by the Japanese in 1942, and liberated by the U.S. Army's 41st Infantry Division in 1945. Fort Pilar now constituted an open-air Catholic church decorated by the Stations of the Cross and other overt Christian symbols. It was maintained in pristine fashion by the Philippine government, even as it overlooked one of the city's poorest Muslim slums.

Just as Fort Pilar faced one Muslim slum, Camp Navarro faced another, this one with known Abu Sayyaf sympathizers. "Forget the crap about it ain't being a culture war," one American master sergeant told me; "in tactical, operational terms, we have no choice but to treat those people as the enemy." That translated into clandestine infiltration on one hand and deliberately maintained paranoia on the other. People drove in and out of Camp Navarro in nondescript vans. A Special Forces A-team in civilian clothes roamed the port, nightclubs, and other hangouts, quietly developing local intelligence assets.

The first thing I noticed about Camp Navarro was how spacious and well maintained it was compared to the rest of Zamboanga, with meticulously cut hedgerows and parade grounds. In the third world, military bases often mean a step-up in economic well-being and social prestige, a refuge from the surrounding poverty and chaos. To wit, coups were a symptom of the early and middle stages of political development, in which the military offered the most organized and effective means of modernization. Because civilian governments in the two decades since Marcos's overthrow were characterized by extremely high levels of corruption and incompetence, military coups remained a distinct possibility here.

Camp Navarro was headquarters for the Philippine military's Southern Command, or SOUTHCOM. In standard colonial fashion, the Philippine armed forces had been organized on the model of the American one, with geographical areas of operational control. Advising Philippine SOUTH-

COM in its war on terror was the American Joint Special Operations Task Force, or JSOTF (the acronym was pronounced "jah-SO-tef"). The JSOTF was a crowded jumble of prefabricated "cheeseboxes" and "blue gooses," or modified shipping containers, each functioning as barracks for two soldiers. Because the monsoon tended to come at night, getting up to use the bathroom meant going from a freezing, air-conditioned shipping container to intense heat and pouring rain. The mess hall served institutional American food, inferior to the spicy seafood found at sidewalk stands all over Zamboanga. The fruit wasn't even fresh. Because of hygienic rules set by American doctors, the fruit had to be flown in from the American base at Okinawa, Japan.

I didn't like the JSOTF. It was claustrophobic, sterile, and impersonal, unlike the cool Green Beret hootches I had become accustomed to in Colombia, which interacted culturally through music and food with the local environment. As a joint command, the JSOTF had Army, Navy, and Air Force personnel, both men and women, often young and unsophisticated about the world outside Camp Navarro. They were guarded round-the-clock by U.S. Marines, distinguished by their high-and-tight haircuts and digital camouflage uniforms, a more complex design than the woodland camouflage of Army and Air Force BDUs.

"Thank God for the Marines," muttered my roommate in the two-man cheesebox, a Green Beret master sergeant from Detroit. "Without them, this place would be a security nightmare. Few of the kids around here would know how to handle themselves outside the base perimeter. The Marines keep them locked up." Though only a high school graduate, the master sergeant was a man of the world. He kept me awake the first night at the JSOTF talking about the execution of policemen in Nepal, ethnic problems in the Aceh region of Indonesia, the robbery of Russian soldiers returning from peacekeeping duties in Bosnia after they had crossed the border into Ukraine, and the old-fashioned esprit de corps of Australian commandos with whom he had trained.

Green Berets like my roommate disliked the unnecessarily big American footprint that the JSOTF represented. "It's what happens when a Navy four-star and an Air Force one-star get to tell Army Special Forces what to do," another Green Beret told me, referring to the PACOM and SOCPAC command structures. The Green Berets felt that the "Washington political correctness in favor of joint commands"—a reaction to the interservice rivalries of previous decades—had simply gone too far in the Pacific theater, and that in the jungly southern Philippines, the Navy and Air Force "aristocracies" were out of their depth.

In fairness to the Navy and Air Force top brass, the JSOTF had a large footprint because it was built and staffed with the assumption of a larger operation than the one which ultimately materialized. After the liberation of Basilan from Abu Sayyaf, PACOM expected the Philippine government to grant permission for U.S. forces to actively comb the other islands of the Sulu chain for remaining guerrillas. When electoral politics in the Philippines closed that option, the PACOM commander, Adm. Thomas Fargo, kept the JSOTF up and running in the hope, which seemed realistic at the time, of Manila's decision being reversed.

In fact, with the closure of the two large and historic U.S. bases in the Philippines in the early 1990s—Clark Air Force Base and Subic Bay Naval Station—the JSOTF had succeeded as a political mechanism for getting an American base-of-sorts up and running, even as it earned the goodwill of the local population by providing free medical care in villages near Zamboanga. "Remember," an Army colonel told me, in defense of the Navy and Air Force approach, "China is nearby and *presence* in the region is everything. The longer the JSOTF can stay here the better."

The JSOTF concept was problematic, though. It indicated how forgetful the U.S. defense establishment could be about successful Cold War efficiencies, such as simply enlarging the ambassador's country team inside the embassy, in order to handle periodic operations like Enduring Freedom. For example, Plan Colombia was run from within the U.S. Embassy in Bogotá without the need for a separate base elsewhere.

Everything inside the JSOTF, from the construction items to the soldiers and marines themselves, was maintained by a lifeline of C-130 cargo planes flying in from the American base at Okinawa. Few sights offered by imperial America were at once more mundane and stirring than the arrival of a C-130 with supplies and reinforcements for U.S. troops in officially hostile terrain. In the moments prior to landing, an MSE (Marine security element) in full kit drops down into the weeds and elephant grass, and secures a perimeter. Then the big bathtub toy of a plane lands and taxis to a halt, its massive propellers never stopping. The hatch opens in the rear and a K-loader quickly drives up to it. Ten-foot-high pallets of food, equipment, and personal belongings are slid off the plane upright. Next comes the long line of soldiers and marines, jogging out of the fuselage in single file and into waiting buses, men and women in BDUs and marine cammies, their expressions green, blank, expectant, nervous, and raceless in their varied ethnicities. Another line, with happier expressions, more comfortable in their surroundings, jogs into the plane, en route home. A John Deere forklift then brings over another assemblage of pallets to slide into the fuselage. The hatch closes and the plane taxis out for takeoff. The whole process takes ten minutes.

During the time I was at the JSOTF, both the commander and deputy commander happened to be Green Berets, Col. Al Walker of Salt Lake City, Utah, and Lt. Col. Dennis Downey from just south of Boston. Col. Walker was a quiet, self-effacing, gray-haired West Pointer; Lt. Col. Downey a delightfully talkative, moon-faced Irishman, a graduate of Norwich Military Academy in Vermont. Both got to the point quickly. There is a saying in the U.S. defense establishment, "Death by PowerPoint." Well, Lt. Col. Downey put together a PowerPoint briefing for me that was anything but dull or insignificant. It was about how fed up he and Col. Walker were with elements of the Philippine military.

With the operation on the island of Basilan complete and high politics between Manila and Washington preventing future ones, the principal function of the JSOTF was ops/intel fusion. In plain English, that meant producing intelligence which led to American recommendations for specific battlefield operations, to be carried out by the Armed Forces of the Philippines against Islamic terrorists such as Abu Sayyaf. Like Colombia, the Philippines was a constitutional democracy that would not permit American troops to fight alongside its soldiers on its own soil. That was considered an infringement of national sovereignty. Thus, all Col. Walker and Lt. Col. Downey could do was advise the Filipinos. But even when real-time intelligence was handed to the Armed Forces of the Philippines on a silver platter, it rarely delivered.

Take the American-advised operation on Jolo Island in the Sulu chain in late December 2002, the subject of Lt. Col. Downey's PowerPoint briefing. It occurred in the same part of Jolo where Capt. John Pershing had conducted successful operations in 1906 against the Moros. The Moros had attacked Pershing's troops with bolos (machetes), Malay krises (wavy-edged swords), and poison darts fired from blowguns.

Downey, a Southeast Asian area expert, who had spent much of his career in the 1st Special Forces Group based out of Fort Lewis, Washington, warmed to his subject: "Jolo constituted the first time in American history that we fought Muslim insurgents. The Moros on Jolo are Tausug speakers, tough and mean-spirited, like the Chechens. When I tell you the details of what went wrong, have some sympathy for the common Filipino soldier—an eighteen-year-old kid paid the equivalent of $35 per month, with $2 extra for combat pay, and poorly led by generals sometimes making fortunes."

After Operation Enduring Freedom—Philippines had ejected Abu Sayyaf from Basilan, five of the ten leading al-Qaeda–trained terrorists in Abu Sayyaf escaped to Jolo, where they conducted kidnap-for-ransom operations to raise money. Facing their tiny army were nine battalions of Philippine Marines and Army Scout Rangers, with helicopters and artillery batteries. On December 23, 2002, an American P-3 surveillance plane identified the terrorists arriving by boat at a Jolo port. The American and Philippine intelligence services tracked them into the interior of the island, to a point where they froze in position. The Americans put forward a plan that had Philippine Marines driving the terrorists into a pocket surrounded on three sides by Army Scout Rangers, thereby setting up a "kill box" without any villages nearby where the terrorists could hide. The Americans established a command operation center for the coming attack at Camp Navarro. But a key Philippine general did not show up. "He was not interested in getting out of bed," Downey said bleakly.

Meanwhile, the Philippine army units designated to surround the terrorists did not move into their blocking positions, as their leaders had promised they would, even as the Philippine Marines began their part of the operation ahead of schedule. By the time the Army units arrived in position, eight hours late, the terrorists had slipped out of the kill box.

"The Filipino army and Marines just hate each other," Downey explained. "There was total lack of synchronization. Their orders are communicated by text messages on cell phones, which are subsequently deleted, so there is no record, no paper trail, no accountability. The incentive for all kinds of corruption is great; nor is anyone punished for these kinds of screwups."

Downey, whether aware of it or not, was describing a typical third world cultural failure, in which a functioning bureaucracy truly doesn't exist, because there are no impersonal rules of behavior that take precedence over labyrinthine personal alliances and bribes. The Abu Sayyaf guerrillas on Jolo, such as Khadaffy Janjalani and Radullan Sahiron—men trained in the ideological hothouse of Afghanistan—had made an end run around their own culture's weaknesses through indoctrination into a militant belief system, and by operating in small, tightly knit groups where no bureaucracy was required.

Still, Downey said that he had been encouraged by the ease in which the enemy could be targeted and Philippine troops mobilized, albeit not moved into position on time. Occasionally, this had led to success, as in June 2002 when Abu Sayyaf leader Abu Sabaya had been sighted on a *banca* off the Zamboanga Peninsula and killed. As in Colombia, despite all the failures, despite all the frustrations with the host country's military, and the limitations on U.S. power, progress was possible, because the average "indig," or native soldier, was brave and selfless.

You never gave up. You stayed engaged, no matter at how low a level, in order to keep enough pressure on the terrorists so that the threat did not escalate to a point requiring a much larger effort, an effort that would need to occur under a global media spotlight. A failed operation on Jolo was still better than no operation at all, since it kept the terrorists on the run. Such was the frustrating essence of imperial maintenance.

Sometimes imperial maintenance could be genuinely inspiring, like the MEDCAPS (medical civic action programs) that the JSOTF operated in the Zamboanga Peninsula to win "hearts and minds," a phrase that officers like Col. Walker, who still chafed a bit at being harassed in New York City while on leave from West Point during the Vietnam War, never used cynically.

The MEDCAP which I observed took place in the village of La Paz north of Zamboanga at an altitude of three thousand feet, an area where the mosquitoes brought dengue fever during the day and malaria at night. Turning inland and uphill into a low montane rain forest, I entered a glittering green world of giant ferns, bamboo and mahogany trees, rattans, tea bushes, and orchids. Pigs scampered beneath coconut leaf houses raised on stilts. Innumerable palms with their sharp fanlike leaves evoked the frightening, nightmarish infinity of nature. In too many places, palm jungles meant either touristic paradises or violent anarchy: St. Bart's or Liberia. Higher and higher into the jungle we drove in our smoke-windowed van, to where people had never before seen a doctor, even if they dressed in cheap Western polyesters with baseball caps.

The MEDCAP had been organized at a school in a clearing. As Col. Walker and I emerged from the van, I saw that several pockets of U.S.

Marines had secured a perimeter. Rain and sunlight sprayed simultaneously through a fine mother-of-pearl mist. In long lines in the rain, people waited to have their teeth pulled, their eyes checked and treated for cataracts, their children examined, and to get medicines for a variety of minor ailments. I overhead a U.S. Navy doctor sadly tell a man that he could do nothing for his daughter's three-chambered heart. But every child was treated for worms and vitamin A deficiency. Lt. Col. Downey was standing with a microphone before an audience of children, teaching them the hokey-pokey while they waited to see the doctors. None of the posters advertising the MEDCAP mentioned the United States or the JSOTF. The front organization was a Taiwan-based, Buddhist NGO (nongovernmental organization), Tzu-Chi, whose Philippine branch had organized the event. Everyone who came went home with a "peace bag," filled with slippers, toothpaste, shampoo, and multivitamins. The doctors were a mix of American and Philippine military medics, as well as civilian physicians mobilized by Tzu-Chi.

Downey explained: "The idea is for us to be in the background, so as to build up the credibility of the national government and the national army in outlying villages like this one. Besides, all of these people here know that without the security provided by United States Marines, none of this would be happening. The NGO and civilian doctors would have been afraid to show up, for fear of Abu Sayyaf."

By late afternoon more than 1,800 people had been treated. I watched one man have twelve teeth pulled. "We do only what we can," Col. Walker said. "My pets at home get better care than these kids," he added, not wanting to overdramatize the significance of the day.

The JSOTF considered such MEDCAPS "force protection" exercises, because they built trust and relationships with surrounding communities that, in turn, provided an informal native intelligence network, like the kind U.S. troops had established a hundred years ago here in Mindanao. The MEDCAPS drove a wedge between the people and the insurgents.

The drive from Camp Navarro, headquarters of the JSOTF, to Camp Malagutay, headquarters of two U.S. Army Special Forces A-teams and one B-team, took less than fifteen minutes. But Camp Malagutay constituted a different world. For me it was like being back in Colombia, only nicer. The A- and B-teams occupied two separate hootches made of artistic coconut wood weave, raised on stilts with iron roofs. Except for the barriers of concertina wire, sandbags, and HESCO baskets, they each had the look of a small South Sea island beach house. Rather than the bland American fare at the JSOTF, the Green Berets lived on curried beef, crabs, and hot sauce. Even better was the company.

Maj. Guy Lemire of San Francisco was an articulate and policy-savvy former noncommissioned officer who had gone to Officer Candidate School. He had a few years of community college, and spoke Thai and Mandarin Chinese. His sergeant major, Brian Walsh, an Army brat from eastern Oregon, was a towering Mr. Clean of a man who barked out opinions that were as indiscreet as they were truthful. The team sergeant for one of the A-teams was a sly, wiry, and laconic Mississippian in civilian clothes, who could stare down an empty alley of Zamboanga and know whether it was Muslim or Christian. I will keep his name anonymous because of the job he did.

After about thirty seconds of polite introductions, Maj. Lemire and Sgt. Maj. Walsh got down to business. Once a Fil officer reached the rank of major, he was done, and thought of nothing but his own career, money, and corruption; 25 percent of the Philippine army's basic weaponry was unserviceable, "because the Fils had no concept of maintenance," even as the U.S. was providing them with state-of-the-art, frequency-hopping radio technology.

Because American military officers, unlike American diplomats, didn't feel the need to be hopeful about the human condition, they tended to be more honest and practical in their analyses. To American diplomats, the Philippines was a democracy; to the American military, beneath the level of President Gloria Macapagal Arroyo, a few of her cabinet ministers, and her military chief of staff, the Philippines was a klepto-oligarchy. But the candor became even clearer and more refreshing as you descended lower through the ranks. In Maj. Lemire's command and intel room, filled with marked terrain maps and soft porn pinups, the candor was like pure oxygen.

Here was Maj. Lemire: "Because the Abu Sayyaf Group has RPGs [rocket-propelled grenades], the Armed Forces of the Philippines says it needs RPGs, too. Bullshit. No it doesn't. RPGs are useless at close range. The response to RPGs is to lay down suppressive fire, and maneuver closer to the enemy. But moving closer to grenade fire is counterintuitive, which means troops have to trust their officers, which here they don't. The truth is that the Filipino army is terrified of Abu Sayyaf. The Fil army does little reconnaissance. It will only initiate battle with a tremendous numerical advantage, and won't do so below the company level. There is no understanding of logistics and maintenance in the Philippine military, of planning for the next day."

In other words, the Philippine military was like the Colombian military, only a bit worse. Meanwhile, there were stories of Abu Sayyaf guerrillas sharing one rifle among four men in the battlefield, making every shot count. The Abu Sayyaf terrorists wore amulets like the Moros a hundred years before. They believed that the blood of hostages whom they beheaded made them stronger. Their irrationality gave them the battlefield discipline that the regular Philippine military lacked.

Sgt. Maj. Walsh and the other noncoms I met at Camp Malagutay were irate that the Filipinos were so bad at maintenance, yet were getting high-frequency radios and night optical devices (NODs) from the U.S. "First, let's see if they can clean and zero in their rifles, and take care to do so, before we give them the gee-whiz stuff," one noncom told me. Another remarked: "Because it's such a lovely, agreeable culture, there are no internal standards, that's why you need growling American sergeants to advise them, or else nothing happens."

At the rifle range one day, I was in the midst of talking with a Filipino lieutenant when a broad-shouldered American sergeant with a commanding glare under a ball cap walked over and stuck his face in the eyes of the Filipino officer and snapped: "Sir, tell your machine gunner that if he wants to break his gun he should keep it on full automatic, just the way he's doing." A moment later the sergeant was back in the Filipino officer's face: "Sir, your man over there is sitting in the kill zone too long, get him out, faster." I liked this Special Forces sergeant from California's San Joaquin Valley. He missed no detail. He had served all over Asia, and had taken time off from military service to work as a bounty hunter back in the U.S. I asked him his assessment of the Philippine military.

"Weak noncoms, badly trained, underpaid," he huffed. "They steal bullets to feed their families. The Thai army is better, and the Koreans and Singaporeans are just plain damn good soldiers. Even with their booze, I found Mongolian troops are superior to the Fils. The Fils are like the Panamanians I've worked with. They need basics, not NODs. You can fight at night without NODs if you use SLLS [Smell. Look. Listen. Silence]. The best time to assault is at night in the pouring rain; the mud hides your sounds and the water your scent. Shooting, moving, communicating, that's the essence of soldiering. You can do it with the most rudimentary technology."

Because the Green Berets' expectations were so low, no one was depressed. "We can make some progress identifying talented cadres," Maj. Lemire assured me, "American-influenced Fil officers who will work their way up the command chain." To repeat: Despite the Hollywood stuff, the primary focus of Special Forces was not commando raids but the instruction of indigenous armies. "Drop us in, and we'll train 'em, whoever they are. Gathering intelligence and building relationships are indirect benefits of that." If the southern Philippines broke away to join a new, radical Muslim state along with parts of Malaysia and Indonesia, or if the Philippine state itself collapsed from within, there would always be an American-influenced cadre here to deal with events. That was the hope.

"As frustrating as things are, if we were not here, somebody else would be, like the Chinese," Sgt. Maj. Walsh said. "What needs to happen is the proliferation of one- and two-man missions, and twelve-man A-teams embedded directly with the Filipino military; that's how we can really get things done, and kill Muslim bad guys."

Hovering over the Special Forces troops at Camp Malagutay was the lugubrious shadow of the JSOTF. The Green Berets provided "security assistance"—that is, they trained the trainers of the elite units of the host nation. As such they were funded under U.S. Title 22, which meant they reported to the State Department and therefore to the U.S. Embassy in Manila, whereas the JSOTF came under the Department of Defense's Title 10, and therefore, theoretically at least, should not have been able to tell the Special Forces troops at Camp Malagutay how to run their lives. Had the JSOTF not been close by—and Maj. Lemire's gang truly wished it wasn't—his troops would have been able to do as they pleased: go out at night, mix more with the locals, exactly what Army Special Forces did everywhere else.

At both Tolemaida and Espinal in Colombia, after a hard day's training, the Green Berets would hit the town almost every night. Here they had to request permission in advance from the JSOTF, and declare in detail a force protection plan in order to visit the tamest of local restaurants. I insisted on going out every night, and Maj. Lemire's boys used that as an excuse to get out themselves.

Actually, Maj. Lemire got along just fine with Col. Walker and Lt. Col.

Downey, the JSOTF commanders. It was the unwieldy bureaucratic arrangement, made worse by their predecessors, which had given him problems.

Each night about eight of us went to La Vista del Mar, a restaurant and club with a panoramic view of the Sulu Sea. We were accompanied by the girls who did the team laundry for $20 per month. These girls were typical *Filipinas:* small-boned, symmetrically featured, and walnut-complexioned beauties, with twangy, mellow Spanish-style voices and subservient oriental manners, a devouring mix of South America and Asia. Though one of the Green Berets slyly disappeared for an hour with a girl into the darkness of the beachfront, with its conveniently noisy winds, otherwise, the evenings were innocent, the consequence of the strict JSOTF regulations and the commonplace logistical problems of shacking up with someone. And that was a shame, at least in my opinion, given the number of single and divorced guys in the group, and the stark fact of a six-month deployment. Had this been the old Pacific Army, some of these men would have taken some of these girls as mistresses.

With sex not an option, the evenings at La Vista del Mar were given over to letting off steam, while enjoying the spicy crabs, the San Miguel beer, and the mesmerizing sea winds. "Don't order the pizza," one Green Beret advised me. "It's so dry that biting into it is like taking communion." A sergeant from Indiana treated us to a grouchy soliloquy about the unfairness of a recent weightlifting competition at the JSOTF. Because the object had been to bench-press a total amount of weight over a large number of repetitions, a certain amount of strategy was involved, and "this narrow-assed, toothpick, pocket-protector-wearing kind of motherfucker," as he put it, "beat out a marine who had played linebacker at the University of Minnesota."

"My daddy's got a new wife," another sergeant told us. "They keep getting younger and younger. This one won't fly in planes. She hates cities. But my daddy's happy. She goes fishing with him. She baits her own hook. That's all he wants."

One sergeant had been the veritable mayor of a small town in Kosovo in 1999. He had to inspect a house, he told us. " 'Fine,' this Albanian woman said, 'but please stay out of my baby's room. He's sleeping.' There was an altercation. The woman became hysterical. I told her I had to inspect the room. 'I'll be quiet, ma'am, I'm not going to hurt your baby.' I picked up the baby and felt under the mattress. There was an AK-47 with the safety off and a blue-tipped armor-piercing bullet in the chamber with a full magazine. When I got to the Balkans, I thought that the Serbs were the bad guys, but the Albanians never ceased to amaze me," he concluded.

"Jimmy Carter," yet another muttered, apropos of nothing, "what a fucking loser. He gives away the Panama Canal without even negotiating and now the PLA [People's Liberation Army of China] is all over Panama with intel operations. Bet your life the Chinese will fight us asymmetrically."*

I raised the subject of Basilan just across the strait, its mountainous outline now a slightly darker ink shade than the night sky. "I was there," a medic at the table said. "We infiltrated villages, built roads, won over the moms and pops by treating their kids' skin diseases, and got info on bad guys in return. It was good stuff." "Only problem with Basilan is that we left," someone else said. "We had to practically force the Fil government to take over the civilian aid projects that we started for the Muslim community. When you visit there in a few days, I'll guarantee you that half the wells we built won't work anymore."

The women at the table were partly ignored. But their good looks and proximity had been something for the guys to look forward to. The Green Beret who had gone off with one of the girls in the direction of the beach suddenly reappeared. Driving back, someone joked about smelling his finger to see where it had been.

———

One of Maj. Lemire's A-teams was allowed the run of the town, though. That was ODA-145, headed by the laconic master sergeant from Mississippi, in white slacks, penny loafers, and a loose summer shirt concealing his 9mm Beretta. ODA-145 was the force protection team for Zamboanga. Over the years and decades, following the bombing of the U.S. Marine barracks in 1983 in Lebanon, of the Khobar Towers complex in 1996 in Saudi Arabia, and other incidents, the U.S. military had become Israeli-like in its distrust of the local environment and its obsession with security. It was ODA-145's job to *get to know people:* to get outside the perimeter, prowl around, find out the normal traffic patterns so that they could spot

* In fact, a Chinese shipping company held the contract for operating the ports at both ends of the Panama Canal.

abnormal ones, develop contacts at the docks and whorehouses, make friends with the local drug-enforcement people for the extra eyes and ears they offered. "No freaking way we're depending on the Filipino military," the Mississippian counseled.

"See those shacks?" he said. "That's Campo Islam. It's dirtier and less prosperous than the Christian areas. You could hide a Western hostage in that confusion for years and no one would know. Down the road is where Abu Sayyaf held Gracia Burnham for a while." The Mississippian had done similar force protection assignments in Thailand, Cambodia, and Malaysia over the previous year. He made snap cultural judgments of the kind that would burn an academic's reputation, but which in the field prove right seven out of ten times.

What concerned him most was not falling into a pattern, not showing up at the same place once too often. That was what may have got Sgt. Mark Wayne Jackson, a member of ODA-145 killed outside Camp Malagutay a few months before.

The Mississippian took me to meet a local Filipino business magnate and former Interpol officer who helped ODA-145 with information here and there. He had an estate and target range by the water where we fired off 9mm and 5.56mm rounds for an hour. This man could afford to look somewhat frail and soft-spoken, I thought, because of the blatancy of his wealth and power. "Why was the Philippines such a corrupt place?" I asked him. He responded in a bored manner with a challenge: "Name a place in the world where the Spanish have been for a long time that is well governed." He added: "Marcos solved the problem of a weak state by creating a huge army. Now the army is such a danger that only a military man can control it and modernize it."

The day wore on. We hit the docks. We got stuck for an hour in Zamboanga's jeepney and trishaw traffic. The Mississippian's sidekick drove the wrong way up a one-way street to finally escape it. We stopped for fast food at a local mall with plate glass windows that had recently been bombed. The Mississippian handed me off to another two members of his team in the evening. They stopped first at a karaoke bar, and later at a whorehouse that the team hadn't checked for a while, shooting the breeze with the owner and *mama-san* about strangers who might have been passing through from Indonesia and Malaysia.

Whorehouses can be insightful, particularly in Asia. Some areas of the world contain a truth, or fact, that everybody knows and quietly admits to, but which no one dares proclaim openly. In Africa, at the beginning of the 1990s, "the advance of democracy as in former communist Europe" was the white lie to which all paid lip service, while the dark truth of "chaos and steep decline" was not spoken about, for fear of sounding racist and without hope. In Asia, the unspoken fact was not something dark or pessimistic, just a bit embarrassing. It was "the girls, girls, girls."

Whether it was journalists or military men, Western men simply loved Asia. I cannot remember how many times I heard an old journalistic hand tell me about how the politics and culture of Asia were "just so fascinating," while noticing that he had an unearthly beautiful Asian wife or girlfriend several decades younger than he. And who could blame him? Particularly in the Philippines, which was a land of smiling and stunning women, many of whom, unlike in Thailand, spoke English well, and where, again, unlike in Thailand, the prevalence of HIV-AIDS was extraordinarily and somewhat unexplainably low. *Filipinas* were known to be so clean in their habits that even the common forms of venereal disease were not all that rampant. The temptations were formidable. As one Green Beret told me after I returned to Manila, "This is the only country in the world where the main tourist attraction squirms up and down on your lap. It's as if the women are kids at a toy store, and we're the last Cabbage Patch dolls on the shelf."

It was a far cry from Yemen, where the women were walking sacks and after a few weeks you found yourself staring at ankles.

The whorehouse in Zamboanga was a typical Asian "fishbowl." The outside was patrolled by shotgun-bearing private security guards. Inside, small groups of men were led by a commanding and buxom *mama-san,* wearing a corsage on her grand pink gown, into large private salons equipped with their own bathrooms and karaoke machines, where an antlike army of beautiful girls in their early twenties, in skimpy black negligees, were led in for the men to choose from. The karaoke machines encouraged a wholesome sing-along kind of popular music—the Beach Boys; Peter, Paul and Mary; the Carpenters—unlike the hard punk rock that made similar places, in prewar Yugoslavia for instance, so unbearable. We were gone in under an hour. I marveled at the self-control of my companions.

At dawn the next morning I found myself on a broken chair under a vast iron shed in rotting heat and humidity by the ferry dock in Zamboanga.

The water was a tableau of fishing nets and *bancas*. The floor in front of me was crowded with garbage and sleeping street people. Next to me were two new traveling companions from the JSOTF, Special Forces Master Sgt. Doug Kealoha of the big island in Hawaii and Air Force Master Sgt. Carlos Duenas Jr. of San Diego. They were the force protection team for my trip to Basilan: Injun Country in the view of the JSOTF, though Abu Sayyaf guerrillas had largely been routed from the island.

I felt the familiar excitement of early-morning sea travel. From here in Zamboanga you could hop cheap and broken-down ferries all the way south along the Sulu chain to Malaysia and Indonesia. Had I been by myself, I might have been tempted to do it. I would certainly have had no qualms about going to Basilan alone. I had gone on my own to far more dangerous places many times. But being embedded with the U.S. military meant giving up some of your own freedom in return for access. Thus, instead of taking a taxi to the dock and jumping aboard the first ferry south across the Basilan Strait, I rode in a darkened van with three soldiers in full kit, in addition to Sgts. Kealoha and Duenas, who, while in civilian clothes, carried Beretta pistols under their loose shirts. Troops of the 103rd Brigade of the Philippine army would meet us at the dock in Isabela, the main town in Basilan. It was all part of the operations plan for my excursion of a few days.

The reasons for this seemingly absurd level of paranoia and organization were several:

- The American military planned and organized for all contingencies, without distinction. That was just the way it operated, and how it minimized risk in a media age when commanders in the Philippines labored "under the tyranny of one casualty," as they put it. For example, one night in Zamboanga, I had left the JSOTF with Col. Walker to have dinner at a local hotel with a visiting U.S. diplomat. En route he packed a cocked Beretta and wore body armor, which he removed only at the last minute, quickly changing into a barong tagalog.
- U.S. soldiers were more valuable hostages than civilians, and simply being embedded made me likewise more valuable, and more of an embarrassment if anything went wrong.
- Special Forces Sgt. First Class Mark Jackson had been killed in a bomb blast outside Camp Malagutay not too long ago, and the JSOTF was simply being extra careful.

Still, I felt that Dana Priest of the *Washington Post* was correct in her observation that the military could get just too protective. For example, she tells about being forced in East Timor to keep her shirtsleeves rolled down and to take malaria pills for a visit of only one day there, even though a Danish humanitarian relief worker had been in the area for months and wore a sleeveless blouse.[32] Force protection had simply gotten out of hand.

Sgt. Kealoha, whose mellow demeanor and wide permanent grin masked a smooth attention to detail, didn't like the fact that the girl at the ferry counter called someone on her cell phone the moment after she had sold us our tickets. "She could have been calling someone in Basilan saying that foreigners were on the way." In this case I couldn't really blame him. Western faces from this point south meant dollar signs for kidnap-for-ransom gangs.

The three of us sat apart on the ferry's upper deck, which was filled with well-groomed middle-class people, giving me yet again the sense that the security precautions were ridiculous. Then a typically good looking *Filipina* carrying a medical textbook sat next to me and asked, "You're not afraid to visit Basilan?"

"Should I be?" I replied.

"Yes, you should. Foreigners get abducted there."

She told me that she was a nurse in the northern part of the island but now lived in Zamboanga and commuted to Basilan a few days a week, afraid to spend the night there. I told her not to worry about me, that I would be met by Philippine soldiers at the dock in Isabela. I was slightly taken aback. In almost every previous instance as a journalist, the moment I had actually arrived somewhere that the outside world considered dangerous, I immediately encountered the most ordinary people going about their daily lives, making me ashamed of my fear.

"Whatever you do," the woman added, "don't go to Tuburan, avoid that area," referring to the anarchic, Muslim-inhabited eastern finger of Basilan that Col. Walker had said was off limits. In the middle of the strait she pointed out the islet of Santa Cruz. "Foreigners were abducted there," she said.

Meanwhile, I was benumbed by the purity of the scene. Beyond the lacquered blue strait crowded with *bancas,* Basilan emerged as a vast line of extinct volcanoes rising sheer above palm jungles. It was a coast of terror as beautiful as could be imagined, with few signs of human habitation. Amid the screen of uninhabited atolls, a perfect white sandy beach came into view that stretched for miles, empty. "Nobody goes to that beach; they're afraid," the woman told me. I noticed a small settlement of thatched, coconut-leaf huts; it looked like a vacation village, but it was an outpost of the 103rd Brigade. Traveling with the military, and particularly with Special Forces, had brought me to the last unspoiled places on earth, the places still too unstable to be touched by tourism.

A tangle of boat-strewn channels and hutments on stilts, with overlapping scrap iron roofs, heralded Isabela. At the dock, hundreds of pairs of eyes stared wondrously and suspiciously at me, their fingers busy texting on cell phones. Again, I was struck by just how off limits this beautiful place was. In almost every other remote and war-ravaged part of the world, I had always come across at least a few intrepid backpackers and relief workers; not here.

Three Filipino soldiers in a Humvee met us at the dock. Suddenly I was careening through crowded and decayed streets, jammed with trikes and motorcycles, and cleansed by fresh sea breezes. Isabela seemed noisy and sleepy at the same time, a backwater in the way that I had found Freetown, Sierra Leone; Port-au-Prince, Haiti; and St. George's, Grenada, many years and decades before: places whose violence and instability were partly a consequence of their isolation. Soon we arrived at the 103rd Brigade outpost, the one I had seen from the ferry. Up close it looked no less idyllic, the kind of place where you expected to find nude Scandinavian holiday makers. Instead I found Philippine Army Col. Bonifacio Ramos and his troops.

Col. Ramos had been the Philippine defense attaché in Washington. As an up-and-comer he was afterwards given a field position in a volatile area, which is where I found him prior to his promotion to brigadier general. "In Basilan," he told me, the sweat pouring down our faces on a rain-darkened veranda, "you cannot define the battlefield, so you might as well organize every community to defend itself."

The Abu Sayyaf guerrillas, Col. Ramos began, had been routed from the island. They were now holed up on Jolo and elsewhere farther south in the archipelago. All that remained in Basilan were a few lawless remnants bent on piracy and kidnapping. The Americans had built roads, schools, and water wells the year before, but they could not stay indefinitely. There was no police force to speak of. And the Manila government had taken two of his five battalions away from him to fight Islamic terrorists in Mindanao.

"Firearms are a prerequisite for living here," Ramos told me. "And as long as people are armed, you might as well organize them into support groups, for defense and intelligence gathering." The vehicle for this was the Citizens Armed Forces Geographical Units, vigilante outfits of the kind that the ethnic Chinese had organized in Zamboanga. It was not as sinister as it sounded. Civil defense is crucial in a counterinsurgency, because it allows individuals to cast their lot in favor of the existing order and against revolutionary upheaval.[33] But these units could not operate in a vacuum. "Without economic development," Ramos warned, "Basilan will die a natural death. It's only when you care for people that you are credible."

Later in Manila, the Philippine foreign minister, Blas Ople, a veteran of the World War II fighting against the Japanese, would have a similar message for me. "The Muslims of Basilan strongly appreciated the humanitarian assistance provided by the U.S. military. Now it is our responsibility to integrate and consolidate Mindanao and Sulu, socially and economically, for the sake of our own national security." The foreign minister referred to the threat of a radical, breakaway Muslim state that could emerge to the Philippines' south, were Indonesia to weaken further.*

But was there any evidence, I asked myself, that the Christian oligarchy in Manila, which ruled under the brand name of democracy even as it presided over corrupt and ineffectual institutions, would actually do that? Almost none at ground level. Yet, in the aftermath of September 11, as PACOM began to plan Operation Enduring Freedom—Philippines, U.S. military officers understood that getting the Philippine government to assume responsibility for its own Muslim citizens would be decisive.

When I was in Honolulu, a Special Forces officer at PACOM recapped for me the significance of what happened in Basilan during the first eight months of 2002: "We were an enabler. We tried to help get the Philippine government to look more benignly on its southern, Muslim population: to treat them as real citizens. The American Joint Task Force set out to be a spine donor. That is, it tried to put some backbone into the Manila authorities so they would better take care of their own people. Success meant that we couldn't take credit for anything. We had to give the credit to the Philippine government. We didn't want credit; that would have ruined the operation. In SF, all we ever want is more missions. For us it is always about

---

* Foreign Minister Ople died a few months after I met him.

access, not publicity. Anyway, speaking personally, getting my name in the paper—even for something good—would make my skin crawl."

PACOM decided to focus on Basilan because it was the northernmost and most populous island in the Sulu chain—the link between the southern islands and the mainland of Mindanao. Were Abu Sayyaf and other Islamic insurgents to be ejected from Basilan, they would be instantly marginalized. Basilan, with a population of 360,000, was important enough to matter, yet small enough for the U.S. to achieve a crucial victory in a short amount of time.

The first thing that Army Special Forces did about Basilan was conduct a series of population surveys. Special Forces surveys are a bit like those conducted by university academics; indeed, many a Special Forces officer has an advanced degree. But there is a difference. Because the motive behind these surveys is operational rather than intellectual, there is a concrete, cut-to-the-chase quality about them that is uncommon in academia. Months are not needed to reach conclusions. Nobody is afraid to generalize in the bluntest terms. Thus, conclusions do not become entangled in exquisite subtleties. Intellectuals reward complexity and refinement; the military, simplicity and bottom-line assessments. For the Green Berets, there was only one important question: what did they need to know about the people of Basilan that would help them kill or drive out the insurgents?

Special Forces officers teamed up with their counterparts in the Philippine army to question local chiefs and their constituents in the island's forty *barangays,* or parishes. They conducted demographic studies helped by satellite imagery. They found that the Christian population was heaviest in the northern part of Basilan, particularly in the island capital of Isabela. Abu Sayyaf's strongest support was in the south and east of the island, where government services were, not surprisingly, the weakest. The islanders' biggest concerns were the lack of clean water, basic security, medical care, education, and good roads, in that order.

Democracy or self-rule was not especially critical for the Muslim population: There already had been elections, many of them, which had achieved little for the average person. The government was elected, but did not rule. Abu Sayyaf had shut the schools and hospitals, and kidnapped and executed teachers and nurses. The survey indicated that, just as I had seen in Colombia, the most basic human right is not freedom as people in the West conceive of it, but physical security.

Next, under the auspices of Operation Enduring Freedom—Philippines, the Zamboanga-based joint task force dispatched twelve Green Beret A-teams to Basilan, backed up by three administrative B-teams. Their mission was to train Philippine army units, which would then conduct military operations against Abu Sayyaf. Doing that meant digging water wells for American troops and building roads so that they could move around the countryside. The Americans also built piers and airstrips for their operations. The Green Berets knew that once they departed, all of this infrastructure would be left behind for the benefit of the civilian population, which was the whole point.

It was precisely in the Abu Sayyaf strongholds where the Green Beret detachments chose to be located. That, in itself, encouraged the guerrillas to scatter and leave the island without firing a shot. By guaranteeing security, the American military was able to lure international relief agencies to Basilan, as well as some of the teachers and doctors who had fled. The American firm Kellogg, Brown & Root, a subsidiary of Halliburton, built and repaired schools and water systems. Special Forces medics conducted medical and dental clinics, at which villagers casually volunteered information about the insurgents while their children were being treated for scabies, malaria, and meningitis, and having their teeth pulled.

The objective was always to further legitimize the Philippine military among the islanders. The Americans went nowhere and did nothing without Philippine troops present to take the credit. When ribbons were cut to open a new road or school, the Americans made sure not to be around.

With discretionary funds the Americans also built several small neighborhood mosques. "We hired locally, and bought locally," a Special Forces officer explained, referring to the labor and materials for each project. The policy was deliberately carried out to the extreme. Repairing roads meant clearing boulders off them. When the Green Berets saw peasants chipping away at these boulders to make smaller rocks, they bought the small jagged rocks (called "aggregate") from these peasants and used them to lay the new roads.

The ostensible mission was to help Philippine troops kill international terrorists. But that was accomplished by orchestrating a humanitarian assistance campaign, which severed the link between the terrorists and the rest of the Muslim population—exactly what successful middle-level American commanders had done in the Philippines a hundred years before. "We changed the way we were perceived," one Green Beret told me. "When we arrived in Basilan, Muslim kids made throat-slashing gestures at us. By the time we left they were our friends. That led them to question everything the guerrillas had told them about Americans."

The Green Berets saw no combat on Basilan. Operation Enduring Freedom—Philippines was an example of unconventional warfare, which, according to Special Forces Lt. Col. David Maxwell, is about "solving complex political-military problems through creative means."

When I arrived in Basilan the Americans had been gone for almost a year. Were their accomplishments long-lasting?

The hospital in Isabela was a short drive from Col. Ramos's headquarters. Prior to Enduring Freedom, there were twenty-five beds and most of the staff had fled to Zamboanga. Now there were 110 beds plus a women's clinic. There was drinkable water and electricity, and the grounds were being landscaped. "Tell the American people that it is a miracle what took place here in 2002," the hospital director, Dr. Nilo Barandino, told me. "What the American people gave to us we will do our best to maintain and build upon. But there is still a shortage of penicillin. We get little help from our own government in Manila."

Dr. Barandino said that Basilan used to be a "paradise for kidnappers," but since the American intervention, kidnapping stopped and the inhabitants of Isabela were going out at night again. A decade earlier he himself had been a kidnap victim.

"I was kidnapped along with my wife and children on November 27, 1992, and released December 24 after the ransom was paid. I'll never forget those dates. All that we had worked and saved for was gone in a day. We were not molested, tied up, or beaten. The Muslim guerrillas were still in an infant state then, just local bandits. The cruelty, the rapes, and the beheadings were techniques they learned from al-Qaeda in Afghanistan later in the decade."

From Isabela, the two American sergeants and I headed southwest in a Humvee loaned to us by Col. Ramos. Everywhere we saw bailey bridges and sections of new roads built under the auspices of Enduring Freedom. If there was an island paradise on earth that surpassed all others, it was here, I thought, with rubber tree plantations and pristine palm jungles adorned with breadfruit, mahogany, and mango trees under a glittering sun.

In Maluso, a predominantly Muslim area on Basilan's southwestern tip, I met a water engineer, Salie Francisco. He jumped in the Humvee with us and took us deep into the jungle to follow the trail of a pipeline constructed by Kellogg, Brown & Root. It led to a new dam, water filtration plant, and school, built under the auspices of the United States Agency for International Development (USAID). The area used to be a lair of Abu Sayyaf. The terrorists were gone. But as Francisco told me, there was no tourism, no jobs, no communications facilities, and yet lots of expectations raised by the Americans.

I saw poor and remote villages of the kind that I had seen all over the world, liberated from fear, but with a new class of Westernized activists beginning to trickle in. "The Philippine military is less and less doing its job here," Francisco said. "We are afraid that Abu Sayyaf will return. No one trusts the government to finish building the roads that the Americans started." He went on: "The Americans were sincere. They did nothing wrong. We will always be grateful to their soldiers. But why did they leave? Please tell me. We are very disappointed that they did so." His smiling, naive eyes cried out for what we in the West call colonialism.

We continued in the Humvee out of the bush and into the port of Maluso, a picturesque firetrap of a town without regular electricity. The aquamarine water was filled with *bancas* stabilized by bamboo outriggings; fishing was the only economy and it wasn't much. A tattered assemblage of unemployed men in Muslim skullcaps milled about. Women wore black scarves. Out in the Sulu Sea I saw a seascape of small islands with beautiful beaches that were reportedly infested by pirates and Abu Sayyaf. A mosque dome shaped like an Ottoman turban caught my eye.

Once again, the most prosperous and well-maintained part of the landscape was a military base, a large Swiss Family Robinson–style tree house of a complex, with fine prospects on the edge of town, inhabited by the 36th Philippine Army Special Forces Company, a combat dive unit trained by the Americans which patrolled the nearby coast. The Philippine base was decorated with inspirational sayings by famous American authors:

Beauty is altogether in the eye of the Beholder
—Gen. Lew Wallace

Destiny is not a matter of chance, it is a matter of will
—William Jennings Bryan

"I use the quotations to boost morale," the commander, Capt. Peter Navarro, told me. He said that since assuming command he was concentrating on the beautification of his post. His company was composed overwhelmingly of Christians from Luzon. Like every other Philippine military encampment I had seen, this one was marked by overt Roman Catholic symbolism. Grace was said before meals. In Basilan, amid the helmet-shaped Muslim headscarves that determined the human landscape of the southern Philippines, Malaysia, and Indonesia, the Christian Philippine military seemed like an occupation force.

As I continued around the island over the next few days, especially in the Muslim region of Tipo-Tipo to the southeast, local officials were openly grateful to the U.S. military for the wells, schools, and clinics that had been built, yet critical of their own government in Manila for "corruption," and for not providing funds for development. True or not, that was the perception.

In southern Basilan, the material intensity of Islamic culture became overpowering for the first time in my journey south. There was a profusion of head scarves, signs for *halal* food, and a large new mosque in Tipo-Tipo paid for by Arabian Gulf countries. Mindanao and the Zamboanga Peninsula had contained pockets of Islamic civilization, and were generally poorer than Luzon to the north. It was the same in northern Basilan. But it was only in Maluso and Tipo-Tipo where it became clear to the traveler that he had entered an Islamic continuum, in which the large Indonesian islands of Java, Borneo, and Sumatra seemed closer to him than Luzon.

While I would learn more about Operation Enduring Freedom—Philippines in the course of my travels, one thing was obvious: America could not change the vast forces of history and culture that had placed a poor Muslim region at the southern edge of a badly governed, Christian-run archipelago nation, just as America could not clap its hands and give governments in the mountains of Colombia and Yemen complete control over their lawless lowlands.

All America could do was insert its armed forces here and there, as unobtrusively as possible, to alleviate perceived threats to its own security when they became particularly acute. And because such insertions were often in fragile third world democracies, with difficult colonial pasts and prickly senses of national pride, American forces had to operate under very restricted rules of engagement.

Humanitarian assistance may not have been the weapon of choice for

Pentagon hard-liners, who preferred to hunt down and kill "bad guys" through "direct action" rather than dig water wells and build schools—projects which, in any case, were likely unsustainable because of the lack of resolve of national governments like that of the Philippines to pick up where the U.S. had left off. But in a world where nineteenth-century-style colonialism was simply impractical and where the very spread of democracy for which America struggled meant that it could no longer operate with impunity, an approach that merged humanitarianism with intelligence gathering, in order to achieve low-cost partial victories, was what imperialism demanded in the early twenty-first century.

Even that was problematic, though, because any overt connection between humanitarian relief and intelligence gathering was illegal, and could put all Western relief charities under suspicion. But the key was not to get hung up in old-fashioned bureaucratic distinctions. There was nothing illegal or immoral about U.S. military officers simply keeping their eyes and ears open at the same time that they were engaged in civil affairs; it was part of what building normal relationships with the locals is all about. The best intelligence gathering is often done passively, not actively.

From Basilan I returned to the JSOTF in Zamboanga, then traveled on to Subic Bay in order to link up with another Green Beret A-team.

Subic Bay is separated from Manila Bay by the Bataan Peninsula. It was while briefly transiting Manila, en route to Subic Bay, that the full force of the poverty and underdevelopment in the Muslim south of the Philippines struck me. Following almost two weeks in Zamboanga and Basilan, I found the modernity and cleanliness of the domestic terminal in Manila simply stunning. The taxi journey from the airport to the ferry station took me past fancy car dealerships and luxurious malls with flashily dressed men and women. Here's where all the money was, I realized, made in one street in Manila and spent in another. In the U.S., the capital and principal cities were wealthier than the countryside, but the countryside was still a seemly place to live, with basic services. In the Philippines there was garish luxury in Manila and its environs, and African-level underdevelopment in the Muslim south. In truth, the Philippines was only Luzon, with Mindanao, Sulu, and the other island groups mere offshore possessions, to greater and lesser extents.

Getting to Subic Bay required a ferry journey across Manila Bay to Orion on the Bataan Peninsula. On the dock at Orion I was met by Master

Sgt. Mark Lopez, the former team sergeant for ODA-125, a combat dive squad, and his sidekick, Sgt. First Class Jim Irish. I was drenched in sweat just standing there. Looking up at the black-green, heavily jungled peaks of Bataan, I imagined what the Death March of April 1942 must have been like, in which as many as ten thousand American and Filipino troops died from disease, starvation, and the wanton brutality of the Japanese conquerors.[34] The drive across the peninsula to Subic Bay took us along part of the route of the Death March, announced by historical markers.

Sgts. Lopez and Irish had just finished conducting a month-long exercise with a Philippine Special Forces unit, and were preparing to return to Okinawa. Mark Lopez was next slated to deploy with the South Korean special forces on a one-man mission. He had just been replaced a few days earlier as the ODA-125 team sergeant. Jim Irish planned to retire soon from the Army. Their Okinawa-based A-team had spent several months on Basilan the previous year.

With his deep tan, baritone voice, bulky muscularity, and beach attire, Lopez, a former surfer from California, fit the stereotypical image of a Special Forces scuba diver. He was self-consciously macho and authentically personable, picking up my train of thought on Manila's colonial attitude toward the Muslim south with the following: "In the Philippines you see the legacy of Spain versus Ottoman Turkey. Luzon is Spanish Roman Catholic; it's where all the Ford plants and other foreign factories are. Mindanao—all the way south to Indonesia—constitutes the Muslim world, influenced by Arab traders from the Ottoman Empire."

Lopez had earned a political science degree from the University of Maryland in his spare time, but was perfectly happy as a noncommissioned officer and had no desire to go to Officer Candidate School. Jim Irish, a fair and towering guy from Pasadena, California, sporting a new tattoo, was the scuba team's technical support sergeant, the equivalent of an auto mechanic for every piece of diving gear. The two drove me to a townhouse-style complex inside a Philippine naval base to meet the other members of ODA-125, who were planning an underwater combat insertion on an offshore island the following night.

In the meantime, I ensconced myself at a small resort hotel on the beach in Subic Bay. The offshore insertion, I knew, was incidental to my purpose here. Training exercises are essentially technical and abstruse; the real purpose of my observing them was the venue they provided for conversation: the "bull session," the "soldier's greatest hobby," as James Jones writes.[35]

I would have a lot of bull sessions at Subic Bay. The setting was perfect for them, and deserves to be described in detail.

———

Subic Bay features scintillating tropical grandeur: a steamy panel of blue and chemical green water trapping the heat, bordered by the junglescapes of Bataan and western Luzon. Subic Bay is testimony to the old saw that nobody acquired nicer real estate than the U.S. Navy and the Catholic Church. A legacy of the Spanish-American War, it was a major U.S. naval base until 1991, when a vote of the Philippine Senate closed it: an assertion of national sovereignty that put thousands of Filipinos employed by the U.S. out of work.

The U.S. Navy loved Subic Bay. So did its Australian counterparts. After the base closure, retired U.S. Navy SEALs and Australian SAS veterans began settling here as expatriates, opening bars, discos, and dive shops.* Australians were particularly prevalent, with leathery tans, rugged musculatures that were beginning to crumble with age, and so many tattoos on their arms they approximated weird shirtsleeves. The Aussies had the game beat.

As one American observed, "Say you're Australian, just retired from the police or military and divorced, with a pension. You're in your late fifties. You move here and set up with a twenty-something-year-old *Filipina*. Living here is inexpensive. Even with alimony payments you're financially better off than if you stayed in Australia."

They were hard workers, though, and quite a few did not fit the stereotype. Take one Australian I met, Brian Homan, had bought a wrecked coaling station with nothing left to it but the rusted iron pierage. He poured three concrete slabs over the pierage to make an enormous deck and opened a bar straightaway. Meanwhile, he built a proper restaurant and scuba center, which included a small museum filled with the remains of old galleons and Chinese junks, as well as sixteenth-century Chinese and Vietnamese pottery he had salvaged from these and other nearby shipwrecks. His next project was an adjacent hotel fronting the bay, with bed-

---

* SEALs: Sea, Air, and Land, the Navy's equivalent of Delta Force. SAS: Special Air Service, an elite commando team.

posts in each room made of old U.S. Navy telephone poles he had found: "Authentic Douglas fir from Washington State," he told me, banging on one with his hand.

The place where I stayed, though not as inventive in its construction, boasted an atmosphere in which, as somone had told me, "the rules of middle-class society simply didn't apply, provided no one infringed on anyone else's peace and security." Families were welcome but not encouraged. The beach bar had no closing bell. It was open twenty-four hours a day, seven days a week. Couples would drift out of their rooms in the middle of the night to have a quiet drink by the sea. What you did was your own business, although there was a security guard on constant patrol against thieves. I left my valuables beside my bed and never worried. There was little random crime in the area anyway.

My hotel and others in the area constituted mildewy, somewhat seedy, pre-luxury-era paradises that were able to go on existing because there was just enough terrorism and political instability in the Philippines to keep global tourism and its regulated standards of behavior far, far away.

There were nearby strip joints with names like Muff Divers. Walking into them was like entering an octopus. Several sets of hands would suddenly be all over you, offering massages and more. The women were not down-and-out as one might expect. I interviewed *Filipinas* in their forties who looked considerably younger and had turned to sex to put children through good colleges and boarding schools. They had specific strategies for investments, future jobs, and cushy retirements. They were not strippers or prostitutes per se. The Philippines offered something subtler: "the girlfriend experience," it was called in Manila. There was an entire class of attractive *Filipinas* who made an excellent living, relative to the standards of the local economy, by becoming companions of Western men. Relationships lasted days, weeks, or months even. Couples were often loyal to each other. Such overtly sex-for-money relationships sometimes evolved into marriages. It was crude by the standards of the middle-class West, and yet quite sophisticated and discriminating by the standards of conventional prostitution.

While the Philippines was an Eden without rival for Western males, for the same reason the wives of American servicemen harbored "a visceral hatred of the place," as one soldier observed. When Subic Bay and Clark Field were in operation as American bases, female spouses who came out here were often in an uproar when they saw what was going on. It led to real "morale problems," as the U.S. military would euphemistically put it: spousal screaming matches, divorces, and the like.

With the bases gone, soldiers interacted more with the locals. It wasn't like the days of the old Pacific Army prior to World War II. But the situation had moved back a bit in that direction. The result, actually, was a better relationship with the immediate environment, a phenomenon which, in fact, has a basis in imperial history.

In *Armies of the Raj,* British military historian Byron Farwell writes that the opening of the Suez Canal, by allowing the wives of British officers in India to conveniently join their husbands, cut the officers off from native society, and became one of the contributing factors leading to the Indian Mutiny of 1857–58 against British rule. "In all societies women have been the conservators of culture," Farwell explains. "When British women began to arrive in India in numbers, they brought with them British attitudes, British fashions, and British morality; they were soon imposing their ideas, standards, and customs upon their new environment."[36] Consequently, British soldiers, many of whom had preferred to be orientalized themselves rather than to Christianize the Indians, now no longer went native, and a new divide opened between them and the locals.[37]

The situation in the Philippines posed a particular dilemma for the American military. Rudyard Kipling noted that "single men in barracks don't grow into plaster saints."[38] Or as one American serviceman whom I met briefly in Manila put it: "I'm thousands of miles from home, I'm away from the base for a few days with a nice hotel room. Do you really think I should go back to my hotel alone tonight?" Another serviceman angrily derided the "Bible-thumpers" in the U.S. military, who, he said, employed all kinds of budgetary and procedural reasons for getting R & R locations moved from Manila to Okinawa, because in Okinawa "everybody knew it was a bit harder to get laid."

In fact, I concluded that the U.S. military was handling this aspect of the Philippine reality fairly sensibly. It was a version of Don't Ask, Don't Tell, applied to heterosexual activity. For example, I noticed that quite a few soldiers got passes periodically, for one reason or another, to visit Manila. One officer whom I would meet there, with many years of experience in sexually charged places like Thailand and the Philippines told me: "I always make sure the medics have lots of antibiotics for venereal disease. I don't go crazy against a guy as long as he doesn't go overboard, as long as he shows up on time for formation, and as long as his wife doesn't start calling and complaining to me. But once it becomes a family prob-lem, then it's a team problem, and an Army problem. And I've got to take action against him."

_____

"The Army was my own idea. Nobody encouraged me in that direction. Nobody was a role model for me while growing up," Mark Lopez ex-plained. Now I was on the beach in Subic Bay, sipping beers at sunset, and he and I spent hours talking. He was part Mexican, part American Indian. He was born in Sacramento, California, and grew up in Yuba City to the north, where "everyone became farmers, loggers, or contractors. I just felt I had to escape that. As a junior in high school I got permission from my parents to join Army ROTC. At first I wanted to become a drill instructor."

Lopez's early years in the Army were spent with the 1st Ranger Battal-ion (Airborne) at Hunter Airfield in Savannah, Georgia, then with U.S. forces in South Korea, and with the 10th Mountain Division at Fort Drum, New York. In 1992 he was accepted into Special Forces. From then on, his only goal in life, he told me in his burly voice, "was to one day become an SF team sergeant. No other job in the world gives you the opportunity to be such a role model and molder of men. You're the glue of the whole squad. Nobody has as much freedom or as much responsibility."

I didn't laugh. Since meeting Mike Fields at Tolemaida in Colombia, I had never ceased to be impressed with the workload carried by Green Beret team sergeants, most of whom held the rank of master sergeant. Later in the Philippines I met a sergeant major, Steve Gregurek, of Nava-sota, Texas. When Gregurek had been at sergeant majors academy in El Paso, Texas, he was asked what his goal in the military was. "I told them that I had already been there. After being an SF team sergeant, there was nothing left to attain in this world."

Team sergeants spent years with their Special Forces detachments, and often never left Special Forces, whereas captains and majors would serve a few years on a team and then transfer elsewhere in the Army, returning to Special Forces only later in their careers, if at all. Sergeants, particularly team sergeants, or master sergeants, were the true repositories of Special Forces tradition.

All Lopez wanted to do was talk about his experiences in Basilan. He and his team had lived in the bush there, marched full pack through man-grove swamps and triple canopy rain forest, rebuilt a mosque, and held medical clinics twice weekly in villages threatened by Abu Sayyaf. His medic, Sgt. Keith Pace of Ann Arbor, Michigan, had, among other exploits, saved a seven-year-old girl's life with a Gatorade enema. "She had spinal meningitis," Pace explained to me. "She was dehydrating fast. I couldn't find a vein for an intravenous solution. I filled an enema with a bottle of Gatorade, lifted her butt, and rammed the Gatorade up her anus. It got into her bloodstream and rehydrated her." Sgt. Pace was personally commended by the Philippine government for his work on Basilan. "I pulled teeth. I treated farm animals. There was no lab nearby. You treated everything empirically. You didn't wait for proof; by that time someone would be dead. If you thought someone had this or that disease, you treated them for it immediately."

Lopez felt that everything his team did on Basilan could have been done at less risk and more effectively without a joint task force. Unloading his frustration under a laterite sunset, he said: "The whole JTF-JSOTF concept violated much of what was taught at the Q course in Fort Bragg," referring to the Green Beret qualification course. "There was relatively little the JTF did that could not have been handled more quietly, efficiently, and with a smaller signature by a Special Forces B-team. The whole point of a B-team is to serve as a forward operating base for several A-teams many miles from their home base.

"The problem," he continued, "wasn't just the PACOM mindset, it was Washington. The Special Operations mission in Basilan was the only hot item in the Pacific theater at the time, so we became the plaything of larger forces. Everybody wanted a piece of it, so it became bigger than it needed to be. Instead of rolling with two-and-a-half-ton trucks into Isabela, we should have come in quietly at night on Zodiacs [inflatable boats used by combat divers] and infiltrated into the countryside with CAFGUs [Citizens Armed Forces Geographical Units]. The JTF represented the kind of heavy-handed approach that had made Vietnam go drastically wrong, and which ignored the lessons of the Philippine War a hundred years ago. It's a good thing that Abu Sayyaf didn't have the teeth or balls to sabotage us."

Everything Lopez told me was backed up by other noncoms from other detachments. Furthermore, Lopez's commanding officer in Basilan, Lt. Col. David Maxwell, would tell me later in Washington that Enduring Freedom—Philippines had operated "ass backwards." The joint task force in Zamboanga "had supposedly set the conditions for our deployment, but there were no conditions to set up until the A-teams were actually deployed on the island."

Tactically speaking, Lopez and Maxwell made sense. But it could also be argued that the larger-than-necessary base complex at Zamboanga delivered political benefits that fell outside a purely tactical analysis; it got the U.S. semi-permanently established south of Luzon for the first time since World War II, positioning it for a future conflict with China.

———

It wasn't far from Subic Bay to Fort Magsaysay in the interior of Luzon, where more Green Beret teams were deployed training Filipinos.* The atmosphere inland was totally different. Subic Bay was exhilarating, Fort Magsaysay depressing. Fort Magsaysay, located near the Japanese prisoner-of-war camp of Cabanatuan, where American survivors of the Bataan Death March had been incarcerated, was flat, with no views or breezes. The heat was crushing. A typhoon system had arrived, submerging the landscape under constant torrential downpours.

The "typhoon blues" had set in around the barracks. Rain lashed the windows. Frogs leapt through the latrines. Some training exercises were canceled. I had plenty of time to talk with Maj. Robert E. Lee Jr. of the Panama Canal Zone and later of Mobile, Alabama, the commanding officer for all Americans at Magsaysay.

Maj. Ed Lee spoke in quick, staccato bursts. He was pale and a bit scrawny compared to the others, with brown hair and a mustache. He was the first member of his family to attend college, at the University of South Alabama in Mobile. His oldest son was named Stonewall, after the Confederate general Thomas "Stonewall" Jackson. He told me that his right-of-passage experience was working for a year as a volunteer for the Southern Baptist mission in a poor African-American section of Wichita, Kansas. "It was my first real exposure to blacks, I mean not from afar. It was a year of learning, day after day, that folks are just folks."

Maj. Lee had conducted training missions all over Asia: South Korea, Singapore, Tonga, the Solomon Islands, the Philippines. . . . He judged cultures and political systems by what he saw of their armies, which wasn't a bad idea. At least it was ground truth rather than abstractions. Armies are usually accurate cultural barometers. America had among the best non-commissioned officer corps in history because the U.S. was the epitome of

* Ramón Magsaysay was the Philippine minister of national defense and later the country's president. In the early 1950s, helped by an American covert action program, he mounted a successful counterinsurgency campaign against the communist Huk guerrillas in Luzon.

a mass middle-class society. Poorly led and corrupt third world countries tended to have militaries in which weapons and other equipment were not maintained. Maintenance—a dull, unpleasant, and yet necessary task—is an indication of discipline, esprit de corps, and faith in the future, because you maintain only what you plan to use for the long term.

Lee, barely audible above the loud typhoon rain, spoke about each Asian army that he had helped train, with the memory of it lingering in his eyes. He was most impressed with Singapore's. "They had a state-of-the-art shoot house. Whenever a soldier got hurt in training, there was an investigation and a detailed explanation given to the family. Life wasn't cheap there. It was valued. Officially, Singapore's a dictatorship, and people in Washington and New York disparage it. Unofficially, it's a civil society.

"Their noncommissioned officer corps is real good," he went on. "Singapore's a meritocracy; lots of future officers are identified out of the ranks in basic training. Chinese, Malays, Indians, they're all mixed together in units. I went there with the idea of Big Brother. But you just cross the border into Malaysia or especially Indonesia from Singapore, and you'll see hordes of beggars and people defecating in the streets and you'll realize why Singapore has those strict rules. You can walk into a movie theater in Singapore without your feet sticking to the floor. Going into Malaysia and Indonesia put things into perspective for me. After those countries, the Big Brotherisms don't bother you much. Anyway, people in Singapore get around the rules. It's not as bad as people write about. You just have to be there."

One kind of training did not halt at Magsaysay because of the bad weather, and it was the most important. It was the CQC (close quarters combat) training conducted by a Special Forces team for a Philippine army light reaction company.

Special Forces soldiers are generalists. They can do everything from digging water wells to negotiating with diplomats to breaking into a house to save hostages. They can infiltrate by water with scuba gear, or from the air with parachutes. They are often in situations of training for one kind of mission, and then have to perform another. Consequently, there are always units in the military that perform specific tasks better than any Special Forces team can. But nobody rivals Special Forces when it comes to their original, classic function: infiltrate an area, and organize and train the indigenes.

Take Charlie Company at Fort Magsaysay, a cluster of Special Forces teams designated for commando-style raids. Whatever one may think, commando training is not interesting. It's the dullest form of repetition. The rifle range may be fun for an hour or two. But spend a day there "transitioning"—that is, switching from an M-4 assault rifle to a 9mm Beretta pistol in one smooth movement, while always hitting the target exactly where you want—and you will see how monstrously tedious it can be to keep your reflexes primed, in order to be a hero. That is what Charlie Company did. By the standards of the Army's Delta Force and some of its Ranger units, of the Navy SEALs, and of the Marines' Force Reconnaissance units, this Special Forces Charlie Company might have been slightly substandard. But those other units only had to fight. Charlie Company could teach indigenes of different cultures how to fight the way it did.

The shoot house used by Charlie Company was a ruined hospital with indoor and outdoor stairwells, and specially constructed movable plywood partitions overseen by a catwalk. Above the catwalk was a corrugated iron roof on which the rain created an uproar. "All units dance," said the sergeant over his hand-held commo gear. "Dance, dance, dance. I have control, I have control. Five, four, three, two, one . . ." Then det cords and flash bangs exploded, breaking down doors with blinding light and smoke, and concussing the air against my chest, as several "stacks" of Philippine soldiers flooded the rooms, firing blue plastic simulation rounds.

The Sim Sit, or simulated situation, was a hostage rescue. The operative concept was DEC (Dominate, Eliminate, Control). To an outsider it looked and sounded like sheer chaos, made worse by the smoke from the flash bangs. But after you observed the same drill a number of times, you began to ignore the sounds and shudder of the det cords and flash bangs, and concentrate instead on the evolving narrative of the rescue, which the sergeant was constantly, calmly critiquing.

Rescuing hostages from an apartment or hotel is a matter of technique, broken down into complex parts that have to be translated into muscle reflex actions. You find as many "breach points" as possible and flood them simultaneously, cutting off escape routes. When you "infil" a room you try to avoid the "bad guy" or hostage who might be directly in front of you challenging you or crying for help. Instead, you go immediately to "the point of domination," a corner from where you can cover half of the room, while your partner goes to the opposite corner to cover the other half. Only when you secure the two points of domination do you deal with the person in the room, friend or foe, because what's in front of you is not the problem. The real problem may be lurking in a corner behind the door.

Because this runs against natural instinct, it must be taught and re-taught, over and over again. Because two are needed to dominate a room, you do not enter a room until your partner squeezes you on your shoulder, to indicate silently that he is right behind you and ready. "Don't wave your hand. Don't say a word to your buddy. Just squeeze him quietly from behind," the sergeant kept repeating. "Each pair can only take one room at a time. So be deliberate. Let the adrenaline subside and think clearly. On the exfil you reclear each room in the same way that you cleared it."

In succeeding Sim Sits, I left the safety of the catwalk and followed a stack through the warren of typhoon-darkened partitions. I listened to the sergeant criticize and encourage his Filipino acolytes with a distinct voice of authority.

"That wasn't too bad. It was pretty good this time. But I still see too much talking and jostling. And when you find a hostage or a bad guy, you may not know who is whom. So don't just pat him down. Squeeze him all over. Squeeze, don't rub. That goes for his package [groin area], too. Don't be shy. *Daba?* It's your life, remember," he said, using the Tagalog word for "get it, understand."

He concluded with, "And remember, guys. We always win. We never lose hostages. We're the good guys. We kill the bad guys."

The clichés were spoken with utter seriousness, without irony. Only to me were they clichés. That's ultimately why these guys liked George W. Bush so much, I realized. He spoke the way they did, with a lack of nuance, which they found estimable because their own tasks did not require it.

At the end of the day, the sergeant and his Charlie Company team demonstrated what a correct Sim Sit looked like. It was beautiful to watch. They became like streams of water, quickly and silently, with an economy of movement, branching off and flooding several rooms simultaneously, squeezing shoulders and advancing, squeezing and advancing, like one seamless muscle reflex.

Away from his job, the sergeant barely talked to anyone. He perked up only when discussing types of bullets, types of infiltration techniques, and so on. He wasn't comfortable talking about much else. He was the perfect policy instrument.

Observing him, I was reminded that the job of diplomats who wear expensive suits and communicate in complex phrases in exquisitely furnished settings is to periodically negotiate arrangements, whereby the ultimate aim, though never spelled out, is to get someone like this sergeant, with tattoos and several bench-press records to his credit, to teach others like himself how to do what he does, for the training in that wreck of a hospital with its gangrenous walls represented the fingertip point of America's security assistance policy for the Philippines.

The sergeant and his team were assets of such importance to the U.S. that the Philippine light infantry company they were instructing had been cut off from the Philippine military's normal chain of command. It had been placed under the direct control of the Chief of Staff, Gen. Narciso Abaya, a West Point graduate known for his upright character. Only by removing whole levels of bureaucracy was it possible to guarantee the integrity of anything here.

My final days in the Philippines were spent at the World War II shrines around Manila. At the American Cemetery and Memorial at Fort Bonifacio (formerly Fort William McKinley) stand the graves of 17,206 American servicemen killed in the Pacific theater in World War II. In addition, on two extensive limestone hemicycles, are inscribed the names of 36,282 Americans missing in action. From the tower of the devotional chapel bells continually peal the "Battle Hymn of the Republic."

On the fortress rock of Corregidor, at the head of Manila Bay, stand the monumental remnants of the Topside and Middleside barracks, home to thousands of American servicemen and bombed in 1942 by the Japanese. Each year the moldy wall fragments become more and more like the medieval ruins at Angkor Wat in Cambodia.

Because the Philippines stood at the heart of the fighting in the Pacific in World War II—and because the Japanese occupation was so brutal—the Americans have always been seen here not merely as colonialists but also as liberators. The words inscribed on the Pacific War Memorial on Corregidor may explain why, ultimately, Americans gave their lives in such numbers in the Philippines and lesser known archipelagoes:

TO LIVE IN FREEDOM'S LIGHT
IS THE RIGHT OF MANKIND

Yet, it was a long way from those lofty words to the reality of freedom in the Philippines at the time of my visit. Coup rumors dominated the headlines for weeks. The last day that I was in Manila there was a mutiny by 296 junior officers, who seized a shopping mall in the financial district of Makati and ringed it with explosives. Their rage was directed against the rampant corruption in President Arroyo's government, in which senior officers were accused of selling ammunition to both communist and Islamic insurgents. Moreover, an international terrorist associated with Jemaah Islamiyah, Fathur Rahman al-Ghozi, had simply walked out of his cell at a maximum security facility in Manila after the requisite payoffs had been made to high-ranking Philippine officials.*

Those young mutinous officers were arguably the most idealistic people in the country. They knew that democracy was only a procedural definition for how the Philippines actually functioned. Almost six decades after liberation from the Japanese, and almost two decades after dictator Ferdinand Marcos had been toppled, the Philippine political system was more accurately defined by the compadre network of sordid personal contacts than by any notion of Western civil society. But those young officers were also incredibly naive, for the worst dictatorships can emerge from an excess of idealism.

Not one American noncom or middle-level officer whom I met spoke to me in terms of "saving" or "improving" the Philippines. Rather, these men saw their charge in terms of developing a cadre of Westernized officers and useful contacts in both the Christian and Muslim communities who could be influential even in the event that the state broke up. None of the Americans were cynical, yet all of them were aware of America's limitations amid vast and roiling cultural and political forces. But they persevered, finding deep personal meaning in their jobs. Soon after I left they found a way to embed individual Green Berets into Philippine units at the battalion level, thus stretching the rules of engagement, so as to better coordinate the hunt for terrorists. Imperial powers know no rest.

* The Philippine Armed Forces later tracked al-Ghozi down and killed him.

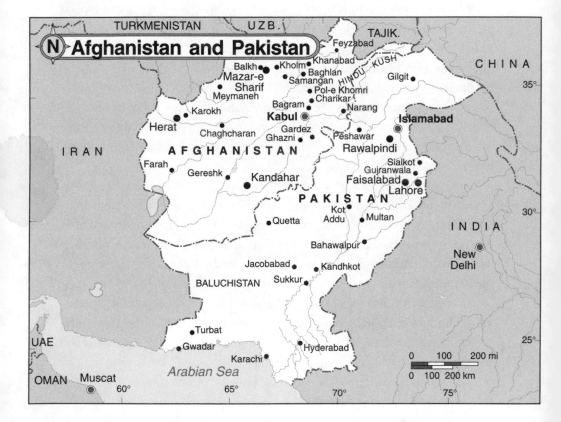

CHAPTER FIVE

CENTCOM AND SOCOM

AFGHANISTAN, AUTUMN 2003

WITH NOTES ON PAKISTAN'S NORTHWEST FRONTIER

"Because al-Qaeda was a worldwide insurgency, America had to fight a classic worldwide counterinsurgency . . . here, amid the field mice and the mud-walled flatness of the Helmand desert, there was only constant trial-and-error experimentation in light of the mission at hand."

By the time I had returned from the Philippines, the postwar stabilizations of Iraq and Afghanistan were in jeopardy. Both the Pentagon and the American public had thought in terms of final victory and victory parades. Yet the fact that more U.S. troops had been killed by shadowy gunmen in Iraq after the dismantling of the Saddam Hussein regime than during the war itself indicated that the real war over Iraq's future was being fought now, and Operation Iraqi Freedom—the American-led invasion of the previous March, featuring hundreds of thousands of infantry troops—had merely shaped the battlefield for it.

The low-intensity violence in Sunni-inhabited central Iraq was an example of how the early twenty-first century constituted a universe in which war, to some degree, never ends because it is inextricable from politics and social unrest. In this universe, first defined by the Prussian general Carl von Clausewitz, the military becomes an unceasing instrument of statecraft even as diplomacy remains a principal weapon of war. Such an admixture of military combat and politics means that cultural and historical knowledge of the terrain is more likely than technological wizardry to dilute the so-called fog of war. As an avid reader of poetry and a product of the Romantic age before the Industrial Revolution—an age which respected the primacy of passion over rationality—Clausewitz had eerily intuited this.

But a never-ending state of war was a principle that Americans repeat-edly found difficult to accept. Indeed, the first Gulf War in 1991 had seen a complete disconnect between America's military aims and its postwar political strategy: by abruptly declaring victory, quickly withdrawing its military forces, not creating a demilitarized zone in southern Iraq to weaken Saddam's surviving regime, and avoiding military links with anti-Saddam insurgents, the administration of George Bush the Elder ended up bolstering the very regime it had sought to undermine during the fighting itself.[1]

Now, more than a decade later, with post-Saddam Iraq an exercise yard for unconventional Economy of Force attacks carried out by small groups of hit men and lone suicide bombers, yet another truth was laid bare: the modern battlefield was continuing to expand and empty out, so that it was characterized by a dispersion of forces.[2] Massive tank and infantry move-ments were of less consequence than the lethal actions of a few individu-als, magnified by a global media.

In Afghanistan, too, a rapid and seemingly decisive military victory had been followed by a dirty and bloody peace. "Militant Islamic extrem-ism," wrote *New York Times* correspondents Amy Waldman and Dexter Filkins, reporting from both Afghanistan and Iraq, was proving to be an ideology that could be "contained but not defeated."[3] Small-scale erup-tions of war, with few enemy troops visible, were now a feature of the Near Eastern landscape. It was something the U.S. would have to get used to, whatever party occupied the White House.

The unrest in both countries had different origins. In Iraq, the Baath party, like the KGB and the Communist party of the Soviet Union, had constituted one huge mafia. When the Soviet Union collapsed, the ruling mafia splintered into many smaller ones, leading to low-level chaos for nearly a decade, manifested in crime, murder, and corruption. The same situation obtained in Iraq, except that Iraq also offered significant numbers of U.S. troops as targets. Moreover, Iraq's sprawling, hard-to-control desert borderlands and its linguistic and ethnic affinities with neighbors like Syria made it possible for al-Qaeda's foot soldiers to slip inside the country and amplify the threat.

As for Afghanistan, the destruction of the state was actually less man-ifest than in Iraq. Even in the best of times (the mid-twentieth century, under the leadership of King Zahir Shah) the Afghan state had existed only partially, and extended to not much more than the major cities and towns, and the ring road connecting them. Contrary to popular wisdom, the Soviet invasion of December 1979 had not ignited the mujahedin uprising. That uprising began more than a year earlier, in April 1978, when the Afghan regime attempted to extend the power of the central government to the villages. However brutal and incompetent that regime's methods were, one had to keep in mind that Afghans had less of a tradition of a modern state than Persians or Arabs.

Warlordism had always been strong in Afghanistan, bolstered in recent decades by the diffuse nature of the mujahedin rebellion against the Soviets, the destruction wrought by the fighting among the mujahedin themselves after the Soviet departure, and the bureaucratic incompetence of the Taliban, who constituted more of an ideological movement than a governing apparatus. Thus, with the state barely in existence even before the American invasion of October 2001, barring some catastrophe like the fall of a major town to a reconstituted Taliban or the assassination of President Hamid Karzai, reading success or failure in Afghanistan would be a subtler enterprise than in Iraq.

The continued turmoil in the Greater Near East, plus my desire to observe Army Special Forces in a more varied role than in Colombia and the Philippines—before I moved on to other branches of the military—was to take me on a two-month journey to Afghanistan. Iraq would wait until early the next year; I was not chasing news, but trying to understand the mechanics of America's security commitments worldwide, on the ground, piece by piece.

Afghanistan and Army Special Forces fell within the domains of CENTCOM (Central Command) and SOCOM (Special Operations Command). Both, as it happened, were headquartered at MacDill Air Force Base in Tampa, Florida.

CENTCOM was an unusual area command in that it was new, had few war-fighting units permanently assigned to it, and yet bore the burden of most of the fighting for the U.S. at the dawn of the twenty-first century. This was in spite of the fact that CENTCOM's area of responsibility was significantly smaller than the other commands, for the Greater Middle East did not compare in square mileage to the vast Pacific; to South America and its oceanic environs; or to Europe, Russia, and Africa—the responsibility of European Command.

But what CENTCOM's area of responsibility lacks in size, it compensates for in strategic importance. It stretches from northeastern Africa across the Middle East to former Soviet Central Asia and Pakistan and comprises that vast desert region which lies east of Europe, south of Russia, and west of China and India. Here the legacies of the Byzantine, Turkish, and Persian empires overlap amid two thirds of the world's proven oil reserves and 40 percent of its natural gas.

While SOUTHCOM and PACOM boast venerable roots in American history—in the building of the Panama Canal and the old Pacific Army before World War II—and while European Command constitutes a legacy of the Allied victory over Hitler's Germany, CENTCOM is without a storied past. It is a creature of the last phase of the Cold War and the challenge posed by extremist Islam, a granite-like ideology as dynamic, inflexible, and ruthless as Soviet communism and European fascism.*

Central Command was activated in 1983 by President Ronald Reagan as a successor to the Rapid Deployment Joint Task Force, which had, in turn, been created by President Jimmy Carter in order to project power in Africa and the Middle East following the Iranian hostage crisis.† In 1990 and 1991, CENTCOM became a household word when under its then-commander, Army Gen. Norman Schwarzkopf, it executed Operations Desert Shield and Desert Storm, respectively the defense of Saudi Arabia and the liberation of Kuwait from Iraqi occupation. In 1992, CENTCOM carried out Restore Hope, the humanitarian intervention in Somalia. And throughout the 1990s CENTCOM enforced the Iraqi no-fly zone.

Along with NATO, CENTCOM had grown into the ultimate coalition manager. Its headquarters, at the point where Tampa Bay opens into the Gulf of Mexico, was distinguished not by its huge nondescript building, but by the enormous expanse of mobile homes, each flying a different national flag, which housed liaison officers from all the countries taking part in Operations Enduring Freedom—Afghanistan and Iraqi Freedom. When one walked inside the main building, not only were the desert cammie utilities (DCUs) that the American soldiers wore different from the dark green

* The comparison between extremist Islam and the granite-like ideology of Soviet communism was made by Bernard-Henri Levy in *Who Killed Daniel Pearl?* (Hoboken, NJ: Melville House, 2003).
† The Rapid Deployment Joint Task Force was specifically promoted by President Carter's hawkish national security advisor, Zbigniew Brzezinski. See Michael R. Gordon and Gen. Bernard E. Trainor, *The Generals' War: The Inside Story of the Conflict in the Gulf* (Boston: Little, Brown, 1995), p. 43.

BDUs of the other area commands, so was the corridor presence of officers from a host of nations, as indicated by their distinctive uniforms. One of my briefers was not even an American, but a Norwegian army major.

CENTCOM's pace of activity made SOUTHCOM and PACOM look sleepy by comparison. People worked longer hours than at the other commands. Most of the higher-ranking officers were not at the Tampa headquarters even, but forward deployed in Afghanistan, Iraq, and elsewhere in the AOR (area of responsibility). Officially, every area command reported directly to the secretary of defense, but CENTCOM's channels of communication to the "SecDef" (as he was called) were simply more direct and seamless.

U.S. Air Force Maj. Michel Escudi, my escort, remarked, "Here you've got a third of the world at your fingertips. Everything is informal with little red tape. All the nations go to the briefings, and that generally goes for the exchange of intelligence, too. If you asked me to diagram the bureaucratic chain of command as it actually works, I couldn't. People just walk in cold on each other's offices."

The U.N. and NATO must have been like this in the early 1950s, I thought, before a formalized rigidity set in. Since the end of the Cold War, CENTCOM had been emerging as an international organization of the kind that elites in the major capitals and financial centers talked about but did not imagine taking shape inside the American military, amid western Florida's tacky sunbelt sprawl. Organizations are at their most dynamic when they are in the process of *becoming*—when they work out of temporary structures and have the sense of the guerrilla outfit about them, disrupting the established order. That was CENTCOM (though NATO, too, had been revitalized somewhat with the entry of former Warsaw Pact countries into its ranks, and by successfully intervening and fighting wars in Bosnia and Kosovo).

Another distinctive feature of CENTCOM was the way that I was treated. At SOUTHCOM and PACOM, whose military operations were largely ignored by the media, I was an oddity, a threat, and a VIP all at once, to be handled with care and lots of planning. At CENTCOM, I was just another journalist being processed through a series of briefings. People barely had time for me.

Special Operations Command, or SOCOM, was activated four years after CENTCOM, in 1987, and thus was even newer. It was forced on a reluctant Pentagon by the U.S. Congress, through an amendment sponsored by

Democratic Senator Sam Nunn of Georgia and Republican Senator William Cohen of Maine.* The two senators had become frustrated with the military's slowness in adapting to unconventional threats. In 1976 the Israelis had carried out a spectacular raid on Entebbe airport in Uganda to rescue hostages taken by Ugandan leader Idi Amin. The following year, the West German military, with help from the British Special Air Service (SAS), performed a similar feat, freeing hostages taken by Baader-Meinhof terrorists at Mogadishu airport in Somalia. In 1980, however, a U.S. attempt to rescue American hostages in Iran was a disastrous failure. SOCOM, like the Rapid Deployment Force and CENTCOM, was yet another consequence of that signal crisis and national humiliation.

The creation of SOCOM marked the most dramatic elevation of Special Operations since President Kennedy had awarded Army Special Forces the green beret. SOCOM comprised not only the various Army Special Forces groups, but the 75th Ranger Regiment, Navy SEALs, Air Force Special Operations squadrons, a provisional Marine detachment, and other commando-style units. The Nunn-Cohen Amendment, at least officially, made SOCOM a war-fighting command as well as a force provider— though in practice SOCOM rarely had operational control of missions in the manner that CENTCOM, PACOM, and the other area commands did.

It was the Global War on Terrorism—and particularly Secretary of Defense Donald Rumsfeld's implementation of it—that made SOCOM a war-fighting command in more than name only. SOCOM was now supposed to be an area command just like the others, but with its area the entire earth, for if al-Qaeda constituted a seamless worldwide apparatus without bureaucratic impediments, so, too, it was thought, should SOCOM.

SOCOM, in theory, was to be the executive arm for the War on Terrorism. Yet, there was an inherent conflict between area commands that had operational control over specific geographic sectors and SOCOM, which could launch operations anywhere, on anybody's turf. Therefore, SOCOM was still a work in progress. Nevertheless, it managed to run operations of some sort in 150 countries in 2003.

SOCOM's was the only command whose budget came directly from Congress, not from the Pentagon.† It dealt with a plethora of government

* William Cohen later served as the secretary of defense in the second administration of President Bill Clinton.
† In 2003 it was $5 billion out of a total defense budget of $364.7 billion, or 1.8 percent. About one third of that $5 billion was for salaries.

agencies in addition to all the uniformed services and area commands. SOCOM's bureaucratic flowchart was numbing in its complexity. Because post–Cold War challenges like nation-building were dependent on interagency cooperation, SOCOM's success or failure as an interagency tool would provide a litmus test of sorts for how well America was able to fulfill its international obligations.

SOCOM's activities were secret to a far greater degree than the other commands. Its "black SOF [Special Operations Forces]" missions against al-Qaeda in the Afghanistan-Pakistan border area were the dagger point of the War on Terrorism. The public affairs officer at SOCOM, Chet Justice, told me that journalists were rare there, and that was just fine with his bosses. Even the meeting rooms at SOCOM had coded locks on them. There was no buzz of activity inside SOCOM as there was at CENTCOM, just secretaries and brawny men in uniforms silently passing each other in the hallways. The command briefing I received began with these words from George Orwell:

> People sleep peaceably in their beds at night only because rough men stand ready to do violence on their behalf.

The SOCOM commander at the time, Army Gen. Doug Brown, a four-star, had been an enlisted man, like his friend Sid Shachnow, the latter whom I had met at the horse farm in North Carolina. Both had gone to Officer Candidate School and risen through the ranks. Gen. Brown's second in command, naval Vice Adm. Eric Olson, was a former SEAL. My conversations with them were off the record, yet the most interesting insight I obtained, oddly enough, was very much on the record. It was SOCOM's four "enduring truths":

- Humans are more important than hardware.
- Quality is better than quantity.
- Special Operations Forces cannot be mass-produced.
- Competent SOF cannot be created after emergencies occur.

Though they seem like clichés, they go against the grain of much of American military thinking in the twentieth century. And they go against what military historian Max Boot critically labels "the army way, the American way, the World War II way: find the enemy, fix him in place, and annihilate him with withering fire power."[4] Contrarily, SOCOM believed that small guerrilla-like groups of men, armed with linguistic and cultural expertise, were more effective than industrial-age tank and infantry divisions manned by citizen conscripts—the heroes of World War II. And because al-Qaeda was a worldwide insurgency, America had to fight a classic worldwide counterinsurgency. Thus, SOCOM commanders thought more about the Philippines of a hundred years ago, about the OSS units in Nazi-occupied France and Japanese-occupied Burma, and the Green Berets in Vietnam and El Salvador than they did about the two Gulf wars, Korea, and World War II.

While the area commands were still wedded to the conventional use of large armies, navies, and air forces, SOCOM was the Pentagon's principal bureaucratic machine of unconventional war (UW). UW entailed not only commando-style raids but softer techniques like the humanitarian work on Basilan Island in the Philippines that had helped root out Islamic insurgents. Violence was not being discarded, but in the future it would be, to quote Sid Shachnow, "complementary rather than controlling."

Success required a long-term continuous presence on the ground in scores of countries—quiet and unobtrusive—with operations harmonized through a central strategy, but with decentralized execution in the manner of the most successful global corporations, be it General Electric or al-Qaeda.[5]

The Afghanistan-Pakistan borderlands were where the jurisdictions of SOCOM and the more conventionally oriented CENTCOM overlapped. How was it working?

This would be my first visit to Afghanistan and the Afghanistan-Pakistani borderlands since the spring of 2000, when I had traveled along the Northwest Frontier and did a profile of Hamid Karzai, then an obscure Afghan tribal leader.[6] Before that, I had reported from Pakistan in the 1990s and covered the mujahedin war against the Soviet Union inside Afghanistan in the 1980s.

Whatever the maps might say, I had learned to view Afghanistan and Pakistan as a single political unit. This was not just the result of Pakistan's intense involvement in the mujahedin war against the Soviet occupation and in the rise of Taliban extremists the following decade, but of simple geography and British colonial history.[7]

Because the transition from the steamy lowlands of the Indian subcontinent to the arid moonscapes of Central Asia is gradual, the border between Afghanistan and Pakistan could never be precise. The border region—a thousand miles long and a hundred miles wide—is a deathly volcanic landscape of crags and winding canyons where the Indian subcontinent's tropical floor pushes upward into Inner Asia's high, shaved wastes. From Baluchistan north through the Pakistani "tribal agencies" of Waziristan, Kurram, Orakzai, Khyber, Mohmand, and Bajaur, near Peshawar—the destitute capital of Pakistan's Northwest Frontier Province—there is an anarchic realm of highwaymen, tribal and religious violence, heroin laboratories, and arms smuggling.

The tribal Pushtuns (also known as Pathans), who controlled the frontier zone of eastern and southern Afghanistan, never accepted the arbitrary boundary between Afghanistan and colonial India (from which Pakistan later emerged): a boundary drawn in 1893 by the British envoy Sir Mortimer Durand. Moreover, the British bequeathed to the Pakistanis the belt of anarchic territories they called "tribal agencies," which lay just east of the Durand Line. This had the effect of further confusing the boundary between settled land in Pakistan and the chaos of Afghanistan. Consequently, Pakistani governments always felt besieged—not only by India to the east but by Afghan tribesmen to the west. To fight India, in the Pakistani view, it was necessary to dominate Afghanistan.

Afghanistan did not truly exist until the middle of the eighteenth century. In 1747, Ahmad Khan, leader of the Abdali contingent of Nadir Shah the Great—the Persian king and conqueror of Moghul India—fled Persia with four thousand horsemen, following Nadir Shah's assassination and the collapse of his regime. Ahmad Khan and his troops fled southeast out of Persia, to Kandahar.

Kandahar was probably the only Greek place name to have survived in Afghanistan. It stemmed from the Arabic form of Alexander's name, Iskander. In 330 B.C., Alexander the Great had led his army through the Kandahar region in search of further conquests, following his victory over the Persian forces of Darius at Gaugamela, in northern Iraq. Kandahar lay in the frontier zone between the Persian historical homeland and the Moghul territories to the east that the Persians and their assassinated leader, Nadir Shah, had vanquished. In this sea of blood and turmoil, Ahmad Khan conceived of an island of order: a native Afghan kingdom that would be sanctioned by whoever would rule next in Persia, in exchange for which he would aggressively patrol the mother kingdom's new territories to the east.

Ahmad Khan was only twenty-four when he became King Ahmad Shah of Afghanistan. In a camp outside Kandahar, as Sir Olaf Caroe tells it, the other Abdali tribesmen "took pieces of grass in their mouths as a token that they were his cattle and beasts of burden."[8] Because King Ahmad Shah liked to wear a pearl earring, he became known by the title Durr-I-Durran (Pearl of Pearls). From this time on, he and his Abdali tribesmen would be known as Durranis.

From Kandahar, Ahmad Shah conquered Kabul and Herat, so the Durrani empire became modern Afghanistan. The Durranis ruled Afghanistan until 1973, when Prime Minister Mohammed Daoud, in a Soviet-assisted coup, overthrew the last Durrani monarch, King Zahir Shah. Zahir Shah would not return to Afghanistan until three decades later as a private citizen, after the dismantling of the Taliban regime by American forces and the election of his tribal kinsman Hamid Karzai as Afghan president.

Hamid Karzai, the headman of the Popolzais, a tribal subgroup of the Durranis, was himself Afghan royalty. Like the original Ahmad Shah, as well as the radical Taliban, Karzai hailed from Kandahar. Kandahar was always considered the pure Afghan homeland, unadulterated by the Persian influences in Herat to the northwest or those of the Indian subcontinent that pervaded Kabul to the northeast.

The Taliban had been so impressed by Hamid Karzai's Kandahari lineage that in the early 1990s, before they came to power, they sought out his support, and in the first days of their rule offered him the post of United Nations ambassador, which he refused.[9] Whereas the U.S. saw the Taliban as radical Islamists, they were also ethnic Pushtuns with deep reverence for tribal heredity. The Taliban lived by the primitive tribal creed of Pushtunwali—"the way of the Pushtuns"—a code more severe than Koranic law. It was the joining of Pushtunwali with Koranic law that produced such a savage end product.

Indeed, the moment you dismissed the importance of tribe and ethnicity you began to misread Afghanistan. From the days of King Ahmad Shah, Afghanistan constituted a fragile webwork of tribes and ethnic groups occupying the water-starved wastes between the settled areas of the Russian Empire in Central Asia, the Persian Empire in the Middle East, and the British Empire in the Indian subcontinent. The killing of 1.3 million Afghans by the Soviets in the 1980s shattered this fragile ethnic web-work. Anarchy was the result. The anarchy continued after Soviet troops departed, leading to the ideologically severe but institutionally weak Taliban government, dismantled by the Americans in order to deny al-Qaeda its principal base of operations following 9/11.

In late 2003, with the state barely functioning despite Karzai's valiant attempts to resurrect it, Afghanistan had been reduced to its constituent ethnic parts. To the north of the Hindu Kush mountains lay the Tajiks, Uzbeks, and Turkomens, all allied with their ethnic compatriots in the former Soviet empire. To the south of the Hindu Kush lay the Pushtuns, allied with Pushtuns inside Pakistan. The unrelenting stream of guerrilla attacks on U.S. and other coalition forces in southern and eastern Afghanistan following the collapse of the Taliban regime was meant, among other things, to drive out the American infidels from this historic Pushtun territory.

The reality of Afghanistan began five minutes away from the luxurious glitter of my hotel in the Persian Gulf emirate of Dubai. One dark October morning at 4:30 a hotel shuttle transported me from a world of fine chocolates, good wines, and the animal scents of expensive perfumes and colognes to Dubai's old terminal, the one used mainly for cargo flights. There I found a horde of Afghans in beards, massive turbans, and *shalwar kameez* (robes and baggy trousers) sprawled all over the departure lounge, their bare feet resting on battered suitcases, while other Afghans, their turbans off, snored in fetal positions on the floor.

In their coarse and costumed splendor, memorialized by Kipling and other writers, the Afghans were like the Yemenis: another unreconstructed people of the mountains and high plains who had never been successfully colonized. The grimy wide-bodied jet that took off from the Dubai cargo terminal, bound for the Afghan capital of Kabul, with every seat occupied, was nearly devoid of women. In the early twenty-first century, such a barren social landscape usually meant violence and unrest.

Two and a half hours later, the plane descended onto a biscuit brown tableland surrounded by ashen hills. As I left the airport in Kabul, the change wrought by American troops quickly became manifest. Near the gateway to the Indian subcontinent, Kabul had always been the most cosmopolitan place in Afghanistan. Thus, the Taliban singled it out for particularly harsh treatment. Women were stoned, banned from school and the workplace, erased from existence practically. Now hundreds of schoolgirls, laughing and smiling, in uniforms and headscarves, crowded the road from the airport. There was colorful new signage advertising consumer goods and civil society groups. Whereas the human image itself had been forbidden by the Taliban, now portraits of the martyred Ahmad Shah Massoud, who had led the guerrilla struggle against both the Soviets and later the Taliban, were omnipresent.

The metamorphosis, superficial and limited to the capital though it was, testified to the power of human agency. Had the Bush administration reacted to 9/11 in a different and less forceful manner, those schoolgirls simply would not have been present on the street.

But I saw it all from a great distance. I was inside a van, riding with American soldiers, both male and female, from the 211th Mobile Public Affairs Detachment, out of Bryan, Texas. They used call signs like "chili" and "beans," and talked about the league play-offs in baseball. From downtown Kabul the van turned east and then north across the Shomali Plain. Singular sawtooth monuments of volcanic gray rock erupted off the high desert floor, swallowed by dust, like bones swiftly disintegrating. The bleached landscape made you thankful for every primary color, whether a red pomegranate or the lapis lazuli blue of a *burka* even.* Less than an hour after I left Kabul, the snow-crenellated ramparts of the Hindu Kush, rising sheer off the tableland to a height of twenty-one thousand feet, heralded Bagram.

Bagram Air Force Base was the headquarters of Combined Joint Task Force 180 (CJTF-180), an American-led alliance of thirty-three countries. Of its 11,000 troops, 8,500 were American, and 5,000 of those were located at Bagram, so the Americans dominated the environment. (The task force was separate from the NATO-led International Security Assistance Force, or ISAF. Whereas ISAF kept the peace in Kabul, CJTF-180 was responsible for the rest of Afghanistan at the time of my visit.)

From 1979 to 1989, Bagram air base had been the nerve center of the Soviet occupation force. The Soviets surrounded Bagram with trenches and minefields, and packed the runways with Hind helicopter gunships that incinerated Afghan villages harboring mujahedin guerrillas. That was until the mid-1980s, when the Americans supplied the mujahedin with

---

* A *burka* is a loose-fitting, all-enveloping cloak with veiled eye slits that devout Muslim women wear in Afghanistan and Pakistan.

Stinger anti-aircraft missiles. Thus did the tide of battle turn, triggering the endgame of the Cold War.

Minefields still littered Bagram's perimeter, along with vast junkyards of wrecked and rusted Soviet helicopters, MiG fighters, fixed-wing Antonovs, air-to-ground missiles, and anti-aircraft guns—the detritus of Russian imperialism.

The van passed through an obstacle course of concrete barriers, sand-filled HESCO baskets, and security checks. It takes so little to reproduce a material culture, I thought. HESCO barriers, a bit of cheap carpentry, rows of portable toilets, Armed Forces Radio, two weight rooms with Sheryl Crow CDs playing in the background, and half a dozen chow halls serving fried chicken, collard greens, and Snapple and Gatorade—and boom! You've got the United States. Or at least a particular country-slash-southern-slash-working-class version of it.

It was in Bosnia where Kellogg, Brown & Root had perfected the instant American military base, a signature item of the nation's late-industrial know-how. It featured aluminum-coated balsa-wood pallets for shower floors, guard towers made of stacked shipping containers, twenty-thousand-gallon synthetic bladders for holding oil and drinking water, and acres of plywood B-huts strangely reminiscent of the tented pavilions of the Ottoman army. Bagram even had its own time zone, Zulu time, equivalent to Greenwich Mean Time. Zulu time was used by the American military at major air bases worldwide, so that they all operated within the same time zone, helpful for the coordination of air assets.

The 250-bed American hospital at Bagram had taken just seventy-two hours to erect. It was a warren of wards, blood and urine analysis labs, and portable hard-walled facilities for X-rays, CAT scans, ultrasound, and microbiology augmentation, all of which lay encased in layers of tenting and giant plenum tubing, which produces a dust-proof environment in the middle of the desert. Manned by Wisconsin reservists, the hospital offered the finest medical care in Central Asia, as well as in much of the Middle East. While it had been set up for wounded coalition soldiers, the Milwaukee-area doctors and nurses spent most of their time treating local victims of the hundreds of thousands of Soviet mines that still littered the countryside.

Except for some of the road crews and the pervasive dust, I would not have known that I was in Afghanistan. Occasionally, I heard the faint echo of the Muslim prayer call from an adjacent village. And that was the real, unspoken, subtle cultural influence working upon the Americans: an Islamic puritanism that activated the puritanical strain within America's own cultural experience. While at Zamboanga in the Philippines troops were allowed a few beers a week and all sorts of stuff happened outside the gates, at American bases in the Muslim Near East there was "no alcohol, no fraternization, period."

But there was another factor behind Bagram's puritanical climate. In the world of the military, the bigger the base, the stricter the rules, and consequently the more uptight and dreary the atmosphere. It reflected the fear of the top brass that large numbers of troops would get out of control without iron discipline. I don't remember how many times I heard it said that being in Bagram was like being in prison. Everyone had to wear rank and salute each other, something I had never seen at Special Forces outposts—or even at the Joint Special Operations Task Force in the Philippines—where rank was nothing and function was everything.

Except for a few quaint, tin-roofed concrete piles and a shrapnel-scarred control tower, you never would have known that the Soviets had ever been here. Construction was ubiquitous: the gravel pit at the base's edge was as large as Ground Zero in lower Manhattan, and getting larger. The Americans were planning for a long stay. Now it was the Global War on Terrorism, but the border with China was close by.

The old Soviet control tower, whose basement had been used by the Taliban for interrogation and torture, constituted the true nerve center of Bagram. From this tower, a team of American Air Force personnel and private contractors directed complex nighttime symphonies of steeply ascending and descending aircraft. The C-130 cargo planes brought troops and almost all of the heavy equipment in from Germany. The CH-47 Chinooks and UH-60 Black Hawks, protected by AH-64 Apaches, helicoptered troops within Afghanistan, though most noticeable on the tarmac were the A-10 Thunderbolts, or Warthogs, which provided CAS (close air support) for ground troops in the thick of battle.

Like the B-52 bomber that has also been around forever, the A-10 is a true hall-of-fame airplane, an ancient ugly duckling with its Gatling guns and twin vertical stabilizers, that since the latter days of Vietnam often turned out to be more useful than the sexiest fighter jets. As dumpy as it looks, once in the air the A-10 is as graceful as any F-15. Because the A-10's self-sealing fuel tank allows it to absorb ground fire without exploding, its pilots can risk flying low within a contained space and thus be instantly available to troops directly underneath. It also helps that the A-10 is slow, so it doesn't disappear over the horizon just when ground troops need it. The A-10s at Bagram were further defined by the graffiti carved on their camera-guided bombs: "To Osama, kiss my ass." Or: "Bought on E-Bay for $7.99."

Without close air support and a few dozen Green Berets this entire American base complex at Bagram might not have existed.*

It was the capture of Bagram, orchestrated by one Green Beret A-team, ODA-555 ("the triple nickel"), that, more than any other single event, led to the collapse of the Taliban regime in November 2001. When ODA-555 had arrived here in late October of that year, Bagram constituted the front line of the war between the Northern Alliance and the Taliban, with the former holding the northern part of the base and the latter the southern part. It was from this control tower that ODA-555's close air support unit called in strikes that decimated thousands of Taliban troops massed to Bagram's south.

As ODA-555's success at Bagram indicated, Afghanistan had been the stage for the most dramatic use of Army Special Forces since the Vietnam War.

The American invasion of Afghanistan in October 2001, a month after the 9/11 attacks, had been greeted with a chorus of dire, historically based predictions from the media and academia about a looming catastrophe. American soldiers, it was said, would fail to defeat the rugged, unruly Afghans just as the Soviets and the nineteenth-century British had. The Afghans had never been defeated by an outsider, nor would they ever be. By mid-November, however, after only a few weeks of American bombing, the Taliban fled the Afghan capital of Kabul in disarray. To say that the Americans succeeded because of their incomparable technology would have been a narrow version of the truth. America's initial success rested on deftly combining high technology with low-tech unconventional warfare.

Afghanistan represented the first time that Army Special Forces were the centerpiece of a major American military effort since El Salvador two decades earlier. But unlike in El Salvador, where, as in Colombia and the

---

* Close air support, during Operation Enduring Freedom in the fall of 2001, involved the much more high-tech AC-130 Spectre gunships, which were converted cargo planes.

Philippines, Special Forces did not fight so much as train those who did, in Afghanistan Green Berets were unleashed to both train and assist in combat operations. Afghanistan constituted a throwback to the early days in Vietnam.

CIA operatives had been the first to arrive: in late September 2001 they were airdropped into northern Afghanistan to prepare for the insertion of Green Beret A-teams from the 5th Special Forces Group, which covers the Greater Middle East and is based out of Fort Campbell, Kentucky. The CIA operatives made contact with the Afghan Northern Alliance. Dominated by ethnic Tajiks and Uzbeks, the Northern Alliance represented the principal opposition to the Pushtun Taliban.

The Northern Alliance had recently suffered a major blow when al-Qaeda assassinated its leader, Ahmad Shah Massoud, two days before 9/11. Massoud, an ethnic Tajik and moderate Islamist, had been Afghanistan's greatest guerrilla asset against the Soviets. The Northern Alliance was essentially an outgrowth of his own military genius. With Massoud dead, it would be the job of 5th Group's A-teams to help fill the organizational gap within the Northern Alliance, as well as to give its Tajik and Uzbek commanders the tactical edge they required against the Taliban, an edge to be provided by high technology.

At the same time, 5th Group teams were preparing to infiltrate the Kandahar region of southern Afghanistan, to help the forces of moderate Pushtuns such as Hamid Karzai.

Upon their arrival in Afghanistan in mid-October 2001, the Special Forces A-teams traveled primarily on horseback, about fifteen miles a day, meeting local commanders and coordinating attacks. In coming weeks each of these small teams would be responsible for the destruction of hundreds of Taliban vehicles and thousands of enemy troops. They were true force multipliers.

The heart of this force multiplication was the three-man close air support units within each A-team, often composed of two Special Forces soldiers and an embedded specialist from the U.S. Air Force. The three operators would usually crouch behind a mound of dirt and set up their equipment: a rubberized spotting scope and a laser designator that resembled a pair of giant binoculars mounted on a tripod. The laser designator shot out a beam to pinpoint the target, so that a laser-guided bomb fired by an aircraft overhead could strike it.[10]

A typical Green Beret/Air Force team would often be surrounded by scores of Taliban troops as close as a hundred yards away in all directions. Amidst the clutter of radios, terrain maps, and mortars, in addition to the scopes and laser designators, the three men would calmly vector American pilots overhead onto the targets.[11] It was such sound-and-light performances that won the A-teams the crucial edge of respect they required from the Northern Alliance as well as from Karzai's troops.

Among the more gifted of such sound-and-light experts was ODA-574's 18 Echo, or communications specialist, Sgt. First Class Dan Petithory of Cheshire, Massachusetts. Sgt. Petithory's adroitness at close air support in southern Afghanistan helped save Hamid Karzai's life. Sgt. Petithory was killed forty-eight hours before the fall of Kandahar, in a blue-on-blue friendly-fire incident when a satellite-guided bomb was incorrectly programmed.* It is a small world that we inhabit sometimes, for Petithory was from the same area of western Massachusetts as I. His father delivered my local newspaper.

A-team members grew beards and longish hair, and wore flat woolen caps from the Hindu Kush known as *pakols.* They went as native as they needed to, in order to be credible in the local landscape. From my own experience living with Afghan mujahedin in the 1980s, it made perfect sense. Inside Afghanistan, no male was taken seriously if he had not grown a beard. Though many conventional thinkers inside the Pentagon were aghast at the news photos of American troops on horseback in native garb, unconventional warriors like Gen. Brown and retired Maj. Gen. Shachnow smiled and understood.

The push into Kabul by the Northern Alliance, assisted by 5th Group Green Berets, began November 11, 2001, and ended victoriously two days later. The territorial gains would be consolidated by the Marines and the Army's 10th Mountain Division. By giving the Green Berets an active combat role, Operation Enduring Freedom in Afghanistan had closed a circle with Vietnam.

If history could stop at that point, it would have been an American success story. But history, like the intertwining of war and politics as defined by the Prussian general Clausewitz, does not stop. By the autumn of 2003 when I arrived in Afghanistan, the Taliban had regrouped to fight a guer-

---

* Also killed in the incident were Sgt. Brian Cody Prosser of California and the team sergeant, Master Sgt. Jefferson Davis of Tennessee. Robin Moore's book *The Hunt for Bin Laden: Task Force Dagger* (New York: Random House, 2003) fills a significant gap in war coverage by detailing this and much else.

202 ROBERT D. KAPLAN

rilla struggle against the American-led international coalition—similar to the struggle that the mujahedin had waged against the Soviets. With hit-and-run attacks across a dispersed and mountainous battlefield, and a new national army that needed to be trained and equipped, Afghanistan still constituted a challenge better suited to Special Operations forces than to the conventional military.

The Joint Special Operations Task Force that functioned within the CJTF-180 was about the same size as the JSOTF at Zamboanga in the Philippines. But after I spent the first two nights at Bagram in one of the hundreds of tents housing CJTF-180's support personnel, the comparatively smaller JSOTF—which lay bureaucratically within, yet physically isolated from, the CJTF-180—felt intimate almost, especially after I had spotted familiar faces from Fort Bragg.* The food was better, as the fruit and vegetables were bought locally. "Yeah, compared to the rest of Bagram, we're living large here," one of the majors from Fort Bragg told me.

Technically, it was a C-JSOTF, a *Combined* Joint Special Operations Task Force, because of the presence of special operators from not only the U.S. but the United Arab Emirates and Lithuania, too. The Lithuanians distinguished themselves by their handy decision to bring a pregnant cat along on the deployment, which produced kittens that in turn killed the field mice in their barracks.

Though the Special Operations community constituted only about 10 percent of the CJTF-180's forces, it was responsible for half of the intelligence gathered, half the prisoners captured, and half the "bad guys" killed. This was not surprising. The bigger the military force, often the smaller the percentage of troops engaged in substantive activities. Washington, in particular, had a way of "piling on," creating an unnecessarily large footprint with high numbers of support personnel. As I would learn upon venturing deeper into Afghanistan, Bagram had just too many upper-level officers micro-managing field operations.

The Special Operations commander at Bagram was Col. Walter Herd, a stiff-mannered Kentuckian with a short crop of iron gray hair and a hard-scrabble border state accent. If the U.S. Army was stereotypical enough to

---

* The sector of Bagram where the JSOTF was located was called "Camp Vance," after Sgt. First Class Gene Arden Vance, a West Virginia National Guardsman killed in the Afghanistan-Pakistan border area in May 2002.

have had an official accent, Col. Herd's might have been it. In his tent, late one night, Col. Herd took less than five minutes to tersely summarize the situation in Afghanistan. As he began, I noticed that on his desk, waiting to be hung, was a black-and-white photo of Col. Cornelius Gardner, a hero of the Philippine War, who, as a commander in southern Luzon, put particular emphasis on civil affairs and indigenous self-government as a tool of pacification, and also blew the whistle on human rights abuses committed by U.S. troops.

"The north of Afghanistan is doing pretty well," Col. Herd told me, "which in Afghanistan means that there's not a lot of massive killing going on. In the north we can focus on political-economic activities." The north, of course, was controlled by the Northern Alliance and by Ismael Khan and Abdul Rashid Dostum, two long-standing warlords. The south and the southeast, however, which were under President Karzai's jurisdiction, Herd called "Injun Country," where Special Operations had fifteen "Fort Apaches" of various sizes: " 'Firebases,' we call them. From these firebases we try to spread peace and sunshine. The object is to seduce who we can and kill the rest. If we succeed, the political-economic stuff can follow like in the north.

"The enemy," he went on, "is the Taliban, al-Qaeda, and the HIG [Hezb-i-Islami Gulbuddin, the Party of Islam faction led by Gulbuddin Hekmatyar]. Everything we do against these ACF [anti-coalition forces] is 'by,' 'through,' and 'with' the *indigs* [indigenous forces]. So we try always to have the ANA [Afghan National Army] with us, and we try to give the ANA the credit for what we do."

The string of Special Operations firebases was mainly located in the vicinity of the Pakistani border region. Third Special Forces Group, supported by 19th Group Special Forces National Guardsmen, manned the firebases in southern Afghanistan, while those in the southeast were manned by 20th Group Guardsmen, helped by some 19th Group members and advisors from 7th Group. As I would be headed first to the southeast, I despaired that I would be mainly with National Guardsmen. Like most Americans, I was ignorant of a subculture of National Guardsmen which was tougher and more experienced than many active duty personnel.

I had a day to kill at Bagram before the helicopter flight to southeastern Afghanistan. I spent it with ODA-2027, a 20th Group National Guard A-team, currently in isolation with a thirty-man Afghan National Army contingent, preparing together for combat deployment. "You'll love these guys," Maj. Jeb Stewart, their commanding officer from northern California, told me. "They're not into the politics of active duty. All they want to do is serve their country, though they'll never talk about it."

Isolation meant that they lived in the same compound with the Afghan soldiers. They fended for themselves, as if already deployed in the field. They had built their own shower unit and bought oriental carpets to decorate their hootch. "They say the compound is haunted," one of the A-team members told me. "I hope the ghosts are naked females with big boobs."

All of ODA-2027 were self-described "guard bums," or "guard whores." In civilian life most were law enforcement officers or firemen, though Capt. Bo Webb, the team's executive officer from South Carolina, had been a real estate agent whose license had lapsed. A graduate of the Citadel, he had, nevertheless, risen through the enlisted ranks by attending Officer Candidate School at Fort Benning. He told me that the team was on a nine-month rotation, including a thirty-day ramp-up and a thirty-day demobilization at the end. Since 9/11 they had been mobilized two thirds of every year. But they had no complaints. They might have been the happiest A-team I had encountered thus far in my travels. And why not: they would be going into a war zone with sufficiently loose rules of engagement as to make A-teams in Colombia and the Philippines drool with envy.

They were mainly from northern Florida—the parts of the state known as "lower Alabama" and "lower Georgia," not to be confused with southern Florida, whose large population of Latinos and retirees from the cold Northeast made it another culture entirely. "Orlando is the DMZ [demilitarized zone] between us and them," Sgt. First Class Chris Grall, a counterdrug instructor for the Florida State Police, told me. He, Capt. Webb, and Team Sgt. Russ Freeman had all been members of ODA-2027 since 1996. "We've been together for much longer than most active duty SF teams," Grall said. Indeed, whereas the Reserve represents the generic civilian world, the National Guard constitutes *the Good Old Boys*.

They had all been in the regular Army or Special Forces prior to entering civilian life. They ranged in age from the late twenties to the mid-thirties. Quite a few were sons of Vietnam veterans. They were avid NASCAR fans. In college football they had intense loyalties, rooting for either the University of Florida Gators or the Florida State Seminoles. They often ate southern: grits and biscuits with gravy for breakfast. Several were divorced at least once. They were all self-described "A" personalities. As Grall explained: "There is a guy in the unit who actually hates NASCAR, and another who hates college football. In our own weird way, we're all individualists.

"It's a great life being a guard bum," Grall continued. "You get to see places tourists never do. We're like tourists with guns." Bosnia, Liberia, Panama, and Honduras were some of the places where 2027 had been deployed.

Kyle Harth, a particularly burly and friendly member of the team, told me this story: "I was in a bar in Naples, Florida. There was this guy even bigger than me wearing a Seminoles cap. What the heck, I thought. I told him, 'That's a pretty ugly cap you got on.' 'Gator fan, uh,' he replied. 'Yeah,' I said. Then he extends his hand and shows me his national championship ring. The guy had actually played for the Seminoles. Wow, I was impressed. But you know what, when he lies to people, I'll bet you he tells them he does what I do."

The truth about these guys was that while some had college degrees, and most had jobs to return to, they defined themselves by their membership in the National Guard and Special Forces, not by what they did in civilian life. September 11 had allowed them to come into their own, to truly define themselves, giving them a social status that they had not had before. Specifically, the War on Terrorism had provided them wider opportunities for merging their law enforcement skills with their Special Forces ones. In the 1990s they had all become fluent in Spanish, hoping to deploy to Cuba when Castro fell. That still hadn't happened. So they were constantly pulling Dari and Pushtu dictionaries out of their cargo pockets, as they instructed Afghan soldiers in the intricacies of assaulting a fort. They ate with their Afghan trainees at lunch and socialized with them at night. While the media was full of lugubrious stories about the great sacrifices being made by reservists in Iraq and Afghanistan, these guys were having the time of their lives.

Maj. Jeb Stewart had called these guys the ultimate patriots. In fact, they constituted something closely related: the great southern military tradition that had produced the gleaming officer corps of the Confederacy, without which the nation would not have been able to fight its later wars quite as well as it had. It is a tradition poignantly described in W. J. Cash's 1941 classic, *The Mind of the South*.

In that book, Cash paints a lyrical and penetrating portrait of the frontier, with its "thin distribution" of population, its raggedy backcountry, and its virtual absence of effective government that the southern plantation system—by appropriating the best land in self-contained units—essentially preserved until late into Reconstruction. For a long time, the South "remained by far the most poorly policed section of the nation," Cash writes. This unpoliced frontier bred a violent mix of romance and individualism, with its "ultimate incarnation" the Confederate soldier, who became every southern schoolboy's "hero-ideal."[12]

Sir Michael Howard writes that the frontier in the United States had produced a "war culture."* The South, according to Cash, was that war culture incarnate. It helped explain why, for example, just two states of the old Confederacy, Texas and Florida, accounted for nearly a quarter of the men and women in the American armed forces in the first years of the twenty-first century.†

ODA-2027 offered the perfect introduction for what I would encounter at the firebases in southeastern and southern Afghanistan.

With troops jammed elbow-to-elbow along the sides, divided by a high wall of mailbags and rucksacks, the CH-47 Chinook, followed by its Apache escort, lifted up off the pierced steel planking that the Soviets had left behind at Bagram. The rear hatch was left open for the M-60 7.62mm mounted gun, manned by a soldier strapped over the edge. Behind the gun, the medieval landscape of Afghanistan fell away: mud-walled castles and green terraced fields of rice, alfalfa, and cannabis on an otherwise gnarled, sandpaper vastness, pockmarked by steep canyons and volcanic slag heaps. The rusty, dried-blood hue of some of the hills indicated iron ore deposits; the drab green colors copper and brass. Because of the drone of the engine, everyone wore earplugs. Nobody talked. Soon, like everyone else, I fell asleep.

An hour later the Chinook descended steeply amid twisted cindery peaks. After it hit the ground, those of us headed for the Gardez firebase grabbed our rucksacks and ran off amid the wind and dust generated by the propellers. At the same time, another group of soldiers, waiting on the

---

* See the Prologue, p. 10.

† *The Economist,* Mar. 22, 2003, p. 28. (Also footnoted in Chapter 2, p. 56.) In fact, that statistic was inflated because tax laws encouraged many troops to declare their residence in those two states. The real truth is that many more came from other states of the Old South, and fewer from Texas and Florida.

ground, ran inside. The crew threw off the mailbags. Then two men placed a hooded figure with a number scrawled on his back and his hands tied in flex cuffs onto the helicopter. In less than five minutes, the Chinook, its engine still beating loudly, roared back up into the sky.

The handcuffed man concealed under a burlap sack was a PUC, person under control, the U.S. military term for its temporary detainees in the War on Terrorism. It had become a verb: to take someone into custody was "to PUC him." The men who had firmly placed the PUC onto the Chinook, en route to Bagram where he would be interrogated, were members of an Army Special Forces A-team at the Gardez firebase. But they didn't look like any of the Green Berets I had so far encountered in my travels. These Green Berets had thick beards and wore traditional Afghan kerchiefs (*deshmals*) around their necks and over their mouths. Covering their heads were either Afghan *pakols* or ball caps with some gas station or firearms insignia. Except for their camouflage pants, M-4s, and Berettas, there was nothing to specifically identify them with the U.S. military. They looked like the photos of the Special Forces troops on horseback inside Afghanistan two years earlier that had mesmerized the American public and horrified the old guard at the Pentagon. They were all gummed with dust like sugarcoated cookies.

I threw my rucksack in the back of one of their Toyota pickups and we drove to the firebase, a few minutes away. There was a science fiction quality to the landscape, which seemed dead of all life-forms. Near the fort were two distinctive hills that the driver referred to as "the two tits."

The Gardez firebase was a traditional yellow, mud-walled fort with the flags of the United States, the state of Texas, and the Florida Gators football team flying from the top of its ramparts. The flags were not necessarily inappropriate. Guardsmen technically are deployed by their state governors. Surrounded by barren hills on a tableland 7,600 feet above sea level, the fort looked like a cross between the Alamo and a French foreign legion outpost. Outside the walls were the familiar HESCO barriers and mountains of "tuna cans," filled with Chinese and Russian ammunition that Special Forces had captured from "the bad guys."

An armed Afghan militiaman opened the creaky gate. Inside, caked and matted with "moondust," as everyone called it, stood double rows of up-armored Humvees, armed ground mobility vehicles, and Toyota Land Cruisers: the essential elements of a new kind of "convoy" warfare, in which Special Operations was adapting more from the Mad Max tactics of the Eritrean and Chadian guerrillas of recent decades than from the cow and oxen tank armies of the passing industrial age.*

Hidden behind the vehicles and veils of swirling dust were canvas tents, a few pissers, a crude shower facility, and the perennial Special Forces standby—a weight room. Like my escorts, everyone here was either a muscular Latino or a white guy dressed like an Afghan-cum-convict-cum-soldier. Half of them smoked. Like Col. Tom Wilhelm in Mongolia, they put Tabasco sauce on everything. Back at home most owned firearms. They bore an uncanny resemblance to the freelance journalists who had covered the mujahedin war against the Soviets two decades earlier here.

"Welcome to the Hotel Gardez," said a smiling and bearded Maj. Kevin Holiday of Tampa, Florida. Maj. Holiday was the commander of this firebase and of another farther south in Zurmat. "Within these walls we have ODB-2070 and two A-teams, 2091 and 2093," he told me in rapid-fire fashion. "Next door, living with an Afghan National Army unit, is 2076. Down at Zurmat is 2074. Most of us are 20th Group guardsmen from Florida and Texas, here for nine months." There was also a tent full of active duty 7th Group guys on a ninety-day deployment—the Latinos. "We're the damn Spartans," Maj. Holiday said, smiling again, "physical warriors with college degrees."

From Firebase Gardez, Maj. Holiday's "Spartans" launched sweeps across Paktia Province, trying to snatch infiltrators from Pakistan. "All the bad guys are coming from Waziristan," said Holiday, referring to a Pakistani tribal agency. "Because of the threat from Pakistan, there is not much civil affairs stuff going on here. It's too dangerous." Officially, the Pakistani government of President Pervez Musharraf was an ally of the U.S. But Musharraf, like his predecessors, and like the British before them, had insufficient control over the unruly tribal areas. *Pakistan is the real enemy* was a phrase that I quickly got used to hearing.

"Who was the PUC they put on the Chinook when I arrived?" I asked Maj. Holiday.

"We hit a compound. It had zero-time grenades, seven RPGs, Saudi

---

* In the history of modern imperialism this was not unusual. At the turn of the twentieth century in the Sahara Desert, the French military found it necessary to shift from "sedentary infantry to mobile, camel-mounted troops." Douglas Porch, *The Conquest of the Sahara* (New York: Knopf, 1984), p. 251.

passports, and books on jihad. The PUC lived there. We've got more people to round up from that hit.

"Everything we do," he went on, repeating a phrase I had heard often already, "is 'by,' 'through,' 'with' the *indigs*. The ANA [Afghan National Army] comes along on our hits. Though the AMF [tribally based Afghan Militia Forces] are the real stand-up guys. They see themselves as our personal security element. Yeah, every time we go out on a mission we try to pick up a few hitchhikers—any Afghan who wants to be associated with what we do. Give the ANA and AMF the credit, put them forward in the eyes of the locals. We have to build up the ANA, it's the only way a real Afghan state will emerge. But it's naive to think you can simply disband the militias."

The mud-walled fort was a "battle lab" for Special Forces, explained Maj. Holiday. The model was El Salvador in the 1980s: build up a national army while at the same time employing the paramilitaries, then help the paramilitaries to merge with the new army. The process would take years, a prospect Holiday relished. Another Special Forces officer, Lt. Col. David Maxwell, who had helped design the Basilan operation in the southern Philippines, had told me: counterinsurgency always requires the three *p*'s—"presence, patience, and persistence."

Holiday, who had just turned forty, seemed the most clean-cut of the fort's inhabitants. A civil engineer with a master's degree from the University of South Florida and three small children back at home, he was chatty, grammatical, and intense. "God has put me here," he told me matter-of-factly. "I'm a Christian," meaning an evangelical. "The best kind of moral leader is one who is invisible. I believe character is more important than education. I have noticed that people who are highly educated and sophisticated do not like to take risks. But God can help someone who is highly educated to take big risks."

Holiday had served with the Army's 82nd Airborne Division before returning to civilian life and joining Special Forces as a Florida National Guardsman. His long months of National Guard duty had not pleased his private employer, so he left his job and went to work as a civil engineer for the state of Florida, where he could wear his Army uniform to work. "You see all this around you," he said, eyeing the dust, the engine grease, and mudbrick walls; "well, it's the high point of my life and of everyone else here."

Truly, looking at the American and Texas flags, the Alamo-style fort, the high-desert landscape with its limitless scale, and the Afghan-cum–Wild West regalia of the troops, they seemed to be living an American myth.

"What about the beards?" I asked.

Maj. Holiday smiled, deliberately rubbing his chin. "The other day I had a meeting at the provincial governor's office," he replied. "All these notables came in and rubbed their beards against mine, a sign of endearment and respect. I simply could not get my message across in these meetings unless I made some accommodations with the local culture and values. Afghanistan is not like other countries. It's a throwback. You've got to compromise and go a little native. Another thing," he went on, "ever since 5th Group was here in '01, Afghans have learned not to tangle with the bearded Americans. Afghanistan needs more SF, less conventional troops, but it's not that easy because SF is already overstretched in its deployments."

Holiday had a tough, lonely job. He was the middleman between the firebase and Bagram. Bagram wanted no beards, no alcohol, no porn, no pets, and very safe, well-thought-out missions. The guys here wanted to go wild and crazy, breaking all the rules just as 5th Group had done in the early days of the War on Terrorism, before the CJTF-180 was stood up; before the Big Army entered the picture, with its love of regulations and hatred of dynamic risk. A monastic existence of sorts had evolved here, with its own code of conduct.

Holiday had to sell the missions and plead understanding for the beards and ball caps with the C-JSOTF, which, in turn, was under similar pressures from the CJTF-180. On one occasion, when the guys were watching a particularly raunchy Italian porn movie during chow, Holiday came in and turned it off, saying, "That's enough of that; keep that stuff hidden, please." An angered silence ensued, but the iron major got his way. Holiday, though an evangelical Christian, was no prude. He was only being sensible. If we are going to flout the rules, he seemed to be saying, we have to at least be subtle about it.

I found a cot inside one of the tents and unraveled my sleeping bag on it, then walked around, climbed the ramparts, talked to people, and in general let myself be amazed by the sawdust landscape and the dust devils constantly kicking up in the direction of the "two tits." Chief Warrant Officer III Neville Shorter helped me get settled, finding me some extra blankets to put over the sleeping bag during the subfreezing nights. Chief

Shorter, an African-American man with a gray beard who had been a real Special Forces stud in his younger years at the dive school in Key West, had aged into a good-natured, fine-mannered gentleman. His mastering, almost mothering type of personality, which quietly directed everything from inventories to vehicle maintenance, was the essence of what James Jones meant when he idealized those who really knew how "to soldier."

I can't remember whether it was Chief Shorter or someone else who warned me that I would have to pass "the sniff test." As I had suspected, not everyone here was Special Forces. There was a sprinkling of OGAs, representatives from other governmental agencies, which usually meant the CIA, Defense Intelligence Agency, and the like. They were in a similar situation as I. To see the front line in the War on Terrorism it was necessary to stay at a Special Forces firebase. And no matter who you were, if the "boys" didn't like you, they made sure you didn't see much. Maj. Gen. Lambert at Fort Bragg, Gen. Brown at SOCOM, and a few others might have gotten me here, but ultimately it would be the team sergeants who decided what I could actually do. And that's the way it should be, I thought.

I had started growing a beard a week before my arrival here. Still, the first days were a bit rough. No, I couldn't go out on this patrol mission, it was too dangerous. No, I couldn't go out on that mission either. While waiting to see if I passed the sniff test, I met "Big Country." Big Country had a big reddish beard, and was from Louisiana. He sported an LSU ball cap. He lived next door in another mud-walled fort, which belonged to the local PRT (provincial reconstruction team), a civil affairs element stood up by the CJTF-180. Big Country was a "terp," an interpreter. He spoke passable Pushtu and gave me a tour of the nearby town of Gardez.

A scraggly dust-bleached growth of eucalyptus and poplar trees in the otherwise milk-coffee color of death heralded Gardez. Then came a massive and venerable glacis, topped by a yawning line of ramparts, where the provincial governor was headquartered, and the Taliban and Soviets before him. The ancient citadel had been, for a short time in the first centuries of the Common Era, the seat of the Kushanids, a dynasty that spread Buddhism throughout the Indus Valley into China. Later, in the early Islamic period, Gardez became a base for the Kharijites, a tribal movement opposed to the centralizing tendencies of the Umayyad caliphs in Damascus. More recently, Gardez was known as a center of the Ghilzai Pushtuns, a major branch of the Pushtuns that was well represented in the Soviet-sponsored regimes of the late 1970s and the 1980s, as well as in the resistance against them.*

By the standards of Afghanistan in 2003, Gardez was a success story: no massive violence, not even an atmosphere of tension. By any other standard Gardez was a wreck: crumbling storefronts lined by water channels where water had not run in decades, and which were now filled with garbage. (Besides a quarter-century of war, Afghanistan was in the seventh year of a drought.) The pungent smells of spices and rotting fruit, the wooden-poled pavilions, the turbans, the felt and topi caps with inlaid mirrors, the garishly painted Bedford "jingle" trucks, and the deep chocolate complexions of the inhabitants all indicated the closeness of India.

Run down by war though it was, Gardez still felt a lot safer than Arauca on the Colombian-Venezuelan border. Roman Catholicism provided Colombia with much less social cohesion than Islam provided Afghanistan.

Beautiful little dark-haired girls in flamboyant-colored fabrics waved at our vehicle. "They're *burka*-ed when they're thirteen, have breast-fed five kids by the time they're thirty. By then, they look like sixty," Big Country remarked. After the Taliban fell, the *burka,* which conceals a woman's face and the rest of her body, had been really removed only in certain areas of Kabul. The fact was that the Taliban, being tribal Pushtuns, were closer to the indigenous culture than many of the Westernized Afghans favored by the Americans. In the Philippines, T & A meant "tits and ass"; in Afghanistan, as U.S. soldiers quipped, it meant "toes and ankles," because that's all you could see.

Big Country pointed to a firetrap of a building housing a restaurant with private rooms, where he held talks with local informers. He took me to where local timber was loaded for transport to Pakistan; the Soviets had deliberately deforested large parts of Afghanistan to deny the mujahedin cover and concealment. The process was continuing, even though it had been outlawed by Karzai's government. "This is the most corrupt place in town," he said.

---

* Pro-Soviet Afghan rulers Nur Mohammed Taraki, Hafizullah Amin, and Najibullah, and anti-Soviet radical mujahedin leaders Gulbuddin Hekmatyar and Rasul Sayyaf were all Ghilzais, prompting one expert to note that in the latter part of the twentieth century power in Afghanistan had passed from the Durrani Pushtuns to the Ghilzai Pushtuns. See Ludwig W. Adamec's *Historical Dictionary of Afghanistan* (London: Scarecrow, 1997), pp. 123–24.

Returning to the firebase, Big Country pointed out a village where he had gone "for shits and giggles"—that is, to climb a mountain, inspect a minefield, and talk and drink *chai* (tea) with the *hajis,* the nickname that American military personnel had given the Afghans. I noticed that Big Country was great with the local kids, stopping the vehicle, shaking hands, talking to them at length, handing out Power Bars and other treats. He wasn't deeply read in the country's history or culture. By academic standards he was no area expert. He had simply glommed on to the language and treated people as people. Thus he was terrifically useful.

When I arrived back at the firebase, a convoy was preparing to leave on a "presence patrol" in the direction of the Pakistan border to the north. "Could I go along?" "No, too dangerous." Then: "Wait, give us a minute." Finally, a sergeant emerged from the operations center and told me to pack my gear, "Yeah, you can come along."

I threw on my body armor—a flak vest with steel rifle plates—and grabbed my helmet and day pack, in which I stuffed some MREs and a sleeping bag, in the event we didn't return by nightfall. Cpl. Dan Johnston, a counter-narcotics policeman from Lake Tahoe, Nevada, handed me a *deshmal:* "You'll need it over your mouth and nose against the dust," he said.*

Knowing what to bring and what to leave behind was always problematic, something made worse by Bagram's utter ignorance of conditions in the field. A public affairs spokesman for the CJTF-180 had told me I should "mentally prepare myself" to ruck many miles if I was to be embedded with Special Forces. But Special Forces, I learned upon arrival at Gardez, did very little rucking in Afghanistan. The desert terrain favored convoys, partly because you couldn't carry enough water in your rucksack to sustain you. I had also been told that Gardez would be warmer than Bagram; it was colder. All I could do was keep filtering my gear. I left my computer and duffel bag behind at Bagram, and split my day pack off from my backpack when I left Gardez.

Another complication was the body armor which I could not take off during patrols, so it was impossible to remove layers of clothing as the day became hotter. With little vegetation to retain the heat, the temperature in Afghanistan dropped at night like the dark side of the moon. You had a

---

* Johnston was one of a handful of 19th Group National Guardsmen at Gardez. Because 19th Group is Utah-based, its ranks are filled with westerners.

choice: you could either freeze at night and in the dawn hours, or bake during the day. I chose to freeze at night.

We were a convoy of eight vehicles. There was one Toyota Land
Cruiser filled with counterintelligence guys (the same category of Green
Beret that in the Philippines had roamed the ports and whorehouses), two
ground mobility vehicles fitted with M2 .50-caliber machine guns, and five
up-armored Humvees: Humvees with reinforced roofs and doors and
mounted guns that had the clunky look of World War II vehicles. I rode in
the Land Cruiser with the counterintelligence guys.

Everyone carried M-4s and Berettas, while some of the 7th Group advisors had shotguns. "We're a bunch of Kuchi nomads trolling for fire,"
one of the counterintelligence guys remarked, referring to the funky,
gypsy-like nomads whose tents littered the Afghanistan-Pakistan border
area. He then organized the cassette music for the trip: Latin salsa and
"Afghan road rage," or "country eastern" as they called the local tunes. We
flew two flags: an American flag on one of the up-armored Humvees and
the Confederate flag on another. "It's not a racist flag, it's a flag of regional
pride," was the explanation I got.

One Green Beret on the convoy besides Chief Shorter was black, and
he joked about the Confederate flag. He told me about a deployment he
had had in South Africa. "The Zulus could not believe that I wasn't one of
them, or that I wasn't from southern Sudan. I had a white Afrikaner translator with me, who explained to them in their tribal language where I was
actually from. The irony that I could only talk to my African brothers
through this so-called racist Afrikaner was not lost on me. Heck, the
Afrikaners are just another African tribe, though their skin happens to be
white."

Within half an hour of leaving Gardez I was matted with dust and my
day pack had turned from black to solid brown. I was fifty-one years old.
Why was I doing this? I was full of doubt my last night amid the pampered
luxury of Dubai. In Bagram, the night before flying to Gardez, I was again
doubtful. But now the past and future, and every other place on the planet
besides here, did not exist. I was living completely for the moment: the ultimate happiness. Every trip followed the same pattern.

The desert receded and we entered a string of villages with fruit or-
chards. Aspen and poplar trees lined berms, turning golden yellow in this
Afghan autumn. Girls in spectacular ruby robes smiled and waved at us.
There was an unbroken line of cannabis fields, with thick bunches of mari-

juana drying on rooftops and piled high in trucks. The guys who worked counter-narcotics in civilian life just loved it. They could not stop snapping pictures. They saw the idea of destroying these crops as sheer lunacy that would only mire the country in deeper poverty.

There were no houses as such, only immense mud-walled forts and compounds just like the firebase, each constituting a hidden maze within. We were in the territory of the Ahmadzai branch of the Pushtuns. Two or three compounds comprised a village, with only a narrow dirt alley separating one compound from another. This was the medieval architecture of paranoia and distrust, even as it provided relief from the wind and blowing dirt. The mid-twentieth-century expert on Afghanistan Louis Dupree had referred to such compounds as "mud curtains" that kept the outside world at bay, because the outside world usually came "to *extract* from, not bring anything into" these enclosed universes. They made Afghanistan an "inward-looking society."[13] The architecture made finding terrorists that much more difficult. "Bin Laden could be in one of these villages and we'd never find him," one of the guys told me, completely serious, gazing at one mud-walled compound after another.

A few hours later we reached Sayed Kurram, less than twenty miles from the border with Pakistan, where there had just been fighting between the Mangal and Totakhel Pushtuns. You could tell if a village was friendly by the behavior of the children: if they came out and waved you were welcome; if they didn't you weren't. Silent streets meant trouble. The worst sign of trouble was if a convoy stopped and the kids slowly filtered away; it might mean an explosive device was about to go off. Special Forces troops always brought along extra Power Bars for the kids on these trips and took pictures with them—anything they could think of to break down barriers.

Sayed Kurram was somewhat friendly, judging by the handful of kids hanging around us. The counterintelligence guys took the lead in talking to the local police, and exchanging some flags and uniforms with them for the sake of goodwill. Presence patrols were not only a way for the Americans to demonstrate that they were here, but also to dissuade bad behavior. The patrols often went to the remotest locations for no other reason than to show that the bearded ones (as Special Forces was known locally) could go anywhere, anytime. The call on the chief of police at Sayed Kurram had a specific reason, though: to collect a stockpile of Soviet artillery and mortars that locals were willing to hand over. Explosives, ordnance, and demolition experts who had come along with the Green Berets took possession of the weapons and would later destroy them with C-4 explosives.

There was much *chai* consumption. Intelligence was best gathered not by asking direct questions, but simply by establishing relationships. The problem was that the counterintelligence guys spoke insufficient Pushtu and had to work through interpreters, making the conversations awkward. Two years into the War on Terrorism, the linguistic situation was a scandal. Only when the other Special Forces groups and representatives from other government agencies could converse with the locals in exotic languages to the degree that 7th Group was able to do in Spanish in Latin America would authentic human intelligence emerge in sufficient amounts.

The real labor began only after dark, when the convoy returned to the firebase: The Green Berets went over every inch of the vehicles and weaponry with compressed air hoses, to get rid of the corrosive dust. It took hours, and was essential after every patrol. U.S. Army vehicles were designed for the soft soil of Central Europe, where it was thought the Soviets would one day be confronted, not for the pulverized crust of the Near Eastern deserts. Mechanical problems were legion, and the mechanics were the true kings of the firebase, especially as the rocks and gravel of this wasteland ruined the suspension systems of the up-armors.

Very late at night we gathered on Bukharan carpets to share in a feast prepared by the local tribal militia, which included lamb kebab, savory pilaf with raisins, spicy dumplings, sweet melons, pomegranates, and so forth. "This is the only pleasure we have. The generals have taken away the rest," one of the sergeants observed. "No beer, no porn, no nothing. If they knew about this meal with the militia they'd probably forbid this, too."

In fact, morale was great, as everyone knew and privately admitted, fighting as they were al-Qaeda, the HIG, and "Johnnie Taliban." Before going to bed, we stood around a potbellied stove to warm ourselves before diving under sleeping bags and blankets in the freezing desert night. "The dismal cold reminds me of deployments in Korea," somebody said. "No, it's better than Korea. We can break doors down and arrest people here," another responded.

The next morning no patrol was scheduled. I had heard that the PRT (provincial reconstruction team) in the adjacent fort was going out on a mission, so I asked Chief Shorter if he would introduce me to the PRT guys. "They don't think much of us bearded ones," the chief warned, "but let's go next door to the 10th Mountain hootch and see." Going out with the PRT was no problem. I was on the road again.

———

The provincial reconstruction teams were a new and trendy concept in the autumn of 2003. The PRTs did the very things that the media loved: civil and humanitarian affairs—nation-building, that is. The PRTs were inter-agency, combining different military units and governmental departments into a single package. They constituted a recognition that in war zones the military, rather than the civilian charities (nongovernmental organizations), was best positioned to carry out civil affairs. The PRTs, while part of the conventional Army, represented a form of unconventional warfare, for humanitarian aid, besides winning "hearts and minds," and thus breaking the link between the insurgents and the general population, was a useful cover for informal intelligence gathering. The global media was less comfortable with this aspect of the PRTs.

The PRT mission in which I took part was composed of the 407th Army Civil Affairs Battalion out of Arden Hills, Minnesota, a combat es-cort from the 10th Mountain Division, Afghan National Army troops, and interpreters. The State Department representative happened to be in Kabul that day, so the only civilian besides myself was a rugged leathery-skinned official from the U.S. Department of Agriculture, who with his bush hat reminded me of the Australian dinosaur hunter in the movie *Jurassic Park*.

We were six vehicles: two Toyota pickups and four scout trucks or Humvees, fitted with MK-19 automatic grenade launchers. The object was to drive south to a remote village in the Shah-i-Kot mountains near the Pakistan border, in order to inspect a school that was under construction. The journey was to take ninety minutes, according to the map. Maj. Dean Fremling, an Airborne Ranger from Milwaukee, was the mission com-mander. The brief he delivered was simple: "If we're ambushed, lay down suppressing fire and keep moving. We'll now have a last-minute piss break. We roll in ten."

Ten minutes later we left the HESCO barriers behind us, and Maj. Fremling began telling me about Ranger school at Fort Benning in the same vein as Col. Wilhelm in Mongolia had done: "I have never been so cold, hot, thirsty, and tired in my whole life." Dean Fremling was bald, hairless, utterly self-effacing, and forgettable looking. He was also lively, talkative, blessed with a great disposition, and full of interesting tales from

Thailand, the Arctic, the Atlas Mountains of Morocco, the Costa Rican jungles, and elsewhere on the planet, where he had either gone on a deployment or as a tourist.

Passing an encampment of Kuchi nomads, he briefed me on a PRT program of vaccinating children and animals against disease. I worried that the Americans were being too altruistic; nobody aside from the people actually helped would know about such programs, even as high-profile projects with political payoffs, like rebuilding the ring road connecting the major cities, were behind schedule.

Next we passed a rock quarry where Maj. Fremling told me he had seen a group of Afghans chipping away with only one shovel. "They said they needed new rocks. No shit, in a wasteland of rocks they needed new ones. They explained that the old rocks had too much dust on them to be mortared. So they wanted new, clean rocks. I was able to get them some extra shovels.

"Stay on the goat trail," Fremling continued, this time into the radio for the benefit of the other vehicles. "Goat shit means we're safe from mines." Then the major complained about his fair complexion and that of the rest of the team. "Most of us are of Scandinavian descent, so we can never blend in with the people of these war-torn countries. We're not like the Puerto Ricans in 7th Group, who look like Pushtuns. There are no counterinsurgencies in Scandinavia."

Fremling took out some Copenhagen chewing tobacco. The landscape got increasingly mountainous, so bare it resembled a child's sandpit. The familiar squads of dark-haired young girls in flowing robes waved at us in a village. "FFN," Fremling said, "Full facial nudity. That's all there is here. But they're not in school. The village elders give us all these excuses. The truth is that outside of the urban areas, most Afghans don't want their girls to go to school." I had heard similar reports from nonmilitary experts, too, who worried that the Americans were becoming resented by the Pushtun population for forcing their values upon it in regard to women's rights.

A stream of clear blue water appeared suddenly out of the ashen wasteland. We gasped in appreciation. Then came more mud-walled fortresses with crumbling towers. The GPS device indicated that we were still far from the school; the road that appeared on the map had been washed away in a flash flood, so we just followed the wadi. One of the pickups could not make it up a hill. As it strained and belched black smoke, the driver said,

"It ain't got enough pony, it's on its fifth radiator, poor girl." It had to be yanked up with a chain at a forty-five-degree angle by a 10th Mountain Humvee. A few hours more of blowing moondust and we arrived at Babukhel, the site of the school. It had taken five and a half hours instead of one and a half. No one was surprised.

The school was supposed to have been 50 percent completed, according to the bill submitted by the Afghan NGO contractor. The foundation appeared finished, along with a security wall, but they were not built correctly, said an expert with the team. "They mixed too much dirt with the cement. One winter and this whole thing is done for. It's not even 20 percent completed. And these are not our construction standards; we certainly don't expect that—they're theirs, the local standards."

Fremling commented, "We won't get back to the base till dark. It'll be an entire day with a convoy just to keep one contractor honest. But that's what a lot of these days are like. The road is gone, the school is far from done. People at home have no idea how difficult the conditions are here." I thought of a remark by a late-nineteenth-century British army colonel, C. E. Callwell, that small wars are "campaigns against nature."[14]

Everything was possible in Afghanistan—with years and patience. The empires that had succeeded in bringing order and a better material life to their colonies had had both of those elements. But it was unclear if the Americans did. A decade-long presence in Afghanistan was not a pessimistic scenario, but an optimistic one.

"We represent the Karzai government," one of the American soldiers said through a terp, as locals gathered around him. "We're trying to get this school built for you." Looking at the villagers with their beards and turbans, and their dead eyes and blank expressions, the fellow from the Department of Agriculture—his gnarled, tanned face caked in dust—quietly remarked: "They have loyalty to no one beyond their tribe. They are easily bent and intimidated by whoever the power happens to be at the moment. They just want to be left alone." We were nothing to them.

On the way back we took another route—never establish patterns, never use the same route twice. This route was much faster, and dustier, if that was possible—a veritable ocean of red and mustard yellow powder, broken only by heaps of black boulders.

Returning after dark I checked in on Col. Tony Hunter, a reservist from South Kansas City, Missouri, who commanded the Gardez PRT out of the

10th Mountain fort. A police officer in civilian life, he was tall, with short gray hair and a conventionally rugged appearance. He provided more background about the PRTs.

"The PRT concept was the brainchild of the CJTF-180 staff," he told me, spitting tobacco juice into a bottle in his hootch. "It was invented to extend the power of the provincial governments. President Karzai had said he wanted it started in Gardez, where there was a high Taliban population and a lot of tribal conflict close to the border with Pakistan. So in December 2002 we stood up four PRT teams.

"Basically," Col. Hunter went on, "the PRT is an Army civil affairs unit that is remoted out, and employs either the 10th Mountain or the 82nd Airborne for base security, depending upon the deployment. The PRT uses humanitarian aid money provided by DOD [the Department of Defense]. It gives us influence without the stigma of occupation. The goal is to civilianize the PRTs by embedding reps from the State Department and USAID.

"You saw the road today," he went on, continuing to spit tobacco. "You saw how bad and difficult it was. A lot of the world is like that. That's why aviation assets will be critical for the future. There will also be a huge need for desert-worthy vehicles for this kind of stuff. We're finding that Toyotas are better than Humvees, and that the commercially sold phones are better than the military-issue ones. We're learning how to adapt to this new world in a low-tech style. Sure, we lose two people a week here in combat. It's the price of doing good work."

When I left Col. Hunter it was completely dark, with no moon out yet. Taking out my red-tinted flashlight to negotiate my way back to the Special Forces fort, I noticed small groups of soldiers holding Christian services with candles under the stars. It was not a holiday—it was something they did every night. Back at the fort, I learned that I had to move tents, as mine was being readied for a team of Navy SEALs arriving the next day for a hit. I moved in with the 7th Group Puerto Ricans, who had extra blankets and a liner for my sleeping bag.

———

The next morning the Green Berets kitted up for another presence patrol, this time down a road known as "sniper alley" near the Pakistan border. One sergeant downloaded the route from a computer into his GPS device. It was so dusty that Alex, one of the 7th Group advisors from Puerto Rico, had to clean not only his M-4, but his magazine loader too. Alex's father and grandfather had fought in Vietnam and Korea, respectively. "We Puerto Ricans have done our share," he remarked good-naturedly.

The mission brief was at 9:30 a.m. "Watch the fucking ridgelines," warned Ed, a police officer from Dade County, Florida, with a gray beard, friendly eyes, and a permanent out-of-bed look. "It can get ugly quick. Decide in advance who the second driver will be if the driver is hit. Every vehicle is responsible for the one in front."

I had a seat in the up-armor driven by team Master Sgt. Henry Peraza, a jocular, dark-complexioned Cuban-American who complained in jest about "white boys" who didn't look Pushtun enough. My job was to feed ammunition to the gunner riding on top in case we were ambushed. Forget about keeping my professional distance. With this bunch, either you helped out or you didn't go along.

"Practice feeding that ammo, Bob," another one of the 7th Group advisors told me. "I will probably run out of ammo, because I'm going to let 'em know just who we are."

I noticed that there were now three American flags flying atop the fort. "What for?" I asked.

"We get more patriotic by the day," someone said.

Another soldier was cleaning his MK-19 .40-caliber auto grenade launcher on a makeshift table. "It's a labor of love," he told me. "It's like a wife or girlfriend. You put all your passion into it, then you move on to the next one and forget." It was an unwritten law, particularly among those from the National Guard, that you needed to have at least one ex-wife to qualify for membership in the Special Forces community. I recall one conversation between a colonel and a sergeant:

"Son, where is the rest of your body armor? Do you want to be killed?"

"Well, sir, according to my alimony settlements, my first ex-wife gets half my retirement income, and the second gets the other half. So I'm not sure."

I put on my body armor and stuffed my cargo pockets with earplugs, Power Bars, and small mineral water bottles. But just as we were ready to leave the compound, the mission was put on hold. A medium-value target had just been positively identified walking into a meeting with the supposedly pro-American provincial governor of Gardez, and the decision was made to PUC him. The presence patrol was canceled in favor of this operation.

Ed, the Dade County policeman, did a "drive-by," checking out the location where the snatch would occur. "The alleys are real narrow; we can't use Humvees. There are lots of kids hanging around; bring Power Bars." Instead of Humvees, two Toyota Land Cruisers were dispatched, with Master Sgt. Henry Peraza driving the lead car. Peraza wore a *shalwar kameez, pakol,* and *deshmal* with body armor underneath. On close inspection this dark-complexioned Cuban-American really didn't look Pushtun. But for a moment or two he could fool anybody, and that was all the time that was needed.

Because only two cars went on the snatch, the rest of us suddenly had nothing to do, and people zoned out in the chow hall watching a really bad science fiction movie.

The Land Cruisers returned several hours later with four PUCs. Peraza and his crew had spent most of their time waiting around, talking to street kids, after they had decided to set up a roadblock in typical state trooper style. "Did they resist?" someone asked. "No," Master Sgt. Peraza said. "Their hands shot up over their heads like jack-in-the-boxes."

The PUCs were brought to a detention facility behind the fort. They were low-priority detainees. After a few days they either had to be released or sent up to Bagram for a higher level of interrogation. In Bagram they could be held only a short period as well, before they were either sent home or on to Guantánamo Bay, Cuba. You could wake them every few hours, disorient them, but that was about it. Well-documented accounts of prisoner abuse by Americans notwithstanding, prisoners knew that in the vast majority of cases the Americans would not mistreat them nearly to the degree that the Soviets and other Afghans had. Usually, an Afghan willing to be uncomfortable for a few days could stiff the American interrogators with impunity. Everyone complained about this.

One of the detainees did talk, though. As a result of the information he had provided, we were suddenly going out on a nighttime hit of a compound just outside Gardez. There would be no time for the steak and shrimp dinner that had been prepared.

Every aspect of these hits was planned, and written up on either a 5-W form for low-risk operations, or in a con-op (concept of operation) for a higher risk attack: what vehicles would be in the convoy, what their order would be in the lineup, where exactly everyone would sit in each vehicle, the blood types and social security numbers of everyone, the communication frequencies (commo freeks) to be used, and so forth. This particular convoy would be searching for a large cache of weapons being held at the home of a sister of a Taliban subcommander who was an HVT—high-value target.

This time I was in an up-armor driven by Sgt. First Class Matt Costen of Austin, Texas. In the darkness the world was consumed by dust and the sound of rumbling engines. "Last piss break before we leave," someone shouted. I was squeezed in the back with sharp points of metal everywhere. My elbows were jammed between the armored door and the ammunition boxes. The dusty boot of the gunner riding on top dangled down into the vehicle, right in my face.

"It's okay to have diarrhea of the mouth, so long as I copy you clearly," a voice said over the multiple-band intra-team radio.

"And away we go, boys and girls," Sgt. Costen announced.

Soon we were amidst bazaar music and nighttime crowds of destitute people who were strolling under weak, flickering lights in the streets of Gardez. We turned into a gridwork of alleys separated by high mud walls. Then it happened like a play in slow motion. Green Berets fanned out of the vehicles covering their assigned fields of fire. Several men in black turbans and beards were PUCed under a high-wattage light along a wall, then made to sit in squatting positions, which they assumed stoically. A terp came out to interview them. When nothing unexpected happened, these operations had little more drama than pulling over to fix a flat tire on the road at night.

Our Humvee was assigned a blocking position. Thus, we spent two hours standing around in the cold as another team entered the compound. I noticed Sgt. Costen's ball cap, "Heritage Firearms." He explained, "It's the place I buy my guns from.

"I was in 5th Group in active duty," he told me, "then worked as a substitute teacher and as a cop in black projects. I'm very religious. I believe we're all from the same creator. After 9/11, Alex Marco—you know, the 18 Delta [medic]—called me and asked if I wanted to join him and Henry [Peraza] and a group of other guys in an A-team, in the 3rd of the 20th [3rd Battalion of the 20th Special Forces Group]. It was because of Alex and Henry that I rejoined the National Guard.

"See those PUCs," Costen went on, "they're probably innocent. Just happened to be at the wrong place at the wrong time. The real object of the mission is to treat them respectfully, so that after they are released they'll tell their families how different the Americans are from the Russians. They know we have to detain them; it's how we treat them that counts. That's what I learned working the black projects: build up rapport in the community." Sgt. Costen then looked up at the brilliant starscape, pointing out the Seven Sisters and Taurus the Bull, with the wound made by Orion the Hunter, which lay near the horizon.

The operation yielded only a few grenades, det cords, and AK-47s. But one of the PUCs would turn out to be a Taliban general who had fought against the Americans in Operation Anaconda in December 2001. The other detainees were released immediately. "The Russians would have shot them," Costen said. Having covered the war in the 1980s, I knew that he had a point.

Everyone was disappointed. "If you want big fish, we need to be over the border in Pakistan; that's where most of the bad guys are," someone repeated yet again. Back at the chow hall we devoured the steak and shrimp that the cook had kept warm, washed down by Gatorade. There was a discussion about which Gatorade flavor was better, the Cool Blue or the purple Riptide Rush. It was almost like discussing different wine vintages. The cold was so severe we could see our breaths.

One of the team sergeants announced: "All right, guys, the general and the colonel are coming down from Bagram to see us tomorrow. So hide your porn and hide your booze, and hide them well. They've got a hard-on for that stuff." That set off a series of complaints against REMFs (rear-echelon mother-fuckers: a World War II acronym, actually). "Will tomorrow be a dog-and-pony show?" I asked. "Worse," I was told, "a real ECE [equestrian-canine extravaganza]."

It wasn't that bad, actually. Col. Herd flew down the next morning with Brig. Gen. Gary Jones, who was visiting from Fort Bragg. Brig. Gen. Jones, the quintessential towering Texan, had recently assumed Maj. Gen. Geoff Lambert's old job as the commander of all Green Berets, and was himself slated for promotion to major general. Along with Col. Herd, Gen. Jones telegraphed his awareness of all the jokes and ribald complaining at his expense. It was part of the process, they both knew. National Guardsmen were particularly unintimidated by the brass, because as civilians they were even less career-oriented than active duty noncoms, who themselves cared little about their reputation except among their fellow NCOs. What made these guardsmen so valuable was that they had no motives whatsoever to be anything but brutally honest. The general and the colonel knew that, and appreciated it.

Maj. Holiday arranged a convoy to take Gen. Jones and Col. Herd two hours south by dust-wracked road to the Special Forces firebase at Zurmat. There, I asked one of the Special Forces trainers about the quality of the newly emerging Afghan National Army.

He told me, "They're better than the Hondurans I've trained. They can do their own night patrols. They hate the Paks, which is good. They really want to mix it up and fight over the border. They're disciplined; they're not thugs. They won't beat you up and steal your money. Wherever we put them, peace breaks out. The bazaar in Zurmat has doubled in size since we deployed them. The only problem is that we need more of them."

Accompanying Gen. Jones and Col. Herd was Lt. Col. Marcus Custer of Mobile, Alabama. "The area where I'm from we call the Red Neck Riviera. Now I know what you're thinking," he told me in laughter. "Yeah, I've got relatives who live in trailers, who've never been thirty miles from their home. I eat grits." In fact, Lt. Col. Custer was an ethnic Cuban who had been separated from his family because of Castro, and was adopted by southerners. "So I'm not really related to *the* Gen. Custer."

Lt. Col. Custer had shown up just as it had become clear that the SEAL mission had been canceled, so he and I moved into my old tent, where we had many late-night bull sessions. Rather than return to Bagram with Gen. Jones and Col. Herd, he had remained at Gardez in order to, as he explained, "help Maj. Holiday get approval for a mission."

Lt. Col. Custer was a 19th Group National Guardsman and a customs officer in civilian life. Like the other guardsmen, his lack of ambition made him doubly honest. "You see," he told me, "there is almost nothing that goes on at these firebases that Maj. Holiday and the other majors are not fully capable of deciding on their own. But that's not how the system works. As a lieutenant colonel, merely by being here I can add a little weight to his request."

One night while cleaning an old Lee-Enfield rifle on a Bukharan carpet, Custer provided me his theory on the problem with the War on Terrorism, as it was being currently waged in Afghanistan. Later, I checked his theory with numerous other sources on the front lines, and it panned out. It wasn't really his theory so much as everyone's—that is, when people were being honest with each other. Sadly, it was a typical American story.

I will put what he and others told me in my own words: The essence of military "transformation"—the Washington buzzword of recent years—is not new tactics or new weapons systems, but bureaucratic reorganization.

In fact, such bureaucratic reorganization was achieved in the weeks following 9/11 by the 5th Special Forces Group based out of Fort Campbell, Kentucky, whose handful of A-teams, with help from the CIA and the Air Force, conquered Afghanistan by themselves.

The relationship between 5th Group and the highest levels of Pentagon officialdom had, in those precious, historic weeks of autumn 2001, evinced the flat bureaucratic hierarchy which distinguished not only al-Qaeda but also the most innovative global corporations. It was an arrangement that the finest business schools and management consultants would have been impressed with. The captains and team sergeants of 5th Group's A-teams did not communicate to the top brass through a yawning, vertical chain of command. No, they weren't even given specific instructions. They were just told to link up with the *indigs* (in this case the Northern Alliance) and help them defeat the Taliban. And to figure the details out as they went along.

The result was the empowerment of master sergeants to call in B-52 strikes. The 5th Special Forces Group was no longer a small part of a massive defense bureaucracy. It had become a veritable corporate spin-off, commissioned to do a specific job its very own way, in the manner of a top consultant.

The upshot was that con-ops (concepts of operation) were approved orally within minutes, whereas now in Afghanistan, two years later, it took three days of paperwork, with bureaucratic layers of lieutenant colonels and other senior officers delaying operations and diluting them of risk, so when attacks on suspect compounds finally took place, they often turned up dry holes.

There was no scandal here, no one specifically to blame. It was just the way that the Big Army—that is, Big Government, that is, Washington—always did things. It was the same reason a Joint Special Operations Task Force had been stood up in Zamboanga, in the southern Philippines, when a much smaller and leaner forward operating base would have done just as well. It was standard Washington "pile on." Every part of the military wanted a piece of Afghanistan.

(Indeed, the further removed I got from Colombia, the more brilliant the Colombia model looked. In Colombia, the Green Berets were frustrated only because the rules of engagement were too restrictive. But that was a matter of high politics, not of military organization. Organizationally, the forward operating base located in the prefab cheesebox on the grounds of the U.S. Embassy in Bogotá and staffed by Lt. Col. Duke Christie's A-team represented the perfect lean and mean structure for managing an unconventional war. Of course, such a bureaucratic structure threatened the Big Army.)

Soon after 5th Group had helped the Northern Alliance take Kabul, the U.S. occupation of Afghanistan was consolidated by the 10th Mountain Division, among other branches of the conventional military. By 2002, a Combined Joint Task Force (CJTF-180) was stood up, with a Combined Joint Special Operations Task Force (C-JSOTF) built inside that. Bagram became a base of thousands of troops, many of them REMFs. The days of the innovative flat hierarchy were over. It was back to the dinosauric, vertical bureaucracy of the industrial age, the greatest single impediment to America's ability to wage a successful worldwide counterinsurgency.

As Lt. Col. Custer explained patiently to me: "It's simply tragic. We don't need Bagram. We have many more people there than we need, and they're clogging up operations. Half of Bagram should be at K2 [Karsi-Khanabad] in Uzbekistan, where people like me wouldn't be draining aviation resources needed by the firebases. CJTF-180 is located just too far forward. Bagram should be a lean FOB with a few shower units; that's it. And these firebases should be AOBs [advanced operating bases] for even smaller garrisons of special operators located even further out. That's UW [unconventional war]."

People referred to Bagram as "the self-licking ice cream cone," which existed for the sake of PT (physical training) in the morning and a PX. If you visited only Bagram, nobody in Special Forces considered that you had even been to Afghanistan.

Custer continued, articulating better what so many others told me: "Big Army just doesn't get it." He smiled, like a persevering parent dealing with the antics of a child. "It doesn't get the beards, the ball caps, the windows rolled down so that we can shake hands with the *hajis* and hand out Power Bars to the kids, as we do our patrols. Big Army has regulations against all of that. Big Army doesn't understand that before you can subvert a people you've got to love them, and love their culture.

"The National Guard units of SF are more like the original SF and OSS than the active duty units," he went on, "because the guard tolerates personal peculiarities. You can't be effective in the War on Terrorism unless you break the rules of the Big Army. Army people are systems people. They think the system is going to protect them. Green Berets don't trust the system. That's really why you see us with all these guns. We know the Kevlar helmets may not stop a 7.62mm round. As they'll tell you in 1st Group, you might as well wear a Thai Buddha around your neck. So we wear ball caps, they're more comfortable. When you see a gunner atop an up-armor, bouncing up and down in the dust, breaking his vertebrae almost, let him wear a ball cap and he's happy. His morale is high, because simply by wearing that ball cap he's convinced himself that he's fucking the system.

"Maybe in the future we'll be incorporated into a new and reformed CIA rather than into the Big Army. Any bureaucracy that is interested in results more than in regulations will be an improvement. You see, I can say these things—I'm a guardsman."

Custer explained the upcoming proposed mission, for which he was helping Maj. Holiday with the con-op. In northern Paktia, a certain *Maulvi* Jalani was making a lot of trouble for the Karzai government.* Jalani was an ally of Jalaluddin Haqqani, a former mujahedin leader associated with Saudi Wahabi extremists such as Osama bin Laden. Maj. Holiday wanted to hit Jalani's compound near Sayed Kurram, where I had gone on the presence patrol a few days earlier.

But Bagram was risk-averse. It wanted helicopters employed in the mission, to reduce the risk of casualties. However, due to bureaucratic changes a generation earlier, Special Forces no longer had its own dedicated air support at the battalion level. It now had to fight for "air" with other Special Operations elements. Since the 10th Mountain Division "owned" helicopters, a piece of the mission could, according to Custer, be farmed out to 10th Mountain in order to get them. This was how different parts of the Big Army did business with each other these days. As the saying went, *Amateurs discussed tactics, and rank amateurs discussed grand strategy, while the professionals discussed logistics.*

Another freezing night sleeping in all my clothes. In the morning I got word of a mission that ODA-2076 next door was executing with its Afghan National Army contingent. I grabbed my body armor and fell in with a crew in a ground mobility vehicle. I rode in the back with two ANA soldiers: an ethnic Tajik and an ethnic Hazara manning a PKM, a Russian

* *Maulvi* is a Pushtun honorific to denote a respected imam or religious personage.

general purpose machine gun.* This really was a national army taking shape, I thought. It was not as if the government had merely recruited local Pushtuns and called it a national army.

Outside the sand barriers, the eight-vehicle convoy halted on the road. After five minutes had passed, one of the gunners peered up at the front of the convoy and proclaimed in a bored, knowing manner: "A cluster fuck. That's what they call this in proper English. They're waiting for final approval by radio from Bagram, even though the mission was chopped last night. Too many fucking layers. Too many chiefs, not enough Indians," he said, as though stealing Lt. Col. Custer's thoughts. "Bureaucracy. Big Government," he went on. "By the time we get moving, every Afghan for miles will know we're going to hit a compound. Fuck."

Passing through Gardez we were mobbed by cheering kids—a good sign. Two years on, the Americans were still welcome in Afghanistan. "Thank you," they kept saying in heavily accented English. We drove through the grit for almost two hours, till we had passed Zurmat. Our skins were like dirty brown shrouds. Five minutes out from the compound a piss break was declared. "A leak in the moondust—the rigors of modern warfare," somebody muttered.

Two compounds were to be hit. Elements of the Afghan National Army and the 10th Mountain Division would man the roadblocks. I was impressed with the efficiency of the ANA soldiers; they moved quickly out of the backs of the vehicles and set up fields of fire in the rice fields. I jumped out of the ground mobility vehicle with Sgt. First Class Cormac Meiners of Raleigh, North Carolina, and followed him along a chain of mud walls inside one of the compounds. There was absolute silence.

It was a typical Pushtun fortress housing several families. In the courtyard lay a vegetable plot and a peach and apricot orchard. Against one wall, near the firewood, stood a bunch of cows decked out with ornamental bangles. The lower level of the rambling mudbrick house was reserved for the animals and for the food stores. The families lived on the upper level, a world of oriental carpets with pillow-lined walls and blankets piled in the corners. We passed through the empty underground storage rooms

---

* The Hazaras are a people of Mongolian origin who live in the mountains of central Afghanistan, and were converted to Shiism several hundred years ago by the Safavid rulers of Iran.

and stomped with our boots on the carpets upstairs, found nothing suspicious, and were faced with the anxious stares of the women and children in tribal robes. Sgt. Meiners told me, "This is like a bad Vietnam War movie."

"What can we do not to offend them culturally?" Sgt. First Class Steve Outlaw of Tallahassee, Florida, asked when it became clear that this place was a dry hole. After handing candies to the kids, the Green Berets cleaned their soles before walking on more carpets. The man of the house had been one of the detainees snatched earlier by Sgt. Peraza's team. "We should have hit this place several days ago," said one soldier, complaining about the delay getting the con-op approved.

Only two rifles were found: an AK-47 and a Chinese-manufactured SKS. The women protested that they needed the rifles to defend themselves. After all, there was no law here of any kind, and such rifles were quite common in Afghanistan. A discussion ensued. They were allowed to keep one rifle. The other would be turned in to the office of the provincial governor and could be reclaimed later, which I certainly did not believe. To win hearts and minds, they should have let the family keep both of the guns.

There had been more success at the other compound, though. Passports and a large quantity of arms and cash were found. A boy came over to us and said that he had seen large numbers of rocket-propelled grenades and other weapons stashed in a third compound. A GPS grid was taken of this third compound, but it couldn't be hit until a 5-W or con-op was submitted and approved. "By that time the weapons will have been moved," one Green Beret told me. "The thing that is really worth doing today we're not allowed to do."

———

Between patrols I read, did laundry, practiced shooting at the range, observed the mechanics at work on the vehicles, and listened to life stories. Not everyone was a law enforcement officer or fireman. One of the 18 Delta medics was a nurse practitioner, another a museum manager, another—as he put it—"practiced law to support my SF habit," and another had two post-graduate degrees and three ex-wives. Quite a few had drifted from one unsatisfying job to the next, and only truly found their métier after 9/11, when they started being called up for duty on an almost permanent basis.

One night, after the moon had gone and it was so black that shooting stars were everywhere, and Mars was particularly prominent in the sky, I was talking to Sgt. Dave Kellerman of Fort Lauderdale, Florida, an air marshal in civilian life. His nineteen-year-old son had recently been awarded a Bronze Star for valor in Iraq, for taking out a machine gun nest while serving with the 3rd Infantry Division. He recited the citation to me by heart almost. "I was so proud, chills still go up my spine," he said. "What more could a father ever want of a son?"

Everyone was a gun aficionado, especially Lt. Col. Custer. The morning after I spoke with Sgt. Kellerman, Lt. Col. Custer took me inside the secured room that held the confiscated firearms: a true dog's breakfast of vintage weaponry, with stacks of rusty chambers and rotting wooden stocks. There were pre–World War I British-built Lee-Enfields, French-built Mosin-Nagants issued to the czarist army, a variety of Russian medium machine guns from both world wars, and so on, all still in use in Afghanistan.

I took one of the oldest Lee-Enfields, known as the SMLE or Smelly (Short Magazine Lee-Enfield), to the range for a hands-on history lesson. What a revolution in weaponry it was! With its "cock-on closing" bolt and stripper clip innovation, this Lee-Enfield could fire almost as fast as today's semi-automatics. "It could drop a man at four hundred yards all day long," Custer said enthusiastically. Yet it was the Soviet-manufactured Kalashnikov assault rifle that truly got the lieutenant colonel going; after he had taken hold of one of the AK-47s and briefed me on every part, I realized that you might learn as much about a culture from its weaponry as you could from its literature.

As Custer demonstrated, while stripping the AK-47 down to its constituent parts, it was a rifle designed for use by fifteen-year-old illiterates whose life was valued cheaply by the designer. "Illiterates won't clean a gun, or at least not meticulously, so the parts are measured to fit loosely. That way the gun won't jam when it's filthy with grime. But it also makes the AK-47 less accurate than our M-16s and M-4s, which have tight-fitting parts and must be constantly cleaned. And because illiterate peasants aim less precisely," he continued, "the lever of the AK-47 goes from safety directly to full automatic, for spraying a field with fire. With our rifles, the lever rests on semi-automatic before it goes to full auto."

The sites on the Russian rifle could not be adjusted for greater accuracy, unlike on American rifles. The Kalashnikov had a bullet magazine that had to be gripped before it could be released, so it wouldn't be lost in the dirt, because magazines were dear in the old U.S.S.R. That made changing magazines slower, and thus further endangered the life of the soldier in combat. In the old Soviet Union, soldiers were more easily expendable than bullet magazines. By contrast, American magazines dropped onto the ground and could be lost, but it made for a faster, more fluent performance by the rifleman.

"The M-4 can hit a man at several hundred yards every time," Custer explained. "The AK-47 is more of an area weapon. We value our soldiers as individuals with precision skills; the Russians see only a mass peasant army."

Custer also observed the evolution of the bullet over the just-departed century, from the "30-odd-6" (.30-06 caliber, or 7.62mm) in the 1890s to the smaller, sleeker 5.56mm. The manufacturers had learned that smaller bullets were faster, and with just a little increase in velocity you got a disproportionate increase in force at impact. Smaller bullets were also lighter, and thus the individual soldier could carry more along with him onto the battlefield. This was Progress.

Alas, the mission with which Lt. Col. Custer was helping Maj. Holiday had been altered and stripped of its teeth by Bagram. What had begun as a hit against an important "bad guy" was transformed into just another presence patrol.

Chief Augustus, another of the warrant officers, provided the background to a crowded chow hall: The CJTF-180 informed President Karzai of the plan to hit *Maulvi* Jalani's compound. Karzai then told the CJTF-180 to wait; he wanted to try to reason with Jalani. Karzai told Jalani to start behaving or the Americans would punish him. But American intelligence indicated that Jalani, rather than heed Karzai, turned around and told the police at Sayed Kurram to get out of town, or he would kill them. Nevertheless, the CJTF-180 approved only a presence patrol to Sayed Kurram, with only twelve Green Berets. When Maj. Holiday indicated that was too small a number to have on hand in the event of an attack, the CJTF-180 said that the number of Green Berets might be increased to twenty-two, but this enlarged patrol was authorized to circle the town only, and stay far from Jalani's compound.

The route we took to Sayed Kurram was different from the one we had taken there on the previous patrol. We drove up a wadi bed into gray draperies of hills, tinged purple at the edges and bearded with scrub pine.

The whole vista, noted Cpl. Dan Johnston, reminded him of hunting trips to Wyoming. Here and there groups of Afghans would emerge from a village and smile at us.

"The Afghans are just great," one soldier said. "They're unfazed by anything, unimpressed, just themselves."

"Yeah, they love guns and love to fight. All they need are trailer parks and beer and they'll be just like us," said another.

The convoy descended from the mountains through cannabis fields and newly tilled poppy plantations. A massive mud-walled fort with Turkic-style towers loomed in the distance, with marijuana leaves drying on its ramparts. I thought of the poppy fields before the Emerald City in *The Wizard of Oz*.

We halted in the middle of the road, in front of what looked like a mine. It wasn't. But the halt led us to a local Afghan intelligence officer, who invited me, one of the counterintelligence guys, and two other Green Berets into his house for green tea, while the rest of the convoy stood guard outside. He served the tea in a carpeted room heated by a dung-fired stove, with aspen beams overhead. I stared at the dust drifting into the tea. The Green Beret from counterintelligence engaged our host in the same kind of conversation that journalists have all the time with their sources, so I felt comfortable joining in.

The journalist and the intelligence officer have different audiences to please: that of the intelligence officer is smaller, narrower in vision, more elite in knowledge, and more technical in scope. But their methods are often similar: get to know someone, get him talking, and some of the truth may dribble out—more truth than if you asked a direct question. You don't question people so much as hang out with them, and get to know them on their own terms. So the counterintelligence guy and I took turns with the man.

The man eventually told us of *Maulvi* Jalani's informal alliance with the former mujahedin leader in Paktia and Khost, Jalaluddin Haqqani, and of the opium profits that were funding the Islamic opposition to Karzai. He believed that the Taliban would not return to power. As pessimistic analyses went, that one was simplistic, he implied. More likely was the coalescing of an Iranian-brokered coalition of anti-American and anti-Karzai forces to include Haqqani, Hekmatyar, and other radical ex-mujahedin leaders, along with disaffected elements of the Northern Alliance, some remnants of the Taliban, and al-Qaeda.

The man wanted us to stay for a meal, but we politely declined, as we had hours of traveling ahead. As usual, the map was useless. The dendritic pattern of dirt roads dissolved into incomprehensibility, so that we found ourselves—in spite of the orders from Bagram—driving smack into the center of Sayed Kurram near Jalani's compound, amid the sickly sweet smells of mint and hashish.

The idea that the CJTF-180 could determine what roads we turned down, in a land where roads were virtually nonexistent, suddenly struck me as ludicrous. Twenty-first-century communications technology worked toward centralization of command, and thus toward micro-management. But the War on Terrorism would be won only by adapting the garrison tactics of the nineteenth century, in which lower-level officers in the field forged policy as they saw fit. Meanwhile, Custer and Holiday were like the ablative tiles on the bottom of the space shuttle, absorbing the bureaucratic heat for everyone. As it turned out, though we had driven right next to Jalani's compound, nobody challenged us.*

The following evening, approval came for a hit near Gardez. Rather than wait, an eleven-vehicle convoy was immediately stood up, and around 9 p.m. we were off. By now I had been on enough raids to know the drill, so after the compound was hit, I drifted away from my assigned vehicle in the dark and proceeded inside the compound itself, to see how the search was progressing. By the outer gate, I ran into Cpl. Johnston, who lent me his night optical devices for a moment.

"Look up into the sky, you won't believe it," he said.

In the Philippines, I had never thought to do that with them. It was a revelation: what you might imagine seeing through a high-powered telescope. The sky was crowded with several times more stars than before.

I returned to reality in the courtyard, where several Green Berets were searching with flashlights for two grenades that one of the occupants had

---

* Some weeks later, Special Forces finally got permission for a direct hit on Jalani's compound. Because it was part of a larger, more conventional offensive, Jalani might have been tipped off in advance and was not found at the compound. The intelligence provided to Special Forces indicated that there were no noncombatants inside, but there was a heavy machine gun which could have destroyed the U.S. helicopters taking part in the mission. Tragically, the intelligence was wrong—there was a group of children in the compound who were killed in the attack. Special Forces captured large amounts of explosives in the attack. Because of the attack, many people in the area began turning in their arms caches for destruction. Among the items recovered were five complete, functional SA-7 portable surface-to-air missiles.

just thrown at them and that hadn't gone off. "Watch where you walk," I was warned. Along the courtyard were darkened rooms, illuminated by blue Chemlites that the Green Berets had left, to indicate which rooms had already been cleared. Inside the house, I peeked into a room where two Green Berets were kneeling on a carpet, going over a pile of documents they had found with a flashlight, being careful not to wake two children who miraculously were sleeping through all this mayhem.

Upstairs, the roof gave on to another series of rooms, where I watched Lt. Col. Custer go through several strongboxes with a bolt cutter. He found soaps, candies, cheap calico cloths, and other family possessions that only to us seemed meager and without value.

As I left the compound, I noticed a counterintelligence officer interrogating one of the male inhabitants. They were both squatting against a section of mud wall illuminated by flashlights attached to the M-4s held by other Green Berets, who had formed a semicircle around the Afghan. He had a long white beard and brown hood over his *pakol*. He looked stoic, unafraid. The counterintelligence officer was asking him simple, stock questions in English: Had he seen anything suspicious? Who were his friends?

Each question elicited a long conversation between the man and the terp. It was clear that the intelligence officer was missing a lot. He didn't speak Pushtu beyond a few phrases. Finally, all he could say to the man was "If you ever have a problem, come and see me at the firebase," as if the man would feel comfortable forsaking his kinsmen and trusting this most recent band of invaders passing through his land, invaders who couldn't even communicate with him.

Here was where the American Empire, such as it was, was weakest. With all of its technology and willingness to send the most enterprising of its soldiers to the most distant parts of the world, it was woefully incompetent in linguistic skills, especially in places and in situations where it counted the most. This was another neglected part of defense "transformation" that had nothing to do with the latest weapons systems.

Early the next morning an eleven-year-old boy who had just stepped on an old Soviet land mine was brought to the front gate of the firebase in the back of a pickup. Suddenly the profanities stopped in the shower unit and in the chow hall, and everything went quiet and efficient, as several of the 18 Delta medics quickly brought the boy into the field clinic, injected him with morphine and a regimen of antibiotics, and went to work on his leg and shoulder. One of the medics did nothing but talk to the boy, telling him through a terp that he would be playing soccer the following week. Within a few minutes, about a third of the boy's body was bandaged, a space blanket was wrapped around him, and internal e-mails to Bagram had spun up a chopper to medivac him there for an operation.

The boy was lucky. His accident had happened close to an American firebase. His limbs were saved in the operation, which took place later that day. He recovered fully. "That's the gold standard," said Maj. Holiday, "what that boy tells people back in his village about how the Americans helped him."

The overwhelming reality of Afghanistan in 2003 was still the Soviet occupation, which had destroyed the tribal infrastructure, deforested the landscape, and sown it with as many as thirty million mines, all in places that the Soviets had not bothered to map.[15]

That day I heard bad news. An internal e-mail had arrived from the firebase at Khost, which lay closer to the border with Pakistan. It was where I wanted to go next. The e-mail, from one of the team sergeants at Khost, informed Lt. Col. Custer that the firebase there was not owned by Special Forces, but by OGAs (people from other government agencies), and that they would have a shit fit if I showed up. In plain English, it meant that the CIA might be using the Khost firebase as a platform for cross-border infiltration into the Pakistani tribal agency of North Waziristan, possibly the "most evil place on earth," as one U.S. military official had put it to me.

North Waziristan was where many of the HVTs (high-value targets) were thought to be hiding. It was where, by all logical standards, the Special Forces firebases really needed to be but weren't, because of the fear of offending Musharraf's regime. From the vantage point of the Gardez firebase, it seemed that the Bush administration policy toward a radical and nuclearizing Pakistan had become as feckless as the Clinton administration's policy toward Taliban-ruled Afghanistan.

The CIA platform at Khost probably, I surmised, was part of an Afghanistan-Pakistan border operation that included the "black," or secret, side of Special Forces, as well as the Army's Delta Force and the SEALs. These elite units, dedicated to the hunt for high-value targets, of whom Osama bin Laden was the foremost, were not subject to the bureaucratic dysfunction that Custer and many others complained about. They functioned much like the 5th Group A-teams in the weeks following 9/11, before the CJTF-180 was stood up. They had their own dedicated air support, and were relatively unfettered by the Pentagon's vertical, at times Soviet-style, bureaucracy.

But this did not solve the larger problem for these reasons:

- Catching high-value targets (HVTs) was dependent on catching middle-value targets (MVTs), and even low-value targets (LVTs), since the MVTs and LVTs provided intelligence on the HVTs. It was like the subway turnstile phenomenon. When New York City mayor Rudolph Giuliani was first elected, he arrested significant numbers of young men for low-level crimes such as jumping turnstiles. In many cases, they turned out to be wanted for more serious crimes, or at least could provide information on those who were. So as long as the Big Army impeded the hunt for MVTs and LVTs, the chances of catching HVTs were reduced.

- If more MVTs and LVTs were not apprehended, HVTs who were killed or captured would quickly be replaced by persons who were currently MVTs and LVTs. Indeed, it was the hunt for MVTs that was the real bread and butter of the War on Terrorism and the effort to stabilize the Afghan regime.

In any case, I was not welcome at Khost. Despondent, I hitched a ride on the back of a truck that was part of a convoy headed for Bagram. It was a bone-breaking, freezing journey in the dust, through a dizzying, almost vertical landscape of sheer rock, a crazed tangle of soft-shouldered hills that heaved upward into winglike formations of gray granite. Then we entered a wide valley of villages that might have been mistaken for archaeological ruins. The road was crowded with jingle trucks carrying vast quantities of timber off to Pakistan. We got into two accidents. In the second, a jingle truck smashed into us sideways, tearing off the iron rail on which I was leaning and sending me flying from one end of the truck to the other. Because of the body armor and helmet I was wearing, not only wasn't I hurt, I barely felt a thing.

In Bagram, it was back to Zulu time, in which noon was 7:30 a.m. and sunset was 1:30 p.m. I began casting about for another trip, which meant hanging around, listening to conversations at the C-JSOTF, until fate intervened.

I had conversations with several civil affairs officers who had just returned from Herat in western Afghanistan and Mazar-e Sharif in the north. In both places, they told me, under the tutelage of the warlords Ismael Khan of Herat and Abdul Rashid Dostum of Mazar-e Sharif, there was relative order and a lot of rebuilding going on.

"Mazar is booming. There really isn't much for the American military to do in those places," one civil affairs officer told me. I was not surprised. It was common knowledge at Bagram that the least stable parts of the country were those ruled by the democratic, internationally recognized government.

In the chow hall, I ran into Col. Herd, and told him my problem with getting to Khost. He had a better idea. He would get me hooked up with the "Third of the Third"—the 3rd Battalion of the 3rd Special Forces Group—currently manning firebases in southern Afghanistan.

The next day, I hiked over to the airfield with my backpack, body armor, and helmet, in order to catch "Flash 43," the next C-130 cargo plane flight to Kandahar.

At the C-JSOTF I had been warned about the departure procedures for the C-130 flights. "When they call your name, if you don't answer immediately, or if you've gone to the head for a minute, they'll scratch you from the flight. The Air Force NCOs [noncommissioned officers] there are bastards," an Army guy had told me. I had to appear four and a half hours before departure; sometimes the planes left early, sometimes late, so you waited six or seven hours. I was shouted at and given contradictory instructions. But so was everyone else. There was nothing to eat. It was like the departure lounge of a dysfunctional third world country. Getting on the aircraft was like being released from forced confinement. REMFs, I thought.

The C-130 is one of the most venerable, dependable aircraft in the history of military aviation. But flying in one is not comfortable. Without windows, the enormous fuselage looks and feels like the darkened hull of a bobbing ship, or the backstage area of a run-down theater, or a creepy basement. It got even darker when the palettes were slid in and the hatch door closed. The plane steeply lumbered into the air, heavily vibrating. The descent after an hour of flying was steeper still, in order to avoid possible ground fire.

The hatch opened at KAF (Kandahar Air Field). In the smoky, glazy heat lay mountains that appeared like crouching dinosaurs on an immense pie-crust plateau. From previous trips to Kandahar fifteen and thirty years ago, I recalled this awesome flatness, periodically interrupted by singular rock sculptures, rising up hundreds and thousands of feet, which defined southern Afghanistan.

Outside the plane, I was grabbed by someone from the 3rd Special Forces Group and driven to the part of the airfield that served as the 3rd Battalion's forward operating base, commanded by Lt. Col. Rand Binford of Houston.

Unlike the original 10th Special Forces Group, which grew out of the legacy of the OSS in Europe, and the 1st, 5th, and 7th groups, all of which were associated with particular parts of the world, 3rd Special Forces Group for a long time had been consigned to Africa, a nonstrategic second-rate theater for a long time in the eyes of the American military. But in recent years, 3rd Group had gotten its area of responsibility extended to the Middle East, and was lately on a roll. It was deployed to northern Iraq during Operation Iraqi Freedom, where it had linked up with the Kurds to attack elements of the Iraqi army's 5th Corps, and it had been deployed twice to Afghanistan following the departure of 5th Group in early 2002. Third Group's profile was now hard-bitten and aggressive.

Lt. Col. Binford's FOB (forward operating base) was the former airport hotel for transit passengers during the bad old Taliban days, a ratty line of arched chambers and grim rooms with fluorescent lights, and cracked and cobwebbed toilets, that seemed perfect backdrops for interrogation and worse. Nearby was a junkyard of destroyed Soviet vehicles and aircraft.

Binford, with short gray hair and an in-your-face expression, told me, in a very deliberate manner: "I'm a blessed commander. I have bust-your-ass, hard-working soldiers, and our job is to kill these fuckers: to kill, capture, destroy, and disrupt the activities of the ACM [anti-coalition militias]. You'll be with a DA [direct action] weapons company. It does smash-mouth combat, often unilaterally, without ANA or other *indigs.* You may find these guys terse, standoffish, and hard on each other. Remember that their job is combat only, and they are professionals at it. Then they come back to their loved ones, retool, retrain, and go back on deployment. I look each wife in the eye before we deploy and say, 'We've done everything we can to train your husband, in order to bring him back safely.' "

On September 11, 2001, Binford had been in the wing of the Pentagon that was destroyed by one of the hijacked jetliners. He had been all over

Africa and the Middle East. We talked about the exploits of the Eritrean guerrillas, whom we both knew well. That got us on to the fighting qualities of the Taliban.

"Guns, drugs, and thugs come out of the opium trade," Binford told me. "Between the drugs and the availability of weapons, the Taliban does not really need outside donors. The drug network sends couriers in and out through a ratline that leads right back to the Central Highlands," he said, pointing on a map to a cluster of mountains in the center of Afghanistan, just north of Kandahar, near where the firebases under his command were located.

"What's with the short hair and clean shave?" I asked, looking at him, feeling out of place because I was heavily bearded at this point in my trip.

He frowned. "You know Bagram," he replied. "They made us shave." He went on: "We're launching a mission in a few days that you'll be on. Yeah, we're going to let you go out and play. The train-ups begin after midnight. The site is called Newark. It's on the southeastern tip of the Central Highlands. A recon element has just gone out there—they were able to wear beards and indigenous garb. You'll hear the details in the briefs and train-ups. Meanwhile, Commander Sherzai of the AMF has invited us to an *iftar* reception tonight. [Ramadan had recently begun with the new moon.] Go along. Look at who's there. Don't ask questions. Just observe. You'll find it interesting."

The reception was just outside the air base at Commander Abdul Raziq Sherzai's fancy new headquarters, distinguished by a full-sized plastic palm tree decorated with Christmas lights: it looked like a prop from Disney World. Sherzai's brother had been engaged in a power struggle of sorts with President Karzai; nevertheless, the Americans had found a need for his brother's militia. The evening was a typical Middle Eastern attempt to seem Western, with awkward, uncomfortable chairs and couches, and tissues in place of napkins at the table. I noticed that beside Afghans and 3rd Group soldiers in uniform, there was a group of Americans, including a woman, all of whom were armed with rifles and guns. They dressed like Pushtuns, with beards and *shalwars;* the lady wore a traditional local dress. Some of them spoke Pushtun. They were referred to somewhat jokingly as Peace Corps workers. I asked no questions.

I had a few hours' sleep before the mission train-up.

The brief was delivered by the mission commander, Maj. Paul Helms of Bossier City, Louisiana, a graduate of Louisiana State University at Shreveport. A tall and dark-haired Air Force brat who had lived around the world, Maj. Helms had a deep, gravelly voice reminiscent of George Clooney rather than a southern accent. He would be in charge as per standard operating procedure; Lt. Col. Binford would remain at the forward operating base.

The mission, Newark, Helms explained, would be serviced by Task Force Hawk, consisting of two CH-47 Chinooks to transport us to the strike zone, and a UH-60 Black Hawk and two AH-64 Apaches to serve as "aerial blocks," and also for close air support if it was needed.

"We're looking for a phone," Maj. Helms said casually, describing the purpose of the mission: "a Thuraya cell phone that we'll dub 'moonbeam.' " Signals Intelligence had picked up a number of interesting calls on the Thuraya regarding Taliban finances and supplies. The user of the phone was a male whom Helms code-named "Nawab." Nawab, apparently, was a legitimate businessman by day and a Taliban moneyman by night.

"We do not know what he looks like. We only know what he reveals in traffic," Helms said. "He walks out into the fields to the north and south of his compound to make his calls, obviously searching for a strong signal. There is a long line of *karezes* issuing from the compound, which may contain contraband and which could take us hours to search," he added, referring to a system of wells and tunnels, originally built for water storage, that are found in Afghanistan, Iran, and western Pakistan.* "Nawab is a facilitator rather than an operator. He's not from the muscle end of the ACM [anti-Coalition militias], so he's not likely to resist. Thus, Newark is considered a CSS [combat service support] site, approved for SSE," sensitive site exploration, which meant a slow and deliberate site search as opposed to a "kinetic strike."

Because women and children had been seen in the compound, any shooting would have to be extremely discriminatory—another reason for a unilateral mission, without Afghan National Army or Afghan militia help.

The dress rehearsal in full kit took place at a mud fort. By the time we arrived everyone was so full of dust, it was as if we had been dipped in a sticky vat of flour. With six A-teams that would each split into two sections, it was like watching a complex work of art. The rehearsal began with

* The more familiar, Arabic term is *qanat*.

"unasseting"—that is, leaving the helicopters—followed by "collapsing in on the target" and the "extraction piece." There were various "button back" maneuvers in and around the compound walls. Rappelling up and down deep water wells while being pulled by an all-terrain vehicle that would come along on the Chinook was also practiced.

The 18 Echo, or commo specialist, in each unit communicated on five separate radio frequencies: the command network which linked the section leaders with Maj. Helms, two separate lines of communication for each section within each A-team, the air net to communicate with the Chinook and Black Hawk pilots, and a fire net to communicate with the Apache pilots for close air support.

The rehearsal was only the beginning of the buildup to Newark. In the afternoon came the "rock drill," when little rocks were moved along a floor to review the mission pattern. The rock drill also went over the operations schedule, a list of several pages of small print that covered each detail of the mission as it was likely to progress, with various fragments built out for everything that might conceivably go wrong. During the rock drill it was decided to bring along two females from the 10th Mountain Division to body search and interrogate "*burka* babes," if that proved necessary.

Later on in the day, there was a separate rock drill, or back-brief, just for the section leaders, and a third drill for the helicopter pilots. During the section leaders' back-brief, the chain of custody for the PUCs was rehearsed: how the PUCs would be transferred from the assault teams to the Army aviators; and how to manage "courtyard control" in the event of large numbers of women and children at the compound. At this meeting each building in the compound, of which there were aerial reconnaissance photos, was given a matrix number in case close air support was necessary. Included in the assault package was an Air Force embed, who carried over a hundred pounds of communication gear on his back, with no extra room for meals ready to eat or a sleeping bag even.

All this was for one operation, involving one MVT (middle-value target), the kind of operation that the battalion did all the time. It was no big deal. It was work.

The guys were not standoffish, as Lt. Col. Binford had warned they might be. In fact, I went through no sniff test at all. I learned later what had happened.

When the battalion found out there would be a journalist among them, there were rude complaints, *another fucking left-wing journalist.* Then an

18 Delta medic, Master Sgt. Corey Russ of Miami—whose family, he told me, were among the city's early settlers in the 1920s—used the NIPRNET to check me out online. He downloaded some of my articles and pronounced me "okay" to the others.

Thus, I became immediately privy to what by now were familiar critiques: *The brass at Bagram is sucking too many resources with their helicopter trips. We can't get enough aviation. Too many levels of decision management up there. It takes three days to get a CONOP approved; what a deterioration since autumn '01. The moment there is something larger than a FOB [forward operating base], there is failure. If only the fucking Big Army hadn't rewritten the UW [unconventional war] manual in the late 1970s. We don't need any F-22s. We need more A-10s and AC-130s. The slower the plane, the better for CAS [close air support]. And we need to send out foot patrols, because even the firebases are too big. But the conventional generals are afraid of higher body counts—they suck up to the media. The Big Army doesn't understand that force protection means force projection. They're killing us in Iraq because they see that we're scared. We need more civil affairs units down here. Just because southern Afghanistan is a war zone doesn't mean you don't build schools and dig wells at the same time that you're fighting the bad guys; that's the essence of unconventional war.*

With all this in mind, it came as no surprise to anyone that Newark was postponed for twenty-four hours, because the helicopters had been reassigned elsewhere. Then it was postponed another twenty-four hours, because Bagram was having second thoughts about the whole operation.

Meanwhile, the cycle of presence patrols, cleaning equipment with compressed air hoses, and guard duty continued unabated. The 3rd Battalion of the 3rd Special Forces Group, with its seven A-teams consisting of only about eighty troops, garrisoned at a few far-flung firebases and backed up by two B-teams, had most of southern Afghanistan to cover. Lt. Col. Binford wanted to expand the battalion's influence farther still, up to the Iranian border, by erecting firebases in Farah Province, west of Kandahar and Helmand.

I used the postponement of Newark to visit Kandahar and Firebase Gecko north of the city, which had been Mullah Omar's base of operations before 5th Group captured it two years earlier.

Kandahar looked more primitive now than it had when I first saw it, in the autumn of 1973. It was still a pungent confection of dust and wood-smoke over broken-down streets, with few buildings more than one story high. A quarter century of war had left it as much a ruin as a proper city, crowded at dusk with trishaws and rickshaws squeezing themselves between a maze of crumbled mud walls. The water channels that had run thirty years before were now dry, and filled with dirt and garbage. All the women except for young girls were hidden under lapis-blue *burkas.* Kandahar had been the Taliban stronghold. It remained the most conservative city in Afghanistan, the rebuke to Kabul's relative cosmopolitanism. It was strange, I thought, eyeing the ratty storefronts separated from each other by aspen poles, and the sidewalks crowded with foodstuffs in old cooking pots; elsewhere in the world, the cities I had seen in my youth had become mostly unrecognizable because of demographic growth, suburban sprawl, and globalization. Yet Kandahar stood still, inside a time capsule of unending conflict.

Beyond Kandahar to the north loomed a *Planet of the Apes* landscape of strangely shaped buttes and mesas, sweeping up from a bright yellow desert that appeared to have little depth, on account of the thin atmosphere and stagy plateau light. Here two A-teams and a B-team had turned Mullah Omar's rambling fortress into a warren of sand barriers and concertina wire.

Mullah Omar's fortress had been the first site objective of the War on Terrorism. At Firebase Gecko, as it was now called, I met Maj. Tony Dill of Pensacola, Florida, the base commander, yet another major with prematurely gray hair, who was at once super-articulate and physically capable—he had parachuted into a stadium during a NASCAR race in North Carolina. I didn't realize when I said goodbye to Maj. Dill inside Mullah Omar's private air-raid shelter that I would be seeing him again a few days later, under very different circumstances.

The next day I walked into the operations center for another briefing on the postponed Operation Newark. But rather than the usual personable atmosphere, everyone was sitting around silent, with long faces, listening intently to scratchy voices coming over the command net.

A presence patrol manned by ODA-371, working out of Firebase Gereshk, to the west of Kandahar in Helmand Province, had been "engaged" by anti-coalition militia, and close air support had been called in.

"Are there casualties?" a voice asked.

Silence. Static. Then: "Yes."

"How many? How bad?"

"One."

"How bad?"

A long silence. "He's seriously hurt."

The room went more silent, if that was possible. "Seriously hurt" was code language in the Special Operations community. If you were KIA (killed in action), your widow got only $200,000 and had to move out of military housing in several weeks. But if you had been "medically retired" before death, your wife got a pension and your children's schooling was paid for through college, among other benefits. It was a cruel system, the curse of Big Government, to such an extent that the law was to be changed. But that hadn't happened yet. So when someone had been critically wounded, the race was on to keep him alive, sometimes for only a few hours, until Washington issued a "control number" which began the retirement process. The nipper net for personal e-mail was immediately shut down and all satellite phone calls forbidden; no chances could be taken that anyone in the U.S. could know what happened until that control number was issued. Only then could the news get out.

The good news was that a control number was issued in time. The bad news was that Staff Sgt. Paul A. Sweeney of Lake Ariel, Pennsylvania, died a few hours later.* War, like travel, was life in compression. You expected one dramatic event, Newark, and you got another, a memorial service.

When ODA-371's dust-ridden convoy of ground mobility vehicles and up-armors arrived at the forward operating base bearing Sgt. Paulie Sweeney's flag-draped coffin, the B-team was there to greet it, and many quiet embraces ensued among grown men. At 7:30 a.m. Zulu (noon local time), everyone walked silently to the airstrip and gathered for the "ramp ceremony" that would transfer Sgt. Sweeney's remains from Mortuary Affairs to the C-130 for the trip home.

It marked the first time that I saw Green Berets actually wearing Green Berets, rather than helmets, ball caps, boonie caps, or patrol caps. Nearby was the old terminal building, where little stone monuments had been erected by President Karzai's new government to the victims of 9/11, and

---

* At the time of his death, Sweeney was promotable to sergeant first class.

to Special Forces, the British SAS, and the Canadian Light Infantry Princess Patricia's Regiment—"damn good regiment, real ass-kickers," an American sergeant told me quietly.

Ramp ceremonies were known to combine spareness and brevity with deep emotion. This was no exception. The coffin with the American flag was placed on a simple plywood dais in front of the C-130's open fuselage. The plane's engine droned throughout. Capt. Lee Nelson, the 3rd Battalion's chaplain, as well as the pastor of the First Baptist Church of Apalachicola in the Florida Panhandle, wearing a camouflage stole, told the assembled uniformed mass: "We gather together to say goodbye to our brother, fallen comrade, staff sergeant, husband, father, and American: Paul Sweeney. Paul's lord and savior, Jesus Christ, believed that nothing is greater than giving life for one's family, country, justice, and the liberation of the oppressed. Here are the words of another warrior, named David, written some three thousand years ago." In a mild southern twang, Capt. Nelson, an awkward and intense man, then recited the Twenty-third Psalm:

> *The Lord is my shepherd; I shall not want.*
> *He maketh me to lie down in green pastures; he leadeth me beside the still*
>   *waters.*
> *He restoreth my soul; he leadeth me in the paths of righteousness for his*
>   *name's sake.*
> *Yea, though I walk through the valley of the shadow of death, I will fear no*
>   *evil: for thou art with me; thy rod and thy staff they comfort me.*
> *Thou preparest a table before me in the presence of mine enemies: thou*
>   *anointest my head with oil; my cup runneth over.*
> *Surely goodness and mercy shall follow me all the days of my life: and I*
>   *will dwell in the house of the Lord forever.*

The chaplain said a few more words, linking the warriors of the Bible with those of Special Forces. Here, according to W. J. Cash, was the "essentially Hebraic" spirit of the evangelical South, which demanded

the Jehovah of the Old Testament: a God who might be seen, a God who had been seen. A passionate . . . tyrant, to be trembled before, but whose favor was the sweeter for that. A personal God, a God for the individualist, a God whose representatives were not silken priests but preachers risen from the people themselves.[16]

Preachers like Capt. Nelson, for instance. For the spirit of the United States military was fiercely evangelical, even as it was fiercely ecumenical. While meals ready to eat were provided that were both kosher and *halal,* and soldiers of all races, religions, and regions of the country were surely welcomed into the ranks, the fact was that not all races, religions, and regional types joined up in equal numbers, so it was that the martial evangelicalism of the South gave the U.S. military its true religious soul.

This was part of a logical historical pattern, for as Cash informs us, southern evangelicalism has always followed the same steady direction— back to the stern Mosaic ideal of the Massachusetts Bay Colony.[17] American power in Afghanistan and elsewhere may have had universalist motives—the advancement of women's rights, a liberal social order, and so on—but the American military, by necessity, played a significant role in that enterprise. And like all militaries, its ranks required a more aboriginal level of altruism than that of the universalist society it sought to bring about.

The moment that Capt. Nelson finished reading the Twenty-third Psalm, the sound system played the thumping, rousing song from the John Wayne movie *The Green Berets,* written by author Robin Moore and Staff Sgt. Barry Sadler in the early Vietnam days, as an honor guard bore Sweeney's coffin into the C-130's cavernous belly:*

Fighting soldiers from the sky,
Fearless men who jump and die,
Men who mean just what they say,
The brave men of the Green Beret.

Trained to live off nature's land,
Trained in combat, hand-to-hand.
Men who fight by night and day,
Courage take from the Green Beret. . . .

---

* Sgt. Sadler, an 18 Delta medic in Vietnam, also wrote a song, "Spit and Polish," making fun of REMFs who cared only about what a soldier looked like.

There was no playing of "Taps," no national anthem, only this song—one that, at the moment, only the cynical would view as corny.

"It never gets any easier, that's why they pay us the big bucks," one of the warrant officers half joked as we all walked back to the forward operating base. Then everyone got back to cleaning and repairing vehicles. The men of ODA-371 rejected a suggestion from the upper echelons for a longer memorial service the following day. They would all pay their tributes in person to Paulie's family when they got home. Meanwhile, they told me, the best tribute to their fallen comrade was to return to their firebase.

Later, at chow, I was sitting with Maj. Helms, lamenting the postponement of Newark, when an aide walked over to say that the major was wanted immediately in the forward operating base. The aide whispered something else to Helms, who then told me to quickly pack my gear.

There was heavy "green-on-green" fighting—Afghans fighting Afghans—going on in the town of Gereshk, located on the strategic ring road west of Kandahar, in Helmand Province. The fighting was moving closer to the firebase, which was held by only seven Green Berets, because the rest of ODA-371 and -375 had driven to Kandahar with Sweeney's remains for the ramp ceremony. It would take three or four hours for them to drive back, during which time the base might be overrun. Thus, two Chinooks with Special Forces troops would fly immediately to Gereshk, to secure the base.

We were stacked tightly into the back of a small truck with all our gear and driven to the airfield, where the Chinooks, which had finally been secured for Newark, were now to fly to Gereshk instead.

"Where's my gun bitch?" someone shouted, looking for the person carrying extra magazines for his squad assault rifle.

When the choppers took off, I was sweating. An hour later, prior to landing, night had descended and I had begun to freeze. Amid the darkness and the loud beating of the rotors, there was the usual frantic fiddling with straps for the web gear, rucksacks, and mounted guns. Night optical devices were adjusted. "Hot landing zone," we all thought we heard the pilot say, meaning there was gunfire.

The hatch opened and we lumbered into the ruler-flat blackness of the Helmand desert. The light of the half moon briefly caught the rotors of the Chinook as it climbed back into the sky. Actually, it was a "rock landing zone," full of small boulders. But less than two miles away we saw the tracer bullets and rocket-propelled grenade fire—and heard the explosions—of the battle currently under way in Gereshk between rival Afghan factions.

"I apologize, I shouldn't have had beans for lunch," someone shouted after we had heard different noises. "At least I'm calling my own shots." We hiked the several hundred yards to the gate of the firebase, where Maj. Helms directed different squads to fan out around a 360-degree perimeter.

I stumbled in the dark behind Helms into the operations center of the firebase, a large whitewashed room, its walls lined with plastic-covered terrain maps and leadership diagrams of the various local tribes. Laptop computers and communications gear lay cluttered on unfinished plywood desks, with camp chairs all around.

"The AMF [Afghan Militia Force] is fighting the local police in the bazaar near the center of Gereshk," an intense-looking chief warrant officer with a long black beard who was manning the comms told Maj. Helms. "The AMF commander is dead with a bullet to the head. His number two is all messed up with multiple wounds. I have no line of communications at the moment with the AMF because the AMF guy with the comms is dead. I'll give you the grid coordinates for the base in case we need CAS [close air support]. We can use the UHF [ultra-high frequency] to vector the gunships. The fighting has moved closer to here." Continuing, he said:

"Take off the fucking body armor, get comfortable; if they overrun us with all the firepower that has just arrived, they can fucking have us."

I threw my backpack, body armor, and helmet in a corner, took a Gatorade from the fridge, and walked over in the dark, using my red-tinted flashlight, to the medical shack, where two 18 Deltas were working on an Afghan covered with whip marks. He also had internal bleeding from being beaten with a rifle butt. "Fluid in the right lung," one medic mumbled, giving the man more morphine. There was blood all over the floor where discarded bandages and guns had been piled up. The room smelled strongly of peroxide. The wounded man was an Afghan Militia Forces member caught and tortured by the police who had just arrived here in the back of a pickup truck.

Soon, two other casualties arrived, one with gunshot wounds through his rectum, the other through his back. It would be a long night, as more casualties were expected to stream in from the fighting.

I decided that I would spend the night shuttling between the operations center and the medical shack rather than at the guard posts; I was not in the mood for a soliloquy from a bored and lonely soldier atop a guard tower. I wanted to understand who was really fighting whom, and why.

When I returned to the operations center, the warrant officer had left, and another intense, darkly bearded noncom, whose right arm was full of tattoos, was manning the communications. "It was the local police who ambushed and killed Paulie," he said. "This freaking firebase is in the middle of the biggest Taliban concentration in the country. Last night there was a heated exchange between the local police and our AMF buddies; the bullets started flying today." Then, he spoke into the radio:

"Corn-day, what's on the freek? I really need some more Copenhagen [chewing tobacco]."

I wasn't comprehending. My confusion increased when a third Green Beret, also with dark hair and a beard, with a studied rabbinical look, stumbled in and began talking breathlessly about an AMF commander who was linked to the radical HIG.

"How can there be HIG in the AMF?" I asked. After all, the HIG was Gulbuddin Hekmatyar, who was pro-Taliban and pro–al-Qaeda, and the Afghan Militia Forces were pro-American.

Looking at me impatiently, as though I were some idiot, he responded: "How can there be HIG in the AMF? How can there be Taliban in the fucking Karzai government we're supporting? Because there are, you know."

Like the others who had remained at the firebase, his eyes were red and dilated. They had all been up for seventy-two hours, and this was going to be another long night. Paul Sweeney's death had been part of a series of events now unfolding in this area of Helmand, a sparsely inhabited desert region where the Taliban did much of its planning, where it rested and re-supplied. Nobody had time to sit down and put the pieces together for me. It wasn't until morning that I understood what they all were talking about.

The sprawling Pushtun areas of southern and eastern Afghanistan were not, in fact, under the control of the internationally recognized government of America's ally, Hamid Karzai. In reality, Pushtun Afghanistan was like a loosely administered tribal agency. Karzai had no more control here than Pakistani president Musharraf had in Waziristan—even less, in fact. Karzai and President George Bush had both made uplifting speeches about democracy, the rule of law, and the adoption of an Afghan constitution, even as the Afghan leader had to fall back on tribal allies, who, in turn, were sometimes connected to the very Taliban regime that Bush and Karzai had deposed.

"To maintain power," one of the noncoms explained calmly to me, as though speaking to a child, "Karzai has to work with people who are not optimal, the same way we had to work with Dostum," the Uzbek warlord who had helped America topple the Taliban in 2001.

Gereshk over the past few days and hours illustrated how there were no clear lines between friends and enemies here. "Our experience with the Kurds in northern Iraq and the Pushtuns in southern Afghanistan is like night and day," explained Capt. Ed Croot of Long Valley, New Jersey. "The Kurds had a defined and organized political structure. Here such structures simply don't exist." Gereshk illustrated yet another aspect of unconventional war: the willingness—the fervor even—of the Green Berets to engage in ambiguities, which these fatigued and frustrated but keenly sentient noncoms and executive officers were doing, it turned out, magnificently.

Though the U.S. was developing an Afghan National Army to provide Karzai's government with further legitimacy, each Special Forces firebase still required an alliance with a tribal militia indigenous to the area, for the daily work of intelligence gathering, base security, and other tasks. These Afghan Militia Forces were crucial to the hunt for middle-value targets, even as the Bush administration, under pressure from both the global media and the Karzai government, wanted to phase them out.

As one noncom at the Gereshk firebase complained: "We are not allowed to give the AMF blankets, food, uniforms, ammo, guns because we are officially phasing out the AMF. What the fuck are they thinking in Washington? The AMF are the only ones protecting our firebases."

The fact that the U.S. supported Karzai did not mean that their interests always coincided. In certain places, Karzai needed to weaken the very same Afghan Militia Forces that the Green Berets needed to strengthen in order to perform their mission.

The militia forces here at Gereshk had proved particularly effective under the leadership of one *Haji* Idriss, described by a Special Forces warrant officer as "small of size, yet great of stature," to such an extent that Idriss was known locally as the *akhund,* the "wise man" in Pushtu. "Idriss's men were quite successful at scarfing up bad guys for us. They helped us PUC twenty-four Taliban. That upset people here, because the Taliban is in leadership positions throughout this area."

The regional governor, Sher Mohammed, was known to have Taliban connections. The police fell on both sides of the pro- and anti-Taliban divide—that is, if such a divide was even definable here. There were indications that the local police were involved in the ambush that killed Sgt. Sweeney. One piece of intelligence even indicated that Sweeney was killed by mistake: the police had shot at the unmarked Special Forces vehicle he was riding in, thinking it was the Afghan Militia Forces.

Signal intercepts told Special Forces that *Haji* Idriss and his Afghan militia assistant, Jan Mohammed, were picked up by the police in Gereshk and told to disarm. When they refused, Idriss was shot in the head and Mohammed was severely wounded. Interrogation of detainees indicated that the order to go after Idriss was given by the chief of police, Bader Khan, and carried out by the assistant chief of police, *Haji* Aruf. The police chief, Bader Khan, was a tribal ally of President Karzai.

To avenge Idriss's death, the pro-American Afghan Militia Forces deserted the firebase in order to attack the police inside the town of Gereshk—the fighting that we had witnessed upon our helicopter arrival. *Haji* Aruf was now calling for American intervention to save him and his police troops from the militia forces. Some of the new detainees that the Green Berets had grabbed this very night were, in fact, captured originally by the militia forces. The Americans asserted control over the detainees for the sake of the prisoners' own protection.

With the arrival of Maj. Tony Dill, whom I had met briefly at Firebase Gecko—Mullah Omar's former fortress—the discussion intensified as to what to do next.

As one of the Green Berets told me, "We have no real friends on the outside." Yet in another sense, it was agreed, the recent fighting had created opportunities. "The last thing we want to do now is to bring the various factions together for a powwow. That could blow up in our faces; these guys are not ready for peace and love."

Maj. Dill spoke:

"The governor knows that we know that he has ACM [anti-Coalition militia, or Taliban] ties. Because of what has just happened, he is in an exposed position. If we let him think the police are all to blame, he can give up the police as low-grade dog food. That's how we'll co-opt the governor. Let's meet alone with him, make him think that we think he's now on the up-and-up."

It was also agreed that the Afghan Militia Forces had to be convinced to remain inside the firebase once the fighting died down, with the promise that Special Forces would, in return, exact some retribution on the local police. New alliances would have to be built up. As in the Philippines, where the Green Berets were faced with rampant corruption on all levels of the indigenous government, no one at this firebase was unduly discouraged. Rather than the clean, black-and-white, zero-defect universe of success and failure through which the Washington and New York power elite often discussed far-flung events, here, amid the field mice and the mud-walled flatness of the Helmand desert, there was only constant trial-and-error experimentation in light of the mission at hand.

The smashmouth combat that Lt. Col. Binford had spoken of had not occurred during my visit. Instead, there had been, as Binford later admitted to me with a wry smile, something equally useful: adaptation to the tribal reality through unconventional war.

Here in this unstable borderland where high desert began its descent into plain, warfare was continuous, of low intensity, and inconclusive. U.S. Army Special Forces were facing the same sorts of challenges that the British had faced with the Afghan tribes on the Northwest Frontier of India in the latter part of the nineteenth century. From Waziristan north through Khyber and Malakand, the British used lightly armed militia and friendly tribal auxiliaries as their first line of defense—exactly as the Romans had done against the Germanic tribes—even as they built forts and improved roads to expand their influence.[18]

The British colonialists, like the Americans I had met, were eminently practical men. While they had conquered parts of this wild territory, "they did not despise it."[19] They knew from personal experience that traditional society, while not necessarily living up to their own values, was nevertheless admirable in its own peculiar way. And so they "did not pretend that their military conquests had produced anything more than the ascendancy of a particular dynasty."[20] They took men as they found them. As Sir Mortimer Durand of the Indian Army once remarked, "Half of my most intimate friends are murderers."[21]

The young Winston Churchill was reading into America's own imperial future when, in 1897, he thus described Afghanistan in *The Story of the Malakand Field Force:*

a roadless, broken and underdeveloped country; an absence of any strategic points; a well-armed enemy with great mobility and modern rifles, who adopts guerrilla tactics. The results . . . are that the troops can march anywhere, and do anything, except catch the enemy. . . . [22]

But, then, what was our alternative?

"The unpractical," Churchill replied, "may wonder why we, a people who fill some considerable place in the world, should mix in the petty intrigues of these border chieftains."[23] Some, whom Churchill calls "bad and nervous sailors," would simply cut and run, even though that would be impossible in the circumstances, whereas others call for "full steam ahead," that is, a dramatic increase in military and other resources until the frontier valleys "are as safe and civilized as Hyde Park." But, as Churchill intimates, there are usually neither the troops nor the money nor the will to do any such thing. Therefore, he concludes, the "inevitable alternative" is a system of "gradual advance, of political intrigue among the tribes, of subsidies and small expeditions."[24]

And that, too, was fraught with difficulties. Consider the eerie similarities between the current challenges and those in the Waziristan of the late 1930s and 1940s, when British troops tried and failed to capture the Faqir of Ipi, a radical cleric who, because of his narrow tribal base, appealed to pan-Islamic ideals in the struggle against colonialist occupiers. Well educated and traveled, the faqir, nevertheless, was able to charm the most primitive tribesmen with a wooly messianic message devoid of any specifics. The faqir, or holy man, whose real name was Mirza Ali Khan, hid out for many years in the network of caves that straddles the Afghan-Pakistani border, inspiring his troops with sermons on religious war. Despite aerial bombardments and the most aggressive infantry tactics, the Faqir of Ipi was never apprehended, dying a natural death in one of his cave hideouts in 1960.[25]

Given the resemblance between the Faqir of Ipi and Osama bin Laden, it was undeniable that in Afghanistan the United States had found itself in a situation for which the only comparisons were with other empires of the past.

But was the U.S. really following the British model?

To an extent, yes. Unfortunately, it was also to an extent following the Soviet model. Rather than power down to the level of small units and expand their activities, the U.S. was maintaining a vertical, multi-layered bureaucracy ruled by conventional general officers with conventional mindsets that was undermining the British-style firebases. In Col. Callwell's *Small Wars,* published in 1896, there is an emphasis on the decentralization of command, the need for mobility, and the need to stay outside the base perimeters and among the local population as much as possible.[26] The CJTF-180 at Bagram was violating all of these principles.

The Soviets had invaded Afghanistan, declared victory, and then were gradually chewed up by unconventional Afghan guerrillas called mujahedin, operating from bases inside Pakistan's tribal agencies. Likewise, the Americans had swept through Afghanistan, declared victory, and were now encountering resistance from "bad guys," whose principal sanctuaries were over the border.

In Washington, everyone droned on about military "transformation." But transformation lay in the past, ever receding, since those precious weeks after 9/11 when the unleashing of 5th Group's A-teams from the bureaucratic straitjacket of the Pentagon allowed for a situation truly up to British imperial standards, as well as to America's own nineteenth-century small wars tradition.

CHAPTER SIX

FROM THE ARMY TO THE MARINES—
FORT BRAGG AND CAMP LEJEUNE, NORTH CAROLINA

WINTER 2003–2004

"I had entered a world stripped to its bare essentials, the inhabitants of which had taken a veritable monastic vow of poverty."

Returning home from Afghanistan, I encountered more discussion in the media about the role of embedded reporters in Iraq and elsewhere: to what degree they might have been manipulated by the military; to what degree they might have lost their professional detachment and begun to identify with the troops they were covering.[1] Taking stock after a year of traveling, while I had been critical in print of how the U.S. military was fighting the Global War on Terrorism, I happily admitted guilt on the second charge.[2]

I should explain: "Every reporter is a citizen of somewhere and a believer in something," said Ernie Pyle, America's best-known World War II correspondent, who was killed during the battle of Okinawa in April 1945.[3] I was a citizen of the United States and a believer in the essential goodness of American nationalism, a nationalism without which the security armature for any emerging global system simply could not have existed. I did not doubt that at some point, perhaps as soon as a few decades, American patriotism itself might begin to become obsolete. I also had no doubt that we were not there yet.

I had served in the military: in the Israeli rather than the American. In Israel in the 1970s, finding life exclusively among Jews in a small country claustrophobic, I discovered my Americanness anew. For a quarter century thereafter, I had been covering wars and insurrections. During this time I made more friends in the American military than in the international media. At the conferences and meetings I attended in the U.S., I encountered military and national security types far more often than fellow journalists. I felt comfortable among soldiers. Stopping in Dubai en route back from Afghanistan, after two days of fine food and hot showers, I felt a bit lonely.

Most journalists had newsrooms to go back to, where they were swept back into a social and professional world that acted as a countervailing force to their reporting experiences. But I had not seen a W-2 form for thirty years. My articles had appeared in *The Atlantic Monthly* for two decades, yet I rarely visited the Boston office and lived out in the country.

I had little interest in breaking news. The last time I had filed a hard news story was back in the Cold War days of yellow telex tapes. I owned no satphone, a standard piece of equipment for embedded reporters. On most reporting trips, I went to places where my cell phone wouldn't work, so I left it behind. The firebase at Gardez had two satphones for the fifty Green Berets. Like everyone else there, I called my family once a week, and talked for a few minutes.

I was not concerned about crossing a professional boundary. My goal as a writer was simple and clear. I wanted to take a snapshot for posterity of what it was like for middle-level commissioned and noncommissioned American officers stationed at remote locations overseas at the beginning of the twenty-first century: a snapshot in words that those sergeants and warrant officers and captains and majors would judge as sufficiently accurate, so they might recognize themselves in it. It should be something, I hoped, that they could give to their grandchildren, saying, "That's sort of like it was, and like those countries were." It did not mean that I ignored tough issues and problems. It did mean that I wrote about *their* problems and frustrations, informed by *their* perspective.

I once heard the columnist George Will say that he harbored an intelligent empathy for the politicians he wrote about, because he often found them more substantial and interesting than his fellow journalists. That's how I felt about the troops. I wanted to think of myself as a traveler in the old-fashioned sense. A traveler accepts the people around him, and whatever happens to him. He never demands or complains; he merely listens and observes. I fell into frequent use of the words "we" and "our" because, although a journalist, I was also a fellow American living among the troops, taking part in most of what they did. World War II military correspondents such as Richard Tregaskis and Robert Sherrod made frequent use of those words for the same reasons.

To say that I was objective would be to deny a basic truth of writing: that to every story and situation a writer brings to bear his entire life experience and professional pressures as they exist at that moment. While a journalist may seek different points of view, he can portray and shape those different points of view from only one angle of vision: his own.

For these reasons, the objectivity of the media as a whole was problematic. The media represented a social, cultural, and regional outlook every bit as specific as the southern evangelicalism of the soldiers I knew. Journalists were global cosmopolitans. If they themselves did not own European and other foreign passports, their spouses or friends or colleagues increasingly did. Contrarily, the American troops I met saw themselves belonging to one country and one society only: that of the United States.

The Deep South was heavily represented in the military, just as the urban Northeast, with its frequent air connections to Europe, was heavily represented in the media. Whenever I did meet New Yorkers or Bostonians in the military, they were usually from the working-class boroughs and outskirts of New York City and Boston—heavily Irish and Hispanic.

In fact, the charge that embedded journalists had lost their objectivity was itself a sign of class prejudice. Even with the embed phenomenon, the media maintained a more incestuous relationship with academics, politicians, businesspeople, international diplomats, and relief charities (among other nongovernmental organizations) than it did with the military. The common denominator among all of these groups, save for the military, is that they spring from the same elevated social and economic strata of their respective societies. Even relief workers are often young people from well-off families, motivated by adventure and idealism. But the military is part of another America, an America that the media establishment was increasingly blind to, and alienated from.*

I am not talking about the poor. The media establishment has always been solicitous of the poor. I am talking about the working class and slightly above: that vast, forgotten multitude of America existing between the two coastal, cosmopolitan zones, which journalists in major media

---

* Obviously, military correspondents—a small part of the media—were an exception to this rule.

markets had fewer and fewer possibilities of engaging in a sustained, meaningful way except by embedding with the military.

The American military, especially the NCOs, who were the guardians of its culture and traditions, constituted a world of beer, cigarettes, instant coffee, and chewing tobaccos, like Copenhagen and Red Man. It was composed of people who hunted, drove pickups, employed profanities as a matter of dialect, and yet had a literal, demonstrable belief in the Almighty.

Most of all, the divide between a media establishment clustered in the Northeast and a military clustered in the South and the heartland brought regional tensions to the surface.

Journeying from my home in the Massachusetts' Berkshires, whose voting patterns put it at the extreme edge of Democratic "blue America," to Fort Bragg and Camp Lejeune, North Carolina, in the heart of Republican "red America," made me think of my experiences crossing the Berlin Wall in the 1970s and 1980s. The change in political attitudes registered in the local newspapers, in the conversations you overheard at restaurants, and in the people you met was that stark and extreme.

I had been shuttling back and forth between Massachusetts and military bases in the South for seven years now, but it was only in 2003, as casualties mounted in postwar Iraq, that the regional differences moved from the background to the foreground of my thoughts.

The southern bent toward militarism, especially in the Tidewater South, and the Greater New England bent toward pacifism were historically long-rooted tendencies, manifesting themselves in the War of 1812, the Mexican War, the Indian wars, both world wars, and the Vietnam War.* Indeed, though the South was opposed to President Franklin Roosevelt's liberalism in domestic affairs, it supported his military buildup against Nazi Germany, even as it was distinctly cool to the isolationist America First committee.[4]

---

* Greater New England means New England proper and regions of the country like the northern Midwest and parts of the Pacific Northwest that had been settled by New Englanders. See Michael Lind's *Vietnam: The Necessary War: A Reinterpretation of America's Most Disastrous Military Conflict* (New York: Free Press, 1999). Chapter 4 presents a penetrating, statistically backed exegesis on the religious, ethnic, and regional divisions over Vietnam and other American wars. For a more general but equally profound observation on the differences between the South and the North regarding military affairs, see Samuel P. Huntington's mid-twentieth-century classic *The Soldier and the State: The Theory and Politics of Civil-Military Relations* (Cambridge, MA: Harvard University Press, 1957), pp. 211–21.

Such history revealed itself in differing attitudes over the casualties in Iraq and the Bush administration's response to them. It had occurred to me in Afghanistan that Americans were actually no more casualty averse than the citizens of other nations. The working class's attitude to casualties was fairly tough, to judge by the soldiers I had met in Gardez and Kandahar. It was the elites that had a more difficult time with the deaths of soldiers and marines.[5]

Many of the people I knew at home were well-off New Yorkers who had moved out of Manhattan; the people I knew at military bases in North Carolina, Tidewater Virginia, and other parts of the South were of working-class origin, with modest military salaries. The latter group had friends and family members, many of them deployed in Iraq and Afghanistan. For them, casualties were not a symbolic issue to be discussed at seminars and dinner parties; they were intensely personal business.

While people where I lived were aghast that the White House had barred photos of the coffins of dead soldiers arriving back in the U.S.—a decision they believed reeked of callousness and political calculation—people I knew in North Carolina said they understood the White House action. They believed it saved lives.

Their logic went like this: In small, unconventional wars, especially in an age of global media and battles televised in real time, the home front was even more important than in previous conflicts. The number of American troops killed by insurgents and suicide bombers in postwar Iraq may have been strategically and tactically insignificant, but the casualties mattered politically, because the steady accumulation of KIAs demoralized the home front. Thus, the greater the impact that these deaths appeared to have on the American public, and especially on the White House, the greater the incentive of the insurgents to keep on killing them, and the more likely that the insurgents' ranks would swell. As one Green Beret in Afghanistan, a southerner, had put it to me after Sgt. Sweeney was killed: "The less emotion the President displays over our deaths, the better for us, here and in Iraq."

Or as some Marine officers simply put it: "We grieve in private."

The ghost of Vietnam hovered over this debate. The administration didn't want the public to see recurring images of flag-draped coffins, as it had in Vietnam. Many anti–Iraq war people I knew in the Northeast had not served in Vietnam. Embarrassment and guilt over that fact helped facilitate their zero tolerance toward casualties. As for those I met in the military, particularly the noncommissioned officer class, because they and their relatives had paid a considerable price in Vietnam, they were free to think pragmatically about the casualty issue—ruthlessly even. Because they were free of complexes, and were closest to the dead and wounded, I trusted their opinion the most.*

On my latest visit to Fort Bragg from Massachusetts, in mid-December 2003, I came to pay off a debt. U.S. Army Special Forces and the John F. Kennedy Special Warfare Center had opened doors for me in Colombia, the Philippines, and Afghanistan. Now I would brief their top echelons on what I thought the defects of Special Forces were, and how I thought Special Forces should evolve over the coming years.

Much of what I had to say did not represent my own ideas as much as those of the noncoms and middle-level officers whom I had met in the field. Because the Army was burdened by so many layers of bureaucracy— and travel to the field, even for the generals' own aides, involved much red tape—journalists like me were occasionally useful for communicating ideas from the bottom to the top of the command chain. My *Atlantic Monthly* colleague James Fallows once noted that the press enjoys unique protection under the Constitution because it is an indispensable part of representative democracy. As an indispensable element of the system, I believed that helping different levels of it to communicate with each other was quite appropriate, especially in wartime.

Hovering in the background of my brief was the issue of money:

Army Special Forces was *hot*. Not only had it played the lead role in taking down the Taliban, and a significant role in Operation Iraqi Freedom, but it was also involved in the capture of thirty-eight of the fifty-five most wanted Iraqis—the so-called deck of cards—including Saddam Hussein himself. Yet this state of affairs had made Special Forces only more vulnerable. It was like Apple about to be overtaken by Microsoft after having just launched the personal computer revolution. To wit, in Gen. Peter J. Schoomaker the Big Army had a truly innovative chief of staff, a man who wanted to make the Army as a whole more like Special Forces. The Marines, too, were consciously reemphasizing their own unconventional

---

* Nearly a year later, an Annenberg Public Policy Center study concluded that 51 percent of the military thought it proper to show flag-draped coffins of troops: a much lower percentage, I suspect, than civilians in New England. Also note that the Special Forces and marine infantry communities tend to be more conservative than other branches of the armed services.

roots. Thus, if Special Forces did not evolve and correct its shortcomings, and stay ahead of the regular Army and Marines, it would go the way of Apple, shortchanged in the Pentagon budget battles.

Having thus gotten the attention of my audience, I told the assembled generals, colonels, sergeant majors, and others that a world of more democracies meant a world of more restrictive rules of engagement. New democracies, besieged by aggressive and newly liberated local medias, could not politically countenance American troops running around on their soil killing people. Therefore, Special Forces had to become much better than it was at winning without firing a shot.

The culture of direct action had taken over Special Forces, and that was bad, I went on. For the real heart and soul of Special Forces was tied to the Kennedyesque vision of embracing their *indig* brothers, and winning alongside them. Special Forces had to move a few steps away from the direct action culture and back toward the culture of the combat advisor.* That meant more one-man missions in which a single Green Beret would be immersed in the local culture during all his waking hours: more Tom Wilhelms, in other words, even if Col. Wilhelm himself was a foreign area officer from the regular Army. In any case, foreign area officers and Green Berets had much in common, I said.

Moving back to the culture of combat advisor meant better linguistic skills. Yet except for the Spanish speakers in 7th Group, I had not been particularly impressed with the linguistic skills of Green Berets. The United States was more than two years into the War on Terrorism. Pushtu should have become a common language by now among Green Berets assigned to Afghanistan. But with few exceptions, even the counterintelligence officers I met barely spoke the language. The situation was no better in the Pacific; almost everyone I encountered in 1st Group knew some oriental language or other, but rarely the one needed in the country where he was currently deployed.

A number of measures had to be taken. Linguistics had to become an occupational Special Forces skill the same as weaponry, communications, medicine, and intelligence gathering. Gifted foreign language speakers had to be cultivated and tracked through the bureaucratic system. They had

---

* This idea was not exclusively mine, but originated in comments made by Gen. Geoff Lambert, former commander of all Green Berets before becoming commandant of the John F. Kennedy Special Warfare Center.

to be awarded special consideration to help them over other hurdles, the kind of practice that an impersonal and overly regulated Army was loath to do. In the Middle East and the Pacific, where numerous languages and dialects were spoken, there needed to be a mix of language expertise within every A-team, so that wherever a team was deployed, it would have at least one or two people on the team who spoke the local language. More emphasis had to be given to cultural training, something the Marines had been doing for years.

Furthermore, A-teams in the field were simply not versatile enough. Linguists, psy-ops, and civil affairs specialists needed to be integrated into counterintelligence teams, just as counterintelligence skills were needed at MEDCAPS and other humanitarian exercises. Humanitarian relief facilitated intelligence gathering, as the exercise on Basilan in the Philippines had shown. There were satisfactory ways to do this that did not undermine current laws. Policing skills—the ability to cultivate snitches, to deal with hordes of teenagers in third world villages, to set up stakeouts and road-blocks—should not be confined to National Guard units, who were over-stretched as it was. Community policing was central to the War on Terror. It had to be a major part of active duty training.

Women, I went on, who were still barred from the ranks of Special Forces, were also needed. Women attracted less notice during stakeouts and intelligence-related operations. Women could search females detained during mission hits. Women were going to be forced on SF anyway at some point. Might as well develop a plan in advance for using them.

That led to another fact of life. The world was changing, especially global demographics. The future was neither white nor black, but coffee-brown mestizo. Special Forces could not go on indefinitely as a bunch of tattooed, muscle-bound white guys, peppered with blacks and Hispanics, who all went around chewing Skoal, Red Man, and Copenhagen. It needed to aggressively recruit from Afghan, Arab, Persian, and other immigrant communities.

In sum, Special Forces needed a dramatic return to its roots, in which small American commando teams made up of Eastern European immigrants had bonded with indigenous forces behind enemy lines in Nazi- and communist-occupied Europe. It needed more people with funny accents like Gen. Sid Shachnow.

I noted that the Jedburgh tradition lived on only in 7th Group in Central and South America, with its Spanish-language skills and Hispanic soldiers. The ethos of not just 7th Group but all of SOUTHCOM, in fact, was particularly appropriate to fighting a worldwide counterinsurgency. SOUTHCOM was known to insiders as a Strategic Patience Theater—that is, SOUTHCOM saw problems like the drug trade as long-term and intractable, where victory was a matter of decades of suppression, and constant application of unconventional warfare, which included the training of *indig* armies. The fact that the media ignored Central and South America actually helped in this effort, for all too often the overall effect of the media was to foster impatience on the home front.

SOUTHCOM and the sub-Saharan African component of EUCOM were underdeployed, even as CENTCOM was overdeployed in the Middle East. I said that it made sense, therefore, to add sub-Saharan Africa to 7th Group's domain and move it away from 3rd Group, which had more than enough on its hands in Afghanistan and nearby countries. After all, Africa and South America were linked to some extent by the Portuguese language, and also by extreme underdevelopment, which led to similar tactical and operational challenges.

My thoughts were put on the agenda for a meeting in January 2004 in Cody, Wyoming, about the future of Army Special Forces. I would not be at the meeting, though. It was time to immerse myself with the Marines. The Special Forces part of my odyssey was over, for the time being.

From Fort Bragg, outside Fayetteville, to Camp Lejeune, outside Jacksonville, was only about eighty miles east through North Carolina as the crow flies. Yet it brought me out of one American military culture and into another: from the Army world of Hoo-ah to the Marine world of Ooh-rah.

Ooh-rah, like Hoo-ah, meant roughly the same thing: "Roger." "Great." "Good-to-go." "How ya doing?" "Stay motivated." The words were a standard greeting that basically meant anything you wanted it to mean except "no" and "It can't be done." And yet each greeting harked back to a different tradition, a different emotion, perhaps, that was key to differentiating the Army and Army Special Forces from the Marines.

The Marines had always been the poorest and scrappiest of the armed services. I remember a visit I had made in the early 1990s to Camp Pendleton, California, where I spent the night in austere, barracks-like quarters. When I made the mistake of telling the Marine driver that, at Fort Leavenworth, the Army had put me up in a lovely suite, he remarked coldly: "Yeah, in the Army people really live the high life."

Whatever sensory deprivation an aesthetic-minded person might experience with the Army or Special Forces, it was more so with the Marines. Whereas Fayetteville, the Green Beret home base (known as Fayette-*nam* during the Vietnam War), was a fairly funky, ratty place, measured against Jacksonville it seemed positively upscale. Jacksonville—a Marine chow hall for all intents and purposes—was a wasteland of crumbling 1970s facades and unpaved parking lots that housed strip joints, tattoo parlors, pawnshops, lock shops, judo centers, and barbershops advertising "military haircuts." Adjacent Camp Lejeune, the principal Marine base on the East Coast, was, likewise, a more blighted version of Fort Bragg. Yet I was not the only journalist for whom being with the Marines felt like a blast of invigorating cold air on an oppressively hot day.

"Good morning, Marine," Marine Capt. David Nevers of Chicago— my escort at Camp Lejeune—said to the Marine guard at the checkpoint to the command headquarters of the 24th Marine Expeditionary Unit.

"Good morning, sir," the guard shot back.

"Ooh-rah," Capt. Nevers replied.

"Ooh-rah," the guard repeated.

Such exchanges repeated themselves throughout the day at Camp Lejeune. With Special Forces, which considered itself somewhat of a bastard child of the regular Army, I had never heard Hoo-ah much. Indeed, one high-ranking Green Beret officer told me that he had joined SF "to get away from that Hoo-ah shit." At regular Army gatherings over the years, I had heard Hoo-ah used mainly as an expression of solidarity during group get-togethers. But Marines exploded in Ooh-rah during one-on-one encounters as though they had deeply internalized it.

When I asked a young female sergeant at Camp Lejeune, a pale and innocent-looking wisp of a girl from Kentucky, why she had joined the Marines, not hesitating half a second even, she barked back: "Because they're the best. And I wanted to be the best." Next to her stood a towering sergeant major, an old-timer who described himself as a "southern redneck." He told me, "You know why we're going to win eventually in Iraq? I'll tell ya. Because Marines are there. And Marines don't fail. We just don't. Because from boot camp on up, we learn and relearn our history and tradition."

Such boastful pride may conceal insecurity within. But that did not seem to be the case with the Marines, to judge by the way they handled journalists. In the Pentagon a few weeks earlier I had run into a Marine general who, after I had told him that I would be traveling with the Marines, said: "Write all about us, warts and all. We don't hide anything. We want the world to know exactly what we're like." Arranging trips with the Marines was simply a matter of telling them where I wanted to go. The Army, as I had learned years before while researching a story about Fort Leavenworth, wanted to manage every minute of your day. The Marines let you go off on your own inside the base. They weren't afraid what you might see by accident.

The United States had marines in the Continental Navy during the Revolutionary War. They were disbanded, though, and reborn as the Corps of Marines in 1798 to fight Barbary pirates in the Mediterranean, hence the line in the Marine Corps anthem, "to the shores of Tripoli." The Marines helped in the 1846–48 Mexican War ("From the halls of Montezuma"). And for three decades beginning with the Spanish-American War of 1898, the Marines staged landings in Cuba, the Philippines, Puerto Rico, Honduras, Mexico, Guam, Samoa, China, Nicaragua, and the Dominican Republic—part of the legacy of America's small wars.

From 3,000 marines in the nineteenth century, the corps had risen to only 11,000 at the time of America's entry into World War I. At the turn of the twenty-first century, with upwards of 174,000 marines, the corps was still by far the smallest and most tightly knit of the services under the Pentagon's umbrella;* it was less than half the size of the Navy and of the Air Force, and slightly more than a third that of the Army. In perhaps the most insightful words written about the Marines, *Washington Post* military correspondent Thomas E. Ricks observes:

> The Air Force has its planes, the Navy its ships, the Army its obsessively written and obeyed "doctrine" that dictates how to act. Culture— that is, the values and assumptions that shape its members—is all the Marines have. It is what holds them together. . . . formalistic, insular, elitist, with a deep anchor in their own history and mythology. . . . Alone among the U.S. military services, the Marines have bestowed their name on their enlisted ranks. The Army has Army officers and soldiers, the Navy has naval officers and sailors, the Air Force has Air Force officers and airmen—but the Marines have officers and Marines. "Every Marine a rifleman," states one key Corps motto. It means that the essence of the organization resides with the lowest of the low, the peon in the trenches.[6]

---

* The Coast Guard fell under the newly created Department of Homeland Security.

In fact, the Marines had fewer officers per enlistee than any of the other services, even as they had twice the percentage of the lowest-ranking troops.[7] More than two thirds of all marines were young enlistees in their first four-year tour. And partly because reenlistment was selective, the corps was kept deliberately young, hungry, and dynamic. It went with the mission: Whereas the Army won wars, the Marines won battles. The Marines were the ones who broke down doors; "the tip of the spear," they called themselves.

Because embassy evacuations and humanitarian relief involved quick insertions and a get-it-done-fast approach, the Marines did those things, too, in southeastern Turkey, northern Iraq, Somalia, Haiti, Sierra Leone, East Timor, Bosnia, Kosovo, Liberia, and Afghanistan.

The Marines were a flattened hierarchy in the manner of the most innovative global corporations, with responsibility pushed out to the farthest edge of the battlefield. *Every marine a rifleman* was the literal truth. Whether a Marine aviator, auto mechanic, or cook, every marine was familiar with infantry skills, and had to keep practicing them. It was a system that suited the guerrilla-style conflicts of the twenty-first century, where battle lines had dissolved and a support unit could easily find itself fighting for its life, as happened during Operation Iraqi Freedom.

The Marines did not quite have the educational opportunities that the Army had, with its vast network of schools and war colleges. The Marines did not have a West Point. Marine sergeant majors did not have a sergeant majors' academy like the Army's at El Paso, Texas. The Marines made do with OJT (on-the-job training). Marine OJT taught everyone the job "one up," so that he could fill the shoes of his immediate superior.

While in Special Forces, a master sergeant was the effective leader of an A-team of twelve men; in the Marines, a lower-ranking staff sergeant led a platoon of thirty-nine men divided into three squads of thirteen, each led by a corporal. They were in turn divided into fire teams of three or four men led by a lance corporal. Most of these noncoms were in their early twenties.

Because the Marines were young, they offered sheer aggression—a not inconsiderable tool in war. Special Forces, on the other hand, with its older and more experienced noncoms, offered deliberation and maturity. Thus, Green Berets may have been better prepared for the nuances of peacekeeping, occupation, and the training of indigenous forces. Still, the Marines had organizational advantages. As I had learned in Afghanistan, Special Forces teams had air support in theory only; they had to fight and bargain for helicopters that were, in fact, owned by the regular Army and joint task forces. But the Marines had, as they put it, "organic" air—helicopters specifically assigned to each unit, giving these young Marine commanders real autonomy and bureaucratic power.

As in innovative businesses, tremendous personal responsibility at the lowest reaches of command was combined with the complete sublimation of the individual within the organizational cult. If you remained an individual, by definition you could not be a marine.[8]

The Army Green Berets with their beards, ball caps, and Afghan dress were individualists; the Marines, with their extreme, "high and tight" crew cuts and digital camouflage uniforms, were standard-issue company men. And yet they both shared something vital, something which deeply attracted me: the history and tradition of Special Forces and the Marines were in counterinsurgency and unconventional war. Special Forces and the Marines, each in its own way, epitomized military transformation. Both these branches of the military combined nineteenth-century techniques with twenty-first-century technology. Because the lessons of conventional industrial age warfare of the twentieth century did not apply to the War on Terrorism, real military transformation would come about only when the Big Army and the Big Navy became more like Special Forces and the Marines, rather than the other way around.

Max Boot writes that like Special Forces, the Marines "focused on people, not weapons systems." Like Special Forces, the Marines saw themselves less as tank drivers or fighter pilots than as warriors. "Although caricatured in certain books and movies as homicidal Neanderthals," Boot goes on, "the Marines were the most intellectually supple of the services."[9] For example, along with Special Forces, the Marines began practicing crowd control and urban warfare long before the urbanization of the planet became a cliché among policy elites.

The greatest intellectual contribution of the United States Marine Corps has been its *Small Wars Manual,* a summary of lessons learned in the many landings, raiding expeditions, occupations, and nation-building exercises in which it took part in the late nineteenth and early twentieth centuries, in the Caribbean, Central America, and the Pacific. Published in 1940 with a restricted distribution, because of its growing relevance the *Small Wars Manual* was declassified in 1972, republished in the 1980s, and updated at the turn of the twenty-first century.[10]

Echoing Clausewitz, the Marine *Small Wars Manual* observes that in small wars neither military operations nor diplomacy ever stops, and the battle plan "must be adapted to the character [that is, the culture] of the people encountered." Small wars "are conceived in uncertainty, are conducted often with precarious responsibility and doubtful authority, under indeterminate orders lacking specific instructions."

As if foreseeing the situation in Iraq, the *Manual* notes that after major fighting,

> hostile forces will withdraw into the more remote parts of the country, or will be dispersed into numerous small groups which continue to oppose the occupation. Even though the recognized leaders may capitulate, subordinate commanders often refuse to abide by the terms of the capitulation. Escaping to the hinterland, they assemble heterogeneous armed groups of patriotic soldiers, malcontents, notorious outlaws . . . and by means of guerrilla warfare, continue to harass and oppose the intervening force in its attempt to restore peace and good order throughout the country as a whole.

To countervail such hostile forces, numerous presence patrols must be organized with the help of native militias, and outposts erected that are "dispersed over a wide area, in order to afford the maximum protection to the peaceful inhabitants" of the country.[11]

Written decades before the War on Terrorism, with experience from even earlier decades, the Marines' *Small Wars Manual* showed the U.S. how to fight unconventionally in both Iraq and Afghanistan.

The Marines were still thinking ahead. They now defined their mission as "Expeditionary Maneuver Warfare, " instead of "Amphibious Warfare." As Capt. Nevers explained, "In the future, because of technology, we won't need to storm ashore like at Iwo Jima, or the way the Army did at Normandy. The sea will be the Navy's giant maneuver space. We won't have to telegraph our location; we will be able to operate from beyond the three-mile territorial limit."

At the moment, military base rights required negotiation with foreign countries, but new planes like the V-22 Osprey might help obviate the need for that; in the Marines' plan, technology would trump diplomacy in specific instances. The Osprey, scheduled to replace the Marines' CH-46 Sea Knight helicopter, could take off vertically like a helicopter from the smallest clearing, in mud or sand—no runway or military base would be necessary; then it could fly like a plane and be refueled in the air.

The Marines, like Special Forces, understood that virtue resided in practicality. Marines were articulate in a very nuts-and-bolts way. In the mid-1990s, at Camp Lejeune, I had listened to a typical "down and dirty" from an instructor talking to a group of Marines about to be deployed to the southern Balkans:

> *You have a meeting, say, at 9:30 a.m. with the local mayor. He'll show up at ten, if he feels like it. His office will be a shambles. You'll want to get his cooperation to do something. But he'll be more interested in what you can do for him. Don't think of it as a meeting with a set time frame. Don't start discussing American policy aims in the former Yugoslavia. You'll get much further bullshitting with him about professional basketball. People in that part of the world love basketball. Ask to see pictures of his family. Always bring pictures of your own family to these meetings. If he offers you a slivovitz, don't give him bullshit about how it's against regulations to drink. Drink with him. He'll have to feel you out, to feel comfortable with you, before he'll want to help you. You may not leave his office till eleven, and you might not have come to an agreement; you may have to meet his family, play with his kids, and drink with him a few more times for that to happen. You will only get the policy done by relating to him as an individual, on his level. And that is what Americans do best.*

Irony, subtlety, and diplomacy were in short supply at Camp Lejeune. "With marines you will always know where you stand. If we have a problem with you, you'll know it," a marine informed me. I had entered a world stripped to its bare essentials, the inhabitants of which had taken a veritable monastic vow of poverty. "In our recruitment drives we don't advertise material or educational benefits like the other services do," Capt. Nevers said. "We just challenge people to be marines."

In the deserts of the Horn of Africa I would meet my first marines in the field. As with Army Special Forces, I planned to get to know the Marines in stages, one deployment at a time.

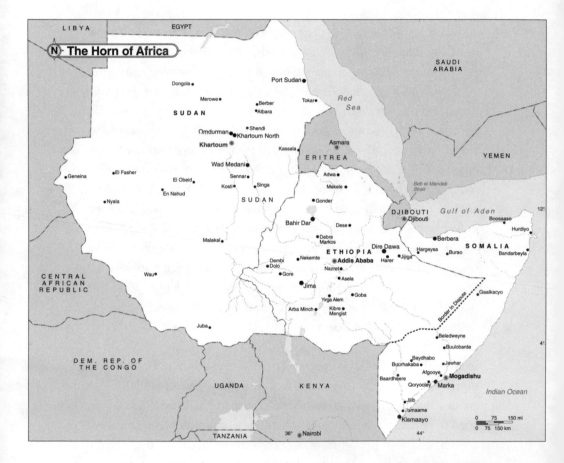

CHAPTER SEVEN

CENTCOM

HORN OF AFRICA, WINTER 2004

WITH NOTES ON EAST AFRICA

" 'Who needs meetings in Washington. . . . Guys in the field will figure out what to do. I took ten guys through eastern Ethiopia. Everywhere people wanted an American presence.' A new paradigm was emerging for the military, one that borrowed more from the French and Indian War and the Lewis and Clark expedition than from the major conflicts of the twentieth century."

jibouti looked like the pictures sent back from space by the Mars Rover: rocky, rust-red desert with brown and gray welts—a place where the planet's ability to support life seemed particularly tenuous. From the air, the villages resembled refuse heaps. But little Djibouti, the size of El Salvador, constituted strategic real estate in the Global War on Terrorism. Only minutes by fighter jet across the Bab el Mandeb Strait from Yemen, it was also close to al-Qaeda pockets in Sudan, Somalia, and Kenya. Terrorists lived off ungovernable areas, and there were plenty of those close to Djibouti. In the early twenty-first century, an American base in Djibouti was as advantageous as one in Central Europe during the Cold War.

Djibouti had been part of the first great Ethiopian empire, that of the Roman-era kingdom of Axum. It shared a border not only with Ethiopia, but with Eritrea and Somalia, too. The ethnic Afars of Djibouti's north were related to the Ethiopians and Eritreans, while Djibouti's Issa community in the south was related to the Somalis. Djibouti existed courtesy of nineteenth-century French imperialism. With the building of the Suez Canal, European powers had scrambled for ports along the Red Sea and the Gulf of Aden. The French got a foothold in the far north of the Somali

coast, which became known as French Somaliland, then as the French Territory of the Afars and the Issas, and finally as the Republic of Djibouti
when independence came in 1977. But the French hadn't left; with three
thousand French troops and foreign legionnaires, Djibouti was the largest
French overseas outpost, rating a billet for a French one-star general. Only
in recent years had French administrators left their posts inside local government ministries.

Had the French not established themselves in Djibouti in the middle of
the nineteenth century, it is unlikely that the British would have backed
Italian ambitions on the coast farther north, in order to counter the French,
in which case modern Eritrea, a creation mainly of Italian colonialism,
probably never would have come into being. Because European divisions
did not always configure with ethnic ones, in recent decades Djibouti had
been wracked by ethnic tensions and civil war, between the Ethiopian- and
Eritrean-related Afars and the dominant, Somali-related Issas.

Those ethnic divides had an obsessive Middle Eastern quality to them,
for the Horn of Africa constituted a loose and wondrous fragment of the
Middle East, whose alkaline volcanic deserts were separated from those of
Arabia by only a narrow band of water.[1] The line of Ethiopian emperors
that ended with Haile Selassie claimed descent from the Hebrew King
Solomon and the Yemeni Queen of Sheba. Here nightmarish grand guig-
nols of conquest and regime-induced starvation were punctuated by a
chilling precision common to the Middle East, but rare in the rest of
Africa. The region's Semitic and Hamitic languages traced their origins in
written form to biblical antiquity. The technical and organizational abili-
ties of the inhabitants were unsurpassed on the African continent. Take the
Amhara of Ethiopia, whom Donald N. Levine in his classic study, *Wax and
Gold,* notes are "not much given to aesthetic concerns. They are practical-
minded peasants, austere religionists, and spirited warriors."[2] Indeed, warfare on the Horn in the final quarter of the twentieth century featured
masterfully orchestrated, set-piece battles with tanks, fighter jets, and helicopter gunships that bore closer relation to the Arab-Israeli wars of 1967
and 1973, and to the Iran-Iraq War of the 1980s, than to any other fighting
in sub-Saharan Africa.

In the mid-1980s, when I first began reporting from the Horn, a famine
of biblical proportions engulfed the region. The media ascribed it exclusively to drought. But the famine was substantially the result of ethnic and

class conflict. In the 1980s, the nineteenth-century empire of the Ethiopian Amharas was finally cracking up, and the regime in the Ethiopian capital of Addis Ababa, fortified by Marxist ideology, was using famine as a means to pressure the rebellious Tigreans and Eritreans into submission. The ethnic divisions never healed. Fighting, which abated in 1991—after which Eritrea officially became independent—resumed from 1998 until 2000, causing tens of thousands of more deaths. Unable to export its goods through Eritrean ports, Ethiopia was dependent on Djibouti for an outlet to the sea. That further boosted Djibouti's strategic importance, and provided it with its first economic windfall.

The second windfall came in 2002 when, with French connivance, the United States stood up the Combined Joint Task Force—Horn of Africa (CJTF-HOA) in Djibouti. At first, it was located offshore on the U.S.S. *Mt. Whitney*. Then the Americans moved onshore to the old French foreign legion outpost of Camp Lemonier. Despite their public spat over Iraq, it had been decided at the highest levels of government in both Washington and Paris that the United States and France needed to cooperate on something real, not merely symbolic, in the War on Terrorism, in order to stabilize their bilateral relationship.

Djibouti and the whole exotic world of the Horn soon evaporated, though; within an hour after my plane had landed, I was ensconced in a crowded tent at Camp Lemonier with ten Marine corporals, lance corporals, and privates first class. For many days they would be my only reality before I ventured beyond the base. The CJTF-HOA was a Marine show to the same degree that the CJTF-180 in Afghanistan had been a Big Army one.

The oldest of the marines in my tent was less than half my age. It was a challenge. The differences between groups of men in their early twenties and those in their mid-thirties are vast. The latter are more settled down, often with growing children and divorces behind them, while the former cannot exist for long without loud soul, hip-hop, and salsa, and constant use of the *f* word. But in the barracks no one remains a stranger. After a day or so, the young marines stopped calling me "sir" and started addressing me by my first name. This was about the time that I had been bitten up by chiggers like everybody else.

Our tent was lost amid many at Camp Lemonier. I might have been back at Bagram, with the same HESCO barriers, sandbags, concertina wire, shower units, gravel pathways, chow hall, and guard towers built of stacked shipping containers—all constructed at breakneck speed by Kellogg, Brown & Root (KBR). KBR was as much a part of the American military empire and the War on Terrorism as any of the armed services. Indeed, KBR's employees tended to be former military, and were known to take considerable risks when the occasion demanded. The architecture, the town planning, and the entire physical ambience of America's overseas outposts at the turn of the twenty-first century were basically an invention of KBR. The average soldier never really saw Afghanistan or Djibouti. His world was the KBR instant city: "Just add water and watch it grow," as the saying on base went.

Camp Lemonier was distinguished from Bagram in that it was much smaller, with 1,400 inhabitants as opposed to Bagram's 5,000. The air here, rather than dry, thin, and cold as at Bagram, was sticky, humid, and hot. Unlike Bagram, nobody used Zulu time. Zulu time was a requirement of the U.S. Air Force, whose time zone reference had to be the same worldwide. But in the Horn of Africa there was much less need for close air support than in Afghanistan.

My "rack" mates belonged to the 2nd squad of the 2nd Platoon of India Company, which, in turn, was part of the 3rd Battalion of the 2nd Regiment of the Second Marine Expeditionary Force (II MEF), out of Camp Lejeune.* India Company, which had seen action in Kosovo in 1999 and during Operation Iraqi Freedom (OIF) in 2003, was in Djibouti as a component of Security Task Force Betio, a reference to the islet in the Tarawa atoll that the Marines had captured from the Japanese in 1943. India Company was responsible for security inside and around the perimeter of Camp Lemonier.

"It all seems complicated but it's really very easy," Staff Sgt. Chad Dickinson of Ilion, New York, explained to me. "In the Marines, we subscribe to KISS—Keep It Simple, Stupid. That's why everything in the Marines is done in threes: three regiments to a division, three battalions to a regiment, three companies to a battalion, three platoons to a company, three squads to a platoon, three fire teams to a squad, and three men to a fire team.† But the most important thing that you have to remember is that our company and our platoon are the best there is in the Marine Corps."

---

* "Rack" is the naval term for bunk. The Marines, being part of the fleet, use Navy lingo.
† This was a useful simplification. For example, while a company had three "line" platoons, there was often a fourth "weapons" platoon. Moreover, fire teams had four men almost as often as three.

Staff Sgt. Dickinson was the 2nd Platoon's leader. His high-and-tight buzz cut revealed fiery red hair. His eyes never seemed to blink. His gaze made me think of a crushing handshake, something that first acquired meaning when I watched him berate the marine in the rack beside mine for a minor infraction. "Don't try me, son, because you'll be sorry," he growled.

"Marines are extremists," Staff Sgt. Dickinson told me. "When I am at home with my wife and it is my turn to clean the bathroom, I clean with straight bleach. The Marines take people who are mean and troublesome, and transform them into people who are just plain intense." When I asked him to call me by my first name, he replied, "If I called you by anything other than 'sir' and my father found out, he'd whoop my ass."

It was "Staff Sgt. Dickinson" to everyone, never simply "Sgt. Dickinson." The Marines never abbreviated rank, as they did in the Army. The rule against abbreviating rank helped uphold distinctions that related to real qualitative differences in responsibility. Staff Sgt. Dickinson was in his late twenties, but the authority that he possessed over the twenty-nine marines in my tent and the two next door made him seem much older.*

Like so many guys I had met in Special Forces and now in the Marines, the older generations of Staff Sgt. Dickinson's family included Vietnam veterans. Staff Sgt. Dickinson's brother was in the Army, and his father-in-law had been a marine. When the economy in upstate New York offered little hope of a job for him, dropping out of college and heading south to enlist in the Marines seemed the natural thing to do. But marines, as I learned the first night in the barracks, were not southern to the degree of Special Forces. They were simply generic working class from all regions of the country.

Much more than Special Forces, marines were tight-lipped and uncommunicative, until it came to their jobs. Then they couldn't stop talking. *Ask them what they do, not how they feel,* I had always to tell myself. Staff Sgt. "Dick" was typical. "I don't really rule the lives of twenty-nine guys," he told me. "I rule only three, the squad leaders. I oversee the rest. What my job really requires is curiosity—about everything that goes on in the platoon." He then continued talking nonstop about gear surveys, and regulations governing haircuts, shaving, and physical appearance in general.

---

* Platoons in the Marine Corps, like Special Forces A-teams, varied in size. With only twenty-nine marines, this was a small platoon.

"When you go home on leave and see the guys you used to hang out with, you see them different—as slobs," he continued. "A marine is always a marine, even in civilian clothes. You always dress neat, you tuck in your shirt. You never walk with your hands in your pockets. But in the field we can flip a switch and turn nasty. Then all our cleanliness is channeled into the cleaning of our weapons and equipment only. Semper Gumby. Always Flexible. That's the real Marine motto."

Staff Sgt. Dick had seen combat the first time as a corporal in the Balkans. The platoon had been trucked in overland from Greece and set up a base in a gymnasium in northern Kosovo. "We did foot patrols in alleys and were shot at by Serb gunmen, who were then killed by our snipers. We carried the bodies away in our ponchos. After Kosovo I reenlisted."

By the time of OIF (Operation Iraqi Freedom) he had become a staff sergeant. Sleeping in "coffin racks" for a month "on ship" en route from Camp Lejeune made the floor of the Kuwait desert a step up in creature comfort. Seven-ton trucks got the platoon to the outskirts of An-Nasiriyah, where it experienced its first firefight with the Fedayeen Saddam. That first night in An-Nasiriyah was their worst in Iraq. Torrential rains caused Staff Sgt. Dickinson's men to bail water as much as dig trenches. It was pitch black. The rain covered up the muzzle flashes. Their night vision goggles fogged up. Rounds buzzed over their heads and next to them. "It's not so much scary as overwhelming. The adrenaline never stops, you go numb, and all of your training falls into place," he explained.

For the most part, though, for the 2nd Platoon of India Company, Operation Iraqi Freedom had been a melancholy delirium of cramped and dust-ridden truck rides with piss breaks every six hours while sweating inside their MOPP suits, interspersed with anxious foot patrols.* Staff Sgt. Dickinson's marines often got no more than one meal ready to eat per day, so they killed chickens and stripped dead cows that they had bought from the *hajis*. While the First Marine Expeditionary Force (I MEF) had marched straight from Kuwait to Baghdad, those of II MEF, which included India Company, were left in the rear to clean up pockets of resistance. They got less publicity, but in some cases saw more combat and had the more interesting experiences.

The platoon went a month without washing until the gunnery sergeant

---

* MOPP: mission-oriented protective posture—gear for chemical and biological attacks.

was able to construct makeshift showers. Their socks became hardened, their bodies black with mud and dirt. They became closer to their fellow marines than they had ever been to their buddies back home. They bled, shat, and vomited together. Without radios or TVs, they discovered reading for the first time in their often poor, misbegotten lives. Every night was "story time," when one of them would read out loud to the others: Larry McMurtry's *Lonesome Dove* from beginning to end.

Most of Staff Sgt. Dick's men were still in their teens, yet they told their Iraq stories to me in the manner of old men talking to their grandchildren. "Iraq made me want to go home and apologize to all the people I had ever been an asshole to; it made me see myself from the outside for the first time," said Richard Cabrera, a twenty-one-year-old corporal from Riverside, California.

Nineteen-year-old Ty Ogden of Saratoga Springs, New York, told me of how an Iraqi girl had come up and given him a flower, which he stuck in his helmet. "The Iraqis were always so nice to us," said another nineteen-year-old tattooed lance corporal, Jeremy Kepner of Utica, New York. "In the morning they brought us fresh tea and pita bread, which we traded for MREs. When we finally got home on leave it was weird. Our old friends suddenly seemed so immature, so naive."

En route home from Iraq, the ship docked in Lisbon, Portugal, for four days. For Lance Cpl. Kepner and most of the others, it was the first time that they had been to Europe. "After months at Camp Lejeune, Kuwait, and Iraq, Portugal blew our minds," he reflected. "The women were so beautiful, the people so polite and well dressed—not like Americans. The buildings were old, like a castle. It made me think. I want to go to college after my enlistment is up."

One day I was sitting atop a Humvee with Lance Cpl. Kepner, waiting to go to the rifle range. I happened to mention that I had been to Colombia the previous winter with the Army's 7th Special Forces Group.

Kepner replied: "That was when my step-grandfather was killed there, in southern Colombia."

It turned out that Lance Cpl. Kepner was the step-grandson of Tom Janis, the Vietnam veteran and Bronze Star recipient who had been executed by FARC guerrillas after his plane had gone down, and whose remains I had seen in the hangar that day at Larandia.

"Yes," Kepner said. "My step-grandfather was buried in Arlington National Cemetery."

Whereas Staff Sgt. Dickinson was the platoon leader, 2nd Lt. Chris Wagner of Hillsborough, New Jersey, a graduate of Towson University in Maryland, was the platoon's executive officer. It was a similar division of responsibilities as that which existed between the master sergeant and the captain of a Special Forces team, which, in turn, was like that between the managing editor and the editor in chief of a newspaper. Staff Sgt. Dickinson was responsible for the minute-by-minute operation of the human machinery, while 2nd Lt. Wagner provided the platoon its basic orientation: he drafted the training schedules and so on. Second Lt. Wagner was like other lower- and middle-ranking officers I had met in the military: officers' training (which for Marines took place at Quantico, Virginia) had, in the process of making him more articulate, also given him a vaguely aristocratic bearing. It was very subtle, and it existed only in relation to the noncommissioned officers, but it was there.

I met 2nd Lt. Wagner for the first time during a field drill at the range. Though guard duty was the oldest job in the Marine Corps, providing security for Camp Lemonier was routine stuff, so a Marine combat unit like the 2nd Platoon had to fill every available hour with training to remain in fighting trim. American soldiers had their first experience in irregular warfare fighting the Iroquois in the heavily wooded terrain of the Ohio River valley during the French and Indian War, but as 2nd Lt. Wagner remarked during the field drill: "You may not see much combat in a wooded environment again. The future is MOUT [military operations on urban terrain]." In front of us, platoon members advanced in the dirt, elbows smacking against the hard desert floor, each marine holding his M-16 in one hand "chicken wing" style, using the other hand to break the fall. For every two marines who laid down suppressing fire, one advanced. *Fire without forward movement is a waste; movement without fire is suicide.* The aim was to keep the fields of fire as narrow as possible, to avoid hitting civilians in this imaginary urban environment. Because it was only a drill, to stay motivated the marines practiced Indian war yells that they had heard in the movie *The Last of the Mohicans.*

The Marines were an example of how government channels the testosterone of young males toward useful national ends. If the military were much smaller than it was, the result might be only more gang violence within the homeland. "I joined because I felt I needed discipline," one of Staff Sgt. Dickinson's squad leaders told me. Not only were the crew cuts, tattoos, and bodybuilder-type physiques of all the marines down to the squad leaders similar, so were their expressions. They bore a metallic intensity like water pouring over rocks in a fast stream.

It was at the range where I saw how the Marines made due. With Special Forces, you'd go out and shoot live fire and rocket-propelled grenades to your heart's content, using the latest M-4 assault rifles with rail systems. The marines shot blank RPGs. They had a limited number of 5.56mm rounds. They did not have the latest helmets, and used older, heavier, and more awkward M-16s. And these were marines who had seen combat in Operation Iraqi Freedom.

Yet this was an afternoon at the range such as I had never experienced. Rather than go out for an hour or two and shoot from a clean berm, we were there six hours in the hot sun, crawling on bare elbows in the greasy African dirt, running from one prone position to another, practicing an assault. Staff Sgt. Dickinson insisted that I experience it firsthand. Lying on my stomach in a prone position, I had trouble aiming because I was so out of breath.

He yelled throughout the day. They were mean yells, especially when two marines fired their rifles on "burst," for marines were taught to always fire deliberately, in order to make every shot count. The discipline never let up. But it was a discipline that instilled not only obedience but also responsibility, because many of these marines commanded others in ever smaller groups.

That evening a fistfight erupted in the barracks and Staff Sgt. Dickinson stormed in. He looked so angry that his face was as red as his hair. Then he turned calm. He spoke to us about his own anger, why it was necessary, and why it was necessary to solve problems within the squad by looking out for each other.

"We fight. I yell. But we're a family. I'm your father and mother. It's the Marine culture. It's why we're still around after two hundred years." These were tough kids from difficult family backgrounds. The Marines were like an orphanage that worked. Cpl. Richard Cabrera was typical. He had joined the Marines to avoid the route that had led his older brother to jail after his father died. His mother was working all the time to support her three children, and Cabrera, being young and ignorant, thought that she hated him because she was rarely around. It was the experience of the Marine Corps, he told me, that made him realize that she had loved him all the time. "All I ever wanted at home was to be missed."

"Column right, column left. Left, left." Staff Sgt. Dickinson called cadence on the hot gravel, as the platoon marched to a formation point to mount up for guard duty. At the formation point each marine neatly piled his helmet and rifle atop his web gear, which in turn was atop his flak jacket—or, as Special Forces had called it, IBA (individual body armor). There was a procedure for everything. It was a small example of how the Marine Corps, more than the other services, stripped away civilian identity.*

Before heading off to their guard posts there was a PME (professional military education). The Vietnamese-born gunnery sergeant, Taun Pham, strutted around, barking in sing-song fashion: "Why is there a need for repetition, gents?" he asked rhetorically. "Because repetition is the way we learn. When an awesome new hip-hop song comes out, what do you do, gents? You listen to it over and over again, until you know the words. You do the same thing with your weapons that you do with a good hip-hop song. You practice loading and aiming and shooting over and over again. And how do you communicate with each other?" he went on. "Through a brevity code. And why do we do that, gents? In order to convey a lot of information quickly. Marines aren't like other people. Marines don't waste time with jibber-jabber. So what do you do when you have to tell someone to shut down the base? You say, 'Sandstorm.' Or if you want to announce that there is an improvised explosive device inside the base? You say, 'Firecracker.' Or if you want someone to have a magazine inserted in his M-16, with the bolt forward, the chamber empty, and the ejection port closed? You say, 'Condition Three.' There is a brevity code for everything, so, like I said, don't waste time with jibber-jabber. Marines should say in a few seconds what it takes others to say in a minute."

For the Marine Corps, the most bureaucratically powered-down of the armed services, the gunnery sergeant was the ultimate rank. The "gunny" was the go-to guy, the captain's technical advisor, the senior enlisted man who handled all logistics, the iron grunt.†

As Gunny Pham continued with his chantlike brief, the officers and

---

* At retirement gatherings, marines who had known each other all their lives still addressed each other by rank.
† The gunnery sergeant was also the last rank in the Marine Corps before the noncom command structure branched off: toward the leadership-oriented sergeant major and the technical-oriented master sergeant.

noncoms went inside one of the tents for their own PME. The session was led by Capt. Charles Cassidy of Evergreen Park, Illinois, India Company's commander. Second Lt. Wagner, Staff Sgt. Dickinson, and the officers and noncoms—so domineering moments before with their corporals and privates—now became subservient. In the Pentagon, a Marine captain was lost amid many other officers. But in the field a captain was a company leader, a truly big deal. Capt. Cassidy's position and responsibility made him seem remote almost. He lectured for over two hours, frequently employing a brevity code. The train of logic and material he packed into his presentation was truly remarkable. In a competition for substance, he would have murdered just about any academic or media pundit. Capt. Cassidy was not interested in what was interesting, only in what mattered.

The subject of the lecture was an imaginary assault on enemy troops that were situated on an elevated plain. The assault route led up through marshy woods and sparsely vegetated ridges. "The terrain comes before the enemy," Capt. Cassidy told us. "The terrain is the most important element because it impacts everything we and the enemy do. The enemy has a different personality, depending upon the terrain in which it must operate." Geographical context was everything, in other words.

Key Terrain, Capt. Cassidy explained, was the part of the terrain that provided an advantage toward acquiring Decisive Terrain. Key Terrain could shift, "because there may be only one fucking machine-gun position holding up an advance, to be replaced later by another machine-gun position." As for Decisive Terrain, "it may not exist at all," because the nature of the enemy configuration may make it impossible to secure success by holding any one piece of ground. Terrain was also divided between an Area of Operation and an Area of Interest. The Area of Interest, in this case the elevated plain, extended beyond the Area of Operation, which was the marshy woodlands and ridges. Key Terrain in this particular assault was situated near the ridgeline where the Area of Operation met the Area of Interest.

The brief went on, becoming increasingly specific as every ridge and path leading up to the plain was described and considered. It followed the unyielding logic of both the *Ranger Handbook* and the *Fleet Marine Force Manual 6-5 (FMFM 6-5)*, the latter known as the "Grunt's Bible."*

---

* The *Ranger Handbook* was the smart sheet for individual tasks; its equivalent was the *Guidebook for Marines*. The *FMFM 6-5* concentrated on squad-level operations.

From the beginning of my journey, I had been meeting men for whom "the mission was everything." Capt. Cassidy's brief clarified the mission further. It showed that the mission had to be tangible; that it had to be finite; that to be successful it need not—and often could not—be perfectly executed; and that, most of all, the mission was about priorities. It assumed, in other words, a messy world with imperfect results.

In such a tactical universe, intentions were meaningless; only effects mattered. This was a universe that featured total accountability, for success and failure were specifically measurable in terms of inches of ground and lives of men. It was a restrictive logic, but not self-delusory like other kinds. Therein lay its power.

It was only a few minutes' walk from Capt. Cassidy's office to that of Marine Brig. Gen. Mastin Robeson, the commander of the Combined Joint Task Force—Horn of Africa, whom I knew from the Army's School of Advanced Military Studies at Fort Leavenworth, Kansas. The Marines of India Company guarded Camp Lemonier, from which Brig. Gen. Robeson launched missions throughout the Horn of Africa and beyond. But while Brig. Gen. Robeson applied himself to larger, strategic matters, the disciplined logic of the Marine field manuals guided his approach. From western North Carolina (though he now lived in Jacksonville), he was tall, trim, and gray-haired, and with a sly, curious expression that made me think of a rifle scope being zeroed in.

The CJTF-HOA labored under "the tyranny of distance," Robeson told me. His AOR (area of responsibility) included not only the traditional Horn of Africa countries—Djibouti, Ethiopia, Eritrea, and Somalia—but also the adjacent real estate of Yemen, Sudan, and Kenya. This subfiefdom of CENTCOM was five times larger than Iraq and Afghanistan combined, yet the American footprint had remained relatively small. "We're conducting an archaeological dig, not doing urban renewal," he explained. "It's about working the fringes, finding needles in haystacks, not dismantling regimes." There was obviously a lot less going on here than in Iraq and Afghanistan, but what was going on—as in Colombia, Mongolia, and the Philippines—was more instructive of how the U.S. military would likely operate in the future.

The Horn of Africa had registered on the American intelligence radar screen long before the 1998 bombings of the U.S. embassies in Nairobi,

Kenya, and Dar es Salaam, Tanzania. Al-Qaeda had been operating around the Horn for years. When Osama bin Laden relocated from Sudan to Afghanistan in 1995, he left a financial support structure behind in Khartoum. Though terrorism thrived on ungovernability, it also required cultural and linguistic access, so that terrorists could blend into the population. In the case of al-Qaeda, Sudan, Somalia, Yemen, and heavily Muslim northern Kenya offered such access.

"This is a region," Robeson told me, "where young al-Qaeda operatives drift into towns and villages, get established, marry local girls, and go to ground." Saleh Nabhan, a key operative in the 2002 attack on the Israeli-owned Paradise Hotel in Mombasa, Kenya, and of the surface-to-air missile launched at an Israeli airliner from Mombasa, fit that description perfectly: one day he had arrived at a coastal fishing village near Lamu Island in northern Kenya, settled in and married a fifteen-year-old local girl, then bought a house with the dowry and laid low for several years. "How many more like him are out there that we don't know about?" the general asked aloud. As it was, CJTF-HOA was tracking more than five hundred terrorists by name. "It's like pulling up a rug and realizing, holy cow, where'd all those cockroaches come from? Once you start playing zone defense in depth, like we're doing in the Horn, it's amazing what turns up."

To a greater degree than Afghanistan even, the Horn was a place for a light and lethal force structure. Robeson had flattened the command hierarchy by collapsing his own staff and that of the CJTF-HOA's Joint Special Operations Task Force (JSOTF) into each other. He had created a single intel-fusion center with representatives from all the countries in the area of responsibility to analyze political, military, and terrorist activities in the Horn and beyond, making for a holistic tapestry unavailable at the State Department or the Central Intelligence Agency.

Less so than the State Department, Brig. Gen. Robeson was unburdened by bureaucratic boundary seams. If terrorists could take advantage of the porosity of borders, why couldn't the U.S. government? And yet U.S. embassies, established according to a system of nation-states, were, by definition, country-centric, with localitis the natural result. The State Department, more than the Pentagon, was also hindered by the Cold War–era divisions of its various "line" bureaus: the Bureau of Near Eastern Affairs, the Bureau of African Affairs, and so forth. Robeson's area of responsibility, on the other hand, overlapped several geographic domains:

the Horn of Africa, the Arabian Peninsula, North and East Africa, and the Pacific. The Horn, Yemen, and Kenya were all inside CENTCOM, which comprised the Middle East and parts of Africa most impacted by the Arabian Peninsula. EUCOM, which handled Europe and sub-Saharan Africa, had allowed Robeson to pursue leads into Tanzania and Uganda. Meanwhile, PACOM had granted Robeson similar access to the Comoros islands.

"Bureaucratically, we're doing things we never did before," Robeson said. "I speak a few times a week to Gen. [John] Abizaid [the CENTCOM commander], and that is the extent of my instructions. It's great to be ignored. It means you can innovate." The newer and more immature the theater of operations, the more opportunity that existed for entrepreneurship.

Djibouti in its own quiet way manifested the ultimate effect of 9/11, an effect that was general and sustaining rather than specific and transitory. Iraq and Afghanistan were about dismantling regimes and consequent nation-building, which, because it grabbed headlines, excited journalists and intellectuals who lived off the news for their debates and discussions. But the Horn demonstrated that the killing of a few thousand Americans on one day two and a half years earlier had provided the U.S. military with the trigger for a new kind of great power role, a role that was precise and subtle, did not involve large numbers of troops, and was not truly about nation-building.

"Just whacking crack houses doesn't cut it anymore," Robeson explained. "The new Economy of Force model we're working on is to whack people quietly, while running a lot of aid projects that generate good publicity in the areas affected." Consequently, Robeson was sprinkling his vast desert and savanna fiefdom with aid missions. U.S. troops, often in civilian clothes, were building schools and hospitals and digging wells; holding MEDCAPS and DENTCAPS for the inhabitants, and VETCAPS for their animals. They were training the indigenous troops of several nations in counterterrorism, establishing local coast guards from Kenya to Yemen, and dispatching clandestine Special Operations teams here and there to snatch and kill "bad guys." September 11 had given the U.S. military the justification to go out scouting for trouble, and at the same time to do some good.

In Ma'rib, the Yemeni badland east of the capital of Sana'a where I had traveled thirteen months before, there had recently been dozens of arrests of al-Qaeda suspects, facilitated by the U.S., which coincided with the insertion of marines to train Yemeni commandos. In the Ogaden desert region of Ethiopia, Army civil affairs teams (CATs) were establishing relationships with local clan leaders who needed help against bandits and refugees seeping in from chaotic Somalia.

"Who needs meetings in Washington?" Army Maj. Trip Narrow of Baton Rouge, Louisiana, told me. "Guys in the field will figure out what to do. I took ten guys for a week through eastern Ethiopia. Everywhere we went people wanted a bigger American presence. They know we're here. They want to see what we can do for them. One four-man CAT [civil affairs team] can accomplish more than a battalion of infantry. Forget the Vietnam baggage," he went on. "It's still about hearts and minds, a Peace Corps role for the military."

Fifteen years after the collapse of the Berlin Wall a new paradigm was emerging for how the American military projected itself abroad, one that borrowed more from the French and Indian War and the Lewis and Clark expedition than from the major conflicts of the twentieth century. Just like the British and the French dealing with the Iroquois Confederacy on the western slopes of the Appalachians and in northern New York State, Americans in the Horn were interacting with indigenous peoples in small numbers, making various deals of mutual self-interest, and killing a few of them when necessary. And like Lewis and Clark, small groups of soldiers and marines were being dispatched to little-surveyed areas, armed with only general guidelines. But because progress was often imperceptible, it was unclear how much defense officials in Washington appreciated the significance of what was going on here.

The new paradigm gave Brig. Gen. Robeson a sort of power that no U.S. ambassador or assistant secretary of state quite had. Not only wasn't he burdened by the State Department's antiquated bureaucratic divisions, but his ability to deal with the region's leaders and strongmen may also have been helped by a cause-and-effect, working-class mind, disciplined by the logic of Marine tactical operations manuals and the classical military education he had received at Fort Leavenworth. Though democracy was gaining in the region, many of the elected leaders with whom Robeson had developed relationships were former guerrilla fighters and military men, men from hardscrabble beginnings who may have had more in common with a Marine brigadier general who had studied business administration at Bryan College in Dayton, Tennessee, and lived in Jacksonville, North Carolina, than they had with a civilian ambassador who had, say, studied liberal arts at an elite university and lived in a prosperous Washington suburb.

The fact that generals like Mastin Robeson were in the diplomatic forefront, somewhat at the expense of the State Department, troubled commentators who assumed the permanence of industrial-age categories of bureaucratic responsibility, categories helped into being by the early-nineteenth-century professionalization of European militaries, which consequently separated them from civilian command structures. But such distinctions appeared to be weakening.

In 1994, two Special Forces officers helped the Paraguayan government to ratify new laws just after Paraguay's constitution had been adopted. On the other hand, it was under the State Department's auspices, not the Pentagon's, that helicopters were leased to the Colombian military to fight narco-terrorists. And just as Robeson was a model for future generals, the model for future diplomats might have been Deane Hinton, who oversaw counterinsurgency operations as ambassador to El Salvador in the early 1980s, and then oversaw efforts to arm Afghan guerrillas as the ambassador to Pakistan in the middle and late 1980s. In both cases, a military strategy would have been unavailing in the absence of a successful interagency strategy, which backed diplomatic initiatives and aid packages with the power of a cocked gun. As military and diplomatic divisions of responsibility continued to break down, the U.S. government was likely to revert to the unified leaderships of the ancient and early modern worlds—what Socrates and Machiavelli recognized as a basic truth of all political systems, whatever the labels those systems claimed for themselves.[3]

With his practical mindset, Gen. Robeson was impressed neither with the appearance of progress nor with scholastic definitions of it, but with progress itself. To wit, like others in the defense establishment, but unlike many in the State Department, Robeson liked the president of neighboring Eritrea, Isaias Afwerki. "Isaias doesn't need bodyguards," Robeson told me. "He goes around alone. He lives in a normal house. He governs an African capital that is crime-free, without slums, even though there are relatively few police. There's no terrorist threat in Eritrea. More than any other country in my AOR [area of responsibility], it has a secular Western sense of patriotism. Isn't that what we claim we want?"*

Eritrea was interesting as a symbol of how the Pentagon and the State Department saw the world differently. My own reporting experiences in Eritrea caused me to initially side with the Pentagon, though, as the human rights situation there continued to deteriorate, even I was fast losing hope. While the State Department defined civil society in terms of generic criteria such as elections, a free press, and the absence of political prisoners, that way of thinking missed vital nuances: President Afwerki did not require a vast security apparatus to protect him as did the prime minister of Ethiopia, Meles Zenawi. Eritrea was arguably the least corrupt of third world countries. It had a record of near-perfect accountability when it came to utilizing international aid, and took care of its handicapped citizens better than any other country in Africa.

As Robeson put it, "Rather than give up on Isaias because he won't conform with our standards of Western democracy, it's in our interest to bring him into the tent, before the human rights situation gets even worse there." He mentioned that the Eritrean leader gave up the disputed Hanish Islands in the Red Sea to Yemen, just as the international community had asked him to. Going on in his mild North Carolina drawl about the tense relationship between Eritrea and Yemen, Robeson remarked: "[Yemeni president Ali Abdullah] Saleh has been a real impressive leader, make no mistake. And the only way he has succeeded is by making deals with one tribe and another. But that's why Isaias can't respect him. You see, Isaias lived in a cave for years during the guerrilla war with Ethiopia. Nobody chooses to live in a cave that long except to defend a strong principle. And so in Isaias's mind, Saleh has no principles, he's just a wheeler-dealer.

"Meles [Zenawi] also lived in a cave for years," he went on, referring to the leader of Ethiopia. "That's why both these guys are so smart. They had nothing to do for years except read."

Indeed, President Bush and Defense Secretary Rumsfeld had met with Zenawi in 2002, making Ethiopia a linchpin in the struggle against al-Qaeda. The Ethiopians were granting overfly rights and sharing intelligence with the U.S., even as troops from the 10th Mountain Division were

---

* Indeed, a religious map of the region put out by the Pentagon showed Eritrea as a separate category all its own, with a single national identity rather than separate religious identities.

training Ethiopian soldiers. Orthodox Christian Ethiopia clearly felt threatened; it was now 50 percent Muslim, with Saudi-financed mosques spreading radicalism, and the Islamic separatist Oromo Liberation Front active in the south of the country.[4]

Robeson showed me a map of the ethnic groups of the Horn. The territory of the Afars overlapped Djibouti, Eritrea, and Ethiopia, and that of the Issas Djibouti, Ethiopia, and Somalia. The numerous Oromos inhabited both Ethiopia and Kenya. The Anuaks inhabited Ethiopia and Sudan, the Digil occupied Somalia and Kenya, and so on. The map looked quaint, but as the Islamic resurgence in Ethiopia evinced, it had urgent political meaning. For example, Somalia was a failed state that had effectively severed into three parts: the Issa-dominated northwest that configured with former British Somaliland; the largely Darood central part called "Puntland" (a reference to the biblical land of Punt, by the mouth of the Red Sea); and the Hawiy-dominated south around Mogadishu, which had been an Italian colony.

Somalia couldn't get any worse. Only the former British northwest had a semblance of government. Robeson was equally concerned with Ethiopia and Kenya. They dominated the region demographically, and had gone from being repressive regimes to weak democracies, as the U.S. had been in the early nineteenth century. Ethiopia still constituted a sprawling empire more than a country, and was ruled by a minority Tigrean. While predominantly orthodox Christian, it had large Muslim areas, as did Kenya. Mosque construction in Robeson's area of responsibility had increased more than eightfold. Sub-Saharan Africa's institutional decline was generating stronger religious identities as the post-colonial state lost its grip on people's imaginations.

Terrorists were the beneficiaries of such trends.

———

Talking with Gen. Robeson, I could not help recalling Donald Levine's mid-twentieth-century portrait of the Ethiopian Amhara, *Wax and Gold*, an ethnographic area study that is one of the finest of the genre. A professor of sociology at the University of Chicago, Levine labeled himself a "pragmatist": someone, he explains, who affirms the human values of modernity, yet conceives of modernity not in fixed ideological terms, but as "relative to the cultural context in which modernization takes place."[5] So while democracy may ultimately be the best system for every society, each society must reform in its own time and in its own way, depending upon historical and geographical circumstances. Because Levine's experience in the Horn was prodigious, and he was unafraid to generalize about human behavior, *Wax and Gold,* researched between 1957 and 1962, has a practical, old-fashioned common sensibility rare in contemporary academic circles.

Wax and gold, Levine explains—*sam-enna warq* in Amharic—"is the formula used by the Amhara to symbolize their favorite form of verse." It is a verse formula built of two semantic layers: the apparent, figurative meaning of the words called the "wax," and the hidden meaning called the "gold." This is the key, he implies, to understanding Ethiopian culture. While the relative absence of ambiguity—clear, straightforward talk—is necessary for the running of a modern society and bureaucracy, the management of social and ethnic tensions requires considerable reliance on ambiguity for interpersonal relations. A culture of deception, according to Levine, has always been the obstacle to Ethiopia's modernization, but also the protector of its relative social peace.[6]

In Ethiopia's "minimal, Hobbesian order," Levine goes on, moral obligations rarely extend beyond the family and tribal circle. Suspicion and secrecy are ever present, partly due to a history of living under the dual threat of Islam and Western Christianity. (Thus, the Ethiopian Orthodox Church concerns itself with "practical justice, not universal love.") Ethiopia, to which Levine was lured by its "extraordinarily handsome people in a setting of great natural beauty," is a hard, cruel place. The author notes "the surly use of authority, the subtle sense of fatalism, the adulation of rank rather than human qualities . . . the narrowness of outlook . . . the interpersonal aspects of the ethos of wax and gold."

The countryside's appearance is proof of this absence of community. There are few venerable urban centers, or villages even, in the Ethiopian highlands, just thinly scattered groups of houses up and down the mountainsides. Instead of clustering, there is dispersion.[7]

Wax and Gold was published a decade before the Ethiopian revolution that toppled Emperor Haile Selassie and brought to power arguably the most systematically murderous regime in the history of twentieth-century Africa, a suspicious and morosely secretive Marxist killing machine that evinced many of the negative cultural traits that Levine had earlier identified in his researches.

Looking at the ethnic map of the Horn and what might transpire there in coming years, I knew that such a book could only grow in relevance, for just as terrain comes before the enemy, in Capt. Cassidy's words, indigenous culture—a reaction to geographical circumstance—must be appreciated before anything can be accomplished with its inhabitants.

———

The diminishing emphasis on central authority had led the U.S. military to forge a presence in far-flung parts of Ethiopia and Kenya. That's what "working the fringes" was all about, according to Brig. Gen. Robeson. Thus, one morning before dawn I slipped out of the penitentiary-like world of the Marine barracks and walked over to the airstrip at Camp Lemonier, boarded a Navy C-20, and by lunchtime was in Nairobi, where I boarded a small commercial prop. Before mid-afternoon I was looking at the top of Mount Kilimanjaro through the plane window. By late afternoon I touched down in the Kenyan coastal town of Manda Bay near the Somali border, where the African bush meets the milky turquoise of the Indian Ocean. Here the Horn gives way to East Africa, and the world of the Muslim Near East melds with that of syncretic sub-Saharan Africa to form the purest Swahili culture. From Manda Bay, I boarded a dhow for the short sail to the island of Lamu, my destination and that of the four-man Army CAT (civil affairs team) with which I was traveling.

Like the Sulu Archipelago in the southern Philippines, Lamu is another lost paradise of empty beaches, aquamarine inlets graced by swirling coral patterns, thatched hutments, and quiet, contemplative alleys hypnotized by the sun and plied by burros. It was saved from mass tourism only by the threat of terrorism and Kenya's reputation for crime.* Muslim dominance was another factor, because it limited liquor licenses on the island.

Lamu, a medieval creation of Arab traders, is the first of the Swahili city-states reached by single-mast dhows sailing from Oman and Yemen. The prevalence of the Persian and the Portuguese in these waters contributed to the cultural eclecticism. Lamu boomed during the centuries of the Arab-dominated East African slave trade. When the slave trade ended, and the British built a rail link from Nairobi to Mombasa south along the coast, Lamu became a backwater, frequented only by a small band of sybaritic Europeans, including the royal family of Monaco. It was in Lamu where Princesses Caroline and Stephanie, with their husbands and hangers-on, attempted to escape from the klieg lights of the paparazzi.

---

* The reputation for crime was somewhat undeserved because crime was limited mainly to Nairobi.

But the Grimaldi sisters soon had company—Arab terrorists and the American military. Both came for the very reason that had made Lamu and other nearby islands fertile ground for the Swahili language and the slave trade—location. For the Arabs, Lamu was the most forward point of cultural access into sub-Saharan Africa. (Swahili, after all, represents a fusion of Arabic and Bantu words and civilizations.) In these island paradises, filled with welcoming Muslim populations, young al-Qaeda operatives with money and good manners could quietly establish themselves. Kenya was an inviting target because of the large concentration of westerners in its major cities. The group that bombed the Israeli-owned hotel in Mombasa worked out of Faza Island, next door to Lamu.

As for the American military, it had a long-standing relationship with the Kenyan one. But the relationship intensified with the collapse of the Berlin Wall and the breakdown of order in adjacent Somalia. Next came the bombing of the Nairobi embassy and then 9/11, as the threat shifted from Soviet domination of Central Europe to radical Islamic terrorism fostered by third world institutional decline.

Edged Mallet, an annual joint American-Kenyan military exercise, was in its fourth year now. Its focus was Kenya's northern coast near Somalia, where at Manda Bay the Kenyan military had an air base and naval station.

Manda Bay required an improved pier and a better runway, which, as it happened, served the interests of the American and Kenyan militaries. It also served the interests of Kenya's new fledgling democracy, which was trying to upgrade services and establish an institutional foothold after the abuses perpetrated by the former ruler, Daniel arap Moi. In an age of democracy, bilateral military contacts were more important than ever. In countries like Kenya, civilian politicians came and went, but leading security and military men remained as behind-the-scenes props. Thus, the better the relationship between American officers and their Kenyan counterparts, the more likely that the Kenyan military would be honest and democratic. As Brig. Gen. Robeson had put it to me, "The success of Kenya's democratic experiment offers the best hope for American security in the region."

A key fact to remember is that the Americans did not require a base of their own; rather, they wanted the Kenyans to have a fully modernized base, so that present and future democratic Kenyan governments would project Kenyan power into the chaotic reaches of Somalia. As for the Americans, they could always use these base facilities if—and only if—

the U.S. maintained a strong relationship with the Kenyan military, and with the local inhabitants of Lamu and Manda Bay. That was where Army Civil Affairs entered the calculation.

Civil Affairs had an obviously civilian connotation. That was the beauty of it. In truth, Civil Affairs was part of USASOC, U.S. Army Special Operations Command, headquartered at Fort Bragg, which also included Special Forces and Psychological Operations. Civil Affairs acted like a relief charity or NGO (nongovernmental organization). It built schools, dug wells, provided medical assistance, and so forth. The four-man civil affairs team that I accompanied to Lamu would be replacing a four-man team that had already been on the island for several months.

These teams had a twofold mission: make a sustained contribution to the island's quality of life, so that the inhabitants would see a relationship with the U.S. as in their best interests; and, more immediately, be the advance guard for U.S. Marines from the U.S.S. *Germantown* coming ashore to repair a school and conduct a MEDCAP.

Lamu was an example of the new paradigm for projecting American power: modernize host country bases for use as strategic outposts, maintain local relationships through humanitarian projects, then use such relationships to hunt down "bad guys." Whether it was upgrading a runway, digging a well, or whacking a terrorist, the emphasis was always on small teams.

The civil affairs teams were usually composed of reservists. Rather than the young, high-testosterone marines I had been staying with, they were more like their Special Forces colleagues in Army Special Operations Command: middle-aged men with civilian skills relevant to the task at hand.

But the people skills required on Lamu were not those the U.S. military usually looked for, even as they were the most important skills to have in a new era of ambiguous war.

A four-man team led by Capt. Steve Stacy of Tiffin, Ohio, a graduate of Ohio State University, would be replacing a team led by Capt. Jeff Rynearson of Orlando, Florida, a graduate of Southern Illinois University. On the plane journey from Djibouti, Capt. Stacy's team did not make much of an impression on me, one way or the other. Stacy's team sergeant, Glenn Elenga of Phoenix, was a friendly, garrulous former Special Forces 18

Delta medic. Sgt. Anthony Diaz of Tenafly, New Jersey, was a handsome ethnic Colombian who planned to do graduate studies at Johns Hopkins University in Washington, D.C. Sgt. Michael McCoy of Las Vegas was just plain quiet and tense. He seemed more suited to direct action than to the softer, humanitarian unconventional war.

It was only when I met the other team at the civilian airstrip in Manda Bay that I realized how much the new team would have to struggle in order to adapt, for the reality of Lamu and the skill set it required hit me at once.

Lamu was just so laid-back. The moment you landed, and the heat and enervating humidity lathered your skin, rotting the back of your shirt, and you saw your first dhow and bougainvillea bush, any tensions or worries you might have brought with you on the plane simply evaporated. Here there was no gritty dust, only fine white sand. It was an Indian Ocean version of what the Greek islands must have been like in the 1950s, before reduced jet fares and *Never on Sunday*—just beautiful scenery, uncorrupted natives, a sensuous concoction of Arab architecture and African styles, and a sprinkle of Western pleasure-seekers.

Capt. Jeff Rynearson, the departing commander, met us at planeside. He had a beefy and relaxed surfer's manner, with a deep tan, longish sunbleached blond hair, and wraparound shades. He was wearing shorts, sandals, and a loud Hawaiian-style shirt. With his "We Are the World" smile, he was like any engaging relief worker or Peace Corps volunteer, except for the Skoal chewing tobacco in his mouth and the 9mm Beretta under his Hawaiian shirt. Capt. Rynearson's sidekick, who at first I thought was a Kenyan security heavy, was Sgt. John Philoctete, an ethnic Haitian from Brooklyn. Sgt. Philoctete had the same jet-black complexion as the locals. He wore a white Muslim-style skullcap and gold chains around his neck.

"*Jambo*," they greeted us, as well as the people they passed on the short walk to the dock, whom they all seemed to know. It was Swahili for "Hello, how are you?"

"*Mzuri sana* [Very good]," came the reply, followed by "*hakuna matata*," which strictly translated as "no problem." But it had a larger connotation akin to "everything is cool." It was seventeen years since I had last been in Kenya, and I had forgotten the electric sense of life that Swahili imparted.

Beautiful African women in black *buibuis* smiled broadly at us. The cotton robes concealed everything but their faces, while accentuating their swaying hips. One girl around seventeen began smiling and talking to Capt. Rynearson. She obviously knew him. "It's sad," he whispered in my ear. "There are a lot of girls here like her. They're at the age when the hormones kick in and they start begging their father to arrange a marriage for them. Then they're finished in this culture."

Looking at the local women, and a few of the fetching European ones by the dock, and smelling their perfume, I remembered that there were marines in the tent in Djibouti who had told me that because of their extended deployments they hadn't been laid in years.

Capt. Rynearson and Sgt. Philoctete represented the future reality of Special Operations: the Peace Corps with guns, the final articulation of unconventional war. An unstated reason the NGOs (nongovernmental organizations, often relief charities) were uncomfortable with the emerging humanitarian role of the American military was that it represented strong professional competition.

Capt. Steve Stacy had the concentrated look of a sprinter before the starting gun sounded, as Capt. Rynearson began talking to him about how to hire a dhow, what to pay the porters, and which of the "Bob Marley clones" with matted hair and colorful woolen caps who were hanging around the dock were trustworthy and which were not. Staff Sgt. Glenn Elenga and Sgt. Tony Diaz were all smiles: Wow, what a deployment, I could hear them thinking; whoever said, "War is hell"? As for Sgt. Mike McCoy, he was stone-faced. I had heard he was disappointed that the team was not sent to Iraq.

Looking at Sgt. McCoy's expression, seeing how pale Sgt. Elenga and Capt. Stacy were, and observing their heavy clothes and Stacy's high-and-tight crew cut he had gotten a few days before at Fort Bragg, I worried that a few days would not be enough for the transition from one team to the other. You wondered who planned these things at Fort Bragg; who it was that ordered Stacy to get a haircut rather than to start growing his hair long and stock up on beach clothes. The problem with the Special Operations community was that it knew intellectually what was necessary for America to project its power stealthily, but it couldn't bring itself to make the necessary cultural adjustments.

The boat that took us across the channel to Lamu was a Jahazi, the largest type of dhow, capable of sailing as far as India. But ocean journeys were rare now because the Somali coast was covered by pirates. With majestic lateen sails and forward overhangs, dhows looked as aerodynamic as the sleekest fighter jets. They littered the channel, which in the sharp, late-afternoon sunlight resembled a sheet of tinted glass running with condensation. The approaching seaboard was cluttered with faded white archways, flowering trees, and small burros. I saw no paved roads and no cars. After disembarking we rested for a moment by a local hotel with potted palms and a dark, cool bar.

Then things happened fast. We met with the district commissioner, James Mwaura, to whom Capt. Rynearson introduced the new team. That was followed by a discussion about compensation to be paid by the U.S. for the destruction of a boat and a fire station, caused by the wind generated by a CH-46 helicopter during Edged Mallet. Next we walked over to the boys' secondary school, where Marine Capt. James Bauch of Cedar Falls, Iowa, explained how a platoon from the 13th Marine Expeditionary Unit (MEU), based off the U.S.S. *Germantown,* had flown in by chopper and in four twelve-hour workdays laid a new roof and refurbished the rest of the building. The marines were now playing basketball with the local kids. Watching the game, Rynearson told me, "This is where we win." At a ceremony for the opening of the new school building the next day, District Commissioner Mwaura would tell the crowd, "In the midst of all the problems in the world, it is important to see the humanitarian hand of the American military."

The island's population was under one hundred thousand. The economy was weak. A few dozen Americans—marines and Army Civil Affairs personnel—going around, spending money in the shops and restaurants, was in and of itself appreciated. Rynearson's team had convinced some of the locals that the U.S.S. *Germantown* should pay a port call. Those locals, in turn, convinced other locals at a community meeting. A Navy SEAL team then arrived to "pop smoke," to keep dhows away from the *Germantown*'s wake. "The SEALs put on a real show for the local kids, throwing a lot of colorful smoke grenades," Rynearson said. Turning to Capt. Stacy, he told him, "Never speak to the community as a group; speak to individuals and have them go to the community. And make sure to call people by their titles here, they like that."

Such details were critical. The endgame was to turn the local media, as Special Operations Command—Pacific had been able to do with the Philippine media during the Basilan operation. Recently, though, things had gone horribly wrong at Garissa, a town in the Kenyan interior near the Somali border. A local mullah had paid off some demonstrators to throw rocks during a MEDCAP, resulting in stories in the Nairobi press about how the Americans were not wanted.

At sunset, we finally arrived at the villa that Rynearson had rented: a white, cubistic masterpiece graced by bougainvillea, geraniums, and sweet-smelling jasmines. We were so close to the equator that on the balcony in the middle of the night I thought it might be possible to see both the Southern Cross and the North Star at opposite points on the horizon.

It was on the balcony where the two teams gathered for a sit-down over beer. Now I met the two other sergeants from Rynearson's team, another ethnic Haitian and an ethnic Nicaraguan, both from Miami, who called themselves Wesley and Max. Wesley, like Philoctete, looked like a local; Max looked like a Lebanese trader. They both had short beards and wore beads and knit caps. There was also someone else present: a Marine force protection specialist whom I shouldn't name. With a short-cropped beard and a café-au-lait complexion, he might have passed for a "bad guy." With no locals around, the noncoms addressed Capts. Rynearson and Stacy as "sir."

The evening breeze was nice and cool. The Kenyan Tusker beer was good, and the bottles were big. When everyone got settled, the force protection guy began dourly: "I'm paid to be paranoid. I'm a marine, so I stay in the box. I don't go out of the box," meaning that he couldn't talk about what was not concrete and immediately definable, unlike Army Special Operations, which was comfortable with nebulosity. "Therefore, here's what I know. The Muslim religious leaders who run the island community are suspicious of us. At the same time they need us to do projects. This house is beautiful, but don't get into the habit of hanging out here, or else you'll really be unsafe. If you guys get snatched, hope somebody will rescue you. But you can't hunker down."

Rynearson cut in: "Don't worry. Even on slow days there will always be someone who wants to show you their school or something. You'll always be busy checking out potential projects. That's the beauty of Civil Affairs. You figure it out on your own. You'll be an easy target, but nobody will do anything in their own backyard. On a scale of one to ten, I'd say the threat level is two."

Then came a long discussion about local contractors and construction materials. It was a disciplined meeting. The new team members took notes. At the end, it was decided that Capt. Stacy would not wear his combat fatigues at the ceremony the next day for the school opening. "Because nobody here knows you yet," Rynearson suggested, "the uniform will be a barrier to becoming accepted." It was no big deal to tell the truth about being an American soldier; it was another to intimidate people with a uniform.

After dinner the new team retired to another part of the villa to meet among themselves. Again, they all had notebooks; Capt. Stacy still had the tense look of an athlete before a race.

"I think," he began, "that we lose the Camel Paks, the military rucks, and the fishing vests. Buy some beach clothes. All of us except for Diaz look too white, too American military. We can't put that in people's faces." The others nodded. "The old team has racial advantages. Looking like some poor, down-and-out Australian or Canadian tourist is the best me and Glenn, for instance, will be able to do. We can grow goatees, they seem big here." More nods. "The one good thing about my lousy Fort Bragg haircut is that my hair will grow back." Some laughter, then Stacy concluded: "This place, this assignment." He searched for the right words. "It will be like herding cats. In Lamu, slow is fast. If we stay uptight, like we are now, if we try to keep people to our schedule, we'll fail. We have to slow down, do things at their speed. It may take some time before we can recommend our first aid project. There will be a lull. The major and the others at Camp Lemonier are going to have to accept that nothing may happen for a while. We can't operate like Capt. Rynearson's team. We'll have to find our own way." More nods.

Capt. Stacy was a pro. He realized fast, as I had, that most of his white bread, standard-issue Army team was out of place in this Bob Marley, everything-is-cool, *hakuna matata* Afro-Islamic environment spiced by the decadent lifestyle of the royal family of Monaco. He knew that they would all, especially Sgt. McCoy, have to adapt fast, to loosen up or be typecast as ugly Americans. He also realized that in the end they could only be themselves.

Later, back at Camp Lemonier, I asked an Army officer about how people were selected to go to a place like Lamu. He replied: "Select? Do you think we have the luxury to select? The Reserve is so overstretched because of Iraq that we're just grabbing bodies to fill slots."

Capt. Stacy's team did come with some advantages, however. For example, Staff Sgt. Glenn Elenga, an avid reader of the tabloids, briefed us on the various marriages of Princesses Caroline and Stephanie, and the colorful reputation of Prince Ernst of Hanover, Caroline's third husband, who spent more time in Lamu than the other royals.

For the members of both these teams, Lamu was merely the most recent in a string of deployments that had brought them all over the globe, to places both known and obscure, violent and potentially so. The marines of India Company could almost have been the sons of these guys, such was the age difference. But even the teenagers back in Djibouti had great stories to tell me, not only about Iraq, but also about Portugal, Kuwait, Bahrain, and other places they had been.

Lying awake as Indian Ocean breezes raced through my mosquito net and the lovely white stucco work, I thought that if you were a male of a certain age during World War II and had not served in some capacity, you would have been denied the American Experience. Now I realized that many of my own generation had been denied it as well, however unwittingly, however unaware of it we may have been. Perhaps it was a safer, more enriching global experience that we were having, but whatever it was I knew now that it was not fully American. The War on Terror was giving two generations of Americans vivid memories of places like Lamu, the southern Philippines, rural Colombia, eastern and southeastern Afghanistan, southern Iraq, and so on. The young marines back in Djibouti had fought in Operation Iraqi Freedom. In not a few cases, they had fathers who had fought in Desert Storm and, yes, grandfathers who had been in Vietnam. World War II was so far distant to them it might as well have been the Peloponnesian War. Yet, as it kept occurring to me in the course of these journeys, for most in my socioeconomic group, World War II was when the American Experience had begun to fade.

The American Experience was exotic, romantic, exciting, bloody, and emotionally painful, sometimes all at once. It was a privilege, as well as great fun, to be with those who were still living it.

Two days later came the MEDCAP that was the culmination of the 13th Marine Expeditionary Unit's onshore visit to Lamu, a visit whose ground-level component had been arranged by Capt. Rynearson's departing team. There were long lines of Muslim women swathed in black cotton with their babies. U.S. Marines provided the security, while Kenyan soldiers organized the crowd inside the King Fahd Hospital, where Kenyan and American military doctors and medics, wearing hospital scrubs deco-rated with the Kenyan and American flags, treated more than a thousand inhabitants of the island in two days.

By now Capt. Stacy's team was beginning to acclimatize. They were wearing appropriate clothes, getting tanned, had stopped shaving, and, more importantly, appeared more relaxed—making friends and learning Swahili. Because the small expatriate community, including the Grimaldis, were capable of spreading nasty rumors, it would be important to befriend them, too. Thus, the team began to hit the bar and restaurant near the villa, for gin and tonics by the moonlit beach.

It was sad to see Capt. Jeff Rynearson and his team depart. They had become veritable kings of the island. Elders had offered to marry their daughters off to them, as they had to al-Qaeda operatives. The old team knew everything that happened around here, down to the rumors about who might have been using the island for money laundering. It was ironic to keep reading stories about unhappy overdeployed reservists, because those in the Special Operations community whom I had met here and in eastern Afghanistan were having the time of their lives.

"You ought to check out of life and remain here," I suggested, only half in jest, to Rynearson. "This is where you belong."

"Don't think I haven't thought of it," he replied, smiling broadly. "I know a local contractor who could build me a glass-bottomed boat for tourists to watch fish and sea turtles. I'd buy two dhows to shuttle the tourists between the boat and the shore. I'd open a pub, renovate an old house, marry a local girl, and become a king. All you need to live as a king here is about $35,000 a year. I've worked it out."

Too bad that the American military personnel system did not allow guys to stay put when they adapted well to a place and had no families to return to, which, for the most part, was the case with Rynearson's team. It was area expertise and adaptation to the local environment—down to the level of the smallest micro-region—that had been one of the pillars of the British imperial system: the sort of expertise and adaptation that could develop only when work was inextricable from pleasure, and eccentricities were tol-erated. That, in turn, required less control from higher levels of command.

A few hours by plane and I was out of the world of pink oleanders against white walls and gin and tonics by a phosphorescent sea, and back to the grainy, black-and-white poverty of the Marine barracks in Djibouti. It was midnight when I got in. I found the guys in the midst of a discussion of how much it cost to lift the suspension of a Silverado versus that of a Jeep: $280 as opposed to $1,000.

I told them about Lamu.

"Shit." They all swooned, but they weren't too depressed. The next day the platoon had the day off and they were going to the beach.

It was one of the saddest-looking beaches I had ever seen. The Mars-like desert simply ended and greenish water began. The tide was low and licks of mud extended far out into the Gulf of Tadjoura, which led to the Gulf of Aden. Black volcanic rocks by the shore lay encrusted with mussels and barnacles. It was like so much strategic real estate—depressing and ugly. There was a ratty bar where the marines laid out their day packs. Soon their tattoo-covered pale and muscular bodies were all over the place.

"I wish I knew more about seashells," a diminutive and bespeckled Pfc. Chris Wrinkle of Hamilton, Maine, told me. Everyone called him just "Wrinkle." Soldiers and marines often called each other by their last names, maybe because their last names were emblazoned on their BDUs. Looking at him knee-deep in the water with his bathing suit, I realized that Pfc. Wrinkle seemed small only because of his wire-rimmed glasses and the especially brawny company he kept. Actually, Wrinkle owned a ropy, muscular physique and had large capable hands.

"I'm weird," he began. "I'm a fourth-generation marine, from a New England military family. Imagine that. I was born at Walter Reed Army Hospital in Washington. My mother and one of my aunts were born at Camp Pendleton. Another one of my aunts was born at Camp Lejeune. My grandparents, parents, and uncles all have stories of Korea, Vietnam, Grenada, Desert Storm . . . but none of my relatives have been deployed for stretches as long as I have in the War on Terrorism. The military has rarely been this busy in our nation's history. I'm proud of that.

"Yeah, I'm small compared to the other guys," he went on. "My grandfather, a Vietnam vet, is even smaller than I am. He told me, 'No grandson of mine is going to be pushed around in the schoolyard. Anyone hits you, hit 'em back and I'll square it with your mother.' There were tears in my grandfather's eyes when I graduated from boot camp at Parris Island. After the ceremony we walked around together and he told me about his experiences there. I signed up for six years and I've seen combat in Iraq. I have as much time in the fleet as Lt. Wagner. If I make staff sergeant, I'll reenlist. But I have no desire to be an officer."

Wrinkle had a large tattoo over his heart: the Marine insignia of the eagle, globe, and anchor, and a large cross. "I'm no Bible-thumper," he told me, referring to the cross. "But I am a believer."

The sun came out after lunch and the beach looked pretty for a moment. Each of the marines drifted off alone, as Wrinkle had done. One corporal whose birthday had been two days earlier lit a Honduran cigar. Another inspected a camel. Another took pictures of us all. The waves lapped. It was a luxury for them just to get off the base.

In coming days I got out and about Djibouti. The capital, Djibouti Town, was sleepy and battered, with gracefully arched white buildings in need of a paint job. It had a charming placelessness. I might have been in Hodeida, Yemen; Cotonou, Benin; or Port-au-Prince, Haiti. The port and airport were being managed by the United Arab Emirates. The Chinese were investing in telecommunications, making loans to the port, and doing all of the major construction. Otherwise, while no one would put it this way, the French were selling Djibouti and the Americans were buying it. The future competition here, as in Mongolia and the Philippines, would be between the U.S. and China.

Like many third world countries that looked small on the map but had rugged landscapes and bad roads, Djibouti was immense. Beyond the capital I found a fantastic landscape of steep canyons and a massive salt lake. Lake Assal was the lowest point in Africa. From a distance its greenish surface looked caked with ice. I had a picnic lunch of MREs at the lake en route back from a MEDCAP that had taken place at Tadjoura, at the top end of a gulf that divides Djibouti's Afar north from its Issa south. Tadjoura was once a busy port before the French built up Djibouti Town in the nineteenth century. Having receded into oblivion, it had a sorry collection of dusty streets and distempered houses by the water that reminded me of photos of Aqaba in 1917, when the Bedouin troops of Lawrence of Arabia captured it from the Ottoman Turks.

Watching the MEDCAP I realized that the U.S. would have an easy time in Djibouti compared to other places. Unlike in the states of the Maghreb, close to France itself, the French had made comparatively little effort to develop this territory of 750,000 people. Because the American military was already covering all of Djibouti with regular MEDCAPS,

DENTCAPS, and VETCAPS, it was fair to say that it had already provided more help to the local inhabitants than the French had in a century and a half of direct and indirect rule. The Americans would not face the problem of rising expectations of the kind that I had sensed in Basilan, following the conclusion of Operation Enduring Freedom—Philippines. Beyond Djibouti Town, the population was composed of pastoral nomads who mainly wanted to be left alone.

In fact, the Americans were more ambitious than the local population. "Could we develop this place?" a Marine staff sergeant asked me as we walked through Tadjoura's destitute streets. "Could we make it a real democracy? Why did the French fail?"

The French hadn't really tried, I told him. I thought to myself that the Americans might only ruin things if they became too ambitious. As Levine writes in *Wax and Gold:* "The experience of history has demonstrated the futility of attempting the revolutionary implementation of a clear and distinct ideal in human society. No matter how bold and sweeping the program, traditional patterns persist tenaciously."[8]

I got back from Tadjoura just as Staff Sgt. Dickinson was beginning a meeting. He was seated in a chair, with marines sprawled around him on their racks in the close, sour air of the tent. The fluorescent lights were on. The generator was droning. He wasn't angry. It was a morale talk.

"I'm not running a bunch of mindless drones," he began. "I value your opinion. Guys have been bitching to me about the training schedule: that it's an insult to those who have fought in Iraq. There's a reason why we have to go over basic fire drills. It's called brain dump. Our brains keep filling with new stuff, so if we don't keep relearning the basics they get dumped. Because we're standing eight-hour posts, our schedules are tight, so the decision was made to use the available training time to keep our rifle skills sharp.

"Ask yourselves, especially the guys who are not reenlisting and are turning fire teams over to others, how would you feel if you learned that your buddy was killed in the next war because you hadn't mentored him enough on the basics? You'd feel like shit, eh? That's why the team leaders need to mentor their riflemen and grenadiers over and over. If only one person out of twenty-nine is not expert on fire and movement, then we fail as a platoon.

"I'm not the one who closes," he continued. "I'm not the one who takes the objective; the ones here who've been to Iraq know that. You guys take the objective: the team leaders and the squad leaders. So if any of you see someone who's not keeping up, who needs help with his fire skills, fucking help him. I don't give a fuck if you're a private first class. If you've got knowledge to impart, you're a leader. That's the Marine way."

"Roger that," everyone responded.

The next morning I was gone, soon to join other marines in Iraq.

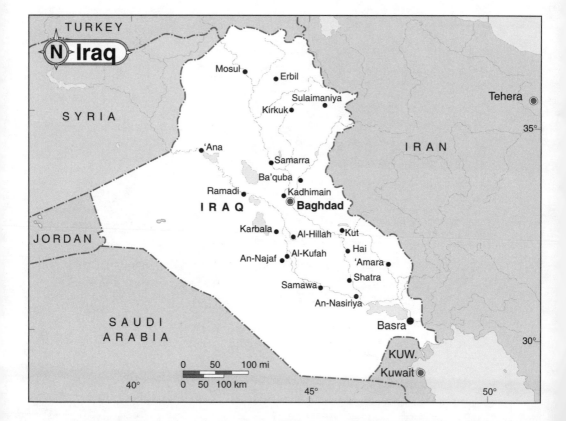

CENTCOM

IRAQ, SPRING 2004

WITH NOTES ON NICARAGUA AND VIETNAM

"I looked around in broad daylight to see the roofscape of Al-Fallujah cov-
ered with thousands upon thousands of old mufflers and tailpipes, guarded
by U.S. Marines, standing atop the city with fixed bayonets. . . . Yet the
American Empire depended upon a tissue of intangibles that was threat-
ened, rather than invigorated, by the naked exercise of power."

The road to Iraq began less in Washington than at Camp Pendleton, California, which along with Camp Lejeune, North Carolina, rep resented the main nodes of Marine strength in the United States. A naval force relatively small in size, the Marines were not spread out over a constellation of bases in the interior continent like the Army. They clustered in only a few places, on the West and East Coasts.

Except for the swaying palm trees and clean Pacific breezes, parts of Oceanside, California, next door to Camp Pendleton, seemed a replay of Jacksonville, North Carolina: pawnshops, tattoo parlors, military surplus stores, late-night convenience hangouts, and greasy spoon joints. I had been home from the Horn of Africa two days before I flew out here from New England.

As in Jacksonville and Fayetteville, I got up at the Comfort Suites, the best hotel in town, and went into the lobby for a breakfast of bad coffee and pre-packaged muffins. The other guests were men in BDUs or off-the-rack suits, the latter government workers or private contractors, usually ex-military. In its own small and sterile way, the morning ritual underscored how far removed the policy nomenklatura in Washington and New York— in its cocoon of fine restaurants and theoretical discussions—was from the frugal necessities of those who actually manned and maintained the Empire.

Washington and New York heralded the world of ideas; places like Oceanside the application of them. Because ideas can be tested only through application, Oceanside was sometimes the more intellectually stimulating.

———

To deploy from Camp Pendleton or Camp Lejeune in significant numbers overseas, which was the case with Iraq, the Marines assembled a MAGTF (pronounced "magtaf"): a Marine Air-Ground Task Force. MAGTFs came in different sizes, depending upon the need. But the key feature of all MAGTFs was their self-sufficiency, with ground combat, aviation, support service, and command components. The largest MAGTFs were the three Marine Expeditionary Forces, or MEFs as they were called, consisting of forty thousand to forty-five thousand marines each.

The First Marine Expeditionary Force (I MEF), based out of Camp Pendleton, covered the Pacific. The Second Marine Expeditionary Force (II MEF), based out of Camp Lejeune, covered the Atlantic. The Third Marine Expeditionary Force (III MEF) was forward deployed in Okinawa, Japan. Smaller than the other MEFs, III MEF had only seventeen thousand marines and was focused on the Korean Peninsula. But all these areas of responsibility were fluid and overlapped. For example, both I and II MEF had seen action in Operation Iraqi Freedom the year before.

Below the MEFs were the MEBs, Marine Expeditionary Brigades of 8,000 to 10,000 marines each. Below them were the MEUs, Marine Expeditionary Units. The MEUs, with about 2,200 marines each, were the real workhorses of Marine deployments in the unconventional post–Cold War world, able to react fast to overseas emergencies with their six-hour Rapid Response Planning Process. The Marines' smallest element was their special purpose MAGTFs, custom fit for just about every situation.

Iraq obviously rated a MEF, the largest kind of MAGTF.

A year earlier, I MEF had been tasked to capture Baghdad. Its ground combat element, the 1st Marine Division, "marched up" from Kuwait to the Iraqi capital, a feat that recalled the ten thousand Greek hoplites under Xenophon who had marched north from Mesopotamia and across Asia Minor in 400 B.C., and "hacked their way through every army that challenged them."[1] The marines advanced on Baghdad under the symbol of the Blue Diamond—the five stars of the Southern Cross against the blue of the evening sky—which commemorated the 1st Division's landing in 1942 at Guadalcanal in the Solomon Islands. The 1st Division also retook Seoul in 1950 during the Korean War, Hue City in 1968 during the Vietnam War, and Kuwait City in 1991 during Desert Storm.

In 2003 during Operation Iraqi Freedom (OIF, in U.S. military parlance), the 1st Marine Division, along with the Army's 3rd Infantry Division, did most of the fighting. Following the ouster of Saddam Hussein, the 1st Division assumed responsibility for stabilizing heavily Shiite south-central Iraq. During that deployment, unlike the experience of the Army in the Sunni Triangle, not one marine was killed. The Marines ascribed their success partly to lessons learned from their *Small Wars Manual*.[2]

The *Small Wars Manual,* it was at least hoped, would guide the division's latest assignment. In the early weeks of 2004, I MEF, with the 1st Division as its ground combat element, was preparing to deploy to western Iraq, an area the size of North Carolina stretching from the Euphrates River to the Syrian border, including part of the Sunni Triangle. This area of responsibility contained 2.8 million people, 80 percent of whom were Sunni and 20 percent Shiite.

While I was at Camp Pendleton, Maj. Gen. James N. Mattis, the 1st Division's commander, delivered his pre-deployment brief to thousands of marines.* He made it clear that not only were the Marines returning to Iraq, they were also returning to their roots as unconventional warriors: a tradition forged long ago in the Philippines and in the Central American "Banana Wars" of the early twentieth century, when the Marines were referred to as the "State Department's troops."

Old black-and-white photos of U.S. Marines in Nicaragua accompanied the brief. Noting Iraq's "confusing, challenging" environment, Maj. Gen. Mattis told his marines that "Chesty Puller faced a similar situation in Nicaragua in 1929 and learned how to be a warrior. He learned on hundreds of patrols over years of fighting where he and his men destroyed the enemy and won the trust of the people."

That history might have been obscure to people in Washington, but it was fresh and relevant to those at Camp Pendleton—perhaps more relevant than the two world wars. Lewis Burwell "Chesty" Puller, born in rural Virginia, grew up worshipping Confederate generals like Robert E. Lee

---

* Whereas Maj. Gen. Mattis, a two-star general, commanded the ground combat element of I MEF, the MEF itself was commanded by Lt. Gen. James T. Conway, a three-star general.

and Stonewall Jackson.[3] He developed a chest "like a pouter pigeon" (hence the nickname). In Haiti, beginning in 1919, Marine Pvt. Chesty Puller led bush patrols composed of native Creole-speaking troops in the struggle against the *cacos*—outlaw gangs opposed to the U.S. occupation. In 1924 he became a second lieutenant, and between 1929 and 1933 he served two tours in Nicaragua, fighting against Augusto César Sandino, the leftist guerrilla leader after whom the Sandinistas were named.

A bandit to the Marines and a hero to radicals throughout Latin America, Sandino threatened Nicaragua's stability, which was crucial to the protection of the Panama Canal. Puller and his gunnery sergeant, William A. Lee, commanded a company of three dozen locally recruited Indians in the fight against Sandino. They marched thirty miles a day, living off the land. "Whenever a chow line formed, Puller and Lee made sure they were at the back; their men got fed first," writes Max Boot in *The Savage Wars of Peace*.

Men wounded or killed were evacuated from the battlefield. Applying the Marine ethos to his native troops, Puller never left an *indig* behind. In 1931, after an earthquake and fire had devastated the capital of Managua, Puller and other marines took the lead in salvage, rescue, and recovery operations. It was just one aspect of the humanitarian side of Marine operations in Nicaragua.

While the political outcome to that early U.S. intervention in Nicaragua was messy, the Marines took pride in it, just as they and the Green Berets took pride in their performance in Vietnam. Though many Americans categorized such interventions as failures and moral disgraces, the Marines knew that the history of those interventions was complex: there were tactics that worked, as well as those that didn't; actions of positive moral consequence, and of negative consequence.

Invoking Nicaragua, Gen. Mattis said he needed "self-disciplined young sailors and marines who can smile to children,* wave to Iraqis who flip you the bird . . . who are tough enough to be kind to the innocent, no matter what the enemy does to us or our buddies. . . . We must win the hearts and minds of the Iraqi people," he went on, repeating a Vietnam War phrase. "Satellites don't give us intel in a counterinsurgency—as you win their trust, the people will give you intel."

Nevertheless, aware of the gritty realities bedeviling the Army in west-

---

* The Marines were a naval force; the medics in each Marine platoon were not marines but "Navy corpsmen," hence the reference to sailors.

ern Iraq at that moment—realities with which the Marines would soon have to deal—Mattis said that in the eyes of Iraqis, Marines had to be seen as *No Better Friend, No Worse Enemy.* He added, "Wave at them, but have a plan to kill them."

Gen. Mattis ended on a religious note. Marines should use the solitude and hardships of the Iraqi desert to strengthen their faith in God: "We, like the people who've gone to the desert before, will know ourselves better and come to have a greater appreciation for each other."

Mattis had the reputation of a "warrior-monk," a spartan fighter with deep moral convictions who was prodigiously well read in history and philosophy, even as he could communicate succinctly with lance corporals. He was a confirmed bachelor; his living quarters at Camp Pendleton were filled with maps and books. On his official résumé he chose to list only his commands, not other career paraphernalia. There was something minimalistic and vaguely Eastern about him—a gene almost, something which I had first detected in lesser degrees in Brig. Gen. Robeson and Capt. Cassidy in Djibouti. With Maj. Gen. Mattis it became sufficiently noticeable for me to identify.

The Prussian-style high-and-tight crew cuts and the cult of German Field Marshal Erwin Rommel that existed within the corps fooled a lot of people. In fact, the U.S. Marines came from the East, from the Orient. That was their spiritual tradition. It was the legacy of their naval landings throughout the Pacific, of the Marine legation guards during the Boxer Rebellion in China, of the "China Marines" in the 1920s, and, most of all, of the very didacticism of the Navy itself, the Marines' sister service, which fit well with Eastern philosophy.

The Army had Clausewitz; the Marines Sun-Tzu. It was a Marine brigadier general, Samuel Blair Griffith II—who had served in China before and after World War II—who translated Sun-Tzu's *The Art of War* in 1963 and Mao Zedong's *On Guerrilla War* in 1978.[*] Marines picked up on the local philosophy the same as they did the local food—not all marines obviously, not even most or many, but enough influential officers here and there so it filtered into the Marine character.

Embracing the local culture seemed to be particularly necessary in western Iraq, "where American military units," as one journalist had written,

---

[*] Lt. Gen. Griffith also earned the Navy Cross on Guadalcanal in September 1942 for "extreme heroism."

"had come and gone so often that they had little time to understand their surroundings," or to form meaningful relationships.* The Marines even had an acronym for the dual tasks that lay ahead—"winning hearts and minds" and "nation-building." It was SASO (stability and security operations). SASO was the buzzword at Camp Pendleton in late January 2004. It represented a hope that the conventional application of military force in "OIF-I"—what the Marines called their deployment in Iraq the year before—would be followed up in "OIF-II" by a more subtle, unconventional use of military force, resulting in the stabilization of Iraq as a democratic society.

As I would see, these hopes died hard.

———

Kuwait was the jumping-off point for my journey into Iraq. An oil-rich Persian Gulf city-state like Dubai, from where I had flown to and from Afghanistan a few months back, Kuwait was different. Dubai had been a veritable luxury shopping mall, punctuated by designer restaurants, nightclubs offering Russian prostitutes, and service up to the highest Asian standards, with international staffs. At times in Dubai, I didn't quite know where I was. Kuwait, however, was more traditional, with no alcohol and little flagrant prostitution, though Filipino cathouses were said to exist on Kuwait City's outskirts. Many of Kuwait's malls catered to a new Arab middle class rather than to a wealthy global elite. Unlike Dubai, whose Arabs and subcontinental Asians seemed like the smiling employees of one vast airport duty-free shop, Kuwait seemed an authentic mixture of Arabia and the Indian subcontinent. In the crumbly, crowded streets near my modest-priced hotel, Kuwait City brought back memories of my first visit to Baghdad twenty years earlier, during the Iran-Iraq War, prior to Saddam Hussein's invasion of Kuwait that had set in motion the destruction of Iraq's nascent prosperity.

My choice of a relatively cheap hotel was deliberate. The hardest, loneliest times on such trips were the days and hours before embedding, when you were particularly sensitive to the creature comforts you were about to give up. Nothing is worse for morale in these moments than luxurious surroundings.

———

* Michael Gordon, *New York Times,* Dec. 12, 2003. Gordon adds: In the Al-Fallujah area, the Army's 82nd Airborne Division had been replaced by the 3rd Armored Cavalry Regiment, which was replaced in turn by the 2nd Brigade of the 3rd Infantry, which handed it back to the 3rd Armored Cavalry and then back to the 82nd Airborne again.

One morning, following a typical Middle Eastern breakfast of *ful* beans, green olives, goat cheese, fresh pita bread, and tea in the dowdy dining room of my hotel, where I seemed to be the only westerner, a Marine lieutenant colonel in civilian clothes drove up to the entrance, threw my backpack and duffel bag into the rear of a sport utility vehicle, and transported me northwest into the desert, the site of Camp Udari, the staging point for the Marine deployment to Iraq. An hour later I was back in the Kellogg, Brown & Root world of tents, palettes, shipping containers, chow halls, and acronyms. Vast lines of seven-ton trucks and Humvees stretched across the horizon, all headed north. The epic scale of America's involvement in Iraq, so much larger than the other deployments I had been covering around the world, became quickly apparent.

The lieutenant colonel quickly passed me and my bags on to another officer, who drove me farther into the desert, to link up with the 1st Battalion of the 5th Marine Regiment, now part of Maj. Gen. Mattis's First Marine Division. The 1st of the 5th as it was called, or simply "1/5," had begun its field isolation the day before. In two days it would be crossing the border into Iraq.

Soon I was amidst two quarter-mile-long lines of Humvees and seven-ton trucks. A sandstorm had started. There was an icy wind. Rain threatened. Several officers and noncoms came up to me, introducing themselves. I was bewildered. It wasn't just their desert cammies, ballistic sunglasses, and high-and-tights that made them look the same; that I was used to. It was also that they all had mustaches. The decision to grow mustaches had been made by 1/5's commander, Lt. Col. Brennan Byrne, who believed that if his men looked a bit like Iraqis, winning hearts and minds might be easier. It would be days before I could distinguish many of his marines individually.

The two lines of humvees and seven-tons constituted Charlie Company, a subdivision of the 1st of the 5th. When I arrived, 1st Lt. David Denial of South Gate, California, was in the middle of a brief. He had an easel against the side of a Humvee, jerry-rigged with armored plates, making the Humvee into what the Marines called a hardback.

First Lt. Denial screamed above the wind and the Humvee's idling engine: "If you're forward of an explosion, haul ass a hundred meters in urban terrain, two hundred in rural; if you're behind an explosion, un-ass a hundred meters in urban, two hundred in rural. If you make contact with the enemy, let me know. I'll do the translation. I speak Army; not much, but I speak it. And explain the ROEs to your subordinate NCOs. This battalion killed civilians last year in OIF-I because in some cases it didn't know the ROEs."

The 1st of the 5th, which comprised just under a thousand marines, was a small part of the 1st Marine Division that would be replacing the Army's 82nd Airborne Division in western Iraq. This formed a major piece of one of the largest troop movements in half a century, with roughly 250,000 soldiers and marines leaving and entering Iraq through the narrow umbilical cord of several bases in Kuwait, over a six-week period. Here was where the mass organizational know-how, borne of several major wars in the twentieth century, paid off for the U.S. military.

About 60 percent of the battalion were veterans of OIF-I. They had fought pitched battles in the oil fields of southern Iraq, slogged through muddy, dusty hellholes like Ad-Diwaniyah, and in a nine-hour battle on April 10, 2003, secured Saddam's palace at the bend of the Tigris in central Baghdad, in the course of which 1/5 sustained dozens of casualties and collected several Bronze Stars for valor. Yet the most significant thing about OIF-I, according to 1st Lt. Richard Wilkerson of Knoxville, Tennessee, was that except for fourteen total hours of hard fighting over a twenty-day period, it was also a *small war.* "Most of the time we were doing SASO: convoy ops, presence patrols, community policing, that is," Lt. Wilkerson said.

The sun sunk so fast over the desert that it was like a searchlight being switched off. Because of the northeast wind I immediately began to freeze. I have never been so cold as in semi-tropical deserts at night. Lt. Col. Byrne held his command brief in the "lee" of a Humvee in the pitch blackness. (A naval force, marines used any opportunity they could find to employ seafaring terminology.) The one-hour meeting dealt with the logistics of a forty-mile-long convoy split into four serials, leaving at thirty-minute intervals, with 250 vehicles spaced a hundred meters apart. Everything from guard duty to battery charging to radio frequency hopping to ammunition draws was gone over. "If the comms shit in bed as comms have a tendency to do, it means we'll have a break in radio contact, so use your fucking hand signals," advised one officer. Thus the meeting went.

The meeting broke up with everyone going off to sleep under their respective cammie nets. Field isolation meant no running water, no coffee or tea, and no chow except for MREs. "Come on," Lt. Col. Byrne told me,

"I'll show you your hootch." He pointed out a cammie net and then disappeared. I couldn't see a thing. A voice asked, "What's your name?"

"Bob," I answered. "I'm a writer."

"Me too. I write haikus and science fiction. But my real passion is har-
vesting venom from pygmy rattlesnakes and reading about feudal Japan. I
started my own computer company in high school but didn't have enough
money to go to college. I love guns, so I joined the Marines. Do you need
anything?"

"I didn't expect it to be this cold in Kuwait. My gear is insufficient."

There was a rustling sound and then I felt a thick sleeping bag in my
hand, and a liner given to me by someone else moving around in the dark.
A minute later I was handed a balaclava.

The haiku writer was Lance Cpl. Mike Neal of the South Side of
Chicago. He handled the M240G medium machine gun mounted atop the
Humvee in which I would travel all the way to Al-Fallujah. The driver of
the Humvee was Cpl. Daniel Pena of Waukegan, Illinois. The commander
of the Humvee and five others, comprising Lt. Col. Byrne's headquarters
and personal security element, was Chief Warrant Officer II David Bednarcik of Allentown, Pennsylvania. All were veterans of OIF-I. They had
fought their way from southern Iraq into Saddam's palace. They called
themselves the "Renegades."

Lance Cpl. Neal and Cpl. Pena were twenty and twenty-one, respectively. Chief Warrant Officer Bednarcik was in his mid-thirties. Because he
was an infantry weapons specialist, he was more properly addressed as
Gunner Bednarcik rather than Chief Bednarcik, the way chief warrant officers are addressed in the Army. All three introduced themselves to me in
the dark; only in the morning would I see their faces.

Stars winked through the cammie net. I got a few hours of sleep.
Reveille was at 5:30 a.m. Immediately thereafter, rifle and other drills
commenced. Then ammunition was handed out for the long journey, and
radio call signs were issued: "Red Cloud," "Apache," "Crazy Horse,"
"Geronimo," and other Indian names. Because of the feverish activity and
excitement of departure, the distinctions between the various categories of
Marine sergeants and corporals that I had noticed in Djibouti seemed less
sharp here.

Before we rolled out, Protestant and Catholic prayer services were
held. At the Protestant ceremony, about several hundred marines huddled

together on the dun flatness of the Kuwaiti desert, as bagpipes sounded "Amazing Grace." Chaplain Steve Pike of Whittier, California, read from Deuteronomy (26:4–10), about the Hebrews' "affliction" in Egypt, and how the Lord had brought them out of bondage. Then he thanked God "for such a dry, hard place" where the Marines could do the "difficult spiritual work necessary to experience the glory of Easter," a few weeks away. He prayed for "the marines, their families, and the Iraqi people." At the end of the service, rumbling lightly over the desert, was the sound of hundreds of voices:

Our Father which art in heaven, Hallowed be thy name. Thy kingdom come. Thy will be done on earth, as it is in heaven. Give us this day our daily bread. And forgive us our debts, as we forgive our debtors. And lead us not into temptation, but deliver us from evil: For thine is the kingdom, and the power, and the glory, forever. Amen.[4]

The congregation dispersed quietly. Lance Cpl. Mike Neal gave me a refresher course on feeding ammunition to a machine gunner in the event we made contact with the enemy. At 1300 hours, a "police call" was announced, when the entire battalion formed a quarter-mile-long line that moved in unison over the camp area, in order to pick up our trash off the desert. The cammie nets were taken down. Marines put on their "flaks" (what Army Special Forces had called "individual body armor"). "Hard cover" (Kevlar helmets) replaced "soft cover" (bush hats; what Special Forces called "boonies").

Ours would be the last of 1/5's four "serials" to break camp. The complex preparations, including the counting of vehicles and "packages" (personnel), reminded me of the organizational procedures that had accompanied one of the last of the great camel caravans to cross Inner Mongolia in the late 1920s, as experienced by Owen Lattimore in *The Desert Road to Turkestan.* If one considered that the age of mass infantry warfare might be drawing to a close, this journey of more than 350 miles through open desert into central Iraq could constitute one of history's last great military convoys.

Finally we were on the road. "Why did you join the Marines?" I asked the driver of our Humvee, Cpl. Pena, a short, soft-spoken, fair-complexioned

Mexican-American with a bulky physique and sweet disposition. He provided a typical story.

"To get away from lots of shit at home. I had bad habits. I would have been in jail by now had I not joined the corps. Just graduating from Waukegan, Illinois, High School was a real struggle for me. I won't reenlist, though. I'm going to college to study business management. I want to go into real estate and be a good citizen. The state of Illinois will pay for my education through the GI Bill."

We traveled north only two hours on Main Supply Route Tampa, or Highway 80—the famed "Highway of Death" for Iraqi soldiers fleeing Kuwait during Desert Storm. Then we stopped for the night at NAVISTAR: navigation starting point, the term that the U.S. military used for the Iraqi-Kuwaiti border. NAVISTAR was a massive fuel and maintenance facility— the mother of all truck stops. A sign at the entrance warned: "Kevlars and flak jackets are mandatory gear for all travel beyond this point."

Lance Cpl. Neal came down from his machine gun position on the Humvee's roof and immediately began talking to me, as he had the night before when we met. He was a big kid with stores of energy, dark hair, and a warm, friendly face that was constantly on the verge of a broad smile. On his shoulder was a big tattoo of a ghoulish monster. "That's Parintachin," he explained, "the crazy little clown that lives inside my head."

Neal's subject now was the nine-hour fight to secure Saddam's palace at the bend of the Tigris in central Baghdad. "It was like the movie *Black Hawk Down* without the rioters. I was RPGed so often I gradually stopped ducking. During one of the lulls I was relaxed enough to eat an MRE and fall asleep for a few minutes. I was so tired and hungry. You get used to anything if it goes on long enough."

NAVISTAR was a vast gravel maze of Jersey barriers that smelled of oil and gasoline. We did a fast-paced quarter-mile march in formation to the chow hall. There was no time to piss even—or you would lose your platoon and never find them again in the dark, as masses of marines and soldiers were being processed through in different directions. The chow hall was airless and overcrowded, with low ceilings and putrefying smells. "This ain't no fuckin' Denny's," a sergeant major screamed over the confusion. "Eat fast, don't talk, and get the fuck out. There are more people waiting to chow down."

The immensity of the redeployment was visually staggering. Outside, engines and generators whined in the dark, as long lines of trucks partially blocked out the stars.

In the order of the convoy, the Renegades led by Gunner Bednarcik were part of the Charlie "stick" of Alpha Company. We were provided a narrow patch of sand between two lines of vehicles to lay our sleeping bags. Reveille would be at 2:30 a.m. There was no place to wash; no heads or Porta-Johns either. By 2:45 a.m. we had packed our gear and marines were fiddling with straps and lubricants, loudly cursing at broken doors and transmission problems.

Iraq was heralded by the lights of burning petrol fires. We rode for hours on the hardball road in the dark. My teeth chattered and my thighs shook from the freezing cold air pouring through the roof hatch where Lance Cpl. Neal sat behind his machine gun. "I'm so cold that my face has frozen into a permanent grin," he shouted down through the hatch.

Dawn brought a landscape of cindery desert and short grass the greenish gray color of mold. As we continued north the desert became increasingly alkaline, with knife-sharp depressions of salt mixed with dried mud. A five-minute piss break was announced through the handheld ICOMs, or intra-squad radios. Hundreds of marines lined up along the road to water the desert. Marines looked at each other and laughed. I ate a cold MRE of Thai chicken for breakfast.

We passed long armored convoys of Turkish trucks bearing fuel and consumer items out of and into Iraq. The construction of the hardball road was the quality of an American interstate, a legacy of Iraq's oil wealth from the 1970s and 1980s before Saddam invaded Kuwait and sanctions were imposed. As the morning wore on, Iraqi civilians appeared along the sides of the highway and in battered minivans, and waved at us. We crossed the Euphrates River between An-Nasiriyah and An-Najaf, entering the heart of southern Shiite Mesopotamia. Here and there were small green areas bordered by irrigation ditches. Iraqis in soiled yet dignified robes and keffiyahs stood beside sheep and cattle, and waved. But for the most part, the dreary moonscape did not cease.

———

Of all the landscapes and geographical situations across the earth, according to the French orientalist Georges Roux, Iraq's is among the least changed throughout history. Roux's book *Ancient Iraq* neatly bridges the gap between the romantic vision of Mesopotamia, based on the first chapters of Genesis, and the rather grim landscape I found there on this and previous visits.[5]

Adam and Eve, it turned out, did not live in a garden paradise but in a turgid mud swamp. The Tigris and Euphrates "flow with such a low gradient that they meander considerably and throw numerous side branches," creating many "lakes and swamps," interspersed with "dreary wastes strewn with dry wadis and salt lakes."[6] The ancient Mesopotamian towns, Roux continues, "were built of nothing but mud."

There is also the early-twentieth-century English traveler Robert Byron's description of Iraq: "It is a mud plain. . . . From this plain rise villages of mud and cities of mud. The rivers flow with liquid mud."[7]

Keep in mind that Iraq has the bone-dry climate of a desert, which is constantly cracking the mud and blowing it into fine dust. Roux notes that temperatures in Mesopotamia, from prehistory onward, reach 120 degrees in summer, and the average annual rainfall is under ten inches, most of which comes in the early spring, causing floods. But since all the land to the west until the Mediterranean and to the east until the Indian subcontinent is riverless and rainless desert, this dreary artery of mud was where ancient civilization developed.

But it did not exactly prosper. Contrary to popular belief, fed by biblical clichés, the valley of the Tigris and the Euphrates did not make Iraq an old and unified land in the way that the Nile Valley made Egypt. Both river valleys may have been the mothers of history and of civilization, narrow lines of life amid desert nothingness, but that is where the similarities ended.

Roux explains that since antiquity the Nile had an annual flood of almost constant volume, with the great lakes of East Africa acting as regulators. Because the Nile "freely inundates the valley for a time and then withdraws," it required only the "cheap and easy 'basin type' of irrigation," in which canal slits were dug and men waited for them to fill up. But the Tigris and the Euphrates had no great lakes at their source to regulate floods. They were two rivers instead of one, with the Tigris born of the snows of Kurdistan and the Euphrates flowing down from the mountains of Armenia. Moreover, their annual flooding occurred too late for the winter crops and too soon for the summer ones. Thus, irrigation in Mesopotamia was a never-ending drudgery involving reservoirs, dikes, and regulator sluices. Even then, unlike Egypt, little was guaranteed. Low waters over a few years meant drought and consequently famine, whereas high waters swept away mud houses as if they had never existed. Roux states that "this double threat and uncertainty" bred a "fundamental pessimism" among Mesopotamia's inhabitants.[8]

That pessimism grew not only out of the perennial struggle against nature, but also out of the struggle of man against man—another thing that did not exist in Egypt. Freya Stark explains: "While Egypt lies parallel and peaceful to the routes of human traffic, Iraq is from earliest times a frontier province, right-angled and obnoxious to the predestined paths of man."[9]

In other words, the Nile has always been a natural migration route. People didn't need to cross it, but to go up or down it. The Nile brought ivory and spices from Africa. The Tigris and the Euphrates brought nothing except their waters. The times that foreign invaders violated Egypt by sea, or by land across the Sinai Peninsula, were few enough to be well remembered—the aggressions of Alexander the Great and Napoleon, for example, which brought learning and economic progress.

But Iraq was never left alone. The valley of the Tigris and Euphrates, as Freya Stark indicates, ran at a right angle to one of history's bloodiest routes of migration. From the Syrian desert in the west came the Amorites, the Hittites, and the medieval Arab armies of the Umayyad caliphs in Damascus: a threat that in modern times has been represented by the rival Baathist regime in Syria. To the east loomed the high plateau of Elam, "the great mountain that strikes terror," from where invaders, including Aryan Kassites, Persians under Darius and Xerxes, Mongol hordes, and Ayatollah Khomeini's Iranians, all marched down into Mesopotamia.[10]

Yet the most important difference between the Nile Valley and Mesopotamia was that while the former was always a demographically cohesive unit, the latter was a nebulous border region where various groups clashed and overlapped. Outsiders have occasionally been inclined to interpret Iraq as a modern outgrowth of an age-old polity, known variously by such names as Sumer, Akkad, Assyria, Babylonia, and the Baghdad caliphate. In truth, as Roux painstakingly documents, each of these civilizations encompassed only a part of present-day Iraq, a part that was often at war with the other parts. The Sumerians, who lived in southern Mesopotamia, fought the Akkadians of central Mesopotamia, and both of them fought the Assyrians, who inhabited northern Mesopotamia. The Assyrians, in turn, fought the Babylonians, who occupied the border region between what had been, in a previous millennium, Sumer and Akkad. This is to say noth-

ing of the many islands of Persians who lived amidst the native Meso-
potamians, forming another source of strife.

Though the ancient Greek historians called the region Mesopotamia,
meaning "the land between the [two] rivers," Roux notes that the inhabitants of Mesopotamia themselves "had no name covering the totality of the
country in which they lived." The terms they used were either too vague
("the Land") or too precise ("Sumer," "Akkad," and so on).[11] Thus, the current division of Iraq between Indo-European Kurds in the northern mountains, Sunni Arabs in central Mesopotamia, and Shiite Arabs in southern
Mesopotamia was—like the divisions that I had seen in Yemen, Colombia,
the Philippines, and Afghanistan—a formidable legacy of both history and
geography.

I reached into an MRE bag and grabbed a fudge brownie for lunch. It had
the consistency of drying cement. During another piss break a growly senior noncom took a back seat in our Humvee after the alternator had gone
bust on his command car. "Fuck this . . . un-fuck that . . . un-ass that . . .
Corporal, you're as fucked up as a football bat," he went on. After gouging
on MREs he fell into a deep sleep, for which I was grateful.

I kept up a running conversation with Gunner David Bednarcik. The
gunner was a stocky, matter-of-fact regular Joe with a shrewd and likable
temperament, the kind of guy I'd trust on anything from setting up presence patrols in an unpacified area to presidential politics. There were rare
moments when he reminded me of the late comic John Candy, of course
without the obesity (in fact, Bednarcik was a long-distance runner). He
was a lifer in the corps, set on doing thirty years, though he would only
half admit it. More than a decade older than Cpl. Pena and Lance Cpl.
Neal, he had a mild, avuncular disposition toward them and the other
"knuckleheads" in the platoon, as he called them.

"I'm from Allentown, Pennsylvania, a place where people are real patriotic," he told me with distinct pride. His family boasted World War II, Korean War, and Vietnam War veterans. Grenada and Beirut had affected him
deeply, so he joined the Marines. A former drill instructor at Parris Island,
South Carolina, and later a gunnery sergeant, he was the ultimate iron grunt.
Yet he also harbored a mellowness that made him a delight to be around.*

---

* Just as this book was going to press, Gunner Bednarcik—back in Iraq for the third time
  in the spring of 2005—was badly wounded and recovering at Bethesda Naval Hospital.

"Parris Island is a machine," Gunner Bednarcik explained, in a reference to Marine Corps basic training. "Drill instructors there are rough because of all the pressure on them to produce competent recruits in a finite period of time. Every minute of the day is micro-managed for the recruits. You can't talk nice to grunts," he intoned in a knowing, authoritative manner, as though confiding a secret to me. "Make no mistake, these are tough kids around you, really tough kids. Unless you're tough with them, they don't respond. The Army wants to train you in order to teach you skills. Fuck that. Marine Corps training seeks to break you down in order to remake you as a better person."

I asked him about one officer in particular, who had seemed a bit distant. "Yeah, I know," Gunner Bednarcik said. "He's a real East Coast marine. You see, Camp Lejeune is close to the flagpole at Quantico [Virginia] and II MEF now has less to do in terms of deployments. The combination makes East Coast marines sticklers for details and regulations"—exactly what I had noticed in Djibouti.

"Camp Lejeune. Jacksonville, N.C.," the Gunner went on, shaking his head with disapproval, "jack shacks, strip joints, the Business of Immorality in other words. Wherever you see the Business of Immorality you know there is a low ratio of available women to young men. Truth be told, Pendleton marines have more fun. The young marines there are right by the interstate, close to Hollywood and San Diego. The best deal for a lance corporal is to do basic at Parris Island and then be posted to Camp Pendleton."

It was after midday. Dried mud oases with whited-out date palm jungles and mud-walled villages appeared under a broad and pasty sky. Women in billowing black robes were walking on berms beside irrigation ditches, with water jugs on their heads. There were donkeys and cattle but no camels. Then came more alkaline desert.

In the late afternoon, exactly thirteen hours after leaving NAVISTAR, we pulled into "Scania," another U.S. military fuel and resupply depot, located two hours south of Baghdad near Al-Hillah. The Jersey barriers, HESCO baskets, and Porta-Johns created the instant sensation of having left Iraq. After refueling, the convoy lined up in eight yawning columns, divided by narrow gravel lanes, where we were told to lay out sleeping bags.

Darkness fell as we stumbled back from chow. Lance Cpl. Neal showed me how to arrange the rifle plates in my flak jacket as a more comfortable surface for sleeping atop the gravel. Using a flashlight in the dark, he showed me a World War I compass that his Marine grandfather had given him, inscribed "Semper Fi, Love Grandpa."

One marine, cursing the sharp gravel, simply laid his sleeping bag on the hood of a truck and fell asleep. Under the stars, we all fell silent as the bagpiper played the "Marine Hymn." Then the loud noises and other chaos of this latter-day caravanserai resumed.

While I was lying in my sleeping bag, one of the Renegades, Cpl. Michael Pinckney of South Kingstown, Rhode Island, came up to me and began to talk: "I'm twenty-three. My generation sucks. They're all soft. They don't care about their identity as Americans. We live in some bad-ass country, and they're not even proud of it. My family flies the flag, but other families don't. Nobody knows what it means to be American anymore, to be tough. I like being home and yet I don't. People at home are not proud of us being in Iraq, because they've lost the meaning of sacrifice. They expect things to be perfect and easy. They don't know that when things go wrong you persevere; you don't second-guess. During OIF-I, we all slept in the rain and got dysentery in Ad-Diwaniyah. But back home, everyone is going to shrinks and suing each other. That's why I like the Marine Corps. If you fuck up, your sergeant makes you suck it up. I don't want to be anywhere else but Iraq. OIF-I and OIF-II, this is what manhood is all about. And I don't mean macho shit either. I mean moral character."

Despite news reports of low morale in the armed services because of overdeployment, with Army Special Forces and the Marines I had met only two kinds of troops: those who were serving in Iraq and Afghanistan, and those who were jealous of those who were.

Reveille was at 5 a.m. After packing our sleeping bags and chowing down, the Gunner gave the platoon a brief on IEDs (improvised explosive devices, including car bombs), which the insurgents often placed on the highway to Baghdad. "All right you knuckleheads, the latest intel mentions Volkswagens, sedans, BMWs, Opels, and red Toyotas as particularly suspicious. I know, I know, that's half the cars on the road. All's I mean is, as Bugs Bunny would say, be *wery, wery* aware."

The next brief came from Sgt. Christian Driotez of Los Angeles. Sgt. D, as he was called, was from a Salvadoran immigrant family. Powerfully built with a hands-on, Charles Bronson–type expression, he was, nevertheless, the mildest, most considerate sergeant I would meet in the Marine Corps, as well as a true leader of men. He had joined the corps, he claimed, because he wanted to make "a fucking difference"—after having seen kids dragged off to fight against their will by left-wing rebels in his family's native country.

"Remember the battalion motto for OIF-II," Sgt. D told the platoon: "*Make Peace or Die*. And make sure you got your fucking ACOG [advanced combat optical gunsight] on your rifles. This is where Iraq really starts. There will be no head calls. So bring empty water and Gatorade bottles to piss in. We're tight, but we're gonna get a lot tighter as the weeks go on. I'm already proud of you guys."

Before we pushed off, the chaplain asked the holy angels to protect us.

We would drive north until the outskirts of Baghdad, then veer west into the heart of the Sunni Triangle near Al-Fallujah. There, at Forward Operating Base (FOB) Mercury, 1/5 would replace the 1st Battalion of the 504th Regiment of the Army's 82nd Airborne Division.

As soon as our serial pulled out onto the main highway, the convoy halted because of a suspected improvised explosive device. Two Army helicopters flew overhead to survey the area and to escort the serial onward. It was a false alarm, though. "Fucking paranoia," Gunner Bednarcik complained. I saw immediately how one person, planting a primitive explosive device, might tie an entire infantry company in knots, even if it had air support. Asymmetry was a basic fact of life in Iraq. And it usually favored the insurgents.

"I want action," Cpl. Pena blurted out.

"No thanks. I've had my fill of shooting civilians," answered Lance Cpl. Neal. "During OIF-I," he explained, "we had strong indications that a vehicle was hostile and I was ordered to fire. It turned out to be an old man who died in seconds. I felt miserable, but under the same circumstances I would have no choice but to do it again."

We were on the outskirts of Baghdad. Pena, Neal, and the Gunner were amazed at the new cars and satellite dishes that clogged the road and rooftops, which they told me had not been here the year before, on the eve of the invasion. The only ugly thing we noticed was the graffiti on the highway overpasses scrawled by the Army's 3rd Infantry Division. The mosques, both Sunni and Shiite, with their glittering faience domes bore the mark of Persian architectural influence: the product of history and geography, as Iran was next door. The golden age of Baghdad at the turn of the ninth century, under the Abbasid caliph Harun al-Rashid, had been, to a significant degree, the upshot of Persian ideas and artisanship.

In early afternoon the low dun walls of Al-Fallujah came into view over the desert. The convoy turned away from the city, though, and headed eastward a few miles: until the apricot-colored desert, partially lost in a haze of chok-ing dust squalls, gave way to a maze of Jersey, Texas, and Alaska barriers, followed by concertina wire, HESCO baskets, and tank treads functioning as speed bumps.* Here and there I saw light scrub and lines of eucalyptus trees. For the marines, this would be their home for months to come.

It was a complex of two bases, really: FOB (forward operating base) St. Mere, and the smaller FOB Mercury. Both had been named by the 82nd Airborne. St. Mere commemorated the village in Normandy, Sainte-Mère-Eglise, that the 82nd had fought for on D-Day. The entire area had been a training facility for the Iranian Mujahidin Khalq (Holy Warriors of the Masses), a guerrilla group supported by Saddam Hussein that sought to overthrow the regime in Teheran. Because Saddam's Iraq was such a highly militarized state, Iraq was cluttered with palaces and military en-campments in which American troops ensconced themselves.

The 1st Marine Division was divided into three regimental combat teams, or RCTs. FOB St. Mere was the headquarters of RCT-1, of which 1/5 formed a part. St. Mere was also the headquarters of I MEF. High-ranking officers were everywhere, therefore. Pena and Neal took one look at the place and muttered disdainfully, "POGs" (pronounced "poges"—persons other than grunts, that is, office types at the regimental, division, and MEF level). "They live high on the hog," Pena said, "not like us grunts who do the real fighting. But we like it that way." The chow hall at St. Mere was the fanciest I had seen thus far in my travels, with separate salad and dessert bars and a big-screen television set permanently to the ESPN sports channel. St. Mere also had a nice PX, laundry facilities, and Kel-logg, Brown & Root shower units.

We left FOB St. Mere after a brief stop and journeyed two miles farther into the desert: to FOB Mercury, 1/5's new home.

Forward Operating Base Mercury was a bleak gravel and dirt expanse with low reinforced-concrete buildings and rows of tents. It was noisy with the groan of generators. There were no amenities. Instead of nice shower and toilet units there were plastic Porta-Johns. The chow hall made you think of a penitentiary. I shared a barracks room with five captains and two warrant officers, along a hallway with busted doors, smashed fluorescent

---

* The size of the state indicated the size of the various cement barricades, Jersey being the smallest and Alaska the largest.

lights, and choking dust. Kit bags were splattered everywhere. "This room looks like a yard sale," one of my rack mates complained in jest after we had moved in. After days of traveling, our "feet funk" was overpowering. Of course, all the deprivations up to this point counted for little compared to those suffered by both the troops and the journalists who had experienced OIF-I.

It didn't help matters that there was often no water in the showers. Living conditions at FOB Mercury would never really improve much over the weeks I was there. Something was always running out—the water, the electricity, the chow even. But FOB Mercury would turn out to be the ultimate stripped-down forward base. It was a place where everyone contributed directly to the fighting effort. It harbored a monastic purity that I had found almost nowhere else in the world among the American military.

The first night there we were attacked by mortars and rockets. It would be a regular occurrence. Problems tumbled down upon the marines before they had even washed and unpacked. The Iraqi barber who serviced the base had just been murdered; the local water contractor had been threatened. The day we arrived there was a shoot-out at a meeting of the provincial council in Al-Fallujah, which couldn't even decide on getting a road built. A number of American soldiers and marines in the city, who had arrived in-country some days before us, were wounded in the process.

One of the captains in my hootch, Jaime McCall of Wilmington, Delaware, had just learned that come the end of June, following the transfer of political power back to the Iraqis, U.S. troops might require search warrants whenever they entered Iraqi houses in pursuit of terrorists. As the battalion judge advocate general, he was sure a compromise could be worked out. Nevertheless, the early consensus in the hootch was that the Bush administration was thrusting too much responsibility upon the Iraqis too soon.

Within hours the details and rigors of the convoy had been forgotten and everyone immersed himself in his new tasks. Because 1/5 would be replacing the 1st of the 504th of the 82nd Airborne in the region between Al-Fallujah and Baghdad, the commander of 1/504, Army Lt. Col. Marshall Hagen of Fosston, Minnesota, spent the next few days showing Lt. Col. Byrne around the AOR (area of responsibility), introducing him to members of the various Iraqi town councils.

It was a unique AOR. Partly because of its proximity to Baghdad, it had more Shiites than perhaps any other place in the Sunni Triangle. The Shiites were generally easier for the U.S. military to deal with. Not only had they been on board for regime change, but their more formalized clerical bureaucracy facilitated the identification of local leaders, and thereby the establishment of communal relationships with the Army and Marines. (It had also facilitated the Iranian revolution in 1978–79, allowing the ayatollahs to form a state within a state even before the Shah fell.)

Army Lt. Col. Hagen's knowledge of the local tribes, clans, and subclans, and the power struggles therein, plus his ability to separate good guys from bad guys on each local council, was considerable—testimony to the fact that even such a conventional force as the 82nd Airborne was capable of adaptation to the most unconventional of circumstances. "I'm no expert," he told me; "there are at least seven different Iraqs, and many layers to each of them. Anyone who calls himself an expert on Iraq is full of shit. The more I learn, the more unfathomable it all becomes."

For the next few days, Lt. Cols. Hagen and Byrne and their staffs were to become inseparable, as the Army unloaded a virtual data dump about the area on the Marines. Intel briefings about such items as the trajectories of incoming mortars and attempts to identify their points of origin would last up to three hours at a time. Hostility between the services, while it still existed, was less noxious now than at any point in American military history—a legacy of the Goldwater-Nichols Act of 1986 that created unified area commands and enlarged the joint staff at the Pentagon in order to force the services to work together.*

The first stop on Lt. Col. Hagen's tour for Lt. Col. Byrne was the West Baghdad City Council meeting, which took place every Saturday in the Mansour district of Baghdad. The council included sheikhs and other leaders of the towns immediately to the west of the Iraqi capital. The route from FOB Mercury to Baghdad took us onto a six-lane highway, past one of the palaces of Saddam's younger son, Qusai, now occupied by several Army Special Forces A-teams. After the palace came the former Saddam International Airport, now a sprawling conglomeration of separate coalition military bases—"Camp Victory" for the Combined Joint Task Force, "Camp Blackjack" for the Army's 1st Cavalry Division, and so on. The whole area was referred to as BIAP (Baghdad International Airport). Just

---

* Senator Barry Goldwater, Republican, of Arizona; Representative Bill Nichols, Democrat, of Alabama.

as the convoy from Kuwait had represented perhaps the last industrial age caravan, BIAP represented the epicenter of perhaps the last great mass infantry invasion.

A few minutes away lay the western edge of downtown Baghdad: decrepit-looking compared to the late 1980s when I had last seen it, the result of more than a decade of economic sanctions. Inside the art gallery where the council meeting was about to begin, I was stunned by the sight of Iraqis chatting loudly in little groups, with cell phones going off all the time. There were men and women in traditional keffiyahs and *abayas* (headscarves), and also in well-tailored suits; unlike the frumpy Eastern European attire of the 1980s when Iraq had been under the security tutelage of the East Germans. The creepy-looking Hollywood uglies—morose-looking security types I remembered from two decades before—were gone. The air of freedom was everywhere in the room, or so it seemed.

Two decades before, council members would have stood apart from each other in nervous silence, waiting to salute the senior official as soon as he entered the room. Now, the moment the council chairman sat down he was peppered with accusations. "We have seen nothing from you. . . . When are we going to see results?" The meeting quickly descended into backbiting.

During a short break, my initial romance with the new Iraq was shattered when a member of the council in a well-tailored suit, Sheikh Dhari al-Dhari, told me:

"People live in fear. There are robberies all the time, carjackings, kidnappings of the members of well-to-do families. The rich families are beginning to move to Amman [Jordan], to escape from the chaos. People don't go out after dark."

Sheikh al-Dhari described a situation reminiscent of Russia and South Africa following the collapse of their authoritarian regimes. As bad as those regimes were, because of their longevity they had made life predictable and people had found ingenious ways to adapt. Because the rules, albeit oppressive, were known, people sometimes found ways around them. But then came liberation and an interregnum of no rules, when nothing was predictable, fostering a new kind of oppression, tied to soaring crime rates.

Actually, Russia and the rest of the communist bloc—much more than South Africa—was the appropriate comparison for Iraq. The ruling Baath (Renewal) party here had been like the Soviet Communist party, its avowed utopian ideology receding deeper into the past as it evolved into a criminal organization. And when that crumbled, smaller mafias and protection rackets came into being that attached themselves to other criminal and terrorist enterprises. The much-trumpeted prisoner release announced by Saddam just prior to the American-led invasion in March 2003 had had a specific purpose: to let common criminals loose all over the country, to prepare the ground for post-invasion ungovernability.

Whereas the Americans were most concerned with terrorism, average Iraqis were just as concerned with common crime. One of the worst areas in the country was the town of Abu Ghraib, just west of Baghdad, where an infamous prison and torture facility was located. Responsibility for the town of Abu Ghraib was split between the 1st Cavalry Division and the 82nd Airborne, the latter of which was handing over its section of Abu Ghraib to the Marines.

Lt. Col. John Ryan of the 1st Cavalry Division got up to address the Iraqis on the council.

"You people can't have security if you can't police your own," Lt. Col. Ryan barked. "You know who the criminals and terrorists are. They're mainly not foreign terrorists. They're your own sons and cousins. You want jobs. Well, there will be no jobs without security. You have to take responsibility for your own neighborhoods. The coalition will be left with no choice but to spend more money in the countryside, where people are more law-abiding and friendly to us, than in Abu Ghraib. We will not feed the mouth that bites us," he went on. "I don't want to search your homes at three in the morning, but you people leave me no choice. Either help us find the criminals or stop complaining about it."

Lt. Col. Byrne hid his head in his hands out of embarrassment. He did not like the insulting tone of the Army lieutenant colonel, who hadn't even removed his flak jacket as the marines and Lt. Col. Hagen had done, and had spoken to the council like a drill instructor to recruits.

"You overthrew the system," one council member shot back, "so it is your job to provide security."

"If you want jobs," Lt. Col. Ryan replied evenly, "help us more with security."

Lt. Col. Byrne addressed the group. His tone was subdued: "I am an American marine. We have a different tradition than the Army. I am honored to be here to serve you. Like you, I am a believer. Before coming here, I met with my chaplain and prayed with him to bless our mission."

But the Army lieutenant colonel turned out to be no less culturally aware than his Marine counterpart. As I found out, Lt. Col. Ryan had tried the soft approach for weeks and had gotten nowhere, even as intelligence mounted about active links between several council members and violent criminals. Lt. Col. Ryan's tough manner was an experiment, he told me later. It was targeted at certain members of the council. Meanwhile, he was meeting privately with other council members.

After the meeting ended, Sheikh al-Dhari told Lt. Col. Byrne that "we need visual examples of progress. The more time that you Americans spend on your own security, the less effort you put into rebuilding, and the less respect the average Iraqi has for you." The sheikh had gotten to the root of the American military dilemma in Iraq, as I'll explain.

In fact, repression had not been the only tool used by Saddam Hussein. He had also bribed the paramount sheikhs of the Sunni Triangle with cash, fancy cars, tracts of land, and other tangible gifts. But the American-led invasion dismantled that entire system. And what had the Americans brought in return to assuage such notables, who for millennia had affected the thinking of their extended clans? The promise of elections? What was that? An abstraction that meant little to many here. In a part of the world where blood was thicker than ideas, it was a difficult step for one Muslim to dime out another Muslim, especially for something as intangible as elections.

Thus, the sheikhs and others, driven by narrow self-interest—as if that should have surprised anyone—made it known that they were open to deals with Syrians and assorted other jihadists, who knew the ingress routes and safe houses along the Euphrates River ratline into Iraq. It didn't help matters that the very militarization of the state facilitated by Saddam had turned Iraq into one huge ammunition storehouse for the supply of rockets and mortars to the jihadists, and the making of IEDs (improvised explosive devices). And with the Iraqi army disbanded, there was now a pool of people with knowledge of ordnance and explosives, and the incentive to use it against the Americans.

I noted the derision with which the council members and other Iraqis present at the meeting looked at us, with our Kevlar helmets and flak jackets further fortified by rifle plates. Simply by being seen with us, they were taking greater risks than we were, and yet they had no such protection, and rarely demanded any. The fact that, a year after the invasion, American marines and soldiers still had to travel around Iraq wearing such protective gear was itself an indication of how little had been achieved.

Because the Bush administration, trapped in an election cycle, could not tolerate more American casualties, unusual security precautions had to be taken which only increased the distance between the American military and the average Iraqi. The willingness to accept a greater number of casualties might have meant faster progress, but the home front in America probably lacked the appetite for that.

Lt. Col. Byrne, a marine brat who had grown up near Quantico, told me: "OIF-I may have been our greatest military victory since World War II. The Iraqi regime was a bunch of animals. How can any civilized person be against what we did? Our defense budget relative to our GDP is now lower than it's been for decades. Objectively, we can stay here at little cost for years helping the new Iraqi government, in order to get the job done. And with sufficient time, we simply can't lose. But will the home front, and the media that influences it so much, allow that? That's the issue."

Keep in mind that this was the early spring of 2004. The Abu Ghraib prison scandal and many other bad things were still in the future, and the marines with whom I was embedded were still more hopeful than hard-bitten. It was a time when Iraqis were still waving at them. Also remember that as a lead fighting unit in the successful 2003 conquest of Baghdad, they had returned here with an idealistic sense of mission. Byrne's comment, and those of other marines with whom I was traveling, reflected how the war was being viewed at a certain moment in time. After I left Iraq, and as the summer arrived, and then the autumn, the military situation would worsen, and embedded correspondents would accurately report a corresponding change in attitudes among marines, registered in growing doubts about the efficacy of the war.

Leaving the council meeting, I noticed the towering, half-completed mosque which dominated the entire Mansour district of Baghdad. Saddam had ordered it built as a monument to himself. On the eve of OIF-I, the mosque was on its way to being one of the largest buildings in the world, hideous beyond all imagining, like the Houston Astrodome surrounded by rocket launchers. I was reminded of Romanian dictator Nicolae Ceauşescu's half-completed House of the Republic in Bucharest at the time that he was toppled.

The architecture of parts of Baghdad told you everything you needed to know about the deposed regime. The presidential palace and the remnants of the nearby Defense and Interior ministries that had withstood American bombing made Baghdad's so-called Green Zone appear like a Babylonian temple precinct built to monstrous Stalinist proportions. Here in wafer-thin yellow brick and blue faience, all forms of megalomania from antiquity to the late twentieth century were united. The eight-pointed star, symbol of the Baath party, was, like the Nazi swastika, everywhere: on bridges, highway girders, overpasses, windows, gates, and other grillwork, evidence of the regime's egotistical desire for dominance over every facet of life. Even in the countryside I would find a world of opulent little palaces surrounded by primitive mudhut settlements: a veritable landscape of antiquity.

The palaces of Saddam and his sons Uday and Qusai, some adorned by immense man-made lakes, had two motifs: Las Vegas hotel-casinos or love shacks for their menagerie of mistresses and rape victims. Indeed, Saddam's son Uday bore a marked resemblance to Ceauşescu's spoilt and depraved son, Nicu, who also violently abused women.

The social and cultural refuse created by the regime was everywhere, overwhelming the American authorities. While clichés abounded about the talent of the Iraqi people and their ability to quickly build a vibrant capitalist society, officers of the 82nd Airborne who had been here for months told another, more familiar story: of how Iraqis, like their Syrian neighbors, had in recent decades not experienced Western capitalism so much as a diseased variant of it, in which you couldn't even open a restaurant or a shop without having connections to the regime. Above the level of the street vendor, in other words, capitalism here would have to be learned from scratch.

After we returned to FOB Mercury from the council meeting, the 82nd Airborne intel shop delivered another three-hour brief and data dump to the marines, this one dealing, in part, with tribal and clan politics. A bewildered Gunner Bednarcik came out of the meeting muttering, "There seems to be no end to this thing. But now I suppose we'll have to see it through, for the sake of our honor." He stayed up half the night, downloading photos of every intersection we had crossed, in order to learn the route better and prepare for ambushes. It would be a ritual of his for several weeks, as we visited all the towns in the area of responsibility for the first time.

Truly, Iraq's tribal reality hit you square in the face the moment you peered into local politics. Because Iraq was among the most backward parts of the Ottoman Empire, with little tradition of central government, tribalism had always been strong here. The Iraqi nationalism that followed World War I was in reality a vague ideological construction, dependent on an intertribal consensus. Tribalism was particularly prevalent near the Bedouin-influenced western desert, part of 1/5's area. The strength of the tribes intensified during the Iran-Iraq War of the 1980s, when the state lost much of its potency amid economic pressures. Because the tribes in the western desert near Al-Fallujah were too strong to destroy, Saddam had no choice but to co-opt them and make them part of his power structure.* It was such traditional loyalties existing below the level of the state that both Marxist and liberal intellectuals, in their pursuit of remaking societies along Soviet and Western democratic models, tragically underestimated.[12] Indeed, a year after the invasion of Iraq, with the country teetering on chaos, among the few groups in Washington without egg on their faces was a subculture of Middle Eastern area experts known as "tribalists."

Unable to sleep the first few nights at FOB Mercury, I walked around the camp under the stars, watching marines wash their BDUs in plastic buckets with their rifles beside them, often the only chance they had to do such chores. Every few hours the ground would shake from a rocket or mortar attack on the base, which everyone quickly got used to, even as there were periodic casualties.

Lt. Col. Byrne's next excursion was to Al-Karmah, nicknamed "Bad Karma" by the 82nd. Located between FOB Mercury and western Baghdad, it was a mini-Fallujah, a town where the soldiers of the 82nd were always getting shot at. Like Al-Fallujah, Karmah was a lawless town on the smuggling ratline to Jordan and Syria, where tribal rule was supreme and no one went to the police for anything. As with Al-Fallujah, Saddam had kept control by turning it into a Baath party stronghold. Both of these towns had a strong sense of local identity. The state of Iraq had usually counted for little in such places, except when it employed high levels of oppression.

---

* The situation was more complicated than that, however. Saddam, by drafting significant numbers of people into the military and hiring many on public works projects, weakened the traditional sheikhs even as he co-opted them. See Patrick Graham's "Beyond Fallujah: A Year with the Iraqi Resistance," *Harpers*, June 2004.

Before departing for Al-Karmah, Chief Warrant Officer Todd Mathisen of Reno, Nevada, a surrogate chaplain, read us Psalm 91, the so-called warrior psalm: because "*He* is my refuge and my fortress. . . . A thousand shall fall at thy side, and ten thousand at thy right hand; *but* it shall not come nigh thee." Mathisen told us that in Hebrew the words "trust" and "refuge" can mean the same thing. "So if you trust in the Lord of the Israelites, gents, you will be protected. Remember, you're on the enemy's playground, the terrain of evil. To trust in the Lord is the best way to hunt down the devil."

After more than a year of travel with the U.S. military, I had become accustomed to such sermons. They revealed a similar emphasis on a Christian God evinced by American troops in their letters home during the Revolutionary War, in the songs the soldiers sang during the Civil War that, as Edmund Wilson noted, "were like psalms," and in the stirring photos of Marines bowing down in prayer prior to the Pacific landings of World War II.[13] Though today's society may be more multicultural than those of the past, that is much less the case regarding the religious makeup of our all-volunteer military. Moreover, for young men living in austere conditions who were not rear-echelon types counting the days to go home but combat troops going out daily to risk their lives, morale could not be based on polite subtleties or secular philosophical constructions, but only on the stark belief in your own righteousness, and in the iniquity of your enemy.

Al-Karmah was heralded by a lovely mosque with a dazzling blue faience dome. Otherwise, it was a shithole. As soon as we pulled into the police station, Gunner Bednarcik had his marines mount the rooftop and fan out in a 360-degree protective fire formation. Lt. Col. Hagen then took Lt. Col. Byrne into the station to introduce the incoming Marine commander to the police chief, Ahmed Abdul Kareen. Kareen was the third police chief in Al-Karmah since the American conquest. The first had proved incompetent. The second had been assassinated. Kareen immediately began asking for more pistols and flak jackets, and complained about car thefts and other crimes that he was unable to stop. The police here had no power to bring in criminals; only the sheikhs could do that.

We moved to another room in the police station where the new town council had been assembled. The talk was about providing seed to the farmers, repairing a cement factory to create several hundred more jobs, landscaping a soccer field for local youth, and ripping out the guardrails on the highway which terrorists were using to plant IEDs. The civil affairs officers whom Lt. Col. Byrne had brought along took notes and asked follow-up questions. The area was too dangerous to interest civilian relief charities.

Outside the police station, I saw that the Gunner was not altogether happy with how the Renegades had manned and maintained their fire positions. "We're new," he told me. "That's what makes us vulnerable. The 82nd knows this place like their front yard. It's only a matter of time before we're tested."

That happened on the next visit to Al-Karmah. Toward the end of the next council meeting, the police fled and the kids on the streets beside the station scattered. Shops shut, bad signs all. A few minutes later, rocket-propelled grenades hit the compound, followed by mortar rounds from the east, and small arms fire from a girls' school to the west. The small arms fire then came at the Renegades from the north, as the beginning of an encircling movement: a classic ambush. The firefight lasted more than an hour. A QRF (quick reaction force) was called in over the radio, including helicopters. Sgt. D was all over the place, zigzagging, carefully firing off rounds, encouraging his men. Cpl. Pena and the others were on the rooftops, shooting. When he returned to FOB Mercury and finally cleared his rifle in the clearing barrel, Sgt. D's smile was so wide it seemed that his whole face would split apart. It was the platoon's first firefight since OIF-I. For the two platoon members who had not fought in Iraq the previous year, Al-Karmah was the place where they had their "cherries popped."

That night Gunner Bednarcik's and Sgt. D's marines were in high spirits, sitting around in camp chairs under the stars, reliving every moment of the firefight. Lance Cpl. Neal told me, "It never fails. You never feel so alive as after you've just been in a close firefight, then had a hot shower, and had your laundry done." He himself had not gotten off a shot that day. "I stayed dry," he explained matter-of-factly. "I had no viable target to shoot at. I'm the machine gunner. I have to be extra careful." In fact, a few days later, one of the town council members would compliment Lt. Col. Byrne on the disciplined shooting of his men. Not one civilian had been hit. It made it easier for the council members to justify to their constituents the American counterattack. Marines were tough young kids from troubled backgrounds, but when the shooting started, I was impressed at how they instantly became mature and calculating thirty-year-olds.

My next visit to Al-Karmah was two days later with Bravo Company, commanded by Capt. Jason Eugene Smith of Baton Rouge, Louisiana, a graduate of Louisiana State University. Capt. Smith, with his determined, rawboned visage, was one of the battalion linchpins.

Organizationally, the Marine Corps was shaped like a triangle; it kept subdividing into threes. Thus, the 1st of the 5th had three infantry companies, or "line" companies: Alpha, Bravo, and Charlie. That wasn't the whole story, though. There was also a weapons company, and a "command element" for Lt. Col. Byrne, managed by Gunner Bednarcik. But the company captains—of Alpha, Bravo, Charlie, and Weapons—were the universal joints for the battalion. Because the Marine Corps had a more powered-down hierarchy than the Army, the company captains were the equivalent of the Army's iron majors.

The infantry captains for 1/5 were variations of the same mold: intense, terse, driven, and generally humorless, like Capt. Cassidy in Djibouti, only more so because of the combat-active environment in Iraq. Because majors and up in the Marine Corps are prisoners of staff work, for the captains this would be their last chance to be in the field with the grunts. Thus, they were all out to prove themselves. Capt. Jason Smith was no exception.

He told his marines, "We're going into Al-Karmah as the first group after the gun battle. We're going to get off the trucks, walk the streets, look people in the eye—to let 'em see the good things about the United States. The kids here refer to the terrorists as 'Ali Babas.'* So be aware when you hear those words. Look for the presence of the abnormal: horns honking, kids fleeing, stores closing. The police chief and many of the townspeople are on the fence. We've got to show 'em the way to go."

As soon as we arrived at the police station, the police fled, running past us in the opposite direction. Stores closed, kids ran, and traffic disappeared off the streets. As I entered the station with Capt. Smith, I braced for a barrage of rocket-propelled grenades. Meanwhile, other elements of Bravo Company were flooding adjacent areas of the town with foot patrols.

Capt. Smith, his translator, and I entered the police chief's office. Another Marine officer followed us inside, but Capt. Smith told him to leave, saying, "I want to talk frankly to the police chief." Tension seemed to suffocate the room.

* Apparently, the term "Ali Baba" was coined by American soldiers who preceded the Marines here, and was picked up on by local kids. See Graham's "Beyond Fallujah."

"I'm here to make sure you fulfill your obligations," Capt. Smith told Chief Kareen. "Why did your men just desert the station?"

"Only civilians fled," the chief replied nervously.

"I didn't see civilians. I saw men in uniform run away," Capt. Smith replied icily in a mild southern drawl. "If I were concerned with my own safety, I'd have stayed home in the United States. I expect a similar attitude from you and your men. You're going to see a lot of the Marines from now on. We know 95 percent of the town are good people, intimidated by the other 5 percent. I am aware of the risk you take by working with us. We are prepared to take the same risk."*

Whereas Capt. Smith's bearing was erect, immobile, and unblinking as he stared laser-like at the police chief, the police chief was bobbing and weaving all over the room, lighting a cigarette, moving from chair to chair, his back curled like a wet noodle, delivering evasive answers. The police chief made demands for more flak jackets and other equipment, which Capt. Smith promised to facilitate. Upon leaving the room, Capt. Smith told me that the police chief was a bellwether challenge: if the Marines were serious about proving that they were the superior tribe in town, the police chief might show more courage. On the other hand, it might just be a matter of getting a new chief. "This guy was appointed," Smith observed. "We might have to find somebody crazy enough to volunteer."

Outside we noticed new Arabic graffiti: "Death to Traitors." "Long live Saddam Hussein." "Kill the Members of the City Council." The information officer with us made a note to return and paint over the graffiti, and replace it with new slogans. The Marines were about to initiate a graffiti war.

No one attacked us, though. Some local kids told us that they saw more than thirty Ali Babas with RPGs and AK-47s run away as soon as the Marines dismounted from their vehicles to commence foot patrols. One officer remarked that a simple change in the TTPs (tactics, techniques, and procedures), such as sending in foot patrols at the same time we entered the police station, is "more effective than all the high-tech shit."

Later at FOB Mercury, 1/5's civil affairs officers were briefed by their outgoing 82nd counterparts about two road-widening projects for Al-

---

* Several weeks later, after assaulting parts of Al-Fallujah, Bravo Company and other elements of 1/5 returned to Al-Karmah. They lived in the community, patrolled regularly, talked to people, collected information, and made some progress toward reclaiming the town.

Karmah, originally slated to cost $32,000 and $75,000, respectively, for which the local contractor was now demanding more money.

"What about bringing in another contractor from Baghdad?" someone asked.

"If you bring in an outside contractor, he'll end up dead," the officer from the 82nd said. It was assumed that the cost overruns were because the contractor and some city council members wanted a slice of the American largesse. "It's like Kosovo," remarked Gunnery Sgt. Mark Kline, an African-American from Kansas City, Missouri, with experience in the Balkans. "The whole system here has been built on graft. All we can do is get these folks out of the ditch they're in, to a slightly higher level of development. What we call corruption is their way of doing things."

I went on a number of Humvee patrols deep into the countryside of central Iraq. It was an extraordinary landscape. My first impression was of a flat, ashen monotony pulverized by the sun. Within that monotony, though, was a pageant of micro-terrains created by ruler-straight, fungal-green irrigation ditches cut into the earth like cuneiform marks; and sluggish rivers, including the Euphrates, whose slate-blue surfaces would harden into a chain of goose bumps in the breeze. Masses of reeds, fatalistic and yielding, twice the height of a man, whispered like time itself in the wind.

"You know what it all reminds me of?" remarked Gunner Bednarcik. "South Carolina. Yeah, real tranquil. Nothing like shrimping in South Carolina. The tide comes in and the shrimp feed in the marshes." A look of ecstasy crossed his face.

The ditches and dams, as well as the wide and navigable cement-lined canals—like the one that stretched from Baghdad all the way to the Syrian border—were impressive feats of engineering, as were the highways, cloverleaf overpasses, and architectural immensities of the Green Zone. Saddam, like the tyrants of Mesopotamia, Egypt, India, and China, was a classic "hydraulic" dictator. According to the early-twentieth-century German political scientist Karl Wittfogel, who borrowed from Karl Marx and Friedrich Engels's theory of "oriental despotism," civilizations of the Near and Far East have manifested an absolutism "more comprehensive and more oppressive than its Western counterpart."[14] This was due to the disciplined social organization required to maintain extensive water and irrigation systems and other public works projects in age-old river valleys. That, in turn, led to the raising of large armies and the building of massive defense works.

Sitting in the back of a seven-ton truck during presence patrols in the Iraqi countryside meant bumps and bruises and dust so fine it billowed up from the tires like smoke. Relief came from the smiling farmers and their families who would gather on the berms under the date palms to wave; as a whole, the rural areas were the most friendly to the Americans, since deep in the Mesopotamian outback the Baath party had been weakest. A year after OIF-I, the fact that hordes of Iraqis in most of the country were still smiling at American troops did not qualify as news. Yet simply because it was a mundane reality did not render it insignificant.

The pro-American sentiment continued despite the lack of demonstrable improvements in people's lives. Farmers complained to the marines about the lack of clean water and functioning schools. For all intents and purposes, the Coalition Provisional Authority (CPA), the civilian arm of the American occupation, had no presence in much of Iraq. To the degree that anything got done in these regions, it was done by the American military.

One day on patrol an Iraqi man waved us down to warn of a suspicious object he had noticed on a bridge we were about to cross. The convoy halted, and several marines went on foot to inspect. They saw an IED. An explosives team was called in, and the object was detonated. It turned out to be a daisy chain of six bombs composed of 120mm and 155mm rounds, primed by a cell phone signal. When the explosives team detonated the 155mm rounds—the same used for booby traps in Vietnam—you could feel the air pressure almost a mile away.

It was the very lifesaving helpfulness of people in the rural areas that sometimes, albeit indirectly, depressed the marines, for despite OIF-II's emphasis on winning hearts and minds, they still wanted to fight. Another day while we were on patrol, word came of 1/5's first casualty of the current deployment. Pfc. Gerardo Perez of Houston had been wounded by a bullet in the shoulder while his platoon was helping another battalion during a firefight in nearby Al-Fallujah. "Fuck, why didn't that happen to us," blurted the marine next to me in the back of the seven-ton. "Fuck him, so he's wounded, he'll live, at least he was in a fight," said another marine. "I'm going to crack your asses for saying those things," their sergeant said. "Don't get us wrong," the first marine told me. "We care about the guy who was wounded. But shit happens. We just want the chance to do what we've been trained for."

I understood the feeling. If you were going to be a journalist, you should want to be where there was real reporting to do, not back in Washington covering press conferences or going on talk shows. And if you were going to join the military, I assumed you would want to fight.

The first WIA (wounded in action) had whetted 1/5's appetite. It was an indicator that, as one marine put it, "the pace would pick up." One senior noncom told me: "Mark my words, this SASO [stability and security operations—nation building] shit is going out the window. OIF-II will turn to be as violent as OIF-I."

The 82nd Airborne finally departed the area. A ceremony was held in the chow hall handing over FOB Mercury to the Marines. Again, the chaplain delivered a benediction. Bagpipes sounded a Christian hymn and the "Marine Hymn," and everybody shouted, "Ooh-rah." The base was promptly renamed FOB Abu Ghraib (not to be confused with the prison), just as St. Mere was renamed FOB Al-Fallujah. The Marines, in keeping with their small wars tradition, consciously wanted to fit in with the local environment wherever possible.

Conditions at the renamed FOB Abu Ghraib got worse before they got better. Water for the showers ran out in the evening and on a few occasions ceased for up to thirty-six hours at a time, even as marines came back from patrols lathered in grime and sweat; nor was the electricity dependable. People had to scavenge for toilet paper and for plastic drinking water bottles even. The Kellogg, Brown & Root–staffed Army bases that I knew from Afghanistan and elsewhere appeared luxurious in retrospect. When the weather turned hot, the water problem became more acute. The Gunner joked that marines turn every place they go into a slum.

Soon living conditions began to improve—somewhat. Meanwhile, more and more HESCO baskets and Texas barriers were brought in to contain mortar and rocket blasts, which were unceasing. The mortar and rocket attacks from the direction of Al-Fallujah and Al-Karmah necessitated night-long patrols that were the essence of drudgery: hanging around in a suspect spot in the darkness, shivering, getting a headache from the night vision goggles, seeing and hearing nothing, then returning bleary-eyed at dawn, only to learn that soon after you left the place, a mortar was launched at the FOB from a nearby spot.*

Ten days after we had settled in, with nighttime attacks continuing, Lt.

---

* Army Special Forces called night vision goggles "NODs" (night optical devices).

Col. Byrne established platoon-sized satellite bases beyond the FOB, which, in turn, dispatched fire teams that camped out at night and went on foot marches through the countryside. In short, the Marines were doing many of the things that Army Special Forces in Afghanistan had wanted to do, but which the regular Army in Bagram wouldn't let them.

"It isn't enough, though," Gunner Bednarcik warned, shaking his head. "We need to put FOBs right in the middle of some of these towns, like Al-Fallujah and Al-Karmah."

Events would prove him right.

On one patrol we found suspicious burn marks by a road near the Euphrates. The marks were in haystacks and berms, both of which could absorb the back blast of a mortar. Being near a road, the attackers could escape before the radar-driven "counter-battery" of the Americans destroyed the site. The perseverance paid off. One morning before dawn, I got up and walked across the FOB's gravel expanse to the Porta-John to take a leak. On the way back, shuffling toward me, guarded by two marines, was a veritable Ghost of Christmas-Yet-to-Come. The hooded PUC (person under control), along with two others, had been caught with IED-making equipment, mortar materials, and a truck filled with sandbags on which a tire rested: the perfect makeshift mobile rocket-launching platform. Because their legs were caked with mud, it was assumed that the mortar caches were located alongside riverbanks and irrigation ditches.

Lt. Col. Byrne was under considerable pressure from his superiors on this issue. Truly, the law of military bureaucracy is that shit rolls downhill. "Your orders are to hunt and kill these fuckers," one general commanded Byrne. "Bring me back dead folk." The higher-ups knew that it was only a matter of time before one of the insurgents got lucky and hit a chow hall with a mortar or rocket during mealtime, or a crowded MWR (moral, welfare, and recreation) facility, killing dozens or more marines in one blow.

One blazing hot afternoon in the camp after a mortar attack, Pfc. Jason Igo, one of the Renegades, called out to me, "Hey, Bob, where ya from?" After I told him, I asked where he was from. "All over," he said. "A military brat, uh?" I responded. "No, I was homeless. I lived in abandoned apartments, backyards, trailers, in Washington, Oregon, Minnesota. . . . I was abandoned at twelve, didn't know my father till I was fifteen. His girlfriend didn't like me, though." Pfc. Igo had fought in OIF-I. He had no plans to reenlist. He wanted to attend a technical college in Arizona. The Marine Corps, he told me, had given him a stability that he had never had before.

FOB Abu Ghraib was a fighting camp, the one that I had been looking for throughout my travels. Once, coming back in the middle of the day from a patrol that had started before dawn, I found the base nearly empty; most of the marines were where they needed to be, outside the perimeter, in the midst of Iraqi towns and villages. If only more American bases in Iraq and elsewhere were like this, I thought—with few creature comforts and consequently a short support tail.

There was a particular sanctity about the chow hall: grim, badly lit, with depressing food, marines jammed together beside long tables, wearing flak jackets, gummed with dust, their rifles and helmets at their feet, every sixth marine or so quietly praying and crossing himself before starting to eat. Second Lt. David Russell of San Antonio, Texas, a graduate of the U.S. Naval Academy at Annapolis—a marine with an unfailingly delightful disposition—told me one evening, eyeing the mess hall: "Isn't this place great! I love being here. It's the new version of the Wild West, minus the booze, the whores, and the fun, of course. But we do have Indians in Iraq—good Indians and"—his voice lowering in mock seriousness— "very, very bad Indians."

One day I went out with 2nd Lt. Russell and the rest of Alpha Company on a foot patrol through Nassir wa Salaam, a predominantly Shiite town in the midst of the Sunni Triangle. Nassir wa Salaam meant "Victory and Peace," a bombastic artificial name that Saddam had given it. Its real name was Haswa, the place of gravel. Haswa was decked with flags and other Shiite regalia. In Iraq even the Sunni mosques, because of the Persian architectural influence, looked Shiite. Thus, it was only through the flags that you could tell from the outside whether a mosque was really Shiite or not: red and black flags for the Imam Hussein, the Shiite martyr massacred at Karbala in A.D. 680; green flags for Abbas, the Prophet Mohammed's uncle and founder of the Abbasid caliphate based in medieval Baghdad; and yellow for the twelfth imam, whom Shiites believe is in occultation and will return to earth at some point.

Our first stop in Haswa was the police station, where the chief told us that as everywhere else in central Iraq since the toppling of Saddam, his town was besieged by a crime wave, carjacking in particular. As marines began to walk the streets they attracted hordes of kids and rough teenagers who had no jobs or schools to go to. They were friendly, but only because the Iraqi Shiite leader, Grand Ayatollah Ali Sistani, had told them to be.

The ICOMs suddenly stopped working. Lt. Russell looked up at the town's sagging electric wires. "Yeah, the power lines here bleed electricity and knock out our intra-squad radios. If we get into trouble now, I can't communicate with the rest of the company. It's an example of how third world infrastructure defeats Western technology and power." As often, the best communication turned out to be shouting.

The intelligence provided to the marines about IEDs was useless. It told them to beware of garbage, junkyards, old white cars, and so forth. But there was garbage and old white cars everywhere, and the whole town was a junkyard. The "latest and greatest" advice was to beware of kids on old bicycles. There were kids on old bicycles everywhere we looked. Here and there throughout the day we saw expensive late-model sedans—the kind used for car bombs. In Haswa every situation the entire day just smelled bad; thus all you could do was relax, give yourself up to fate, and enjoy the scenery.

Lt. Russell remarked wryly, as though seeing all this from a safe distance: "I remember reading about foot patrols in Vietnam. Over six months the casualty rate from booby traps would be 30 percent, and yet no one ever saw the enemy. That's the kind of stuff that drives you insane. An enemy you can see focuses your organizational skills and actually reduces stress."

Alpha Company's commander was Capt. Philip Treglia of Elida, Ohio. "We will divide responsibility three ways on this patrol," he told his men. "One marine smiles, talks with the kids and the *hajis,* and does the public relations. The marine behind him has the responsibility for intel, like registering the GPS position for any guy with a beard who won't shake hands or gives you a stink stare. The third marine never takes off his sunglasses. His hand is on the trigger all the time. His only job is security."

Angry complaints from passersby assaulted our ears. "We have no water or electricity" . . . "The city council that you Americans established was supposed to provide us with services, but it stole the money. They are a bunch of thieves" . . . "The city council was supposed to build us a soccer field, they're all bastards. Do something!" . . . "My house was broken into, can you find and arrest the culprit?" . . . "My daughter has an irregular heartbeat, can I take her to your military doctor?" In one section of town, anger over water cutoffs was so passionate that Lt. Russell ordered his platoon to distribute a mineral water bottle to one person in every household. As he later admitted, it was a well-intentioned but ineffectual action. But he felt that he just had to do something.

The theme throughout the day was the same: the citizens of this ratty, crumbling, fly-and-garbage-strewn, overcrowded Shiite hellhole of seventy-five thousand were dumbfounded and disappointed that the Americans, who had done what none of them thought possible—swiftly dismantle Saddam's totalitarian regime—now couldn't even get the tap water running or the garbage collected.

I saw mounds of chopped-up automobile parts and trash everywhere. Yet here and there were new rooftop satellite dishes. Women stood silently in the alleys, hidden under *abayas*, just staring at us. People seemed increasingly aware of the outside world, and therefore increasingly dissatisfied at their predicament, even as their town teetered on the brink of chaos and lawlessness, and the city council had lost all legitimacy. Haswa—Nassir wa Salaam—was Liberia or Sierra Leone without the violence. Only tribe and religion held society together here.

"To rule this place," Lt. Russell observed, "requires an infinite capacity to give, and an infinite capacity to hurt."

Two days later came the Haswa City Council meeting. In a grim room with busted windows, Marine officers and council members—men in keffiyahs and Western suits, and women with kerchiefs—filled boxy brown sofas. Syrupy tea was offered in small glasses. I expected Lt. Col. Byrne and Maj. Larry Kaifesh of Chicago, the battalion civil affairs officer, to read the riot act to the council for its delinquency in providing constituents with basic services. But it didn't happen, for the problems turned out to be frustratingly complicated.

The water pumping station was short of electricity. The pumps were out of order. Pipes were broken. Under the new democratic regime, proper tenders for all this work had to be submitted; that would take time. Some of the tenders already submitted turned out to be fake. One of the contractors had absconded with money. Meanwhile, nearby towns were pleading for water hookups, further straining the system. The council was like the one in western Baghdad. Its members were either well-meaning, albeit ineffectual, or not well-meaning at all. A mixture of passivity and intrigue undermined the discussions. The council members became passionate only when asking the marines for personal favors: obtaining weapons licenses and satellite phones.

Listening to all the steps required to get the tap water running, I reflected that Saddam was able to break through bureaucratic logjams by employing fear and coercion. In fact, Iraqis cared more about the tangible necessities of daily life, like water and electricity, than about less tangible things like democracy. Democracy here would be a much slower process than in the Balkans, which represented a far more advanced region of the old Ottoman Empire.

Some of the departed Army officers had confided to me that they got results only by dealing directly with the tribal leaders, even as they paid lip service to the new democratic councils. Marines were coming to a similar conclusion. "This SASO shit just isn't working," one noncom told me yet again. "I hope we go back to fighting, like in OIF-I."

He soon got his wish.

On March 31, 2004, a few weeks after 1/5 had arrived from Kuwait, a van with four American contractors was ambushed in Al-Fallujah. The vehicle was blasted with small arms fire and set alight. Frenzied crowds dragged the burned bodies through the streets. Two of the four were hung from a nearby bridge. Some of the body parts were cut off with shovels. Headlines in the United States compared the incident to the killings of Americans eleven years before in Mogadishu, Somalia.

There was relatively little talk about the incident at FOB Abu Ghraib. Marines digested the news silently; discerning what the consequences would be for 1/5 wasn't that difficult. The next day, April 1, Lt. Col. Byrne disappeared for many hours behind closed doors at the headquarters of the Regimental Combat Team at FOB Al-Fallujah. It was Capt. Jason Smith who quietly pulled me aside in the barracks and told me that 1/5 would be going into Al-Fallujah.

The briefing on April 2 at Camp Abu Ghraib's Combat Operations Center was low key and terrifically business-like. The taking of a middle-sized city of 285,000 is an amazingly complex affair. Was there enough barbed wire on hand to create makeshift detention facilities? "We need wire, wire, and more wire," Byrne said, "and that means we need a lot of stakes and pile drivers." Were there enough translators, MREs, mineral water bottles, ammo, power amps, blue force trackers, and so on? An "assload" of refugees was assumed, which would require a whole logistics operation of its own. And how many marines should be left behind to secure the FOB in case of an attack? The attack on Al-Fallujah itself was just one of many details to be worked out.

A pattern set in that should not have been surprising, but which was extraordinary to actually observe: The more it became apparent that the battalion was really going to war, the quieter and more deliberate the discussions became. Marines kept more to themselves, busy packing; deciding what gear to take and what to leave behind could determine life or death days from now. People washed and groomed themselves, assuming it would be the last time for quite a while. In the shower I ran into the Navy doc, Lt. Cormac O'Connor of Indianapolis, Indiana. He prayed that he wouldn't be busy in the coming weeks. It was a vain hope, he realized.

Power devolved to the head of the "Three Shop," the Operations section of the battalion: Maj. Pete Farnum of Tipton, Iowa, whose tall, rather hulking, and quietly capable demeanor gave him a particular air of authority.* Maj. Farnum drove the briefings over coming days, variations of which would be part of those given the President of the United States, for the assault on Al-Fallujah, which was a political decision taken at the highest levels, would be worked out in detail here at FOB Abu Ghraib, at the nearby headquarters of the Regimental Combat Team, and at the FOB of another battalion (the 2nd Battalion of the 1st Marines) that would be included in the operation. The RCT building at FOB Al-Fallujah was suddenly besieged by men in civilian hiking clothes and bearing either M-4 assault rifles or Glock pistols: Army Special Forces, Delta, CIA, FBI, and other elements that would have pieces of the Marine-led attack on Al-Fallujah.

The process was like writing and performing a symphony whose complexity demanded that the main briefs be "fragged out" into smaller ones, dealing with different aspects of the task. For example, I attended a meeting dedicated to one matter only: arranging for Navy construction battalions to transport portable bunkers and other equipment to be used at the checkpoints set up around the city prior to the assault.

All the elements came together fast because of a factor largely missing from civilian life, the incontestability of command; meetings quickly resulted in priorities, which in turn led to decisions. As soon as the ranking officer decided on something, the debate moved on to the next point.

"Armies have always been viewed with suspicion in democratic societies because they are the least democratic of all social institutions," writes the military historian Byron Farwell. "They are, in fact, not democratic at

* The One Shop was Administration, the Two Shop Intelligence, the Four Shop Logistics, and so forth. All were headed by first lieutenants, except for the Three, which was headed by a major, reflecting the preeminence of Operations.

all. Governments which have tried to . . . blur the distinction between officer and man have not been successful. Armies," Farwell goes on, "stand as disturbing reminders that democratic processes are not always the best, living and perpetual proof that, in at least this one area, the caste system works."[15] That was certainly true in the planning of the attack on Al-Fallujah.

At the Combat Operations Center, the room was packed as Maj. Farnum delivered his penultimate brief before 1/5 departed for Al-Fallujah. Among those in attendance were the four battle captains who would bear the heaviest load of risk and personal responsibility for the assault: Alpha Company commander, Capt. Philip Treglia; Bravo Company commander, Capt. Jason Smith; Charlie Company commander, Capt. Wilbert Dickens of Rich Square, North Carolina; and Capt. Blair Sokol of Newark, Delaware, the commander of Weapons Company.* Capt. Sokol, awarded the Bronze Star for valor in OIF-I, was a towering, taciturn man who had been a football lineman at the Naval Academy. He was also a tactical genius-in-the-making. This time he would remain slightly in the rear, in order to run the other three captains, and principally to deal with "deconfliction" issues:

When three companies assault a city in order to box in the enemy, the biggest danger is often not the enemy itself but friendly fire. And with 5.56mm rounds able to travel several miles before losing velocity, avoiding friendly fire in city streets—and at the same time orchestrating an attack from different directions—requires an uncommon instinct for spatial geometry.

Once more, Maj. Farnum went over the basics of the plan. The 1st of the 5th would bear responsibility for capturing the southern half of Al-Fallujah, the part below a main thoroughfare that the U.S. military had dubbed "Michigan." The northern half of the city would be taken by the 2nd Battalion of the 1st Marines, or 2/1. But because the southern half of Al-Fallujah contained a sparsely populated industrial zone and an adjacent commercial area, both of which could be captured relatively easily, 1/5 would be the first battalion to establish a substantial foothold in the city.

Prior to the assault, nine traffic control points would be set up around Al-Fallujah to create a "blocking cordon," isolating it and preventing in-

* Pronounced New-*ark,* to distinguish it from Newark, New Jersey.

surgents, for the most part, from leaving or entering. Following that, the two battalions would occupy the city's outskirts, using the new forward operating bases to prosecute raids for HVTs (high-value targets). Concomitantly, there would be IO (information operations), whose underlying message would be to convince the city's inhabitants that the Marines represented the "superior tribe" there. Selling democracy not just in Al-Fallujah but elsewhere in the Sunni Triangle was an idea that had been losing traction for some time now.

One officer told me: "This is a flash-bang strategy. Stun the bad guys with aggressive fire, then psy-ops the shit out of them, always coming back to the theme of the inevitability of the superior tribe."

The final stage would be the handover of the city to the new Iraqi Police, the new Iraqi Army, and the American-created Iraqi Civil Defense Corps (ICDC). Marines listened politely to this, but I don't think they believed it. The ICDC and the Iraqi Police in the Al-Fallujah area were said to be deserting in droves, at the company level no less. I had found that the ICDC and the police were loyal where the Americans were strong and disloyal where there was a perception of American weakness. People in all cultures gravitate toward power and are susceptible to intimidation by thugs and chieftains. But the chieftain mentality was particularly prevalent in Iraq.*

As Maj. Farnum went through his brief, it dawned on everyone inside the room that Operation Valiant Resolve, as it was code-named, represented the opposite of what the Marines had come to Iraq to do. Instead of nation-building—what the Marines called SASO—they were about to lead a theater-level attack on a large urban area, with assistance from the CIA and the Army's Delta force, 5th Special Forces group, and the psy-ops branch of Special Operations Command. Air assets would include AC-130 spectral gunships, Marine Cobra and UH-1D Huey helicopters, unmanned Pioneer surveillance planes, and Air Force F-15s.

The truth was, that what the Marines called OIF-II had quite literally

---

* Actually, one of the finest expositions of the chieftain phenomenon can be found in Bing West's 1972 classic about Vietnam, *The Village* (New York: Pocket Books), pp. 328–29: "In Dai Loc district . . . one night in early November the VC had laid waste several villages with the thoroughness and savagery of Apache raiders, despite the nearby presence of a Marine battalion. As a consequence of the fear thus instilled, the people afterward refused even American medcaps for their wounds. One general thought that the disruption proved his point that the people went with the winner—the incident at Dai Loc had happened because the people had not been provided security. 'Give them security,' he said, 'and they'll give you information and cooperation.' "

become OIF-II. Like Desert Storm, Operation Iraqi Freedom of 2003 had been a relatively painless and dazzling success only because it was incomplete. In both cases, victory was declared before the hard part of the operation had been attempted. In 1991 in Desert Storm, key Republican Guard units had been left intact, allowing the regime to survive; in OIF-I, cities and towns like Al-Fallujah and Al-Karmah had largely been bypassed, without eradicating pro-regime elements in those places.

It was a classic American syndrome: an aversion to sustained engagement overseas that leads to more carnage, rather than less. The Americans wanted clean end-states and victory parades. Imperialism, though, is about never-ending involvement. And deny it all they wanted, American officials were in an imperial situation, even if the Bush administration and the troops themselves, to say nothing of the public, were uncomfortable with the word.

Maj. Farnum reiterated that Operation Valiant Resolve was not retribution for the butchery of March 31. "It's just that the problem of Fallujah has festered to the point where dealing with it represents a pivot opportunity to improve the atmosphere in the entire AOR."

He then deferred to Lt. Col. Byrne, who, because of his higher rank and the fact of his command over the battalion, needed to succinctly inspire the grunts for close-quarters combat against jihadists and the most hardened elements of the old regime. "Gents, let me tell you what this is really about. It's about killing shitheads. The CG [commanding general of the 1st Division, Jim Mattis] has changed the op order from 'capture or kill' the enemy to 'kill or capture.' He wants the emphasis on 'kill.'

"You'll be facing interesting folk," Byrne continued. "Guys who fought in Grozny [Chechnya], in Afghanistan, guys who aren't all that interested in giving up. I made everyone grow mustaches for the sake of cultural sensitivity. Now I want you all to shave them off. We're going on the offensive."*

He then stood up, signaling the end of the brief. Everyone else stood up and shouted, "Ooh-rah."

Outside, Lt. Russell, in his ever-chipper manner, noted a difficult truth: "This is one where we have no idea whether there will be lots of casualties within days, or no one will even shoot at us." The biggest worry was that

---

* Preliminary intelligence given the Marines at the time indicated that there may have been a few individuals inside Al-Fallujah who had fought in the places Byrne mentioned.

just one well-placed IED would cause a "cluster fuck," or traffic foul-up, which, in turn, would facilitate a major ambush. Al-Fallujah was the ultimate challenge that the U.S. military had been studying and prepping for since the end of the Cold War, when MOUT (military operations in urban terrain) first came into vogue.

But some high-ranking marines were uncomfortable with that realization. After all, most of the precedents were bad: Mogadishu, Grozny, Jenin . . . You were ambushed as in Mogadishu in 1993, barely won through indiscriminate slaughter like the Russians in Grozny in the mid-1990s, or won relatively cleanly, in view of the circumstances, like the Israelis in Jenin in 2002, but nowhere near clean enough to satisfy world public opinion.

Actually, there was a model to be followed, at least partially, one that Lt. Col. Byrne occasionally alluded to, and which harked back to one of the most glorious chapters in Marine history. It was the twenty-six-day battle for Hue in Vietnam, that began January 31, 1968, during the Tet offensive. According to the *Marine Corps Gazette,* Hue bears no less a positive connotation than the battles of Belleau Wood, in France in 1918, and Tarawa, in the central Pacific in 1943.*

A former imperial city of the once-unified Vietnam with 140,000 inhabitants, located near the Demilitarized Zone, Hue had been stormed by 12,000 Viet Cong and North Vietnamese regulars. They rounded up South Vietnamese soldiers, government officials, and other American sympathizers, clubbing or shooting up to 6,000 of them to death. American soldiers and marines, including the 1st of the 5th, counterattacked, leading to a month of brutal, theater-level urban combat that featured three undermanned Marine infantry battalions fighting house-to-house. The Marines, in helping to take back the heavily fortified urban center, helped to kill 5,113 of the enemy and expel almost another 5,000, while suffering only 147 killed and 857 wounded: results that they would have qualified as an historic victory in either of the two world wars.† Of the 6,000 prisoners and civilians slaughtered by the Hanoi government, 3,000 mass graves were discovered. The indiscriminate North Vietnamese massacre of thou-

---

* Belleau Wood was where the Germans gave the Marines their notorious nickname, *Teufel-Hunden* (devil dogs).
† This was in addition to the dozens of soldiers killed and more than 500 wounded.

sands, as well as the Marine and Army heroism inside the city, went relatively unnoticed in the America media, though, compared to coverage of the massacre at My Lai, which happened a month later, in which a U.S. Army platoon killed 347 innocent civilians.[16]*

Al-Fallujah might be like Hue, I thought. As at Hue (and Stalingrad, too) snipers on both sides would provide a force-multiplier effect. Like Hue, it would be a messy squad leader's war, a struggle of privates first class and corporals rushing from street to street, where the enemy would hide within crowds, firing mortars and rocket-propelled grenades, and mosques would be used as enemy fortresses in a similar way that Buddhist temples had been at Hue. It would be a battle where a certain percentage of the local inhabitants would sympathize with the insurgents, but where the majority would flee or lie low, just trying to survive.[17]

More briefings followed at lower levels of command. Each company captain briefed his staff noncoms on their specific routes and objectives in the city, and the radio frequencies and call signs to be used. Briefs were also held on the placement of heavy guns and snipers. The engineers had to decide where to drop dirt and spike strips for the roadblocks. The order of the convoy to the battle zone had to be established, divided by "sticks" and "serials," just as before the departure from Kuwait. By the evening of April 4, the officers had already gone several days with little sleep. This was before the operation had begun.

"Stepping time" was scheduled for 1 a.m. on April 5. At 7:30 p.m. April 4, Capt. Jason Smith assembled Bravo Company in a V formation in front of the red company flag. He told his 150 marines that they should be grateful for the opportunity now given them. Then a chaplain, Navy Lt. Wayne Hall of Oklahoma City, blessed Bravo: "Today is Palm Sunday," he began, "the day of Jesus' triumphal entry into Jerusalem, where he broke the bounds of Hell. Tonight commences your triumphal entry into Fallujah, a place in the bounds of Hell. This is a spiritual battle, and you marines are the tools of mercy." As he invoked the holy spirit, the 150 marines dropped to one knee and bowed their heads, removing their bush or field caps as they did so.

I told Capt. Smith that I would link up with Bravo the next day, after accompanying Lt. Col. Byrne to Al-Fallujah's outskirts. Capt. Smith's face

* The coverage of My Lai did not appear until revelations began to surface in late 1969.

was glowing in rapture. This was the moment he had lived for. Bravo had been selected to be the tip of the spear for the assault inside the city, just as Bravo Company of the 1st of the 5th Marines had been the first inside the citadel of Hue thirty-six years earlier.[18]

By 9 p.m. the camp was silent, as many marines slid away to take power naps. In the shadows cast by the full moon I noticed scout-snipers painting their faces in green cammie stick.[19]

A few hours later, we "stepped" outside the gate.

The weather had turned cold and windy. The dust of the desert looked like snow in the moonlight. In under an hour, the Renegades arrived at a point in the desert half a mile outside Al-Fallujah, where a communications team set up a temporary command post for Lt. Col. Byrne. Al-Fallujah was a line of twinkling yellow and bluish lights, where the sound of small arms fire and RPGs could be heard intermittently: Charlie Company, commanded by Capt. Wilbert Dickens, had already made "contact" with the enemy at the "cloverleaf," a highway intersection outside the city to the northeast.

It was too cold and cramped in the Humvee for me to sleep. Along with Gunner Bednarcik, Cpl. Pena, and Lance Cpl. Neal, I listened to the news of the cloverleaf engagement on the battalion "tac" (tactical radio network) throughout the night. Catnapping in daylight and staying up all night would become a pattern over the coming week. Night fighting favored the Americans, armed with night vision goggles. As Lt. Col. Byrne had told me, "The bad guys only have what God gave them. We have what Raytheon gave us."

At dawn, coughing and freezing, I walked over to Byrne's Humvee. He was sitting in the back seat, his head half hidden inside a balaclava, shivering and coated with dust like the rest of us. He was listening and talking to three different radio nets at once. Military command is about making split-second executive decisions, the consequences of which might psychologically immobilize your average CEO, and making those decisions during periods of extreme physical discomfort.

I asked Byrne why the Marines had not shut down Al-Fallujah immediately after the murder of the contractors, to prevent the perpetrators from escaping the city: what the Israelis would likely have done. Instead, they had waited five days.

He explained: "In the West Bank, the Israelis have 'flooded the zone,' dividing it into sectors and checkpoints. Because the Israelis are already there in such numbers, it's less trouble for them to cordon off a city. But we are spread thin throughout Iraq. For us to cordon off a city takes a special effort. If we do that every time there is an outrage, soon the enemy will be dictating our every movement."

Indeed, the Marines were doing this operation on a shoestring, initially with two battalions, when they really required three: Hue, a city with half the population of Al-Fallujah, had been invested with nearly three Marine battalions. As I had observed in Afghanistan, there were just too many support troops concentrated near the capital, and too few fighting elements dispersed throughout the countryside. Nothing angered me more than to enter a vast chow hall at Camp Victory, the headquarters of the military coalition at Baghdad airport, and see it teeming with troops choosing different kinds of fine cakes for dessert, and then to travel in the countryside and see barely a U.S. presence at all. The U.S. military was everywhere burdened by a top-heavy bureaucracy, with too many layers of staff that needed pampering. Thus, it was organizationally miscast for dealing with twenty-first-century insurgencies. In both Afghanistan and Iraq, as I had seen, the U.S. military had set up structures it was historically comfortable with, not those particularly suited for the challenge at hand.

I spent the first half of April 5 touring various traffic checkpoints with Byrne, and listening to casualty reports (eight wounded so far). In midafternoon, regimental and division-level commanders powwowed with Byrne and his company captains by the side of his Humvee in the desert, a mile outside Al-Fallujah. A snatch of the conversation:

ONE OFFICER TO HIS HIGHER-UP: "Sir, we have a problem with an ICDC commander. He's still sitting on the fence about whether to commit his men to this fight."
HIGHER-UP: "Tell him we'll incarcerate his fucking ass and then send him to Baghdad to beg on the streets the rest of his life. By the way, keep your men disciplined. I don't want reports of shooting or mistreating civilians. Remember, your men are going to be under a lot of pressure."

It was decided that when Bravo Company penetrated the city along with Alpha and Charlie, all fanning out in different directions in the industrial zone of southeastern Al-Fallujah, marines would affix bayonets to their M-16 assault rifles. The point was mainly psychological: to show the people of Al-Fallujah that the marines truly meant business. As one high-ranking officer told me, "Folks here have been conditioned to seeing the U.S. Army patrol the main roads in large vehicles. We aim to dismount and enter on foot with bayonets."

After the division and regimental commanders left, Byrne and his captains went over the radio call signs: "Geronimo" for the lieutenant colonel and the Renegades, "Apache" for Alpha Company, "Blackhawk" for Bravo, "Red Cloud" for a platoon from Weapons Company that would assist Alpha and Bravo, "Little Wolf" and "Crazy Horse" for two counter-mechanized units, and so on.

As the sun was setting and word came of three KIAs from Charlie Company by the cloverleaf, I said goodbye to Lt. Col. Byrne and walked with Capt. Smith a few hundred yards through the desert to where Bravo Company was assembling for the night attack.

———

Capt. Smith briefed his lieutenants and staff noncoms, then conducted comms rehearsals. They lit cigars and had a smoke together before dispersing to their various Humvees and seven-tons. Smith handed me over to 2nd Lt. Joshua Palmer of Banning, California, who escorted me to the seven-ton in which I would be riding.

Second Lt. Joshua Palmer, like 2nd Lt. David Russell, was a polished, well-spoken, and well-read college graduate in his early twenties, who had joined the corps out of a true sense of idealism. I remember the serene glow in his eyes. He talked easily with his men, who had not the education that he had. Like Capt. Smith, 2nd Lt. Palmer was the picture of contentment that evening. The two of us sat together in the front of the seven-ton, talking about books and listening to the sounds of rockets and mortars above the drone of the truck engine, trying to forget how cold we were. Al-Fallujah lay a quarter of a mile away.

Al-Fallujah was known as the "city of mosques," with more than two hundred in the city and surrounding villages, making it a regional center of Sunni Islam. Its name, though, might have had a pagan derivation: *Pallugtha,* an Assyrian word for "division," a reference to a side branch of the Euphrates that no longer existed. Al-Fallujah marked a northern border of the kingdom of Hammurabi (1792–1750 B.C.). From antiquity, one of the two major land-based trade routes that connected Mesopotamia to Syria and the Mediterranean began near here. Because of the city's reputation for tribal independence and smuggling, Saddam had to work to keep the city under control. Thus, it was made into a Baath party stronghold.

At midnight the trucks began to move, zigzagging without lights to avoid mortar hits as we crossed the short patch of desert to where the city streets began. In a moment we were outside the walls of the soft drink factory which satellite photos and other intel had indicated would make a suitable forward operating base for Lt. Col. Byrne and 1/5. Immediately Bravo began rounding up PUCs, including some Sudanese nationals. But the factory was taken without a fight.

Byrne soon arrived to take command of his new post, a sprawling cluster of one-story buildings protected by an outer wall. With him was Col. John Toolan of Brooklyn, the RCT-1 commander. Col. Toolan tried to inspect the area to the east of the compound, but his up-armored Humvee immediately came under intense bombardment, silenced by the guns of a hovering AC-130 Spectre gunship called in by a forward air controller on the ground.* All of this happened within the space of a few minutes.

I found Capt. Smith just as he had begun to lead Bravo's advance deeper into the city on foot. Streets and buildings were blacked out. Marines fanned out into alleys under the moonlight, as mortars and rockets sounded in the northern half of the city, a half mile away, where we could see tracers.

It was organized confusion, as Smith kept trying to ascertain the boundary seams between Bravo and Alpha directly to the south and behind us. Against a surrealistic urban landscape of howling stray dogs and the sand-encrusted remains of rusted automobiles and cement mixers, marines in their desert cammies crouched motionlessly at every intersection, like so many gray boulders, peering through their night vision goggles, their rifles covering designated fields of fire.

Smith's forward contingent of Bravo moved out of the industrial zone and into an area of low-end stores. Yet the whole of Al-Fallujah still looked like one big automobile chop shop. Just before dawn, when the

---

* The AC-130 in particular is a magnificent asset, an attack cargo plane designed to fly for hours at a time above the battlefield, carrying tens of thousands of pounds of ammunition for its 25mm and 40mm guns. Because it can hover for hours, its crew gets to understand the battle space, talk to the ground-based forward air controllers, and be intimately involved in the fight. The Big Air Force is no fan of this rather antiquated plane. But old-fashioned counterinsurgency is part of the U.S. military's future. Thus, the AC-130 could continue to prove more useful than some of the high-tech jets and other gizmos in the Air Force's arsenal.

prayer call sounded from nearby mosques, we reached "Michigan," the broad thoroughfare that marked the northern edge of 1/5's responsibility. It would be days before the other battalion—2/1—might be able to reach it from the other side.

Smith immediately began ordering marines onto rooftops; he wanted "guardian angels" everywhere when daylight arrived. Because there was a shortage of lightweight portable ladders, marines had to scramble onto each other's shoulders.

Smith; his 1st sergeant, Scott Van De Ven of Grayling, Michigan; a radio operator whose name I neglected to write down; and I scrambled onto a roof, only to find that rather than the flat empty space we had anticipated, this roof and every other one nearby was cluttered with rusted and discarded mufflers and tailpipes, to such an extent that we all had to pitch in and make space just to lie down and rest, in shifts. I managed an hour's sleep. I used one of the rusted mufflers as a pillow and awoke covered in filth. I looked around in broad daylight to see the roofscape of Al-Fallujah covered with thousands upon thousands of old mufflers and tailpipes, guarded by U.S. Marines, standing atop this part of the city with fixed bayonets.

Mosques and factories loomed in the distance. It was truly ugly: the classic terrain of radicalism, occupied by the lumpen faithful.[20] Islamic radicalism should be distinguished from Islamic conservatism. Conservatism is about tradition, often featuring a high degree of aesthetics, and is notably represented by the royal courts of Morocco, Jordan, and the Gulf states. But radicalism germinates from a break in tradition, when *Dar al-Islam* (the House of Islam) finds itself amid the alienating anonymity of early-industrial-age slums and shantytowns, where traditions can be maintained only by reinventing religion in a more abstract and ideological form. Indeed, Al-Fallujah's ancient-looking factories had a Cold War, Eastern Bloc quality to them that reminded me of 1980s Romania.

First Sgt. Scott Van De Ven immediately began calling over the intra-squad radios for water, chow, and radio batteries. Capt. Smith had other concerns: the marines were spread out too sparsely at intersections and on the rooftops, even as suspicious late-model cars began prowling the area. The bad guys were casing our locations. Smith immediately demanded the establishment of roadblocks over the ICOM and battalion "tac." The empty streets and closed shops were signs that we would soon be attacked.

It was impressive the way the insurgents, as well as the local population at large, could gather information about the marines so quickly. British Col. Callwell wrote at the end of the nineteenth century that indigenous forces are helped by a system of intelligence that seems to issue from the soil itself:

> News spreads in a most mysterious fashion. The people are far more observant than the dwellers of civilized lands. By a kind of instinct they interpret military portents. . . . Camp gossip is heard by those who are attracted by the ready payment which supplies brought to a civilized army always meet with, and it flies from mouth to mouth till it reaches the ears of the hostile leaders.*

Smith ordered marines off the rooftops and to new locations. He and his men broke into an automobile repair shop, where Bravo established a POS, or forward headquarters "position." Stripped-down MREs and water soon arrived by truck. I had just poured water into the heating filter for a Country Captain Chicken MRE, and was preparing to remove some clothing layers beneath my flak vest, as the weather had turned hot after a freezing night, when RPG and small arms fire rattled the scrap iron that formed the roof of the filthy garage headquarters.

The fire directed at us did not let up. Over the ICOM, Smith learned that it was coming from a mosque on Michigan about three hundred meters away. The mosque was gridded for a possible air strike, and everyone began a fast march toward it.

Smith did not really have to order the marines straight into the direction of the fire. It was a collective impulse, a phenomenon I would see again

---

* C. E. Callwell, *Small Wars: Their Principles and Practice* (1896; reprint, Lincoln: University of Nebraska Press, 1996), pp. 52–54. The fact that the U.S. military needed to adapt to such frustrations of counterinsurgency was somewhat ironic, given that unconventional guerrilla warfare had been part of the American military tradition since the French and Indian War of the mid-eighteenth century. On the western slopes of the Appalachians, English settlers mustered light infantry, ranger, and reconnaisance units, often small and nimble, working with Indian auxiliaries against the French and their Indian allies. And that tradition did not die, for the American Revolution itself, not to mention the many small wars that followed, saw the U.S. military fight both as insurgents and as counterinsurgents. It was only the two world wars, with their emphasis on mass infantry movements, that finally obscured this vitally useful legacy, forcing it to be painfully relearned in places like Afghanistan and Iraq. See Fred Anderson's *Crucible of War: The Seven Years' War and the Fate of Empire in British North America, 1754–1766* (New York: Knopf, 2000), p. 411.

and again over coming days. The idea that marines are trained to break down doors, to seize territory and beachheads, was an abstraction until I was there to experience it. Running into the fire rather than seeking cover from it goes counter to every human survival instinct—trust me. I was sweating as much from fear as from the layers of clothing I still had on from the night before, to the degree that it felt like pure salt was running into my eyes from my forehead. As the weeks had rolled on, and I got to know the 1/5 marines more as the individuals they were, I had started deluding myself that they weren't much different from me. They had soft spots, they got sick, they complained. But in one flash, as we charged across Michigan amid whistling incoming shots, I realized that they were not like me; they were marines. It is no exaggeration to say that Capt. Smith and Bravo literally *rode to the sound of the guns.*

We ran through several residential lots until we were just outside the gates of the mosque. It had a Persian-style blue dome though it was Sunni. Then the firing stopped. One of Smith's corporals, Robert Dawson of Staten Island, New York, led a squad of nine marines inside the mosque. His men detained two people and found some arms, but most of the gunmen had fled just as Smith's men and other marines were closing in on it.

"I want to IO the shit out of this place tomorrow," Smith said, referring to information operations—dropping leaflets, painting graffiti. The point was "to let them know that if they flagrantly use mosques for offensive operations, their mosques lose their protected status," he told me.

We crossed back to the southern side of Michigan amid sporadic fire. I had stopped ducking—you do get used to anything. A car approached. It was the mayor, Mohammed Ibrahim al-Juraissey, and his bodyguard. The mayor asked if it was safe for him to continue down the street. Out of the blue he started complaining about the reporting of the local al-Jazeera correspondent. There was something bizarre and dreamlike about this. Smith, ignoring the bit about al-Jazeera, told the mayor: "We tried our very best, sir, to shoot them [the gunmen in the mosque]. But we are new to the city. Next time we will be more efficient."

Directly across the street from the mosque, on the southern side of Michigan, was an apartment building which the marines had suspected was being used to fire on them. They had searched it and ordered a large family with children and babies into the courtyard. Smith approached the male head of the family to apologize. Smith stood erect now, except for a slight hunch in his shoulders, his hands deep in his pockets, a position I would see him take often when he was deciding, thinking, or about to say something important. He stared unblinking at the man, the same way he had at the police chief in Al-Karmah.

It was sometimes hard to imagine someone as serious and intense as Capt. Jason Smith. And yet there was a courtly quality about him, too. I thought of a Confederate officer.

Through his Iraqi translator, Smith told the man: "Sir, we are truly sorry that we had to ask your family to leave the building. You can all go back in now. We will compensate you for the inconvenience. We are United States Marines, a different breed than you are used to. We do not take kindly to people shooting at us. If you have any information about the Ali Babas, please share it with us. If you know any of the Ali Babas personally, please tell them to attack us as quickly as possible, so that we may kill them and start repairing sewers, electricity, and other services in your city."

After the translation was completed, the man, looking dumbfounded, gripped Capt. Smith's hand and wouldn't let go. Smith wasn't kidding about the compensation. Lt. Col. Byrne had been given a hoard of ready cash to use as he saw fit in order to win allies in the city. Byrne already had plans to pay the owner of the soda factory. "I'm going to give him rent, make repairs, buy a lot of his soda, and pay his employees for all the days they missed work because of us."

Walking back to the garage across an open space, we were set upon by an RPG and an intense barrage of small arms fire. We ran for cover and crouched against a building. Then we saw a body in the street. Amid the chaos, a marine had accidentally killed an Iraqi civilian who was suspiciously running away. Smith got angry at the marine. "Did he have a weapon? No! So where in the ROEs does it say you can shoot at him?" Everyone became somber. I felt bad for the marine who had fired the shot—any civilian would have felt bad for him, if he or she had experienced the complexity and confusion of this urban battle space, and the split-second life-or-death decisions required. Another luxury car passed, tracking our movement. "It's like trying to grab a fistful of water," Smith remarked, looking at the car.

Back at the garage, I finally got to strip off my excess layers of clothing. I had sweated so much that the glue holding together the laminated press credentials around my neck had melted and destroyed them. I ate my Country Captain Chicken, now cold. I didn't care. The moment that the danger had passed, I realized I was starving.

Smith took out a packet of instant coffee powder and poured it dry on his tongue, chasing it down with mineral water. Then he conducted a debrief.

Again, slightly hunched, with hands in pockets, he spoke in his slight southern drawl: "I find it encouraging that while our units were separated, we quickly got organized and moved on the objective. But the moment the objective was cleared, we let our guard down. We took too long crossing the open space, got fired upon, and shot a civilian. I know we have been running on empty without sleep and little food or water. But I expect more of marines. We are going to spend the night doing foot patrols. We are going to stop suspicious vehicles. The Ali Babas don't take chances. They left the mosque as soon as we closed in on it. They look for targets of opportunity. We won't give them any."

I noticed 2nd Lt. Palmer, the young marine with the serene look in his eyes who had been with me the night before in the truck, talking about books. He had slipped into the garage with a few of his men. Despite the turmoil and absence of sleep, he was upbeat while talking to me. I heard another marine say, "We're in shape to handle this without much sleep. Thank God Capt. Smith PT-ed the shit out of us at Camp Pendleton," referring to physical training.

Indeed, Cpl. Nicholas Magdalin of Chicago, who had been attached to Bravo and was now with the Renegades, told me that back at Camp Pendleton, when the company "wasn't working well together, Capt. Smith took us on a field op. He fucking broke us. I mean broke us. We were so desperate," Cpl. Magdalin went on, "that in order to survive the hike we started helping each other as never before, the stronger guys carrying the packs of the weaker guys. It made us really come together as a team. Seeing that, Capt. Smith finally allowed us to rest, telling us that 'there wasn't anything we couldn't do, no matter the odds, if we had unity.' "

After I had finished my MRE we were attacked again by RPGs, mortar, and small arms. Again, everyone moved in the direction of the fire. This time it was two blocks away to the north, on Michigan. The crack of bullets can be a good sound. It often means outgoing, and in any case usually means it is a safe distance away. The whistle and swish of bullets is bad; it usually means incoming and close by. Running down a back street with one of Capt. Smith's lieutenants, we heard the latter sound. Both of us jumped into a sewer ditch.

This firefight, like the previous one, lasted more than an hour, though they both seemed much longer. On a few occasions, I caught glimpses of the insurgents—in black pajamas and fedayeen-style keffiyahs—who were shooting at us. The combat was that close.

There was no sweeter sound than the drone of the AC-130 overhead. It meant help was on the way. Then came the thudding, drilling noise of its guns—help itself. I thought of the two forward air controllers, Capts. Chris Graham of Miami and Don Mareska of Moscow, Idaho, two backslapping friendly pilots who, only a few weeks before, had been downcast with me in the chow hall over the fact that in this SASO environment, they wouldn't have the opportunity to use their skills. Now they were the stars of the show. Mareska would be slightly wounded in the leg the next day.

The AC-130 was one of the few advantages the marines had. Almost all of the fire and explosions I heard were incoming. The insurgents could fire indiscriminately and blame collateral damage on the Americans, whereas the Americans I saw picked and chose their shots carefully. There was zero toleration for civilian casualties, though it was an impossible standard to always meet.

I wasn't back at the garage for more than half an hour before the third sustained, intense firefight of the day commenced. Two marines were wounded. I rode in a Humvee truck with them back to the soda factory. The truck got stuck for a moment crossing Michigan, which had become a free-fire zone. A hail of bullets descended on us. Luckily the side panels were up-armored. I lay flat against my stomach.

Through all the attacks that day, April 6, 2004, Bravo Company had gradually advanced its lines deeper into the city. There was nothing fancy about this: the marines slugged it out three steps forward, two steps backward. This was the classic, immemorial labor of infantry, little different from the way it had been practiced in Vietnam, World War II, and earlier back to the Greeks and Romans. Commanders inserted grunts and waited for them to be attacked, using the opportunity to break the enemy over the contact line. Whereas elite assets like Delta were high maintenance and required specific high-value targets, there was still a place in this world for old-fashioned infantrymen.

Back at the soda factory, the new FOB headquarters, I learned that there were still no units available to relieve Bravo. Capt. Smith's marines would have to fight on, with little sleep. I again thought of the throngs of troops at Camp Victory.

The Renegades had their Humvees outside the walls of the forward operating base, guarding it against attack. As there was no running water for a shower, soon after I returned I went back outside the perimeter to visit with Bednarcik, Pena, and Neal. "Sit with us for a while and relax. You need it," one of them said. That's when the 122mm rocket landed fifty feet away.

As with gunfire, the thud of an explosion can be a good sound; it means that you missed it. But the swoosh and airflow of an incoming rocket means *oh shit, it's over,* as you cower in the longest split second you'll ever know. That's the sound we heard. The Humvee rocked; fortunately it was up-armored. Lance Cpl. Neal, a bundle of delightful energy who had not stopped talking for weeks, went silent for a while, whereas Lance Cpl. Nathan Favorit of Watertown, Minnesota, the machine gunner in the next Humvee, who was usually so quiet that not even Lt. Col. Byrne could draw him into a conversation, suddenly exploded in chatter. "I tried to get Neal on the ICOM. 'Talking Guns [Neal's call sign], this is Bastard Guns, please, please come in.' For a moment there was no response. My God, I thought you guys . . ."

For weeks I had lived with constant rocket and mortar fire. It was maddening because you had absolutely no control over your destiny, unlike in firefights where you could run, duck, dive into a ditch, or hug a wall. Rocket and mortar attacks represented the utter randomness of life compressed beyond all imagining, with devastating, unalterable consequences. At St. Mere, a Navy doc had been talking outside with his father on a cell phone when he was killed by a mortar blast. At the cloverleaf, a rocket that had traveled almost ten miles killed a man who would have gotten away unscathed had it landed even a few feet away, on the other side of a blast barrier. Should I walk to the chow hall or Porta-John in this direction or that? It might be a decision that determined whether you lived or died.

I walked from the Humvee back inside the base, found a small storeroom that smelled like cat shit—the only room unoccupied by marines—and opened my sleeping bag. Still in my flak jacket, I went to sleep for a few hours on the cement floor using my helmet as a pillow.

The next day, as rocket and mortar fire continued intermittently on the base, which still had no Porta-Johns and only a sporadic trickle of cold running water, we got a visit from twelve stars' worth of Marine generals: Maj. Gen. Jim Mattis (two stars) and Lt. Gen. Jan Huly (three stars), Lt. Gen. James Conway (three stars), and Gen. Michael Hagee (four stars). Hagee was the Marine Corps commandant, one of the Joint Chiefs of Staff. He had traveled to the base from Washington with Huly, the Marines' deputy commandant for plans, policies, and operations. Conway was the I MEF commander, and Mattis the division commander. It said something for the Marine Corps that the commandant would come all the way from Washington to what one officer termed "this shithole." (Conditions at the soda factory later improved to the point where one journalist would describe it as "relatively luxurious.") Cpl. Magdalin, who happened to be nearby when their armored vehicles rolled in, had his picture taken with them. "Even if I am killed tomorrow, my life is now complete," he told me in disbelief.

The four generals, along with Col. Toolan, the RCT-1 commander, and Lt. Col. Byrne, pored over a satellite map of Al-Fallujah which they spread out on the hood of a Humvee. The plan was for 2/1 to come down from the northern part of the city and 1/5 to move in from the south and east, in order to box the insurgents against the Euphrates River, which flows north to south along the city's western edge. The bad news was the following:

- There was no such thing as a friendly mosque in the city. Mosques were storage depots for explosives, and their ramparts and minarets were used by snipers and other gunmen.
- The American-trained Iraqi Civil Defense Corps in the area were not only deserting, but cooperating with those inside the mosques.
- It was not the high-tech stuff, but the basics that the U.S. military had neglected. The Marines were short of Arabic translators, bolt cutters for breaking into shops in their rear, and 5.56mm ammo even. (The bolt cutters would arrive the next day, and ammo soon after.)
- The plan for taking the city down was realistic militarily, but high politics in the form of cease-fires threatened to intrude.

What the Marines did have going for them was a particular warrior spirit that was less the product of American patriotism than of Marine Corps tradition joined with the traditional camaraderie of the grunts— what I had experienced with the Renegades the night after their firefight in Al-Karmah.

Democracy may have been an additional factor. Citizens of democracies eschew wars but, once they embark on a war through democratic consultation, show a propensity to fight to the bitter end. This has been true since the days of ancient Athens, and it has made democratic troops the fiercest in combat.[21] Vietnam was not really an exception. By wide majorities, as attested by Harris polls, Americans supported continued heavy bombing of North Vietnam until late in the war, and President Nixon's victory over George McGovern's surrender strategy in 1972 was a blowout. The soldiers and marines I encountered during months of travels with the military—whose parents and grandparents had fought in Vietnam—thought of that war as every bit as sanctified as the nation's others. As for those who saw Vietnam differently, they were generally from the more prosperous classes of American society, classes which even back then were in the process of forging a global, cosmopolitan elite.* By the time of Iraq this new global citizenry was more deeply established, calling into question the age-old ability of individual democracies to persevere in a sustained and difficult war.

The grunts' unpretentious willingness to die was also the product of their working-class origins. The working classes had always been accustomed to rough, unfair lives and turns. They had less of an articulated and narcissistic sense of self than the elites, and could subsume their egos more easily inside a prideful unit identity, of the kind that uplifted an entire platoon—the organizational layer at which the Marine Corps functioned best.

These marines, in fact, were as old as antiquity, as old as their fellow marines who had stormed Guadalcanal and Iwo Jima and Hue City; as old as their Army brethren who had stormed Omaha Beach. They were the same people. Their intent, unquestioning visages were dead ringers for those in black-and-white World War II movies. Working-class existence had functioned as the Great Preserver of the oldest, simplest virtues: un-

---

* See James Fallows's 1975 essay in *The Washington Monthly* "What Did You Do in the Class War, Daddy?" He describes a busload of Harvard draftees at the Boston Navy Yard armed with carefully manipulated medical records to show their lack of fitness for duty, while another busload of working-class kids from Chelsea went smoothly through the induction process. See, too, Peter Beinart's "Two Countries," *The New Republic Online,* May 5, 2004. There is also Swarthmore professor James Kurth's "The Late American Nation" (*The National Interest,* Fall 2004). He explains that the global economy began producing business and cultural elites in the early twentieth century, but was stopped in its tracks by World War I, a worldwide economic depression, and World War II. By the 1960s, however, this globalization process resumed, with the rebirth of transnational identities. The sixties' youth revolt was a partial consequence of that.

blinking courage and straightforwardness, which was both revealed and obscured by the profane language they used.

Finally, there was the unapologetic, literal belief in God absent for the most part among the elites, a faith both tempered and uplifted by the democratic experience, which endowed the grunts with stores of compassion.

To wit, a mood of depression set in at the soda factory when it was learned that a six-year-old Iraqi girl, whose family lived nearby, had been killed by a mortar intended for the American base. It was the same depression that I had observed within Bravo after the Iraqi civilian had been mistakenly shot by a marine. The number of KIAs in the battalion from the Al-Fallujah fighting had by then reached a half dozen, and the wounded had crept up into the dozens.

One of the dead was 2nd Lt. Joshua Palmer, who was shot in the neck and abdomen while leading his platoon into a house from which marines were taking fire. He had been slated for promotion to 1st lieutenant in two days, but in his typical understated manner kept the news to himself. He was recommended for the Navy Cross. To think that any humane and peaceful global order is possible without such men would be self-delusory.

———

I went out more times into the city to see Capt. Smith. As Bravo advanced westward, deeper into downtown Al-Fallujah, the POS (forward "position") moved from the garage to a small warehouse with hardened cement walls. Because it had a high ceiling, Smith had to get near the roof in order to facilitate radio transmissions. Thus, on one occasion, Lt. Col. Byrne, I, and some other reporters who had recently arrived found Smith squatting atop a metal bookcase, speaking on the battalion tac as RPGs and gunfire registered outside on the street. He looked well rested after four hours of sleep, the most he had had in a week. "Blackhawk Two, this is Blackhawk Six, I need Red Cloud backed up. For the moment, it's a Red Cloud and Little Wolf show."

Smith then spoke over the ICOM, directing a Bravo platoon to the 905-degree grid, a few blocks farther to the west. Having returned to Iraq intending to bond with the local culture in the classic tradition of unconventional war—partly by growing mustaches and giving their forward operating bases Arabic names—circumstances had forced the marines to revert to direct action, and thus Al-Fallujah had become a familiar American urban space. Points on the map were identified not by any local landmark, but by their GPS grids. Streets had been given American names, like Michigan. Contact points with the enemy were color coded. And so I followed Smith and Byrne to "Violet," an intersection where Alpha Company would link up with Bravo, where the commercial part of southern Al-Fallujah edged into the residential part. Here Bravo intended to go "firm" for a while: dig in and establish yet another POS.

We were now a hundred meters away from the point of contact with the enemy. Two Marine M1A1 Abrams tanks stood fifty meters away. We all crouched against a wall as bullets whizzed by. But as the marines consolidated the position, the whistles turned to cracks and we stood up and relaxed a bit. Someone took a leak. Through binoculars, men armed with RPG launchers, wearing checkered keffiyahs around their faces, could be seen surrounded by women and children, taunting us. Only the snipers tried to get shots off.

The third world urban environment was like the Old West, I thought, when the cavalry invested Indian encampments only to find the braves periodically surrounded by women and children. However much the cavalry tried to spare the lives of noncombatants, the inevitable collateral damage among civilians raised profound moral questions, especially among humanitarians back east, who, because of the dissolution of the mass citizen army at the end of the Civil War, no longer felt close to this smaller, horse-borne volunteer force beyond the Mississippi.[22]

Byrne's Humvee pulled up, with Cpl. Magdalin at the wheel. Byrne and Smith began conferencing with the base over the battalion tac. Smith wanted to move the two tanks southward to draw enemy fire away from Bravo, allowing his men to farther advance. But he did not have direct command over the tank unit, so the request had "to go up through staff" before the tanks right next to him could move. Eventually they did. Even here in the midst of the battlefield there was an issue with cumbersome management.

Moreover, Bravo and the other infantry companies were dangerously scattered throughout the southern half of the city, so much so that the enemy could easily infiltrate the large warren of streets to the rear between Bravo's newly advanced position and the base about a mile away to the southeast. The company commanders would deal with this problem by standing up nonstop nighttime satellite patrols, despite the sleep deprivation afflicting many marines.

Another Marine battalion, the 3rd Battalion of the 4th Marine Regiment, would arrive in a few days from western Iraq to assist 1/5 and 2/1. But that redeployment, in turn, would make marines vulnerable in another part of their AOR. One hundred thirty thousand American troops in Iraq were simply not enough to deal with a fraction of that number of insurgents. It wasn't only because insurgencies, *pace* nineteenth-century British Col. Callwell, arise from the soil itself, and thus have whole categories of advantages that a military force from the outside, alien to the culture, lacks. It was also because, as the large number of American troops near Baghdad International Airport attested, the U.S. defense establishment, despite all the talk of reform and transformation, was still organized for World War II and the Korean War, with too many chiefs at massive rear bases and too few Indians at the edges. It was the same problem that I had observed in the Philippines and in Afghanistan. It just existed on a bigger scale in Iraq.

I thought again of the Indian wars, and of military historian Robert M. Utley's criticism of how the Army had responded to the massacre of Custer's 7th Cavalry—the 9/11 of its day:

> An enemy powerful enough to inflict so appalling a disaster seemed at the time to demand heavier armies than had yet been fielded. But once again the campaign demonstrated truths that so often eluded the frontier generals: heavy conventional columns rarely succeeded against the unconventional foe; the logistical requirements of provisioning so many men and horses so far from their bases usually turned such operations into exercises in self-preservation.[23]

The Army of that era never truly learned the lesson that small units of foot soldiers were more effective against Indian braves than large mounted regiments, burdened by the need to carry forage for the horses. The Sioux and their allies were ultimately vanquished not because the U.S. Army fully adapted to the challenge of an unconventional enemy—it didn't—but because of the flooding of the Old West with settlers, who were, in turn, aided by the railroad.[24] This time, however, the U.S. military would have to do better.

I last saw Capt. Jason Smith of Baton Rouge, Louisiana, in the middle of a street in Al-Fallujah that was popping with small arms fire, his hands deep in his pockets, his expression hardy and purposeful. T. E. Lawrence called doubt "our modern crown of thorns"; Smith betrayed none.[25] He was enunciating orders through the ICOM and conferring through the battalion tac: *Blackhawk, Apache, Red Cloud, Crazy Horse* . . . He might have been the subject of an oil portrait executed by Frederic Remington, or an officer of the old Confederacy that still inhabited the soul of the American military, invigorating its fighting spirit. His expression, his whole demeanor, was that of an earlier, less complicated age.

And yet, as necessary as Capt. Smith and others like him were for the United States and for the world, he was not ultimately the answer to the challenge raised by that vast crowd of the proletarian faithful I had seen strolling by the sea in the Yemeni port city of Mukalla at the very beginning of my travels. How to deal with that crowd? The answer existed in parts only, of which I had caught glimpses in Mongolia, on Basilan Island in the southern Philippines, on Lamu Island in Kenya, and elsewhere, for when imperialism is most obvious, as it was in Iraq, it was also most vulnerable and under siege.

In truth, Iraq in 2003 and 2004 was less a replay of Vietnam than of the Indian Mutiny against the British in 1857 and 1858, when the orientalists and other pragmatists in the British power structure, who wanted to leave traditional India as it was, lost sway to Evangelical and Utilitarian reformers who wanted to modernize and Christianize India—to make it more like England. But such attempts to bring the fruits of Western civilization to the Asian subcontinent were met with a violent revolt against imperial authority. Delhi, Lucknow, and other Indian cities were besieged and captured before being retaken by colonial forces.[26] Yet the debacle did not signal the end of the British Empire, which continued on and expanded even for another hundred years. Instead, it signaled the transition from an ad hoc imperium fired by an intemperate, evangelical lust to impose its values to a calmer, more pragmatic and soldiering empire built on international trade and technology.

The lesson was clear: The more subtle and cautious its application of power, the greater would be America's sustaining impact. The United States could hold sway over the world only quietly, off camera, so to speak. The focus of the media klieg light on Al-Fallujah, following my departure there, was central to the decision—made at the highest levels of the U.S. government—to call a cease-fire that would end the Marine assault. This happened just as the Marines, strengthened by the arrival of a whole new battalion, may have been about to overrun the insurgents.

To be sure, the decision to invest Al-Fallujah and then pull out just as victory was within reach demonstrated both the fecklessness and incoherence of the Bush administration. While a case can be made for either launching a full-scale marine assault or continuing the previous policy of individual surgical strikes, a case cannot be made for launching a full-scale assault only to reverse it because of political pressures that were easily foreseeable in the first place.[27] But in larger historical terms the Al-Fallujah drama also demonstrated the weakness of nation-states against the thundering new forces of a global media. Take Al-Jazeera, the independent, Qatar-based network whose characterizations of the fighting added to the political pressure on the White House to halt the offensive. Al-Jazeera was itself an example of the very political freedom that the U.S. sought to encourage in the Arab world. The more we succeeded in our quest for open societies, the more those open societies would seek to restrain us—and consequently the more quiet and devious our military behavior would have to be.

The American Empire of the early twenty-first century depended upon a tissue of intangibles that was threatened, rather than invigorated, by the naked exercise of power.[28] Or as Army Col. Tom Wilhelm had told me in Mongolia, an empire of behind-the-scenes relationships was all that was possible anymore.

I left the soda factory in Al-Fallujah just as the cease-fire was announced and more journalists began to arrive. From St. Mere I hitched a ride at midnight on a C-46 Sea Knight helicopter to an air base farther west, only to learn that military flights from there to Kuwait had stopped weeks before. There was little food and only a soiled cot on a concrete floor to sleep on. Twenty-four hours later, I caught another helicopter ride to another base deeper into Iraq's western desert, where an Air Force C-130 bound for Kuwait was due to stop over the next day. I spent the night in an open tent. It was freezing and there was a dust storm. The Air Force plane was a no-show. But a civilian cargo plane arrived, en route to Sharjah in the United Arab Emirates. It was an Antonov with a Russian crew and they agreed to take me. They smoked even more than the marines did, but the strong tea, black bread, and sausages that they offered tasted good after weeks of MREs and Gatorade. One of the hatch doors didn't seal properly upon closing, and they stuffed it with oily rags. "No problem," one of the Russians said dismissively as the plane took off.

The plane landed at the far end of Sharjah airport, reserved for cargo planes. I said goodbye to the crew and made my way in the dark to the civilian arrivals terminal. I hadn't bathed properly for a long time, and my clothes and backpack were layered in dust. Suddenly, I was under bright lights amid noisy crowds of prosperous Europeans on holiday, clad in fine clothes and jewelry and smelling of expensive perfumes and colognes. It was a half-hour taxi ride to a luxury hotel in Dubai. In the lobby, on the way to my room, I noticed a newsstand. The front pages were all about Al-Fallujah. I felt like a person at the center of a scandal that everyone was reading about, in which even the most accurate, balanced accounts were unconnected to what I had actually experienced and the marines I had experienced it all with. I felt deeply alienated. After I ate and showered and scrubbed my backpack, I didn't want to talk to anyone. All I wanted to do was write.

There was still so much I had to see. Places such as Indonesia, Korea, and even an area command or two still beckoned, not to mention other armed services. I had only begun my journey. I remember what one of the Marine generals visiting from Washington had told me before I left Al-Fallujah:

"Go home and rest a few weeks in the world of porcelain shitters. Then come back for more."

THE INTERIOR CONTINENT

O n late winter nights a lively group of young men and women gather round the tables at the High Noon Saloon and Brewery in Leavenworth, Kansas, escaping from the snowdrifts and ransacking prairie wind. Green Berets, Army FAOs (foreign area officers), and others spending their required year or two of study at nearby Fort Leavenworth talk loud above the karaoke music in the adjoining room. They swap stories about intrepid French tourists in Cambodia, tensions on the Saudi-Qatari border, the Maoist rebellion in Nepal, training missions that might one day materialize in Libya, getting sick in Afghanistan, chewing ghat in Somalia, and the awful Korean winters—worse than those in Kansas. I recall a young married couple, both Army majors, he a graduate of the Citadel, she of West Point, both from service families—her mother had been a nurse in Vietnam. They would be moving to European Command in Stuttgart, they told me. They could help arrange travel in their AOR, which included the Sahel countries of Africa.

The outside streets, lined with brick warehouses, are named for the North American Indian tribes with which the U.S. Army negotiated truces—Cheyenne, Pawnee, Seneca, Dakota, Choctaw . . . Two hundred years earlier Lewis and Clark camped nearby. From here the first white settlers moved into Indian Country. Fort Leavenworth, where the tallgrass prairie meets the short grass of the Great Plains, was the starting point for Manifest Destiny.

But nobody at the High Noon Saloon talks about "Are we an empire or not?" Rather, people talk about which indigenous armies are better than others, how successful the Marine training mission in the Caucasus was, tensions between the Army and the Air Force in East Asia, and so on.

Here, as at Fort Bragg, Camp Lejeune, and Camp Pendleton, places where people wear BDUs rather than dress greens, the talk is about application rather than conceptualization. Here you find out what is really going on in the world, where a traveler should be headed next, and who could help him get there. Here, in the interior continent, western Iraq seems closer than western Kansas during the Indian wars.

AUTHOR'S NOTE
AND ACKNOWLEDGMENTS

This is the first volume of a series of books about traveling with the American military. Less than a quarter of the material in this volume has been excerpted in *The Atlantic Monthly* magazine, and never more than half of any individual chapter.

My exposure to the American military began in the early 1990s at the School of Advanced Military Studies at Fort Leavenworth, Kansas. I went there at the suggestion of Army Col. (now Lt. Gen.) Jim Dubik, Col. (now retired Lt. Gen.) Randy House, and Army Chief of Staff Gen. Gordon Sullivan. At Fort Leavenworth I formed a friendship with Professor Robert Berlin. A year did not pass when I did not return there. The contacts I made at Fort Leavenworth would lead me eventually to this project.

I have been lucky with my long-term relationships, without which this undertaking would not have been possible. Literary agents Carl D. Brandt and Marianne Merola have been with me from the germination of this project, as they have for all my others for the past seventeen years. Random House has been the hardcover publisher of the last seven of my eleven books. I will always be grateful to Jason Epstein for beginning that association, just as I am grateful to William Whitworth for bringing me to *The Atlantic Monthly* in 1985.

Joy de Menil, my longtime editor at Random House, and Ann Godoff were generous boosters of this idea at its inception. Afterwards I was lucky in the extreme to fall into the hands of Kate Medina and Gina Centrello. Kate's cool encouragement never ceased. She helped me shape the manuscript without intruding upon it, thus allowing me to relax mentally to a degree I never have with an editor while writing a book. Charlotte Gross did a painstaking job of copyediting. I also appreciate advice and help from Frankie Jones, Jonathan Karp, Danielle Posen, and Robin Rolewicz at Random House.

Cullen Murphy of *The Atlantic Monthly* has edited my magazine articles for twenty years. He has nurtured and advised me on every book that I have ever written. It was Cullen and the late Michael Kelly, killed while covering the war in Iraq in 2003, who commissioned the series of articles that began this initial volume of military books. At *The Atlantic,* Yvonne Rolzhausen's research was indispensable. Help also came from Toby Lester, Emerson Hilton, and Sue Parilla.

Long periods of travel devour money in direct and indirect ways. The Smith Richardson and John M. Olin foundations provided generous amounts of it, as they have for previous projects going back to 1986. I thank their staffs, especially Nadia Shadlow and James Piereson, who never ceased in attempts to get me extra funding. Grant funds were administered by the Foreign Policy Research Institute (FPRI) in Philadelphia, which made few demands on me for this service. My relationship with FPRI and its directors, Harvey Sicherman and Alan Luxenberg, has also been a fruitful and long-standing one. At FPRI, I thank Michael Noonan for his military expertise and other help.

Though my agent, Carl Brandt, first gave me the idea for a book about "traveling with the military," it was Army Lt. Col. Ralph Peters (ret.) who got me started. Ralph burst into my room at Fort Myer in Arlington, Virginia, one morning and said: "This is what you should do, and here is how you should do it."

Unwilling to be interrupted, Ralph proceeded to outline an editorial structure that would organize my work for years to come. While Ralph is known to op-ed–page readers and talk show audiences for his strong and spicy opinions, it is his literary faculties that I have always admired most.

James P. Thomas, a deputy assistant secretary of defense for resources and plans, is the kind of young civil servant of whom the taxpayer can be proud: self-effacing, exceptionally analytical, temperamentally nonpartisan, supremely pragmatic, and particularly helpful in the early phases of this volume. Any administration, Republican or Democratic, would be the poorer without him. As Jim himself once told me—only somewhat in jest—having worked in the Pentagon for both the Clinton and younger Bush administrations: "I come with the building, like the furniture."

Maj. Gen. Geoffrey C. Lambert, commander of Army Special Forces (Airborne), trusted me without guarantees on my part, and broke down bureaucratic barriers to get me to many places around the world. He was truly a godsend. The same goes for Marine Maj. Gen. James N. Mattis, commander of the 1st Marine Division. If Homer were alive today, he'd be writing odes about Jim Mattis.

Army Majors Rob Gowan and Cynthia Teramae, as well as Marine Capt. Dan McSweeney, were not there to share in my experiences, but they all did so much to get me overseas, and were delightful to work with in the process. I have Cynthia and her husband, Army Chief Warrant Officer Jerry Teramae, to thank for a memorable few days in Honolulu. As I write, Marine Maj. Tim Keefe and Army Maj. Gen. Karl Eikenberry are working their hearts out, trying to put together journeys for me to Sahelian Africa and Pacific military bases for the early chapters of volume two in this series. I thank Army Maj. Don Bridgers for being a hidden hand in facilitating my visits to the Philippines, in order to explore an operation that he played a significant role in designing.

Because so many officers and grunts of the 1st Battalion of the 5th Marine Regiment were so helpful to me, I simply cannot name some without slighting others, or naming every marine of 1/5. Thus I thank them all as a group, particularly the Renegades. It was one of the great honors of my life to share their trials and tribulations in Iraq.

Indeed, rarely have I so thoroughly enjoyed the company of a group of people as much as I have Americans in uniform. They showered me with large and small kindnesses: an extra blanket or sleeping bag, the last seat on a C-130, a flashlight, a glass of vodka hidden under the floor when the regulations forbade it. Many a name below is associated with an overseas memory for which I am the richer, or with logistical and bureaucratic help back in the U.S. Their ranks are those at the time I met them. I have left out those mentioned more than briefly in the book:

Army Lt. Col. Mark Beattie, Army Lt. Col. Curtis Boyd, Army Maj. Gen. Jerry Boykin, Marine First Sgt. Donald Brazeal, Marine Col. Brooks Brewington, Army Gen. Doug Brown, Marine Staff Sgt. Matthew Butler, Army Maj. Roger Carstens, Army Lt. Col. Rick Choppa, Army Lt. Col. Ken Comer, Army Maj. Dan Cullison, Army Col. Rodney Davis, Marine Col. Stephen Davis, Air Force Maj. Gen. David Deptula, Army Col. Peter J. Dillon, Air Force Master Sgt. Carlos Duenas Jr., Army Maj. Fred Dummar, Army Maj. Mitchell Edgar, Army Sgt. Eric Jose Estrada, Army Col. Stan Florer, Army Sgt. First Class Jim Gentry, Army Sgt. Maj. Steven Gregurek, Army Col. Timothy Heinemann, Army Col. Kevin Higgins, Marine Lt. Gen. Jan Huly, Army Lt. Col. Ferdinand Irizarry, Army Cpl. Dan Johnston, Army Master Sgt. Doug Kealoha, Marine Lt. Eric Knapp, Army Maj. Gen. Stanley McChrystal, Army Lt. Col. Thor McNevin, Army Lt. Col. Dave Maxwell, Air Force Maj. Todd Miller, Army Lt. Col. Sean Mulholland, Army Lt. Col. John Murphy, Army Lt. Col. Kevin Murphy, Army Maj. Trip Narrow, Marine Brig. Gen. Robert Neller, Marine Capt. David Nevers, Naval Vice Adm. Eric Olson, Army Chief Warrant Officer Keith Pang, Army Maj. Rick Reese, Air Force 2nd Lt. Eric Saks, Air Force Lt. Anna Siegel, Marine Lt. Col. M. A. Singleton, Army Chief Warrant Officer Mike Stewart, Army Col. Sam Taylor III, Army Maj. Paul Warren, and Army Sgt. Maj. Jeff Wright.

Additional help came from Marshall Adair, Tiffany Bartish, Anthony Dolan, Randy Gangle, Kathy Gannon, Georje Jacob, Chet Justice, Andrew Krepinevich, Chuck Melson, Robert A. Putz Jr., Ambassador Francis Ricciardone, Mike Vickers, Peter Willems, and Robert Work.

My assistant, Elizabeth Lockyer, has organized my working life to such an extent that—up to a point—she has become a second *me,* allowing me to travel for months at a time, unimpeded by messages and mail piling up, making me as free as I was decades ago when the phone rarely rang and faxes and e-mail did not exist.

My wife, Maria Cabral, and my son, Michael, have put up with my long absences for twenty years, providing a sense of love and stability for which I am truly grateful.

GLOSSARY

ACF: anti-coalition forces in Afghanistan and Iraq.

ACM: anti-coalition militia in Afghanistan.

ACOG: advanced combat optical gunsight. Provides precision sighting in any lighting.

AC-130 Spectre gunship: heavily armed U.S. Air Force aircraft converted from a C-130 cargo plane, used to protect a ground force and for mop-up operations. Turbo-propelled, it can circle for hours but is vulnerable because it is slow and flies at low altitude. Think of it as an airborne tank.

ACV: armored combat vehicle. Enclosed military vehicle with cannon that moves on caterpillar treads or four-wheel-drive wheels.

Afghan-Arab: Arab veteran of the Afghan war against the Soviet Union in the 1980s.

AH-64 Apache: the U.S. Army's primary attack helicopter, with a twin engine, four blades, and high technology; it can perform multiple missions in any weather, day or night.

AK-47: lightweight and compact Russian assault rifle that fires 7.62mm cartridges. One of the first assault rifles (1947), it is reliable and easy to use and maintain in the field. Also called Kalashnikov, after its designer.

Ali Babas: term coined by U.S. soldiers in Iraq to refer to looters, terrorists, and other opponents.

AMCIT: American citizen.

AMF: Afghan militia forces (tribal).

ANA: Afghan National Army.

AOB: advanced operating or operations base. In Special Operations, a small temporary base in another country used for command, control, and/or support training or tactical operations. Usually subordinate to a forward or main operations base.

AOR: area of responsibility. Geographical area for which a military unit has authority.

A-team: a U.S. Army Special Forces twelve-man team that operates in a remote, often hostile area with little or no outside supervision. Also called ODA (Operational Detachment Alpha).

A-10 Thunderbolt: a versatile U.S. Air Force ground attack aircraft, nicknamed "Warthog." Highly survivable, it is used to provide close air support.

AVR: active vehicle restraint. Retractable barrier at entrances and exits that can withstand being crashed into. Also called a Delta barrier.

bailey bridge: bridge made of portable, interchangeable prefabricated steel panels for fast, easy assembly by military engineering units.

banca: a small wooden-hulled boat of the Pacific Ocean, especially the Philippines, usually a diesel-powered dugout canoe with bamboo outrigging.

barong tagalog: a loose, light, long-sleeved formal men's dress shirt of the Philippines, often with an embroidered collar and facing, worn with the tails hanging out.

BDU: battle dress utility. Camouflage uniform formerly known as combat fatigues— green in the tropics, tan in the desert.

Bedford "jingle" truck: a four-wheel-drive truck built for rugged terrain, usually adorned with colorful stickers and chimes, and garishly painted.

Beretta: 9mm lightweight semiautomatic pistol that has been the standard U.S. Army sidearm since 1985.

BIAP: Baghdad International Airport.

bravo: weapons.

B team: command and control of Special Operations A team. Also called ODB (Operational Detachment Bravo).

burka: a loose, all-enveloping garment with net holes for the eyes worn by some traditional Muslim women in public.

CAFGU: Philippine Armed Forces Geographical Units; Philippine paramilitary force.

Camel Pak: backpack canteen.

CAS: close air support.

CAT: civil affairs team. Responsible for developing relationships between the U.S. military and civil authority in the country in which it serves. A CAT provides humanitarian aid—building roads, schools, and schools, arranging for medical clinics, and so on.

CENTCOM: Central Command.

C-4: a very powerful plastic explosive that is easy to hide and difficult to detect.

CG: commanding general (U.S. Army).

CGSC: the U.S. Army Command and General Staff College, Fort Leavenworth, Kansas.

Charlie: engineer.

CH-47 Chinook: a U.S. Army cargo and troop transport helicopter.

CJSOTF: Combined Joint Special Operations Task Force. Task force made up of special Operations forces of the U.S. and another country or other countries.

CJTF-HOA: Combined Joint Task Force–Horn of Africa.

CJTF-180: Combined Joint Task Force 180. U.S.-led alliance of thirty-three countries in Afghanistan responsible for security outside Kabul.

claymore mine: anti-personnel mine set just off the ground and designed to propel balls (shrapnel) in a preset direction. It offers protection from ambush and infiltration.

GLOSSARY

ACF: anti-coalition forces in Afghanistan and Iraq.

ACM: anti-coalition militia in Afghanistan.

ACOG: advanced combat optical gunsight. Provides precision sighting in any lighting.

AC-130 Spectre gunship: heavily armed U.S. Air Force aircraft converted from a C-130 cargo plane, used to protect a ground force and for mop-up operations. Turbo-propelled, it can circle for hours but is vulnerable because it is slow and flies at low altitude. Think of it as an airborne tank.

ACV: armored combat vehicle. Enclosed military vehicle with cannon that moves on caterpillar treads or four-wheel-drive wheels.

Afghan-Arab: Arab veteran of the Afghan war against the Soviet Union in the 1980s.

AH-64 Apache: the U.S. Army's primary attack helicopter, with a twin engine, four blades, and high technology; it can perform multiple missions in any weather, day or night.

AK-47: lightweight and compact Russian assault rifle that fires 7.62mm cartridges. One of the first assault rifles (1947), it is reliable and easy to use and maintain in the field. Also called Kalashnikov, after its designer.

Ali Babas: term coined by U.S. soldiers in Iraq to refer to looters, terrorists, and other opponents.

AMCIT: American citizen.

AMF: Afghan militia forces (tribal).

ANA: Afghan National Army.

AOB: advanced operating or operations base. In Special Operations, a small temporary base in another country used for command, control, and/or support training or tactical operations. Usually subordinate to a forward or main operations base.

AOR: area of responsibility. Geographical area for which a military unit has authority.

A-team: a U.S. Army Special Forces twelve-man team that operates in a remote, often hostile area with little or no outside supervision. Also called ODA (Operational Detachment Alpha).

A-10 Thunderbolt: a versatile U.S. Air Force ground attack aircraft, nicknamed "Warthog." Highly survivable, it is used to provide close air support.

AVR: active vehicle restraint. Retractable barrier at entrances and exits that can withstand being crashed into. Also called a Delta barrier.

bailey bridge: bridge made of portable, interchangeable prefabricated steel panels for fast, easy assembly by military engineering units.

banca: a small wooden-hulled boat of the Pacific Ocean, especially the Philippines, usually a diesel-powered dugout canoe with bamboo outrigging.

barong tagalog: a loose, light, long-sleeved formal men's dress shirt of the Philippines, often with an embroidered collar and facing, worn with the tails hanging out.

BDU: battle dress utility. Camouflage uniform formerly known as combat fatigues— green in the tropics, tan in the desert.

Bedford "jingle" truck: a four-wheel-drive truck built for rugged terrain, usually adorned with colorful stickers and chimes, and garishly painted.

Beretta: 9mm lightweight semiautomatic pistol that has been the standard U.S. Army sidearm since 1983.

BIAP: Baghdad International Airport.

bravo: weapons.

B-team: command and control of Special Operations A-team. Also called ODB (Operational Detachment Bravo).

burka: a loose, all-enveloping garment with net holes for the eyes worn by some traditional Muslim women in public.

CAFGU: Citizens Armed Forces Geographical Units; Philippine paramilitary force.

Camel Pak: backpack canteen.

CAS: close air support.

CAT: civil affairs team. Responsible for developing relationships between the U.S. military and civil authority in the country in which it serves. A CAT provides humanitarian aid—building roads, sewers, and schools, arranging for medical clinics, and so on.

CENTCOM: Central Command.

C-4: a very powerful plastic explosive that is easy to hide and difficult to detect.

CG: commanding general (U.S. Army).

CGSC: the U.S. Army Command and General Staff College, Fort Leavenworth, Kansas.

Charlie: engineer.

CH-47 Chinook: a U.S. Army cargo and troop transport helicopter.

CJSOTF: Combined Joint Special Operations Task Force. Task force made up of Special Operations forces of the U.S. and another country or other countries.

CJTF-HOA: Combined Joint Task Force—Horn of Africa.

CJTF-180: Combined Joint Task Force 180. U.S.-led alliance of thirty-three countries in Afghanistan responsible for security outside Kabul.

claymore mine: anti-personnel mine set just off the ground and designed to fire metal balls (shrapnel) in a preset direction. It offers protection from ambushes, assaults, and infiltration.

COLAR: Colombian army.

commo freeks: communications frequencies.

comms: communications.

con-op: concept of operation. Written plan for a military attack.

C-130: a four-engine U.S. Air Force troop and cargo transport aircraft that can airdrop into a combat zone.

CSS: combat service support. Fire support and operational assistance to combat units.

DA: direct action—that is, combat.

delta: U.S. Army Special Forces medic.

Delta barrier: see AVR.

deshmal: a traditional Afghan kerchief.

DMZ: demilitarized zone.

DOD: Department of Defense.

ECE: equestrian-canine extravaganza (dog-and-pony show).

echo: communications.

18 Delta: U.S. Army Special Forces medic.

18 Zulu: U.S. Special Forces team sergeant responsible for his group. Has the rank of "master sergeant."

EUCOM: European Command.

exfil: exfiltration.

firebase: a secured site that is usually remote and isolated.

FMFM 6-5: *Fleet-Marine Force Manual 6-5.* Concentrates on squad-level operations. Also called "Grunt's Bible."

FOB: forward operating or operations base. In Special Operations, a base established in a friendly territory to extend command and control of communications, or to provide support for training and tactical operations.

foxtrot: intelligence.

freek: (radio) frequency.

ger: a Mongolian circular domed felt tent. Also called a *yurt.*

ghat: a shrub cultivated in Africa and the Middle East for its buds and leaves, which are chewed as a stimulant. Also spelled khat.

GMV: ground mobility vehicle.

GPS: global positioning system. Navigational system that uses satellite signals to fix the location of a radio receiver.

GWOT: Global War on Terrorism.

hajis: military slang for Afghans and Iraqis that may be used as an endearment or a pejorative, depending on the context.

HALO: high altitude, low opening. Ability to jump from a high altitude and not open a parachute until reaching a low altitude.

HESCO baskets: large wire-mesh baskets that are filled with sandbags to create barriers.

HIG: Hezb-i-Islami Gulbuddin. Party of Islam faction led by Gulbuddin Hekmatyar.

Humvee: U.S. Army all-purpose four-wheel-drive vehicle.

HVT: high-valve target.

ICDC: Iraqi Civil Defense Corps.

ICOM: integrated communications; intra-squad radio.

I MEF: First Marine Expeditionary Force.

indigs: indigenous troops in a given country.

intel: intelligence information.

IO: information operations. Includes dropping leaflets, making signs, broadcasting.

iron major: a major or other middle-level officer, often the workhorse of the U.S. military.

ISAF: International Security Assistance Force. NATO-led peacekeeping force in Afghanistan, responsible for security in Kabul.

jambiya: double-edged, heavy ornamental dagger with a curved blade carried by Yemeni men on their belts.

jeepney: in the Philippines, a jeep converted into a bus.

jihad: Islamic holy war.

jingle truck: see Bedford "jingle" truck.

JMC: joint military command.

JSOTF: Joint Special Operations Task Force.

JSTAFF: Joint Staff at the Pentagon.

JTF: joint task force.

Kalashnikov: see AK-47.

Kevlar: strong lightweight fiber used for protective apparel, including helmets. It is flexible and comfortable.

K-loader: truck that carries cargo to and from the cargo ramp of a plane or dock.

LVT: low-value target.

MAGTF: Marine Air-Ground Task Force. Self-sufficient, it has ground combat, aviation, support, and command components.

Makarov pistol: 9mm service sidearm of the Soviet Union during the Cold War that is compact and easy to use and maintain.

MEB: Marine Expeditionary Brigade.

MEDCAP: medical civic action program. Free medical care for local people in the area where it is set up.

medivac: to transport the wounded or sick for medical care, usually by helicopter.

MEF: Marine Expeditionary Force.

MEU: Marine Expeditionary Unit.

M-4: light, compact 5.56mm assault rifle used by some U.S. Army and Special Operations units. It can be operated in close quarters.

M1A1 Abrams: the main U.S. Army battle tank. Provides mobile firepower for armored divisions. Also used by Marines.

MOPP: mission-oriented protective posture. Flexible protection system against nuclear, biological, and chemical contamination.

MOUT: military operations in urban terrain.

MRE: meal ready to eat.

M-3 medical kit: three-fold carry kit.

M-16: U.S. Army 5.56mm assault rifle, lightweight and easy to use.

M-203: 40mm grenade launcher used with M-16 series rifle.

M-249: "Minimi" compact 5.56mm machine gun used by the U.S. Army and Marines that is light enough to be carried by one man and can fire for long periods.

MVT: middle-value target.

NAVISTAR: Navigation Starting Point. Massive U.S. military fuel and maintenance facility at the Iraq-Kuwait border.

NCO: noncommissioned officer.

NGO: nongovernmental organization.

NOD: night optical device.

NORTHCOM: Northern Command.

ODA: Operational Detachment Alpha. See A-team.

ODB: Operational Detachment Bravo. See B-team.

OIF-I: Operation Iraqi Freedom-I. U.S. military invasion of Iraq in spring 2003, characterized by the use of conventional military force.

op: military operation.

OSS: Office of Strategic Services. U.S. intelligence agency from 1942 to 1945, forerunner of the CIA.

PACOM: Pacific Command.

Pak: Pakistani.

pakol: round, flat lamb's-wool cap worn by tribal men of the Hindu Kush and in the Afghan-Pakistani border region.

Peltor: earphone that filters out gun sounds but not voices on the firing range.

PKM: general-purpose Russian 7.62mm machine gun.

POG: person other than a grunt—that is, an officer type at the regimental, division, and expeditionary force level. Sometimes spelled "pogue."

POS: temporary support position in a combat zone.

Predator: small, unmanned reconnaissance aircraft operated by remote control that can be in the air up to twenty-four hours. It has been armed with laser-guided anti-tank missiles to assassinate targeted individuals.

PRT: provincial reconstruction team. Made up of different military units and government departments, it is responsible for nation-building-type activities.

psy-ops: psychological operations.

PUC: person under control; detainee in the War on Terrorism.

rack: U.S. Navy term for bunk.

RCT: regimental combat team.

REMF: rear-echelon motherfucker. A World War II acronym.

ROE: rules of engagement.

RPG: rocket-propelled grenade.

SASO: Marine acronym for stability and security operations—"winning hearts and minds" and "nation-building."

SEAL: commando team of the U.S. Navy. ("SEAL" is an acronym for "sea, air, land.")

SecDef: secretary of defense.

SF: Special Forces. Highly trained branch of the U.S. Army that specializes in unconventional warfare. Popularly called Green Berets, though they don't often refer to themselves as such.

shalwar kameez: pajama-like trousers *(shalwar)* gathered at the waist and ankles, and worn underneath a long loose tunic *(kameez)* by Pushtun men and women.

Sim Sit: simulated situation.

SLLS: Smell. Look. Listen. Silence.

SOCOM: Special Operations Command.

SOCPAC: Special Operations Command, Pacific.

SOF: Special Operations Forces.

SOP: standard operating procedure.

SOUTHCOM: Southern Command.

SPETSNAZ: Russian special forces.

SSE: sensitive site exploration. A slow and deliberate site search.

terp: interpreter.

TOC: tactical operations center. Command post where general and special staff direct support operations.

trishaw: in Asia, a light vehicle with three wheels that is pedaled to transport passengers or goods.

TUFF bin: a polyurethane-insulated container used to transport and hold personal items.

UHF: ultra-high (radio) frequency.

UH-ID Huey: U.S. Army attack and transport helicopter used extensively during the Vietnam War.

UH-IN Huey: U.S. Army and Marine gunship helicopter.

UH-69 Black Hawk: the primary U.S. Army front-line utility helicopter, used for air assault, troop and cargo transport, electronic warfare, and medical evacuation. Successor to the UH-1 Huey.

USAID: United States Agency for International Development.

UW: unconventional warfare.

wadi: in arid regions of Southwest Asia and North Africa, a streambed that is dry except during the rainy season.

Zodiac: inflatable boat.

Zulu time: military time, numbered in hours to twenty-four and expressed in four digits—for example, 2300 is 11 p.m. Equivalent to Greenwich mean time.

NOTES

Prologue: Injun Country

1. See Robert M. Utley, *Frontiersmen in Blue: The United States Army and the Indian, 1848–1865* (1967; reprint, Lincoln: University of Nebraska Press, 1981), p. 5.
2. Gen. Wesley K. Clark, *Waging Modern War: Bosnia, Kosovo, and the Future of Conflict* (New York: PublicAffairs, 2001), p. 86. Furthermore, the term "strategic corporal" was coined by Marine Gen. Charles Krulak in 1999.
3. Erich S. Gruen, *The Hellenistic World and the Coming of Rome* (Berkeley: University of California Press, 1984), p. 7. Gruen is commenting on an essay by Paul Veyne about Roman imperialism. James (now Jan) Morris, *Farewell the Trumpets: An Imperial Retreat* (New York: Harcourt Brace, 1978), p. 91.
4. Gruen, *Hellenistic World and the Coming of Rome,* pp. 286–87.
5. Francis G. Hutchins, *The Illusion of Permanence: British Imperialism in India* (Princeton, NJ: Princeton University Press, 1967), p. 196.
6. Bernard De Voto, *The Course of Empire* (1952; reprint, New York: American Heritage, 1980), p. 228.
7. Ibid., p. 266.
8. Robert M. Utley, *Frontier Regulars: The United States Army and the Indian, 1866–1891* (Lincoln: University of Nebraska Press, 1973), p. 172.
9. International Institute for Strategic Studies (London); *U.S. News & World Report,* Oct. 6, 2003; and Victoria Thompson, research associate, Council on Foreign Relations, in Max Boot, "Bush Funding Request Would Keep Iraq on Recovery Road," *USA Today,* Sept. 29, 2003.
10. Byron Farwell, *Mr. Kipling's Army: All the Queen's Men* (New York: Norton, 1981), p. 115; Eliot A. Cohen, "Why the Gap Matters," *The National Interest,* Fall 2000.
11. John Keegan, *Six Armies in Normandy: From D-Day to the Liberation of Paris* (New York: Viking Penguin, 1982), p. 24; Robert D. Kaplan, "Fort Leavenworth and the Eclipse of Nationhood," *The Atlantic Monthly,* September 1996, p. 86.
12. John Keegan, *Fields of Battle: The Wars for North America* (New York: Knopf, 1996), chap. 5, "Forts on the Plains."
13. Ibid., p. 270.

14. Winston S. Churchill, *The Story of the Malakand Field Force: An Episode of Frontier War* (1898; reprint, New York: Barnes & Noble, 1993), p. 3.

15. Quoted in Robert M. Utley and Wilcomb E. Washburn, *The Indian Wars* (New York: American Heritage, 1977), p. 165.

16. Brian W. Dippie, *The Frederic Remington Art Museum Collection* (Ogdensburg, NY: Frederic Remington Art Museum, 2001), p. 13.

17. Ibid.

18. De Voto, *Course of Empire*, p. 266.

19. Michael Howard, *The Invention of Peace: Reflections on War and International Order* (New Haven, CT: Yale University Press, 2000), p. 28.

20. Ibid., pp. 28–29.

21. Eric Hinderaker, *Elusive Empires: Constructing Colonialism in the Ohio Valley, 1673–1800* (New York: Cambridge University Press, 1997), p. xi. See also Fred Anderson, *Crucible of War: The Seven Years' War and the Fate of Empire in British North America, 1754–1766* (New York: Knopf, 2000), p. xxi.

22. John Julius Norwich, *A History of Venice* (New York: Vintage, 1982), pp. 282–83, 508, 594.

23. Robert Work, Center for Strategic and Budgetary Assessments, briefing on America's overseas bases, Washington, DC, June 19, 2003. This passage is based on his analysis.

24. Ibid.

Chapter 1 — CENTCOM: Yemen, Winter 2002

1. Jane Fletcher Geniesse, *Passionate Nomad: The Life of Freya Stark* (New York: Random House, 1999), pp. 167–69; Malise Ruthven, *Freya Stark in Southern Arabia* (Reading, UK: Garnet, 1995), p. 19; Freya Stark, *The Southern Gates of Arabia: A Journey in the Hadramaut* (London: Murray, 1936). See her acknowledgments.

2. Winston S. Churchill, *The Story of the Malakand Field Force: An Episode of Frontier War* (1898; reprint, New York: Barnes & Noble, 1993), p. 103.

3. See my report "Supremacy by Stealth," *The Atlantic Monthly,* July/August 2003.

4. *The Economist: World in Figures,* 2001.

5. Freya Stark, *The Southern Gates of Arabia* (New York: Modern Library, 2001), p. 6.

6. Michael Jenner, *Yemen Rediscovered* (London: Longman, 1983), p. 56.

7. James (now Jan) Morris, *Farewell the Trumpets: An Imperial Retreat* (New York: Harcourt Brace, 1978), p. 317; Ruthven, *Freya Stark in Southern Arabia,* p. 9.

8. Ruthven, *Freya Stark in Southern Arabia,* p. 9.

9. M. C. Ricklefs, *A History of Modern Indonesia Since c. 1200* (Stanford, CA: Stanford University Press, 1981), p. 89.

10. Marguerite Yourcenar, *Memoirs of Hadrian* (1951; reprint, New York: Noonday, 1990), p. 109.

Chapter 2—SOUTHCOM: Colombia, Winter 2003

 1. Gen. Shachnow would later publish his autobiography, with Jann Robbins, *Hope and Honor* (New York: Doherty, 2004).

 2. Livy, *History of Rome,* trans. Evan T. Sage and Alfred C. Schlesinger (Cambridge, MA: Loeb Classical Library, 1938), 42.34.

 3. A. J. Simons, *The Company They Keep: Life Inside the U.S. Army Special Forces* (New York: Free Press, 1997), p. 29.

 4. Col. Aaron Bank, *From OSS to Green Berets: The Birth of Special Forces* (New York: Simon & Schuster, 1986), pp. 25, 74.

 5. Dana Priest, *The Mission: Waging War and Keeping Peace with America's Military* (New York: Norton, 2003), p. 135.

 6. *Public Papers of the Presidents of the United States, John F. Kennedy* (Washington, DC: U.S. Government Printing Office, 1962), p. 453. Quoted in Richard H. Shultz Jr., *The Secret War Against Hanoi: The Untold Story of Spies, Saboteurs, and Covert Warriors in North Vietnam* (New York: HarperCollins, 1999), p. 270.

 7. Simons, *The Company They Keep,* p. 215.

 8. A. J. Bacevich, James D. Hallums, Richard H. White, and Thomas F. Young, *American Military Policy in Small Wars: The Case of El Salvador* (Washington, DC: Pergamon-Brassey's, 1988), p. 16.

 9. Stephen Peter Rosen, "An Empire, If You Can Keep It," *National Interest,* Spring 2003; Edward Luttwak, *The Grand Strategy of the Roman Empire: From the First Century A.D. to the Third* (Baltimore: Johns Hopkins University Press, 1976).

10. Barry Asmus, *The Best Is Yet to Come* (Atlanta: Ameripress, 2001), p. 97.

11. Bacevich et al., *American Military Policy in Small Wars,* p. 25.

12. Frank Safford and Marco Palacios, *Colombia: Fragmented Land, Divided Society* (New York: Oxford University Press, 2002), p. 360.

13. Col. Joseph R. Nuñez, *Fighting the Hobbesian Trinity in Colombia: A New Strategy for Peace* (Carlisle, PA: U.S. Army War College, 2001), p. 31.

14. United States Army Infantry School, Fort Benning, Georgia, *Ranger Handbook,* July 1992, pp. 6-31–6-35.

15. Martin van Creveld, *The Art of War: War and Military Thought* (London: Cassell, 2000), p. 25.

16. *Journal of Special Warfare,* October 1993.

17. Joseph Conrad, *Nostromo: A Tale of the Seaboard* (1904; reprint, Middlesex, UK: Penguin, 1963), p. 195.

18. Safford and Palacios. *Colombia,* p.7.

19. Ibid., p. 278.

20. Alma Guillermoprieto, *Looking for History: Dispatches from Latin America* (New York: Pantheon, 2001), p. 52.

21. Mark Bowden, *Killing Pablo* (New York: Atlantic Monthly Press, 2001), p. 11.

22. Dr. Richard W. Stewart, USASOC historian, "Special Forces in El Salvador, 1980–92: A Synopsis," John F. Kennedy Special Warfare Center and School, Fort Bragg, North Carolina, p. 5.

23. "El Salvador: Military Assistance Has Helped Counter but Not Overcome the Insurgency; Report to the Honorable Edward M. Kennedy, U.S. Senate" (Washington, DC: General Accounting Office, Apr. 23, 1991), pp. 3, 4, 26, 21.

24. Stephen E. Ambrose, *Band of Brothers: E Company, 506th Regiment, 101st Airborne from Normandy to Eagle's Nest* (New York: Simon & Schuster, 1992).

25. Strategic Forecasting LLC, "Colombia: Growing Crisis in Arauca?," Jan. 30, 2003.

26. "Security in Venezuela: A Lack of Clarity on Terror," *The Economist,* Mar. 22, 2003.

27. Linda Robinson, "Terror Close to Home: In Oil-rich Venezuela, a Volatile Leader Befriends Bad Actors from the Mideast, Colombia, and Cuba," *U.S. News & World Report,* Oct. 6, 2003.

28. *Ranger Handbook,* section 5-11.

29. Ibid., sections 6-19, 6-20.

Chapter 3—PACOM: Mongolia, Spring 2003

1. The main source for historical background in this chapter is René Grousset's *The Empire of the Steppes: A History of Central Asia* (1939; reprint, New Brunswick, NJ: Rutgers University Press, 1970).

2. B. Batbayar (Baabar), *History of Mongolia* (Cambridge, UK: University of Cambridge, Mongolia and Inner Asia Studies Unit, 1999), p. 8.

3. Grousset, *Empire of the Steppes*, p. xxix.

4. Ibid.

5. Ibid., p. xxiv.

6. Batbayar, *History of Mongolia*, p. 29.

7. Edward Gibbon, *The Decline and Fall of the Roman Empire*, vol. 6, *1776–88* (New York: Knopf, 1994), ch. 64, part 3.

8. Grousset, *Empire of the Steppes*, p. 225.

9. Geoffrey Moorhouse, *On the Other Side: A Journey Through Soviet Central Asia* (New York: Henry Holt, 1990); mentioned also in my book *Eastward to Tartary: Travels in the Balkans, the Middle East, and the Caucasus* (New York: Random House, 2000).

10. Gibbon, *Decline and Fall of the Roman Empire*, vol. 6, ch. 64.

11. Ibid., part 4.

12. Batbayar, *History of Mongolia*, p. 32.

13. Grousset, *Empire of the Steppes*, pp. 256–57.

14. Gibbon, *Decline and Fall of the Roman Empire*, vol. 6, ch. 64, part 4.

15. Grousset, *Empire of the Steppes*, p. 280.

16. David Lattimore's 1995 introduction to Owen Lattimore's *The Desert Road to Turkestan* (Boston: Little, Brown, 1929).

17. Owen Lattimore, *Studies in Frontier History: Collected Papers, 1928–1958* (London: Oxford University Press, 1962), p. 14.

18. See Peter Hopkirk's chapters on the Mad Baron, and bibliography, in *Setting the East Ablaze: Lenin's Dream of an Empire in Asia* (London: Murray, 1984). Also Fitzroy Maclean's *To the Back of Beyond* (Boston: Little, Brown, 1975), and Charles Gallenkamp's *Dragon Hunter: Roy Chapman Andrews and the Central Asiatic Expeditions* (New York: Viking Penguin, 2001), pp. 123–24.

19. Hopkirk, *Setting the East Ablaze* (New York: Kodansha, 1995), p. 137.

20. See Gallenkamp's biography, *Dragon Hunter.*

21. Byron Farwell, *The Gurkhas* (New York: Norton, 1990), pp. 12, 51.

22. Roy Chapman Andrews, *Across Mongolian Plains: A Naturalist's Account of China's "Great Northwest"* (Amsterdam, The Netherlands: Fredonia, 2001), pp. 62–63.

23. Barbara W. Tuchman, *Stilwell and the American Experience in China, 1911–45* (New York: Macmillan, 1970), p. 185. And it wasn't only Stilwell who made this observation. So did Owen Lattimore on the first page of *Nomads and Commissars: Mongolia Revisited* (New York: Oxford University Press, 1962).

24. Peter Fleming, *News from Tartary: A Journey from Peking to Kashmir* (1936; reprint, Evanston, IL: Northwestern University Press, 1999), p. 18.

25. Gallenkamp, *Dragon Hunter,* p. 141.

26. Chapman Andrews, *Across Mongolian Plains,* p. 5.

27. Ibid., p. 8.

28. Lattimore, *The Desert Road to Turkestan,* p. 101.

29. Tuchman, *Stilwell and the American Experience in China,* pp. 88–89.

30. Fleming, *News from Tartary,* p. 252.

31. Ahmed Rashid, *Jihad: The Rise of Militant Islam in Central Asia* (New Haven, CT: Yale University Press, 2002), p. 95.

32. In addition to Rashid, see Shirin Akiner's *Tajikistan: Disintegration or Reconciliation?* (London: Royal Institute of International Affairs, 2001).

33. Lattimore, *The Desert Road to Turkestan,* p. 149.

34. Chapman Andrews, *Across Mongolian Plains,* p. 186.

35. Marco Polo, *The Travels of Marco Polo* (New York: Library Publications), p. 57.

36. Lattimore, *Nomads and Commissars,* p. 16.

Chapter 4—PACOM: The Philippines, Summer 2003

1. Brian McAllister Linn, *Guardians of Empire: The U.S. Army and the Pacific, 1902–1940* (Chapel Hill: University of North Carolina Press, 1997), pp. 51, 65, 68, 73, 115, 185, 248, 253.

2. James Jones, *From Here to Eternity* (1951; reprint, New York: Delta, 1998), pp. 15–17, 492.

3. GlobalSecurity.org, reprinted in *The Atlantic Monthly,* July/August 2003.

4. Max Boot, *The Savage Wars of Peace: Small Wars and the Rise of American*

Power (New York: Basic Books, 2002), p. 55. This book offers the best compendium of American imperialist expansion in mainly small seaborne conflicts, as well as much needed revisionism on the wars in the Philippines and Vietnam.

5. Ibid., chs. 2, 3.

6. Stanley Karnow, *In Our Image: America's Empire in the Philippines* (New York: Random House, 1989), pp. 12, 119.

7. Brian McAllister Linn, *The U.S. Army and Counterinsurgency in the Philippine War, 1899–1902* (Chapel Hill: The University of North Carolina Press, 1989), p. 27; Richard C. Welch, *Response to Imperialism: The United States and the Philippine-American War, 1899–1902* (Chapel Hill: University of North Carolina Press, 1979), pp. 133–47.

8. Boot, *Savage Wars of Peace,* p. 128.

9. Samuel K. Tan, *The Filipino-American War, 1899–1913* (Quezon City: University of the Philippines Press, 2002), p. 248.

10. Regarding the details of the war, I have relied heavily on Linn's *The U.S. Army and Counterinsurgency in the Philippine War,* as well as on Boot, Karnow, and other sources.

11. Taft Papers, series 21, letter dated July 14, 1900; Linn, *The U.S. Army and Counterinsurgency in the Philippine War,* p. 22.

12. Linn, *The U.S. Army and Counterinsurgency in the Philippine War,* p. 46.

13. Ibid., p. 57.

14. Ibid., p. 76.

15. Ibid., p. 85.

16. Ibid., p. 170.

17. Boot, *Savage Wars of Peace,* p. 125.

18. Karnow, *In Our Image,* p. 140.

19. Boot, *Savage Wars of Peace,* p. 127.

20. Karnow, *In Our Image,* p. 197.

21. Tan, *The Filipino-American War,* p. 256.

22. Ibid.

23. James Fallows, "A Damaged Culture," *The Atlantic Monthly,* November 1987, pp. 49–58.

24. Karnow, *In Our Image,* p. 14.

25. Thomas McKenna, *Muslim Rulers and Rebels: Everyday Politics and Armed Separatism in the Southern Philippines* (Berkeley: University of California Press, 1998), pp. 80–81.

26. Ibid., p. 85. Also see Tan, *The Filipino-American War,* pp. 192, 200.

27. Linn, *Guardians of Empire,* pp. 35–36.

28. Tan, *The Filipino-American War,* p. 177.

29. McKenna, *Muslim Rulers and Rebels,* pp. 43, 44, 104, 112, 143, 144.

30. Raymond Bonner, "Philippine Camps Are Training Al Qaeda's Allies, Officials Say," *New York Times,* May 31, 2003.

31. See Maria A. Ressa's *Seeds of Terror: An Eyewitness Account of Al-Qaeda's Newest Center of Operations in Southeast Asia* (New York: Free Press, 2003).

32. Dana Priest, *The Mission: Waging War and Keeping Peace with America's Military* (New York: Norton, 2003), p. 367.

33. A.J. Bacevich, James D. Hallums, Richard H. White, and Thomas F. Young, *American Military Policy in Small Wars: The Case of El Salvador* (Washington, DC: Pergamon-Brassey's, 1988), p. 40.

34. Karnow, *In Our Image*, p. 302.

35. Jones, *From Here to Eternity*, p. 172.

36. Byron Farwell, *Armies of the Raj: From the Great Indian Mutiny to Independence: 1858–1947* (New York: Norton, 1989), pp. 59–60.

37. Niall Ferguson, *Empire: The Rise and Demise of the British World Order and the Lessons for Global Power* (New York: Basic Books, 2003), p. 136.

38. Byron Farwell, *Mr. Kipling's Army: All the Queen's Men* (New York: Norton, 1981), p. 209.

Chapter 5—CENTCOM and SOCOM: Afghanistan, Autumn 2003

1. Michael R. Gordon and Gen. Bernard E. Trainor, *The Generals' War: The Inside Story of the Conflict in the Gulf* (Boston: Little, Brown, 1995), p. xv.

2. Williamson Murray and Maj. Gen. Robert H. Scales Jr., *The Iraq War: A Military History* (Cambridge, MA: Harvard University Press, 2003), p. 248.

3. Amy Waldman and Dexter Filkins, "Two U.S. Fronts: Quick Wars but Bloody Peace," *New York Times*, Sept. 19, 2003.

4. Max Boot, *The Savage Wars of Peace: Small Wars and the Rise of American Power* (New York: Basic Books, 2002), p. 293.

5. Lt. Col. David Maxwell, 1st Special Forces Group, unpublished paper, "How to Fight Counter-Insurgency."

6. Robert D. Kaplan, "The Lawless Frontier: The Tribal Lands of the Afghanistan-Pakistan Border Reveal the Future of Conflict in the Subcontinent, Along with the Dark Side of Globalization," *The Atlantic Monthly*, September 2000.

7. This and the following paragraphs draw heavily on my "Lawless Frontier" and my book on Afghanistan and Pakistan, *Soldiers of God* (Boston: Houghton Mifflin, 1990). See bibliography in *Soldiers of God* for more.

8. Olaf Caroe, *The Pathans, 550 B.C.–A.D. 1957* (London: Macmillan, 1958), p. 255.

9. Kaplan, "Lawless Frontier."

10. Robin Moore, *The Hunt for Bin Laden: Task Force Dagger* (New York: Random House, 2003), p. 5.

11. Ibid., p. 200.

12. W. J. Cash, *The Mind of the South* (1941; reprint, New York: Vintage, 1991), pp. 31–34, 38, 43–44, 121–122.

13. Louis Dupree, *Afghanistan* (Princeton, NJ: Princeton University Press, 1973, 1980), pp. 248–49.
14. C. E. Callwell, *Small Wars: Their Principles and Practice* (1896; reprint, Lincoln: University of Nebraska Press, 1996), p. 44.
15. Kaplan, *Soldiers of God,* p. 30.
16. Cash, *Mind of the South,* p. 56.
17. Ibid., p. 57.
18. Byron Farwell, *Armies of the Raj: From the Great Indian Mutiny to Independence, 1858–1947* (New York: Norton, 1989), pp. 68, 197–98.
19. Francis G. Hutchins, *The Illusion of Permanence: British Imperialism in India* (Princeton, NJ: Princeton University Press, 1967), p. 3.
20. Ibid.
21. Farwell, *Armies of the Raj,* p. 192.
22. Winston S. Churchill, *The Story of the Malakand Field Force: An Episode of Frontier War* (1898; reprint, New York: Barnes & Noble, 1993), pp. 203–204.
23. Ibid., p. 104.
24. Ibid., pp. 214–15.
25. See Alan Warren, *Waziristan: The Faqir of Ipi and the Indian Army: The North West Frontier Revolt of 1936–37* (Karachi, Pakistan: Oxford University Press, 2000).
26. Callwell, *Small Wars,* pp. 84, 115, 133, 136, 207.

Chapter 6—From the Army to the Marines—
Fort Bragg and Camp Lejeune, North Carolina, Winter 2003–2004

1. Among other articles, see H.D.S. Greenway's "Embedded with Their Satphones," *New York Times Book Review,* Nov. 23, 2003.
2. See, for example, my criticism of the Army's strategy: "Think Global, Fight Local: Our Force Is No Longer Light and Lethal in Afghanistan," *Wall Street Journal,* Dec. 19, 2003.
3. Quoted in James Tobin's introduction to *Reporting America at War: An Oral History,* comp. Michelle Ferrari (New York: Hyperion, 2003).
4. Michael Lind, *Vietnam: The Necessary War: A Reinterpretation of America's Most Drastic Military Conflict* (New York: Free Press, 1999), p. 115. See Lind's footnotes as well.
5. My experiences in Afghanistan generally tracked with the views of Lawrence Kaplan (no relation) in his article "Willpower," *The New Republic,* Sept. 8, 2003.
6. Thomas E. Ricks, *Making the Corps* (New York: Touchstone, 1997), p. 19.
7. Ibid.
8. Ibid., p. 64.
9. Max Boot, *The Savage Wars of Peace: Small Wars and the Rise of American Power* (New York: Basic Books, 2002), p. 334.

10. *Small War Manual: United States Marine Corps, 1940* (1940; reprint, Manhattan, KS: Sunflower University Press, 1996).

11. These quotes are all taken from the *Small Wars Manual,* sections 1-6, 1-7, 1-8, 6-1, 6-2, 6-20.

Chapter 7—CENTCOM: Horn of Africa, Winter 2004

1. The historical and geographical background in these paragraphs is adapted from an early book of mine, *Surrender or Starve: Travels in Ethiopia, Sudan, Somalia, and Eritrea* (Boulder, CO: Westview Press, 1988; reprint, New York: Vintage, 2003).

2. Donald N. Levine, *Wax and Gold: Tradition and Innovation in Ethiopian Culture* (Chicago: University of Chicago Press, 1965), p. 5.

3. Robert D. Kaplan, *Warrior Politics: Why Leadership Demands a Pagan Ethos* (New York: Random House, 2001), p. 116. In Chapter 9, I go into more detail about the reasons, both technological and historical, driving civilian and military command chains together.

4. See Joshua Hammer, "Keeping the Faith," *The New Republic Online,* Feb. 2, 2004.

5. Levine, *Wax and Gold,* p. 13.

6. Ibid., pp. 5, 17, 250–51.

7. Ibid., p. ix, 82, 174, 242, 251–52, 284.

8. Ibid., p. 16.

Chapter 8—CENTCOM: Iraq, Spring 2004

1. Bing West and Maj. Gen. Ray L. Smith (USMC ret.), *The March Up: Taking Baghdad with the 1st Marine Division* (New York: Bantam, 2003), pp. 2, 3, 18; Xenophon, *The Persian Expedition,* trans. Rex Warner (Middlesex, UK: Penguin, 1949).

2. Michael R. Gordon, "Marines Plan to Use Velvet Glove More Than Iron Fist," *New York Times,* Dec. 12, 2003.

3. The biographical background on Chesty Puller is drawn from Max Boot's *The Savage Wars of Peace: Small Wars and the Rise of American Power* (New York: Basic Books, 2002), pp. 244–48.

4. Matthew 6: 9–13.

5. Georges Roux, *Ancient Iraq* (London: Allen & Unwin, 1964; Harmondworth, UK: Penguin, 1982); citations are to the Penguin edition. The following graphs of historical background are drawn from my book *The Arabists: The Romance of an American Elite* (New York: Free Press, 1993).

6. Roux, *Ancient Iraq,* pp. 23, 27, 35.

7. Robert Byron, *The Road to Oxiana* (1937; reprint, London: Picador, 1981), p. 46.

8. Roux, *Ancient Iraq,* pp. 24–25.

9. Freya Stark, *Islam To-day,* ed. A. J. Arberry and Rom Landau (London: Faber & Faber, 1943).

10. Roux, *Ancient Iraq,* p.136.

11. Ibid., p. 20.

12. See the various essays on Iraqi tribalism in Faleh H. Jabar and Hosham Dawod, eds., *Tribes and Power: Nationalism and Ethnicity in the Middle East* (London: Saqi, 2003), pp. 8, 82, 90, 113–14, 138, 283.

13. See, in particular, Richard M. Ketchum, *Saratoga: Turning Point of America's Revolutionary War* (New York: Henry Holt, 1997), p. xii; Edmund Wilson, *Patriotic Gore: Studies in the Literature of the American Civil War* (1962; reprint, New York: Norton, 1994), pp. 92–97; and Robert Sherrod, *Tarawa: The Story of a Battle* (New York: Duell, Sloan and Pearce, 1944), photo insert.

14. Karl A. Wittfogel, *Oriental Despotism: A Comparative Study of Total Power* (New Haven, CT: Yale University Press, 1964), p. 1.

15. Byron Farwell, *Mr. Kipling's Army: All the Queen's Men* (New York: Norton, 1981), pp. 79–80.

16. See Keith William Nolan, *Battle for Hue: Tet 1968* (Novato, CA: Presidio, 1983), pp. ix, 181–85; Victor Davis Hanson, *Carnage and Culture: Landmark Battles in the Rise of Western Power* (New York: Doubleday, 2001), pp. 394–98.

17. Nolan, *Battle for Hue,* pp. 29, 82, 143, 164; Hanson, *Carnage and Culture,* p. 395.

18. Nolan, *Battle for Hue,* p. 167.

19. For a description of marine snipers and their equipment see Anthony Swofford, *Jarhead: A Marine's Chronicle of the Gulf War and Other Battles* (New York: Scribner, 2003); esp. pp. 54–58, 121–22, 135–36.

20. See Olivier Roy, *The Failure of Political Islam,* trans. Carol Volk (Cambridge, MA: Harvard University Press, 1994), pp. 75, 80, 82, 84, 195, 196.

21. See Hanson, *Carnage and Culture.*

22. See Robert M. Utley, *Frontier Regulars: The United States Army and the Indian, 1866–1891* (Lincoln: University of Nebraska Press, 1973), pp. 51, 59.

23. Ibid., p. 271.

24. Ibid., pp. 49, 289, 291.

25. T. E. Lawrence, *Seven Pillars of Wisdom: A Triumph* (1935; reprint, Harmondsworth, UK: Penguin, 1977), p. 360.

26. See Francis G. Hutchins, *The Illusion of Permanence: British Imperialism in India* (Princeton, NJ: Princeton University Press, 1967), pp. 196–97; and Niall Ferguson, *Empire: The Rise and Demise of the British World Order and the Lessons for Global Power* (New York: Basic Books, 2003), pp. 137–38, 151–53.

27. See Lt. Gen. Conway's own criticism of the administration, which came several months later, as reported by Rajiv Chandrasekan in "Key General Criticizes April Attack in Fallujah: Abrupt Withdrawal Called Vacillation," *Washington Post,* September 13, 2004.

28. See Fred Anderson's brilliant ruminations on imperial control in *Crucible of War: The Seven Years' War and the Fate of Empire in British North America, 1754–1766* (New York: Knopf, 2000), pp. 741–42.

INDEX

ABOUT THE AUTHOR

ROBERT D. KAPLAN is a correspondent for *The Atlantic Monthly* and the author of ten previous books on foreign affairs and travel, which have been translated into many languages; these books include *Balkan Ghosts, Eastward to Tartary, Warrior Politics, The Coming Anarchy,* and *The Ends of the Earth.* He lives in western Massachusetts.

ABOUT THE TYPE

This book was set in Times Roman, designed by Stanley Morrison specifically for *The Times* of London. The typeface was introduced in the newspaper in 1932. Times Roman had its greatest success in the United States as a book and commercial typeface, rather than one used in newspapers.